CROWOOD AVIATION SERIES

ANTONOV AN-12 CUB

Yefim Gordon and Dmitriy Komissarov

The Crowood Press

First published in 2004 by
The Crowood Press Ltd
Ramsbury, Marlborough
Wiltshire SN8 2HR

www.crowood.com

© Yefim Gordon and Dmitriy Komissarov 2004

All rights reserved. No part of this publication may be reproduced or transmitted in any form or by any means, electronic or mechanical, including photocopy, recording, or any information storage and retrieval system, without permission in writing from the publishers.

British Library Cataloguing-in-Publication Data
A catalogue record for this book is available from the British Library.

ISBN 1 84037 350 4

Typefaces used: Goudy (*text*), Cheltenham (*headings*), Univers Condensed (*captions and boxes*).

Typeset by Servis Filmsetting Limited, Manchester, England

Printed and bound in Great Britain by CPI, Bath

Contents

Introduction		4
1	THE PREDECESSORS	6
2	THE WINGED 'UKRAINE'	19
3	BIRTH OF AN AIRLIFTER	41
4	MISSION VARIETY	48
5	CLONING THE CUB: CHINESE VERSIONS	92
6	AN-12 ANATOMY	97
7	IN TIMES OF WAR AND TIMES OF PEACE, OR FORTY YEARS OF SERVICE	109
8	CUBS AT HOME . . . (CIS OPERATORS)	127
9	. . . AND ABROAD (NON-CIS OPERATORS)	147
Appendix I	Accident Attrition	169
Appendix II	An-12 Drawings	180
Notes		186
Index		189

Introduction

The Antonov An-12 belongs to the category of outstanding aircraft. Its emergence was remarkably timely; it featured a good technical level and was manufactured in sufficient numbers. Easy to fly and undemanding in operation, it earned world renown not only for the Antonov design bureau but for the Soviet aircraft industry in general. From the mid-1960s onwards there was not a single major event in the history of the Soviet Union, and later Russia, where the An-12 aircraft was not involved. It served in a multitude of roles, ranging from development of sparsely populated areas to direct participation in military conflicts and *coups d'état*; for several decades this machine, along with its American counterpart, the Lockheed C-130 Hercules, remained a mainstay of the world's transport aviation – civil as well as military.

Surprisingly, the Soviet Union, which was the first to establish airborne troops as a separate arm, possessed no dedicated military transport aircraft until the end of the 1950s. This role was fulfilled by heavy bombers and passenger aircraft specially adapted for the purpose. During the Great Patriotic War this task was performed mainly by converted Tupolev TB-3 bombers of pre-war vintage and PS-84 (Lisunov Li-2; NATO codename *Cab*) passenger aircraft. The latter type was a licence-built Douglas DC-3 Dakota derivative featuring a different powerplant and other changes. Later they were superseded by the Tupolev Tu-4D (a conversion of the Tu-4 *Bull* bomber adapted for transport and paradropping tasks) and the Ilyushin Il-12D (a purpose-built military assault transport version of the Il-12B *Coach* twin-engined airliner). True, big assault gliders such as the Tsybin Ts-25 and Yakovlev Yak-14 were also constructed, but they could not obviate the need for transport aircraft and take over their role completely.

The Tu-75 assault transport aircraft – again a derivative of the Tu-4 bomber – was designed, built and tested by Andrey Nikolayevich Tupolev's OKB-156,[1] but series manufacture failed to materialise. Shortly after the beginning of flight tests the sole prototype crashed, killing the crew of four captained by General A.I. Kabanov, vice-chief of the Tupolev OKB's flight test facility.

In addition to the Tu-75, several other projects of dedicated transport aircraft were under development at the end of the 1940s. Thus, in 1944–8 a design bureau led by Robert Lyudvigovich Bartini worked on the T-108 and T-117 piston-engined military transport aircraft and on the T-200 heavy transport aircraft featuring a compound powerplant (with piston engines as the main powerplant assisted by turbojets). Implementation of these projects, however, proved to be impracticable because the Bartini OKB was closed down by that time.

The situation changed in the early 1950s when the USA was already operating the Fairchild C-119 Flying Boxcar dedicated military transport on a mass scale, and series manufacture had begun of the 'classic' Fairchild C-123 Provider military transport, and the Lockheed Company commenced the development of a new-generation machine – the turboprop-powered C-130.

A new military doctrine evolved in the USSR with due regard to the changing world political situation which contained a requirement for increased troop mobility. To this end, plans were made for modernising and expanding the transport aviation to meet exigencies of contemporary warfare. On 17 April 1953 Marshal Dmitriy Fyodorovich Ustinov, the then-Minister of Defence Industry of the USSR,[2] having familiarised himself with a TsAGI report on the assembly of two YC-130 prototypes, wrote on the report: '*To Comrade Khrunichev. Must confer with you*' (TsAGI = *Tsentrahl'nyy aero- i ghidrodinamicheskiy institoot* – the Central Aero- and Hydrodynamics Institute named after Nikolay Yegorovich Zhukovskiy. Mikhail V. Khrunichev was then Minister of the Aircraft Industry). This served as the first official go-ahead for the work which eventually resulted in the creation of a Soviet dedicated transport aircraft powered by turboprop engines. Several design teams, including the design bureaux led by Oleg Konstantinovich Antonov, Vladimir Mikhaïlovich Miasishchev and A.N. Tupolev were asked to develop projects of specialised turboprop-powered transport aircraft. There was no contest as such, but in the end it was the Antonov OKB that received this task from the Government.

The An-12 was not the first transport aircraft developed by this OKB. Design work on transport machines for the Soviet Air Force commenced in Kiev in the first half of the 1950s. The first aircraft to be put into series production was the An-8 twin-turboprop military transport (described in this book), which, however, was not built in large numbers. Nevertheless, the creation of this machine determined the chief specialisation of the Antonov OKB's further activities – the development of transport aircraft and airliners. The first among these were the four-engined An-10 civil airliner and its stablemate – the An-12 military transport aircraft which was built in nearly 40 versions for various military and civil uses in the course of its long and glorious service career.

Within a short period the Antonov OKB succeeded in evolving its own concept of transport machines. The aircraft possessed a considerable cargo-carrying capacity; it was capable of transporting bulky cargoes at high speeds and yet could make use of unprepared airstrips for landing. For a long subsequent period the transport aircraft created by the Antonov design team came to feature the characteristic layout of a high-wing monoplane with wing-mounted engines. (When asked in a television interview in 1984 why all of his aircraft except the An-2 *Colt* utility biplane were high-wing designs, Oleg K. Antonov responded with a question: 'Have you ever seen a low-wing bird?') Placing the engines and propellers high above the ground enhanced the reliability of the powerplants, the lift/drag ratio and operational safety. Ground vehicles could freely move about under the high wings, which made it possible to park the aircraft closer to each other on the airfield. Moreover, in the event of a wheels-up emergency landing the wings housing the fuel tanks remained intact, which reduced the risk of a fire breaking out.

The An-12 has been operated by the air forces and airlines of many countries of the world and has gained a reputation as a thoroughly efficient and reliable means of transport. To this day it can be seen at numerous air bases, not only in Russia but also in other CIS countries, as well as on different continents. Quite a few airlines persist in making use of this relatively cheap and undemanding aircraft for transportation purposes. Unfortunately, not infrequently the An-12's career was marred by tragic incidents which were caused mainly by weather conditions, or by human error, or by the failure to observe certain rules that are imperative for any aircraft – such as extending the service life of certain assemblies, timely repairs, performing maintenance by the book, etc. However, many machines remain operational to this day, which in itself testifies well to the qualities of an aircraft that first took to the skies nearly half a century ago.

The Lockheed C-130 Hercules was the closest Western counterpart of the Antonov An-12; the common layout is no coincidence, since both aircraft were developed concurrently to meet exactly the same requirements. (Dmitriy Komissarov)

CHAPTER ONE

The Predecessors

DT-5/8 assault/transport aircraft project

As already related in the Introduction, in the late 1940s and early 1950s several Soviet aircraft design bureaux started work on projects of dedicated military transport aircraft. In December 1951 the design bureau (OKB) of aircraft factory No. 153 in Novosibirsk led by Oleg K. Antonov prepared an advanced development project of the DT-5/8 assault transport aircraft powered by two turboprops (DT = *desahntno-trahnsportnyy* [*samolyot*] – assault transport aircraft). The machine had a maximum load-carrying capacity of 8 tons (17,640 lb); it was provided with an undercarriage capable of negotiating difficult terrain and featured a big rear cargo door permitting both the unloading of troops and materiel after landing and for paradropping them in the air. Pinning big hopes on this project, Antonov also took an active part in the 'promotion' of the work on creating a turboprop in the appropriate power class.

It should be noted here that the 5,163 ehp TV-2 turboprop[3] – virtually the only turboprop engine available in the USSR at that time, created in 1947–50 by Nikolay Dmitriyevich Kuznetsov's OKB-276 with the participation of German designers – was handicapped by a short service life and low reliability. Eventually this led to a tragedy: on 11 May 1953 the first prototype of the Tu-95 *Bear-A* bomber powered by four 2TV-2F coupled engines crashed owing to disintegration of the reduction gear. In June 1952, therefore, a year before the crash of the Tu-95, aircraft designers O.K. Antonov and Mikhail Leontyevich Mil (the future renowned helicopter designer) and aircraft engine designer Aleksandr Gheorgiyevich Ivchenko wrote a letter addressed to M.V. Khrunichev, the Minister of the Aircraft Industry, in which they stated: 'To enable the development of assault transport helicopter, high-speed airliner and assault transport aircraft projects it is necessary to create a turboprop engine with a power output of the order of 3,000 hp. Bearing in mind that the development of the engine must to some extent be ahead of the work on aircraft, it would be expedient to commence the work on it immediately. We request you to support our proposal.'

The performance targets submitted in the DT-5/8 project generally met the requirements posed by the Soviet Air Force's airlift branch (VTA – *Voyenno-trahnsportnaya aviahtsiya*). On 11 December 1953 the Council of Ministers of the USSR issued Directive No. 2922-1251 requiring the Antonov OKB (which, after moving to the premises of the Kiev Machinery Plant No. 473 (KMZ No. 473 'Trood', Labour) was renamed GSOKB-473)[4] to create a transport aircraft powered by two turboprop engines. The appropriate Order No. 278 was issued by the Ministry of Aircraft Industry (MAP – *Ministerstvo aviatsionnoy promyshlennosti*, or *Minaviaprom*) on 23 December. The Government directive contained more precise basic specifications for the aircraft. The mentioned documents also tasked Ivchenko's OKB-478 with perfecting the TV-2 turboprop (N.D. Kuznetsov's design bureau was overburdened with work on the development of the TV-2F (*forseerovannyy*, uprated) and with work on creating a new, more powerful and 'purely indigenous' turboprop for strategic bombers). In turn, the issuance of the official requirements necessitated some revision of the DT-5/8 project.

An-8 *Camp* military transport aircraft prototype (*izdeliye* P)

At GSOKB-473 the new version of the military transport aircraft received the in-house designation '*izdeliye* P'[5] or *samolyot* P (Aircraft P). A.Ya. Belolipetskiy was appointed the machine's chief project engineer. The aircraft was to be powered by a new version of the TV-2 engine

The uncoded prototype An-8 as originally flown, with 5,163-ehp Kuznetsov TV-2T turboprops driving AV-58 four-bladed reversible-pitch propellers. The large size and distinctive bulged shape of the engine nacelles are evident in this view. (Yefim Gordon archive)

The An-8 prototype taxies on a snow-covered airfield during manufacturer's flight tests. Note the instrument landing system (ILS) aerial ahead of the flight-deck glazing. (Yefim Gordon archive)

designated TV-2T; the engines drove AV-58 four-bladed reversible-pitch propellers.

The Design Bureau did not have the production facilities or the required number of specialists for fulfilling such a complicated task. At O.K. Antonov's initiative, aircraft engineers from Moscow, Riga, Leningrad, Taganrog and Voronezh started arriving in Kiev as early as the beginning of 1954. In April the design team accepted into its ranks the first big batch of new graduates of the Kharkov Aviation Institute (KhAI). Plant No. 473 placed one of its workshops at the disposal of the OKB, to be used as a prototype production facility.

Antonov was especially worried by the fact that his design team lacked the experience of creating an aircraft of that kind. The chief designer approached Andrey N. Tupolev and Sergey Vladimirovich Ilyushin (head of OKB-240), requesting that technical drawings of the Tu-16 *Badger* medium bomber and Il-28 *Beagle* tactical bomber be sent to his OKB; he also asked that specialists from Kiev be allowed to study the design features of these aircraft directly at production plants.

Shortly thereafter one group of designers from Kiev came to Aircraft Factory No. 30 (MMZ No. 30 'Znamya Trooda', the Banner of Labour)[6] at Moscow-Khodynka to study the Il-28, while another group arrived at the Kazan Aircraft Factory No. 22 named after S.P. Gorboonov producing the Tu-16. Antonov also received assistance from Robert L. Bartini, who had already accumulated some experience in designing dedicated transport aircraft when projecting the T-108, T-117 and T-200. 'We were on good terms,' Antonov recalled later, 'and I wrote a letter asking if we could get from them the technical drawings of the freight hold floor. They had failed to turn these drawings into hardware, but we did it on the An-8 with some minor modifications. The floor's design concept was very interesting: the longitudinal beams of girder-type construction passed through the fuselage frames. As a result, the floor turned out to be very sturdy and lightweight, and it did not give cause for any complaints.'

Thanks to the experience thus obtained, the Kiev designers managed to avoid many mistakes when designing 'Aircraft P', and substantially reduced the time required for creating the new machine.

The special features of the aircraft under development confronted the design team with a number of tough problems, which necessitated a large amount of theoretical and experimental studies. A matter of particular complexity was the design of the aft fuselage with the large cargo hatch, which was 7.4 m (24 ft 3 in) long and 2.95 m (9 ft 8 in) wide. The open fuselage contour was ill suited for tackling the loads created by the empennage. Methods of calculating the strength of a stressed fuselage section of that kind were evolved under the direction of Ye.A. Shakhatooni; then a 1/10th-scale model was built, reproducing precisely all units and joints, including the riveting. Strength tests conducted on the model made it possible to select the optimum design of the hatch section in terms of weight. Subsequently, during static tests, the fuselage withstood 102 per cent of the design load.

To study the mutual influence of the aircraft and the cargoes paradropped by it,

The An-8 prototype in flight, still with TV-2T engines, showing the flat-bottomed fuselage. It is easy to see why the freighter earned the nickname *Kit* (Whale) in Soviet service. (Yefim Gordon archive)

flight tests were conducted under the direction of A.P. Eskin and V.N. Ghelprin, using scale models of the fuselage of *izdeliye* P. Two 1/5th-scale models housing dynamically similar models of cargoes were suspended under the lower wings of the An-2F prototype (a stillborn artillery spotter version of the An-2 relegated to test duties), and models to 1/10th scale were mounted between the upper and lower wings of the An-2. During flights at different speeds and angles of attack models of cargoes were dropped and the trajectories of their fall were photographed. These experiments, coupled with the theoretical calculations conducted under the direction of A.Yu. Manotskov, made it possible to evolve requirements for the transport and paradropping equipment and for parachute systems. Later, safe methods of paradropping heavy materiel were developed – in particular the parachute extraction method, making use of drogue parachutes.

New high-lift devices (double-slotted flaps with a fixed second slot) and a special heavy-duty undercarriage giving rough-field capability were developed for 'Aircraft P'. According to calculations, the aircraft was expected to possess good airfield performance and the ability to tackle difficult terrain during take-off and landing. This would enable the aircraft to operate from unpaved airfields and thus considerably extend the sphere of its use.

The advanced development project of 'Aircraft P' was completed in July 1954, and on 26 October 1954 the mock-up review commission headed by Air Major-General V.I. Lebedev held its session with the participation of representatives of the customer (the Air Force). The mock-up was presented with alternative powerplant options: it had a TV-2T turboprop on the port wing and a 6,830 kgp (15,057 lb st) Lyulka AL-7 turbojet under the starboard wing. The commission came to the following conclusion: 'The mock-up of a transport and assault aircraft powered by two TV-2T turboprops (manufacturer's designation 'Aircraft P') presented by chief designer O.K. Antonov is approved.' On 17 November Air Marshal P.F. Zhigarev, Commander-in-Chief of the Soviet Air Force, endorsed the commission's protocol. However, some documents reveal that the situation with the future manufacture of the aircraft and the construction of a flying prototype was far from cloudless. On 30 December 1954, therefore, the chief designer of GSOKB-473, O.K. Antonov, wrote to Gheorgiy M. Malenkov, Chairman of the Council of Ministers of the USSR:

> Even though the design work on the aircraft is proceeding ahead of the schedule approved by the Minister, construction of the aircraft entrusted to Plant No. 473 has not properly got under way. [...] The state of affairs in developing the turboprop engine for the aircraft gives rise to serious concern. OKB-478 Chief Designer A.G. Ivchenko has not yet received the required number of TV-2 engines for their reworking and development. It should be noted that production of turboprop engines is of great importance for the transport aviation as a whole, since by virtue of their low fuel consumption they have every prospect of becoming the main powerplants for airliners and transport and assault aircraft in the nearest 10 to 15 years. In England the Viscount and Britannia passenger aircraft powered by turboprops have been built. In the USA, which is lagging behind England in this respect, large-scale work is being conducted with a view to installing turboprops on a number of transport and passenger aircraft.

Presumably the letter had some influence on the course of events. As early as the following year the Ivchenko OKB had adapted the TV-2 engine to suit 'Aircraft P'. The powerplant passed bench running in TsAGI's T-104 wind tunnel and was later put through its paces on one of the Tu-4LL engine testbeds (c/n 225402). The new version of the turboprop, designated TV-2T, had a take-off power rating of 6,250 ehp (some documents quote it as 6,500 ehp).

The prototype of *izdeliye* P was built in

co-operation with many of the country's aircraft factories. Construction of the fuselage and final assembly of the aircraft were conducted at GSOKB-473's prototype production facility. At the end of 1955 Chief Designer O.K. Antonov and Director of Plant No. 473 V.A. Stepankov signed a document stating that the first prototype of the aircraft was ready for ground and flight testing. A.Ya. Belolipetskiy was appointed deputy chief designer for flight testing, with R.S. Korol as his assistant.

At the beginning of February 1956 the new machine, already bearing the official designation An-8, was formally rolled out in a festive setting. The staff of the Design Bureau arranged this event to coincide with the chief designer's 50th birthday. However, during preparations for the first flight, leaks were revealed in the fuel tanks, which necessitated returning the machine to the workshop to rectify the fault.

On 11 February 1956 the prototype An-8 took to the air for the first time, piloted by a test crew from the Flight Research Institute named after Mikhail M. Gromov (LII – *Lyotno-issledovatel'skiy institoot*). The crew comprised captain Yakov I. Vernikov (Hero of the Soviet Union), co-pilot V.P. Vasin, navigator P. Kondratyev, radio operator Chizhikov, flight engineer I.M. Morozov and leading engineer (in charge of testing) Yevdokimov. After taking off from Kiev-Svyatoshino (the factory airfield of Plant No. 473) the aircraft, despite some malfunctions in the flap control system, flew to Kiev-Borispol airport, where the manufacturer's flight tests began on the following day. The machine was also tested at Kiev's other airport, Zhuliany, and at the LII airfield in Zhukovskiy near Moscow. Ya.I. Vernikov, G.I. Lysenko and Yuriy V. Koorlin were the project test pilots at this stage.

It is worthy of note that the first public demonstration of the aircraft took place already at that time. On 18 August 1956 the An-8 prototype took part in the annual Air Display at Moscow's Tushino airfield together with another new piece of Soviet aviation hardware – the first Soviet jet airliner, the Tu-104 *Camel*.

Manufacturer's tests, the last stage of which was conducted by a crew captained by test-pilot I.Ye. Davydov, were completed on 2 October. Thereupon the prototype machine was transferred to the Red Banner State Research Institute of the Air Force (GK NII VVS – *Gosoodarstvennyy krasnoznamyonnyy naoochno-issledovatel'skiy institoot Voyenno-vozdooshnykh sil*) for State acceptance trials, which were completed on 27 November 1956; the final protocol of the State commission was endorsed on 15 December. Military test pilots V.K. Grechishkin and A.G. Terentyev, as well as test navigators M.K. Kotliuba and B.V. Lootsenko, had taken part in the State acceptance trials.

As it turned out, 'Aircraft P' possessed quite commendable performance. It could transport up to 11 tons (24,250 lb) of cargo, including lorries, artillery pieces and armoured personnel carriers, and they could be delivered both by unloading after landing and by paradropping. 'Aircraft P' had every chance to become the first Soviet dedicated transport aircraft, superseding the Tu-4D and the Il-14T/Il-14D *Crate*, which were ill suited for the purpose.

Legend has it that when A.N. Tupolev, the doyen of Soviet aircraft designers, was shown the freight hold of the prototype 'Aircraft P', his comment was brief: 'A good shed'. Presumably this was meant as praise. And not only because Antonov's designers had received valuable assistance from the staff of Tupolev's OKB-156, who had supplied their colleagues with drawings of a number of units and assemblies (wings, empennage, flight deck and navigator's station glazing); above all, it was a recognition of the merits of the aerodynamic layout of a radically new aircraft evolved by Antonov.

Nevertheless, the State commission chose not to recommend putting the An-8 into production and Air Force service in as-was configuration. There were quite a few reasons for that. Among other things, the State acceptance trials revealed unsatisfactory spinning characteristics, insufficient directional stability, shimmy oscillations on the nose-gear unit, poor controllability during landing in crosswinds exceeding 6 m/sec (12 kt), substantial elastic deformation and backlash in the control system, etc. Self-induced auto-oscillations in all three axes occurred during straight and level flight, making piloting difficult and causing pilot fatigue.

Rudder hypercompensation was also noted at deflection angles exceeding 12°. The latter defect was instrumental in bringing the machine to the verge of a crash in one of the test flights. The day's task was to check the aircraft's lateral stability at the altitude of 4,000 m (13,120 ft). When the pilot applied left rudder the aircraft was 'seized' by an unknown force all of a sudden and dragged to port. All attempts to restore straight flight using the rudder failed, and the machine was plunging more and more into a steep spiral. The situation looked hopeless and the crew were on the point of baling out when the pilots suddenly discovered an unorthodox way of tackling the situation – resorting to differential thrust. Gradually the aircraft stopped slipping, levelling out at an altitude of barely 500 m (1,640 ft).

The original powerplant proved catastrophically unreliable, forcing the Antonov OKB to re-engine the An-8 with 5,250-ehp Ivchenko AI-20D turboprops driving AV-68D propellers. This is probably the first prototype following modification. (Yefim Gordon archive)

THE PREDECESSORS

This view makes an interesting comparison with the one on page 6. Note the shorter and slimmer engine nacelles with forward-mounted oil coolers and the new taller vertical tail. (Yefim Gordon archive)

The upgraded An-8 during rough-field trials, showing the different window placement port and starboard. Of note are the tandem faired altimeter antennas under the centre fuselage, the rod aerials of the tactical radio navigation (TACAN) system under the nose and outer wings, and the holder for a cine camera beneath the starboard wingtip. (Yefim Gordon archive)

Yet, the main reason for the refusal to accept the aircraft for service was the poor functioning of the TV-2T engines, caused by the low stability of their gas dynamics at altitudes in excess of 6,000 m (19,690 ft). Starting of the powerplant was unreliable and its running at high altitude unstable; this was compounded by the low service life (turbine blades burned out after a mere 5 or 6 hours). Experimental technical features incorporated in the design of this engine made it impossible to eliminate these shortcomings. The TV-2T could at that time be replaced only by the new Soviet Kuznetsov NK-4 or Ivchenko AI-20 turboprops, but their power output was obviously insufficient. A four-engined version of *izdeliye* P was proposed, but the idea was rejected. Under these circumstances A.G. Ivchenko, chief designer of OKB-478, proposed that the TV-2T engine be replaced by an uprated version of the less powerful but more reliable turboprop developed in his design bureau – the AI-20, originally delivering 4,000 ehp for take-off. After studying the behaviour of this engine in boosted (contingency) modes, OKB-478 stated that it was possible to create an upgraded version, the AI-20D (*dorabotannyy* – updated) with a take-off rating of 5,500 ehp. Ivchenko's proposal was accepted, and as early as 4 April 1957 the Soviet Council of Ministers issued Directive No.373-184 prescribing that the shortcomings noted on the prototype An-8 be eliminated and the aircraft be re-engined with AI-20Ds, whereupon the machine was to be put into production at Aircraft Factory No. 84 in Tashkent.

In the period between July and 23 October 1957 the Antonov OKB was busy installing the modified AI-20D engines (delivering 5,250 ehp for take-off) with AV-68D four-bladed reversible-pitch propellers on the available An-8 prototype. Concurrently the area of the fin fillet was increased and the fin itself was replaced by a new one borrowed from the An-10 four-engined passenger aircraft then under development (see next chapter). The horizontal tail span was increased by 800 mm (2 ft 7.5 in), the leading-edge slats were deleted, and changes were made to some airframe components, accompanied by increasing the strength margin. Finally, anti-spin strakes were installed on the upper rear fuselage. The modifications cut the aircraft's empty weight by 3 tons (6,613 lb), which was mainly because of the installation of lighter engines. In June 1957, before these modifications were put into effect on the prototype, GSOKB-473 started transferring the reworked technical drawings of the An-8 to the production plant.

An-8 *Camp* production military transport

Series production of the new An-8 military airlifter started in 1957 at MAP Aircraft Factory No. 84, named after the famous test pilot Valeriy Pavlovich Chkalov, in Tashkent, and lasted until 1961 when the type was supplanted by the An-12 on the Tashkent production line. A directive of the Soviet Council of Ministers issued on 6 March 1958 envisaged the construction of three An-8s at Plant No. 23 in Fili, an area in the western part of Moscow, but six months later this work was discontinued. To master the production of the An-8, differing radically in its design from the Il-14 which Plant No. 84 had been manufacturing previously, new production techniques were introduced for the stamping and forging of large structural members, for the extrusion of long sections, for the chemical milling of skin panels, for the manufacture of flap tracks and carriages, and of the welded flight deck glazing frame, etc. In May 1957 a special workshop was set up for manufacturing bulky and long parts.

On 29 July 1959 the State Committee for Aviation Hardware (GKAT – *Gosoodarstvennyy komitet po aviatsionnoy tekhnike*), as the former Ministry of the Aircraft Industry was known during the Khrushchev era,[7] issued an order, in keeping with which a branch of the GSOKB-473 was set up at the Tashkent aircraft factory to efficiently support the series production of the An-8. The group of specialists sent from Kiev to Tashkent comprised V.F. Yeroshin (branch chief), V.A. Bessonov, V.A. Privalikhin, Ya.N. Prikhodko, B.N. Shchelkunov, V.T. Chmil and others. Soon the number of employees of the Antonov OKB's Tashkent branch reached 150 persons.

By the end of 1958 the plant had manufactured ten production An-8s. After the first five (some sources say eight) production aircraft had left the assembly line, all subsequent An-8 examples featured a fin height reduced by 480 mm (18.9 in). Production rates steadily increased. Thus, as many as 75 machines were built in 1960, and overall production in Tashkent totalled 151 An-8s (148, according to other sources) between 1958 and 1961.

An-8s built in 1958–9 were allocated seven-digit construction numbers (manufacturer's serial numbers): e.g. CCCP-69348 manufactured on 6 August 1959, c/n 9340503; the first digit denoted the year of manufacture, the next two (34) were a code for the Tashkent Plant No. 84,[8] followed by the production batch number and the number of the aircraft in the batch (ten per batch). From February 1960 onwards a new system with alphanumeric c/ns was introduced for some reason: the first digit denoting the year of

This early-production An-8 coded 10 Blue (c/n 9340504) is preserved at the Soviet Air Force Museum (now Central Russian Air Force Museum) in Monino near Moscow. (Yefim Gordon archive)

Soviet Airborne Troops (VDV) personnel board An-8 '11 Red'. Unusually, this aircraft has had the tail turret removed and the resulting aperture and tail-gunner's station windows faired over; this was more characteristic of An-8s transferred to civil operators! (Sergey and Dmitriy Komissarov archive)

manufacture was followed by a letter denoting the batch (in Cyrillic alphabetical sequence; transcribed into Latin, these were Batches A, B, V, G, D, Ye and Zh in 1960 and Batches Z, I, K in 1961); next came the familiar code 34 and the number of the aircraft in the batch **written backwards**. For example, CCCP-27209 manufactured on 21 February 1960, c/n 0A 3460, is the sixth aircraft in Batch A, which is, in effect, Batch 8; CCCP-69315 manufactured on 1 April 1960 (c/n 0A 3401; the second An-8 to have this registration) is the tenth and last aircraft in the same batch.[9]

Military An-8s had the c/n stencilled on the starboard side of the forward fuselage, just aft of the flight deck, and on the starboard side of the fin; civil-registered examples normally carried the c/n on the fin only. Additionally, the c/n was reportedly embossed on a metal plate attached to the rear bulkhead of the flight deck.

Coming back to the initial period of series production, it should be noted above all that, despite a large volume of bench and flight testing, attempts to obtain the promised power rating of the AI-20D engine were to no avail. However, the production plant was already completing the first five (or eight?) examples of the An-8 which were structurally similar to the modified prototype. Therefore MAP and the Air Force took the joint decision to introduce the An-8 into service with the engines derated to 5,180 ehp. The take-off weight of the aircraft was also limited to 38 tons (83,800 lb), as compared to the initial 42 tons (92,600 lb) for the version powered by TV-2T engines.

In August 1958 the first production machine (c/n 8340101) was rolled out in Tashkent, and at the end of the year it was flown by the plant's test crew (N.S. Gavritskiy, G.D. Zhdanov, Yu.M. Sorokin, A.N. Myahkov). It differed from the prototype by introducing changes in the undercarriage control system, the fuel-tank vents, the pressurization and de-icing systems. In addition, this machine had the skinning of the fuselage sides reinforced in the propellers' plane of rotation, and the maximum rudder deflection angle was reduced.

In the summer of 1959 test pilots I.Ye. Davydov and N.A. Sharov commenced factory tests of a production An-8 (c/n 9340304) which was submitted for State acceptance trials in June. In August of the same year it was joined by the next production machine (tactical code 92 Red, c/n 9340305; leading engineer Lysenko, pilot Bryksin, navigator Alekseyev). On 30 October the State acceptance trials were successfully completed. Derating the engines impaired the performance considerably. Suffice it to say that the maximum payload was limited to 8 tons (17,640 lb), although the normal payload of 5 tons (11,000 lb) remained unchanged. The top speed, range and service ceiling deteriorated and the inadequate power-to-weight ratio precluded the continuation of take-off from Class 3 (unpaved) runways in the event of an engine failure.

(**Note:** Until the mid-1950s Soviet military aircraft had three- or four-digit *serial numbers*. These allowed more or less positive identification, since they tied in with the aircraft's construction number – usually the last one or two digits of the batch number plus the number of the aircraft in the batch. In 1955, however, the VVS switched (probably for security reasons) to the current system of two-digit *tactical codes* which, as a rule, are simply the aircraft's number in the unit operating it, making positive identification impossible. Three- or four-digit tactical codes are rare and are usually worn by development aircraft only, in which case they still tie in with the c/n or fuselage number (manufacturer's line number).[10])

During manufacturer's flight tests, which lasted from 25 March and 6 May 1959, the aircraft's single-engine handling was investigated in different flight modes (with the propeller of the inoperative engine both in feathered condition and in autorotation mode). That same year OKB-478 worked on uprating the AI-20D engine to a take-off rating of 5,700 ehp with automatic feathering of the propeller in all flight modes; yet the required engine for the An-8 never materialised. In 1959 the four-engined An-12 military transport successfully completed State acceptance trials and was recommended for service introduction. Nevertheless, so acute was the shortage of aircraft of that category that the An-8 was also adopted for service in the military transport aviation of the USSR.

After the An-8's Tushino début in 1956 the NATO Air Standards Co-ordinating Committee (ASCC) allocated to it the reporting name *Camp* (C for Cargo, or Commercial, depending on the type of aircraft). In the Soviet Air Force it was unofficially known as Kit (Whale), a reflection on its size and weighty appearance.

Until the mid-1950s the structural layout of the An-8 was markedly different from that of all Soviet transport aircraft in operation or under development at the time. The main point of difference was the all-metal large-diameter fuselage with an unpressurised cargo hold measuring 11 m (36 ft 1 in) in length and a cargo door 2.95 m (9 ft 8 in) wide and 7.4 m (24 ft 3 in) long. Designing a big hatch for an aircraft represented a fairly complicated engineering task. Nevertheless, such a design was evolved and introduced into production, and it served as a basis when designing similar cargo hatches for the subsequent transport aircraft developed by the Antonov OKB.

The cargo hold of the An-8 was spacious enough to accommodate bulky military equipment, such as artillery pieces of up to 122 mm (4.8 in) calibre, 120 mm (4.7 in) and 160 mm (6.3 in) mortars with GAZ-63 four-wheel-drive trucks, two ASU-57 self-propelled guns, a D-211 bulldozer, a ZiS-151 6 × 6 truck and BTR-40 (4 × 4) and BTR-152 (6 × 6) armoured personnel carriers. In the case of troop transportation the cargo hold accommodated up to sixty fully equipped troops or forty paratroopers. The aft fuselage incorporated a tail gunner's station with a PV-23U powered turret designed by Fedoseyev and mounting two 23 mm (.90 calibre) Afanasyev/Makarov AM-23 cannon. Six crew members, apart from the gunner, were accommodated in the pressurised front cabin, which was partly protected with armour.

The high-set wings of trapezoidal planform were swept back 6° 50' at quarter-chord, with an incidence of +4° and zero dihedral; they utilised TsAGI S-5-18, S-3-16 and S-3-14 airfoil sections with a thickness/chord ratio of 18% at the root and 14% at the tips. Twenty bag-type fuel tanks with a total capacity of 12,850 litres (2,827 imp. gal.) were housed in the wing torsion box.

The An-8 featured an RBP-2 panoramic navigation/ground-mapping radar (NATO codename *Toad Stool*) in a teardrop-shaped chin radome. Other avionics and equipment included an ARK-5 Amur (a river in the Soviet Far East; pronounced like the French word *amour*) automatic direction finder, an MRP-56P Dyatel (Woodpecker) marker beacon receiver, an RV-2 Kristall (Crystal) radio altimeter, a Sirena-2 radar warning receiver (RWR), an SP-50 *Materik* (Continent) instrument landing system, an SPI-1M receiver/indicator unit for determining the aircraft's position, and an SRO-2 Khrom (Chromium) identification friend-or-foe (IFF) transponder (NATO *Odd Rods*). A PDSP-2S Proton-M receiver was provided for finding the route to the drop zone; NKPB-7 and AIP-32 bombsights ensured precision paradropping. Placed in the aft fuselage were a Gamma-54T gun-ranging radar and a VB-257 ballistic computer.[11]

To enable aerial photography and paradropping at night, provision was made for carrying four FotAB-100-80 flare bombs on KD-353A racks in the forward portions of the main-landing-gear fairings; additionally, six 10 kg (22 lb) TsOSAB-10 marker bombs were carried on DYa-SS-A

CCCP-06190, one of the last An-8s built (c/n 1K 3410), at Moscow-Domodedovo in the late 1960s, showing the anti-spin strakes on the aft fuselage and the skin reinforcement strips in the propellers' plane of rotation. Unusually, the aircraft does not carry the Soviet flag and Aeroflot titles. (Yefim Gordon archive)

racks in the aft portions of the same fairings. The An-8 was equipped with cameras for day- and night-time photography.[12]

The aircraft had a tricycle undercarriage with a twin-wheel nose unit steered by the rudder pedals. All units retracted aft, the four-wheel main-gear bogies rotating aft through 180° in the process to stow in neat lateral fairings. As compared to other aircraft the An-8 had a very narrow wheel track (in relation to the wingspan) – just a little more than half of the recommended one. Nevertheless, this new feature found acceptance in aviation and fully proved its worth.

Although the An-8 was adopted for squadron service, development was to continue for a long time yet, necessitating further flight tests. In particular, in November 1960 test pilots S.G. Brovtsev and V.N. Davydov conducted State acceptance trials of a modified de-icing system. To enhance the aircraft's operating autonomy, a TG-16 auxiliary power unit (APU)[13] developed by the Kazan Machinery Design Bureau (*Kazahnskoye proyektnoye byuro mashinostroyeniya*; now the *Aviamotor* Joint-Stock Co.) was installed in the aft portion of the port main-gear fairing. The anti-spin strakes on the rear fuselage were deleted because their effectiveness proved low.

In 1959 the An-8 achieved initial operational capability with the 12th Red Banner *Mginskaya* Guards Military Airlift Division (GvVTAD – *Gvardeyskaya voyenno-trahnsportnaya aviadiveeziya*, ≅ military airlift group).[14] The 374th and 229th Military Airlift Regiments (VTAP – *voyenno-trahnsportnyy aviapolk*, ≅ military airlift wing) based in Tula and in the small town of Teykovo (Ivanovo Region) were the first to re-equip. In 1961 two more regiments began conversion to the An-8, one of them being stationed at Krechevitsy airbase near Novgorod[15] (Leningrad Defence District) and the other in Zavitinsk near Chita (Transbaikalian DD).

Mastering the An-8 in service units was accompanied by a fair share of difficulties. During the first three years of operation alone the military transport aviation of the Soviet Air Force lost five aircraft of the type, three of them crashing because of powerplant defects. Unfortunately, conversion of service pilots to the type took its toll of human lives. On 14 October 1959, when a 374th VTAP An-8 (tactical code unknown, c/n 8340205) was coming in to land near Tula, one of the pilots accidentally locked the elevators in a neutral position, which resulted in a crash. A year later another An-8 crashed near the same airbase (and again during final approach) due to a failure of the starboard engine's control linkage.

Incidents and crashes continued in the subsequent years. On one An-8 a hydraulic fluid leak caused a total hydraulics failure. Grasping the situation, the resourceful crew topped up the hydraulic system with kerosene and made a safe landing. A tragicomical incident occurred near Krechevitsy AB in February 1962. Twenty minutes after take-off one of the engines cut, followed half an hour later by the other engine. The crew wasted no time in baling out. Meanwhile, left to its own devices, the aircraft glided to the ground and made an off-field landing on its own. True, it suffered some damage because the landing was uncontrolled, after all. Numerous crashes and incidents quickly earned the aircraft a bad reputation.

A lot of trouble was provoked by self-induced braking of the wheels. For instance, on 9 August 1979 the port mainwheels of An-8 CCCP-69314 (c/n 0B 3420) owned by the Omsk Engine Production Association unaccountably braked after a late-night landing at Moscow-Domodedovo airport, overheating and bursting into flames. The fire quickly burned through the fuselage side

Grey-painted An-8 CCCP-13357 (c/n 1Z 3440) belonged to MAP aircraft factory No. 116 in Arsen'yev, the Far East. Like most civilian *Camp*s, this one has been demilitarised. (Yefim Gordon archive)

CCCP-13361 (c/n 1I 3430) owned by MAP's Moscow United Flight Detachment/201st Flight illustrates the typical livery of civil An-8s; the grey Air Force finish was livened up by the addition of a blue cheatline. (Yefim Gordon archive)

and spread to the freight hold; the passengers accompanying the cargo panicked and started jumping out while the aircraft was still in motion. The result was tragic: two passengers ran into the port propeller, losing their lives; and the 19-year-old aircraft was completely destroyed by the fire.

Civil operations of the An-8 which began in the 1970s were likewise marred by accidents and incidents. For example, on 11 October 1990 An-8 CCCP-69320 (c/n 0V 3420), belonging to the Novosibirsk Aircraft Production Association named after V.P. Chkalov, crashed near Novosibirsk-Yeltsovka, the factory airfield, when both engines flamed out on short finals. Half a year later, on 16 May 1991, An-8 CCCP-13330 (c/n 0G 3490) owned by the Komsomolsk-on-Amur aircraft factory crashed at Irkutsk-2 airfield. The last crash at the time of writing occurred on 20 April 2002 in Pepa, Democratic Republic of Congo, when an An-8 registered in the Central African Republic as TL-ACM (c/n 9340706) crashed after colliding with a bird on take-off.

Nevertheless, many of the type's problems were gradually resolved. For instance, after many years of operation fatigue cracks appeared in the fuselage skin of some aircraft in the propellers' plane of rotation; the cure was to further strengthen the area by riveting on prominent external metal strips.

An unwelcome peculiarity of the An-8 was its high external noise level with a characteristic quality to the sound. Because of this it was easy to identify the An-8 among other turboprop-powered aircraft, even without seeing it, just by the sound of its engines. On the other hand, as distinct from the similarly powered Be-12 amphibian, the noise level in the cabin of the 'Whale' was relatively low.

Nevertheless, the *Camp* undeniably had its strong points. For example, the An-8 demonstrated its ability to tackle difficult airfield terrain when airlifting military materiel from waterlogged unpaved airstrips in Belorussia in November 1959. Flight and ground crews also took a liking to the machine because the propeller de-icing system featured a tank for 100 litres (22 imp. gal) of denatured alcohol; predictably, the liquid was not infrequently diverted for other uses.

The An-8 has been in operation for more than 40 years. During this time it has not taken part in long-distance flights, nor has it established any world records. And yet it became the Soviet Air Force's first dedicated military transport and a stepping stone towards the more advanced An-12. The 'Whale' was used on the biggest scale in 1962, when the *Stal'noy Shchit* (Steel Shield) military exercise of the Warsaw Pact nations was held on the territories of Poland and the former East Germany.

Starting in 1970, however, the An-8 was progressively phased out. The main reason was the introduction into squadron service of the more advanced and reliable An-12 aircraft. A few An-8s soldiered on with the Naval Aviation and the PVO (**Protivovozdooshnaya oborona** – Air Defence Force), but the majority of the surviving *Camps* (more than 100 aircraft) were transferred to the civil register, serving with the transport elements of certain ministries and agencies. These included the Ministry of Aircraft Industry, the Ministry of General Machinery (MOM – *Ministerstvo obschchevo mashinostroyeniya*, or *Minobschchemash*) responsible for the Soviet space and missile programmes, the Ministry of Shipbuilding (MSP – *Ministerstvo soodostroitel'noy promyshlennosti*) and the Ministry of Electronic Industry (MRP – *Ministerstvo rahdioelektronnoy promyshlennosti*, or *Minradioprom*).

MAP aircraft were used by the aircraft factories in Arsenyev (No. 116), Irkutsk (No. 39), Komsomolsk-on-Amur (No. 126), Kuibyshev (No. 18),[16] Novosibirsk (No. 153), Omsk (No. 166), Rostov-on-Don (No. 168), Ulan-Ude (No. 99) and Ulyanovsk, the Kaluga Engine Production Association, as well as the Moscow-based Transport Aviation Production Association. **MOM** enterprises operating the An-8 included the Kirov Machinery Production Association, named after the 20th Congress of the Communist Party, the Voronezh and Zlatoust Machinery Plants (all three were branches of the NPO Energiya concern), the Omsk Engine Production Association (Plant No. 29) and the 'Strela' (Arrow) Production Association in Orenburg.[17]

Many machines remained in service well into the 1990s, and some were used by Russian private airlines. However, towards the end of the century all airworthy examples had been transferred to the registers of Liberia, Equatorial Guinea, Djibouti, Sri Lanka, Angola, Swaziland, the Central African Republic and Congo-Brazzaville because the An-8 was banned from flying over the territory of Russia. From time to time these aircraft put in an appearance in Kiev to have their service life extended by the Antonov OKB, now known as Antonov Aviation Scientific and Technical Complex. In 2001 the Antonov Design Bureau withdrew the An-8's type certificate, but a handful of examples remained operational, albeit illegally.

An An-8 coded 10 Blue (c/n 9340504)

An-8 CCCP-69331 (c/n 9340708) of the Ministry of General Machinery's 'Strela' (Arrow) Mechanical Plant located in Orenburg was not demilitarised, unlike most of its sister ships. Many civil *Camp*s were registered in the 69xxx block. (Yefim Gordon archive)

Basic specifications of the prototype and production versions of the An-8		
	'Aircraft P'	An-8
Powerplant	2 × Kuznetsov TV-2T	2 × Ivchenko AI-20D
Power, ehp	2 × 6,250	2 × 5,180
Length overall	30.81 m (101 ft 1 in)	30.744 m (100 ft 10.39 in)
Height on ground	9.12 m (29 ft 11.05 in)	10.045 m (32 ft 11.47 in)
Wingspan	37.00 m (121 ft 4.69 in)	37.00 m (121 ft 4.69 in)
Wing area, m² (sq. ft)	117.2 (1,260.2)	117.2 (1,260.2)
Take-off weight, kg (lb):		
normal	39,450 (86,970)	38,000 (83,774)
maximum	42,450 (93,585)	41,000 (90,388)
Maximum payload, kg (lb)	11,000 (24,250)	8,000 (17,640)
Maximum fuel load, kg (lb)	10,350 (22,817)	9,960 (21,957)
Maximum speed, km/h (mph):		
at sea level	500 (310.5)	432 (268.3)
at 7,000 m (22,965 ft)	620 (385.0)	561 (348.4)
Time to 8,000 m (26,246 ft), min	21.6	24.1
Climb rate at S/L, m/sec (ft/min)	9.5 (1,870)	9.5 (1,870)
Range, km (miles):		
with a normal payload (5,000 kg/11,020 lb)	3,310 (2,055)	2,800–3,400 (1,739–2,111)
maximum	4,020 (2,496)	4,410 (2,739)
Service ceiling, m (ft)	10,800 (35,430)	9,600 (31,500)
Take-off run, m (ft)	540 (1,770)	700 (2,300)
Landing run, m (ft)	550–400 (1,805–1,310)	450 (1,480)
	350–400 (1,150–1,310)*	

*using reverse propeller pitch for braking

was donated to the Soviet Air Force Museum (now the Central Russian Air Force Museum) in Monino, south-east of Moscow, after completing its service in the PVO units of the Transcaucasian Defence District. One An-8 is preserved in the Alley of Labour Glory (an open-air museum) of the Tashkent Aviation Production Association named after V.P. Chkalov.

Three special-mission versions of the An-8 were built, and there were also several projected versions which never left the drawing board.

An-8 RINT aircraft

At least one An-8 painted in the overall medium grey Air Force colour scheme and registered CCCP-55522 (c/n unknown) was converted for radiation intelligence (RINT) duties. It carried two RR8311-100 standardised air-sampling pods looking like rather large cylinders with a movable nosecone and a door like a car throttle at the rear to adjust the airflow; a paper filter inside trapped radioactive dust particles for later analysis. Originally developed in 1964 for the Yakovlev Yak-28RR *Brewer-E* RINT aircraft, the RR8311-100 could be carried by other types, including the Antonov An-24RR *Coke*, Tupolev Tu-16R *Badger-K*, Tu-95KM *Bear-C*/Tu-95K-22 *Bear-G* and Yak-25RRV *Mandrake*.

The *Camp* had the pods installed in a rather unconventional way – under the tail-gunner's station, which obviously made fitting and removing them a quite complicated procedure requiring high work platforms. No separate designation is known for this variant.

The existence of the RINT version was revealed on 11 May 1966 when Republic of Korea Air Force (RoKAF) Northrop F-5E Tiger fighters intercepted CCCP-55522 over international waters off Ullung Island. The reason for its presence in the area was a nuclear test which China had held two days earlier.

An-8T fuel carrier

In 1959 a single production An-8 (identity unknown) was converted into a fuel transporter version called An-8T (*toplivovoz* – fuel carrier). This aircraft could transport all kinds of automotive, aircraft and rocket fuels. Depending on the mission, the cargo hold was equipped with two 5,300-litre (1,166 imp. gal) tanks for petroleum products or with a special 5,000-litre (1,100 imp. gal) reservoir with a gross weight of 8,000 kg (17,636 lb) for oxidants based on nitric acid, or with a liquid oxygen (LOX) reservoir grossing at 11,000 kg (24,250 lb). The need to ensure fire safety and protect the airframe from corrosive oxidant vapours necessitated special measures. The cargo hold was equipped with a firefighting system and the fuel reservoirs were shielded with a special casing. The free space between the reservoirs and the casing was to be ventilated with a specially arranged air stream. However, the problems of fire safety and protection from toxic substances were never solved, and the An-8T remained in prototype form.

An-8RU military transport

Another production *Camp* (c/n 1Z 3470; the registration looks like CCCP-55517 on the only available photo, but has also been reported as CCCP-55521) was modified with a view to increasing the maximum TOW to 42 tons (92,590 lb) while retaining the standard An-8's climb rate during take-off with one engine inoperative. To this end two SPRD-159 solid-propellant rocket boosters (*startovyy porokhovoy raketnyy dvigatel*) delivering a thrust of 4,300 kgp (9,480 lb st) apiece were mounted beneath the tail-gunner's station in a large flat-bottomed fairing. The modification was effected in 1963 by the Tashkent aircraft factory at the initiative of Kh.G. Sarymsakov, a designer from the Antonov OKB's Tashkent branch who received support from the head office in Kiev.

Designated An-8RU (*s raketnymi ooskoritelyami* – with rocket boosters), the aircraft passed joint State acceptance trials held by the Air Force and GKAT. Tragically, on 16 September 1964 the prototype crashed at Kiev-Gostomel, the flight test and development facility of GSOKB-473, while performing a take-off with a simulated engine failure.

Twenty seconds after brake release both boosters were ignited when the speed had reached 220 km/h (136 mph); six seconds later, when the aircraft was doing 264 km/h (164 mph), the pilots shut down the port engine. However, the propeller failed to feather automatically and started autorotating, creating tremendous drag. The crew were unable to counteract the steadily increasing left bank and sideslipping with the flight controls. At 16.45 local time the An-8RU slammed into the ground with 70–80° left bank at a distance of 1,850 m from the brake release point and exploded in a fireball. The entire crew – captain A.F. Mitronin, co-pilot A.M. Tsygankov, navigator V.N. Popov, radio operator P.S. Melnichenko, flight engineer N.A. Petrashenko and test engineer B.L. Skliarskiy – lost their lives. This was the first fatal crash in the history of the Antonov OKB. All further work on the An-8RU was discontinued.

An-8 airliner version project (*izdeliye* N)

Of all the 'paper aeroplanes' based on the An-8, the airliner version came closest to reaching the hardware stage. This version, bearing the manufacturer's designation '*izdeliye* N', was developed simultaneously with the baseline '*izdeliye* P' transport and assault aircraft and in response to the same directive documents. The two aircraft differed only in the design of their fuselage: the passenger version had an elongated pressurised fuselage of circular cross-section; the cabin accommodated 57 passengers in a high-density layout or 30–46 passengers in layouts with increased comfort. Interestingly, all the seats were aft-facing; this feature was intended to enhance the passengers' safety during a crash landing.

An-8 CCCP-69340 (c/n 0G 3430) belonging to the Novosibirsk aircraft factory No. 153 looks resplendent in Aeroflot's 1973-standard livery which was worn by some civil examples. Note how the skin reinforcement strips stand out against the white top of the fuselage. (Yefim Gordon archive)

Provision was made for converting the airliner into a transport aircraft with a maximum load-carrying capacity of 7,700 kg (16,975 lb). Hence a cargo door was provided in the aft fuselage, to be used as a baggage hatch in the passenger version.

According to the project, 'Aircraft N' was to have the following basic specifications: a maximum speed of 650–700 km/h (403–34 mph), a range of 3,500 km (2,170 miles) with a 4-ton (8,818 lb) payload, a service ceiling of 9,000–11,000 m (29,530–36,090 ft), a 650 m (2,130 ft) take-off and landing run and a maximum TOW of 39 tons (85,980 lb).

Work on the aircraft was discontinued at the full-size mock-up stage. This decision was influenced in part by Nikita S. Khrushchev, the then First Secretary (i.e. chairman) of the Communist Party Central Committee, who, after inspecting the mock-up of the *izdeliye* N in the summer of 1955, expressed the wish that O.K. Antonov develop a four-engined passenger aircraft so as to ensure greater passenger safety.

An-8M ASW aircraft project

The An-8M anti-submarine warfare aircraft (the M stood for either *modifit-seerovannyy*, modified, or *morskoy*, naval or maritime) was projected in accordance with a Council of Ministers directive dated 20 July 1958. In accordance with its intended mission – to seek and destroy enemy submarines – the machine was to be fitted with a special search and tracking equipment suite, including an Initsiativa-2 (Initiative-2) search radar. The armament consisted of depth-charges which would be dropped through special hatches in the freight hold floor. The crew included a mission equipment operator.

An-8Sh navigator trainer project

Work on the An-8Sh navigator trainer (*shtoormanskiy* – for navigators) proceeded in accordance with a Council of Ministers directive issued on 18 March 1959. The aircraft was intended for group training of cadets of navigator schools and for proficiency training of navigators in service units. Eighteen additional workstations were to be accommodated in the freight hold; of these, sixteen were intended for the trainees and two for the instructor navigators.

An-8PS maritime SAR aircraft project

The An-8PS (*poiskovo-spasahtel'nyy* – search and rescue, used attributively), the design work on which was begun in accordance with a Council of Ministers' directive dated 31 July 1959, was intended for locating and aiding persons in distress at sea or in land areas with impassable terrain. In various versions the aircraft could provide aid for between 240 and 675 persons in distress. It was envisaged that this task would be tackled by paradropping rescue teams, life rafts and life buoys, food supplies, medicines, etc.

CHAPTER TWO

The Winged 'Ukraine'

An-10 Ookraïna airliner prototype (*izdeliye* U; *Cat*)

This poor but interesting shot from an old Soviet newspaper shows the prototype of the An-10 Ookraïna (The Ukraine) as originally flown – with a shallow dorsal fin and short vertical tail. (Sergey and Dmitriy Komissarov archive)

One of the first photos of the An-10 published in the Soviet press. Though heavily retouched (and apparently distorted, making the fuselage look much too tubby!), this view is interesting in that it shows the prototype taxiing at an early stage of the trials. (Yefim Gordon archive)

The An-10 prototype (SSSR-U1957) in modified form with a taller tail and endplate fins on the stabilizers to improve directional stability. Note the automatic direction finder 'towel rail' aerial on the forward fuselage. (Yefim Gordon archive)

SSSR-U1957 taxies over an unpaved airfield during trials. Note the aft location of the oil coolers characteristic of the Kuznetsov NK-4 engines and the design of the flight-deck glazing. (Yefim Gordon archive)

The prototype at a late stage of the trials. The original *Ookraïna* nose titles have been replaced with *An-10* titles. (Yefim Gordon archive)

Production aircraft were powered by AI-20 engines with AV-68 propellers. (Antonov OKB)

Head-on view of a still unpainted production An-10 undergoing pre-delivery tests at the Voronezh aircraft factory. (Yefim Gordon archive)

The twin-engined *izdeliye* N airliner described in the previous chapter had a successor. This was the four-engined *izdeliye* U ('Aircraft U') airliner. It had the distinction of being the first turboprop-powered airliner to be flight-tested in the USSR, the first Soviet series-produced turboprop passenger aircraft, the first turboprop airliner to enter service in the USSR – and the first such aircraft to be phased out subsequently.

A four-engined airliner, said GSOKB-473 Chief Designer Oleg K. Antonov, should be created in such a way that it would be easy to evolve a transport aircraft from it. His belief was that a single project should be developed, but in two versions differing only in the aft fuselage design and equipment fit. This approach made it possible to considerably speed up the design work and preparations for mass production, reducing the expenses involved; it also facilitated conversion of the flight and ground crews to these aircraft and simplified operation. In addition, airliners sharing a common undercarriage with a military transport aircraft could operate from a wider network of airports, including the ill-equipped and unpaved provincial airfields, which would endow local air routes with the same level of comfort as on trunk routes. Finally, should war become imminent, the airliners could be easily converted into the military transport version by simply substituting the 'civil' rear fuselage with the 'military' one.

The Soviet head of state Nikita S. Khrushchev, who made a trip to the Ukraine in 1955 and visited the GSOKB-473, among other things, found this idea attractive since it promised so many advantages. Recalling his meeting with Antonov, he emphasised: 'This designer talked economics to me.' Apparently such a conversation was a rare phenomenon in those days, therefore it impressed Khrushchev greatly. Soon, as related in the previous chapter, work on the *izdeliye* N twin-engined airliner was discontinued and on 30 December 1955 the Soviet Council of Ministers issued a new directive requiring Chief Designer O.K. Antonov to develop what may be called 'twin brothers' – the 85-seat An-10 airliner and the An-12 military transport, two versions of the same basic design. The said document required engine designers Nikolay D. Kuznetsov and Aleksandr G. Ivchenko to develop the NK-4 and TV-20 (later renamed AI-20) turboprop engines which aircraft designer Sergey V. Ilyushin was to install on his new Il-18 Moskva (Moscow; NATO *Coot*) airliner.

In effect, for the first time in the post-war years a contest was being organised in the USSR for the best civil airliner. Each of the contenders had its 'selling points': the Il-18's advantage lay in its low fuel consumption when operated on trunk routes, whereas the An-10 was expected to operate from a wide network of airfields and have a military transport version.

The An-10, allocated the in-house designation '*izdeliye* U' and the popular name *Ookraïna* (the Ukraine), was intended to serve medium-haul routes 500–2,000 km (310–1,240 miles) long. The main special feature of the future airliner was its ability to operate from grass airstrips, since the construction of paved airstrips was just getting into its stride.

By that time the staff of the GSOKB-473 already totalled 1,500 employees, including nearly 250 designers, most of whom had graduated from aviation institutes. To help them in mastering the intricate art of creating an aircraft, special groups were formed which, as related in the previous chapter, were sent to aircraft plants in Kazan (No. 22) and Moscow (MMZ No. 30). There, as arranged with A.N. Tupolev and S.V. Ilyushin, the young specialists studied technical documentation on the Tu-16 and Il-28 bombers. This is why many elements in the design of the

A fine shot of an early-production An-10 *sans suffixe* (CCCP-11165; c/n 9401303?) in service; the colour scheme is identical to that of the prototype. Passengers embark via the rear door while mailbags are loaded through the forward entry door. Note the different design of the flight-deck side windows which was typical of production aircraft. (Sergey and Dmitriy Komissarov archive)

An-10 *sans suffixe* CCCP-11144 (c/n 8400506) taxies out for take-off. (Yefim Gordon archive)

The improved An-10A superseded the original model on the Voronezh production line in December 1959. Outwardly the A was almost identical to the An-10 *sans suffixe*, save for some changes in the window placement. CCCP-11206 (c/n 0402305), a late-production A, is seen here extending its undercarriage prior to landing; note the two small windows near the tail which were one of the external recognition features. As a point of interest, this aircraft was reregistered CCCP-34385 after transfer to MAP. (Yefim Gordon archive)

An-8, An-10 and An-12 later proved to be similar to the respective design features developed by Moscow design bureaux (for example, the navigator's station in the extreme nose of all three Antonov machines bore a striking resemblance to the nose of the basic Tu-16 *Badger-A*). Thus, a unified school of aircraft design gradually emerged in the USSR.

N.S. Troonchenkov and V.N. Ghelprin were appointed chief project engineers for the An-10 and the An-12 respectively. The general arrangement team was headed by N.A. Nechayev, the fuselage team by S.D. Yelmesev, the wing team by A.A. Batoomov and the undercarriage team by N.P. Smirnov. A.M. Kondratyev was responsible for the development of hydraulic systems, I.A. Pashinin and M.S. Galperin for the electrical equipment, V.A. Danilchenko for the avionics. Since all the passenger equipment, including the seats, was developed in-house, a special team headed by N.A. Pogorelov was set up for this purpose. O.K. Antonov himself took part in solving the main problems, such as determining the general arrangement and the design features of the most complicated single assemblies. Being endowed with a fine artistic taste, he paid special attention to the passenger cabin interior, the decor of which incorporated many ethnic Ukrainian motifs.

The fact that GSOKB-473 was located on Ukrainian soil had one more consequence which was of far greater importance for the destiny of the An-10 and An-12. It consisted in the choice of the engine type for these aircraft. The NK-4 engine developed by the Kuibyshev-based OKB-276[18] seemed very promising, with high specific performance characteristics and an output of 4,000 ehp. On the other hand, the identically rated TV-20 (AI-20) engine developed by Ivchenko's OKB-478 (which was located in the southern Ukrainian town of Zaporozhye),[19] albeit less advanced, relied on proved technical features. For some reason an opinion prevails that, thanks to Ivchenko's wisely cautious conservative approach, his engine was superior to that of his rival in reliability and operational safety. However, to this day no documentary proof has been found of the alleged 'unreliability' of the NK-4.

In the Antonov OKB each of the two engine types had its supporters and opponents. Some aviation historians believe that Antonov, being in two minds, took the decision that the first prototype of the An-10 should be powered by NK-4s and the first prototype of the An-12 by TV-20 (AI-20) engines. However, this was not the case. There is documentary evidence that the chief designer envisaged mounting Kuznetsov turboprops on the first two An-12 transports, and only the subsequent aircraft of this type were to be powered by Ivchenko engines. A certain part in this matter was also played by the Central Committee of the Communist Party of the Ukraine. Their reasoning was simple: since the aircraft is being created in the Ukraine, its engines should also be 'Ukrainian'. Understandably, O.K. Antonov, whose enterprise was situated in Kiev and depended to a large extent on the goodwill of the Ukrainian leadership, could not ignore this 'opinion'. Thus, the AI-20 engine was launched on a service career that proved to be long and successful.

In May 1956 the advanced development project of *izdeliye* U was submitted for approval, and the full-size mock-up was endorsed five months later.

The first prototype bearing the non-standard registration CCCP-Y1957 (i.e. SSSR-U1957 in Cyrillic characters; c/n unknown)[20] entered flight test on 7 March 1957. The maiden flight was performed by test pilots Yakov I. Vernikov (LII) and I.Ye. Davydov (GSOKB-473). Many features of the machine were unusual for a passenger aircraft of that time: the large fuselage diameter of 4.1 m (13 ft 5.5 in), the high-set wings with a span of 38 m (124 ft 8 in) and the short landing gear. In those years only two other airliners – the Soviet Tu-114 *Rossiya* (Russia; NATO *Cleat*) and the British Saunders-Roe Princess flying boat – could boast such a wide fuselage. The comfortable cabins featured carpeted floors; the seats with lightweight and strong aluminium alloy frames incorporated ashtrays, individual reading lamps and even sockets for headphones to allow you to listen to the radio without disturbing your fellow passengers.

For take-off at maximum AUW the aircraft needed an airstrip no more than 700–800 m (2,300–2,625 ft) long – even if it was unpaved. The landing run was even shorter, being just 500–600 m (1,640–1,970 ft). Besides, the An-10's radio navigation and radar equipment and flight instruments were advanced by the standards of the day. Pressurised cabins and an air-conditioning system enabled cruise flight at high altitudes, ensuring comfort and proper conditions for the crew and passengers.

The manufacturer's flight test programme was completed by I.Ye. Davydov and V.A. Kalinin. As noted above, the aircraft was powered by NK-4 engines driving AV-60 four-bladed propellers which had passed bench-testing ahead of the AI-20. In the course of flight-testing the prototype got a taller vertical tail to

Directional stability problems with the type persisted, necessitating a further redesign of the tail unit. Here CCCP-11160, one of the last An-10s *sans suffixe* (c/n 9401201), is seen as released from the factory. Before... (Yefim Gordon archive)

THE WINGED 'UKRAINE'

...and after. The same aircraft following an upgrade, seen taxiing past a sister ship at Moscow-Sheremet'yevo in 1965; note the new splayed ventral fins and the absence of endplate fins are well visible. Note also the ultimate blue/white livery with 'feathers' worn by the type. (Sergey Komissarov)

The An-10A fleet underwent an identical upgrade. Here CCCP-11177, an early-production example (c/n 9401704), is seen seconds before touchdown. Before...
(Boris Vdovenko)

enhance pitch and directional stability. However, this proved insufficient, and so large hexagonal endplate fins were fitted to the stabilisers.

In July 1957 the An-10 prototype was demonstrated for the first time to journalists and the general public at Moscow's Vnukovo airport. The same year, the aircraft entered series production at MAP Factory No. 64 in Voronezh. By the end of the year the plant had manufactured three aircraft powered by NK-4 engines; the latter was because the definitive AI-20 engines were not yet available.

Until 1964 State acceptance trials of the first Soviet airliners powered by turbojet and turboprop engines were held, not by the Civil Air Fleet Research Institute (NII GVF – *Naoochno-issledovatel'skiy instituoot Grazhdahnskovo vozdooshnovo flota*), as was the established practice in the 1930s and at present, but by GK NII VVS situated at Chkalovskaya airbase, east of Moscow. The second prototype An-10 (which was also the first production machine) bearing the registration CCCP-Λ5723 (i.e., SSSR-L5723; c/n 7400101)[21] first flew on 5 November 1957 with I.Ye. Davydow in the captain's seat. In 1958 it was ferried to Chkalovskaya AB, and its NK-4 engines were replaced by AI-20s in the course of the manufacturer's flight tests. (Later the same path was followed by the creators of the famous Il-18 airliner. Initially S.V. Ilyushin would not hear of the AI-20, but operational experience with the first production Il-18As powered by NK-4s revealed that these engines still needed a lengthy development process, which eventually led to the installation of AI-20 engines from the Il-18B version onwards.)

State acceptance trials of the An-10, which began in January 1959, were conducted by GK NII VVS project test pilots Kuznetsov and Fyodorov, engineer Sorokin, test navigators Zhitnik, Zatsepa and Vasilyev. The aircraft was also flown by military test pilots Golenkin, Azbiyevich, Yakovlev and Dedukh, as well as by Zakharovich, a civil pilot. GK NII VVS pilot E. Golenkin performed high-alpha and stalling tests of the An-10, flying the machine at critical angles of attack. Proceeding from the results of the trials which were completed in June 1959, the new aircraft – the first Soviet turboprop airliner – was recommended for series production, which had by that time already got into full swing at Plant No. 64 in Voronezh.

Flight testing of the *Ookraïna* was accompanied by frequent incidents. The first serious incident took place on 22 July 1957, shortly after the demonstration of the aircraft at Moscow-Vnukovo. When SSSR-U1957 was landing at the LII airfield in Zhukovskiy the starboard main undercarriage unit failed to lock in the down position, collapsing on touchdown.

On 21 February 1958 the prototype came close to being written off in an accident at Kiev-Sviatoshino, the airfield of Plant No. 473. While performing an emergency landing with No. 3 engine abnormally running at full throttle, test pilots I.Ye. Davydov and V.A. Kalinin miscalculated the final approach and made a crash landing. The port outer wing panel and No. 1 engine nacelle were destroyed, and the fuselage and the port main gear unit suffered some damage as well. This time the An-10 prototype was in need of more lengthy repairs (fortunately it was deemed repairable).

Two months later, on 29 April, one more incident occurred, but the crew coped admirably with an extremely difficult situation, avoiding a crash by a narrow margin. The port flap disintegrated owing to a manufacturing defect, and only the quick reaction of the crew captain allowed the flight to be completed safely.

With its high-set wings and large-diameter fuselage (by the standards of the day), the An-10 differed markedly from all existing passenger aircraft. This layout, as demonstrated by research conducted in the towing basin of a TsAGI branch specialising in seaplanes, ensured safe ditching with stable hydroplaning, even in rough seas. Fortunately, however, this property was not put to the test during the

...and after. These photos show the red/white colour scheme worn by many An-10s; note also the ADF strake aerial. (Yefim Gordon archive)

An-10A CCCP-11185 was retained by the Antonov OKB as a trials aircraft for testing new design features. (Antonov OKB)

operational career of the An-10 (nor the An-8 and An-12).

An-10 Ookraïna production version

Starting in 1958, the NK-4 engines were supplanted on production aircraft rolling off the Voronezh assembly line by the more reliable 4,000 ehp AI-20As driving AV-68 propellers. The Ivchenko engines had a longer service life and compared favourably to the Kuznetsov engine in terms of weight, power output, ease of production and in some other respects. Outwardly the AI-20-powered version could be identified by the oil coolers located under the front ends of the engine nacelles; on the initial NK-4-powered aircraft the oil coolers were located well aft. Also, the cabin window placement was different on production An-10s. The prototype featured 15 windows on each side (2 windows + an emergency exit with a window + 1 window + an entry door with a window + 3 windows + an emergency exit + 2 windows + another entry door + 3 windows to port and 2 windows + an emergency exit + 1 window + 8 windows + a large cargo door with a window + 2 windows to starboard). Production aircraft had one window less on the starboard side (1 + exit + 1 + 8 + door + 2).

Most of the defects revealed during the flight testing of the An-10 could be easily rectified in series production; however, two of them necessitated additional and rather lengthy research. It was discovered that when the aircraft reached Mach 0.62 a rather dangerous buffeting arose, for which reason the pilots were forbidden to exceed this speed, even though the engine power available was more than sufficient for that. Besides, insufficient longitudinal stability manifested itself during landing approach. As the An-10 came in for landing with the flaps extended, even an insignificant but abrupt 'push' of the control column would cause the nose to 'fall through' and the pilot had to be extra-careful and more precise in calculations at this crucial stage of the flight.

On 27 April 1959 the An-10 performed its first route-proving flight. Exactly a month later the aircraft took off on a publicity tour which took it from Kiev to Moscow, Tbilisi, Sochi/Adler (the two cities share the same airport), Kharkov and thence back to Kiev. The type's first scheduled flight (from Moscow-Vnukovo to Simferopol) took place on 22 July 1959, and on 17–24 December of that year An-10 CCCP-11172 (c/n 9401602) made a demonstration flight to the USA, bringing 44 saplings of trees endemic to the USSR as a gift from Khrushchev to President Dwight D. Eisenhower. On 10 September of the same year, after successfully completing operational trials, the new aircraft was officially put into service by Aeroflot, the sole Soviet airline.

The pilots of the Ukrainian Civil Aviation Directorate (CAD) were the first to master the An-10. Following suit, several other Aeroflot directorates in the Russian Federative Soviet Socialist Republic and other Union republics simultaneously started operating this machine on medium-haul routes.

During the initial period of its operation the aircraft won favour thanks to its large payload and good field performance. As noted earlier, the machine was well suited for operation from unpaved airstrips. It has to be stressed that in the conditions of the Soviet Union this was of great importance. In 1959 even Kiev-Borispol, the main airport of the Ukrainian capital, had no paved runway – to say nothing about other cities big and small where paved runways were at best under construction, or only grass airstrips were available. If one resorts to 'Soviet' parlance (i.e. officialese yuckspeak characteristic of those times), the An-10 *brought the air transport on its wings to those places*. Without indulging in enumeration, it can be mentioned that in the Ukraine alone

A number of Aeroflot An-10s were used for carrying small cargoes; this version was called An-10AS. Here a cargo-configured *Cat* is seen offloading sacks of fresh newspapers and magazines at Rostov-on-Don in 1962. (Novosti Press Agency)

An-10A CCCP-11185 was later converted into the prototype of the 132-seat An-10B. The appropriate nose titles are only just discernible in this view. (Yefim Gordon archive)

these included the majority of regional centres.

The aircraft could operate in a mixed cargo/passenger configuration (52 passengers, 1,040 kg/2,290 lb of baggage and 9,080 kg/20,020 lb of cargo) or, if need be, in pure cargo configuration, carrying 15 tons (33,070 lb) of cargo, and the aircraft could be reconfigured very quickly in field conditions. This, coupled with other advantages, made the machine truly versatile. On shorter trunk routes with intensive passenger traffic this versatility made it possible to venture on the concept of an 'airbus' expected to be able to land on any more or less suitable field. Not infrequently, tickets were sold right on the spot, in the passenger cabin, and the airliner took off after all the seats were sold. Low tariff rates, where the price of the ticket was on a par with the price of a railway ticket in a sleeping car to the same distance, as well as the initially high profitability of the machine, justified hopes for the whole concept to prove economically viable.

According to calculations made by specialists, the seat-mile costs of the 85-seat An-10 were considerably lower than those of the turbojet-powered 50-seat Tu-104A *Camel*, mainly thanks to the former type's higher seating capacity. However, the introduction of the stretched Tu-104B seating up to 100 passengers negated this advantage – in fact, the Tu-104B proved to be more economical than the Antonov machine. It should be noted that the Tu-104B's high fuel efficiency manifested itself only at high altitudes, deteriorating markedly at medium and low altitudes. Conversely, the An-10 offered high fuel efficiency both at medium and at relatively low altitudes.

Interestingly, the in-flight entertainment (IFE) systems of modern airliners *ain't nothin'* new. The passenger cabin of a regular in-service An-10 registered CCCP-11171 (c/n 0401503) was equipped with a film projection screen – a feature which won universal approval on the part of both passengers and aircrews. Nevertheless, passengers were of the opinion that flying in the An-10 was less pleasant than in the various versions of the Tu-104 (mainly because of the An-10's greater sensitivity to turbulence and the annoying vibrations in the passenger cabin). The seats most favoured by the passengers of the An-10 were the ones in the rear cabin, where the engine noise was less strong.

The considerable structural commonality of the An-10 and its transport derivative, the An-12, was a liability in certain respects. For example, early production An-12s had their centre fuselage structure hermetically sealed (as on the pressurised An-10), even though the freight hold was unpressurised – with an attendant increase in manufacturing costs and complexity. In turn, the An-10, owing to the placement of the cabin floor on the same height as the freighter's cargo floor, featured an excessive passenger cabin volume at the expense of the baggage compartments' capacity. All this entailed an unnecessary increase in airframe weight, especially in the case of the An-10. The An-10's payload/TOW ratio was appreciably lower as compared to the Il-18, as repeatedly pointed out by Sergey V. Ilyushin, who considered the whole concept of the An-10/An-12 to be flawed for this very reason.

Nevertheless, O.K. Antonov consciously put up with certain weight penalties, regarding them an acceptable price for the advantages listed above. From the present-day point of view this attitude is extremely vulnerable, but in the days when the country had plentiful supplies of kerosene and any project was judged mainly as to whether it was conducive to 'speeding up progress', the concept of the An-10/An-12 'twins' looked very attractive and even economically sound – after all, it made it possible to create powerful military transport assets by manufacturing innocuous passenger aircraft.

As already mentioned, on 22 July 1959

Aeroflot started revenue operation of the An-10. Thus, everything indicated that one of the world's best aircraft in its class had emerged. In 1958 the An-10 was awarded the Gold Medal and a diploma at the World Exhibition in Bruxelles. In 1960–61 the An-10 made demonstration trips to many countries of the world. (In 1961 it was accompanied by the Il-18. Not one of these trips resulted in an An-10 sale; the Il-18, on the contrary, attracted numerous export orders.) When the An-10's existence became known to the West the type was allocated the reporting name *Cat*.

It is known that at least one An-10 was successfully transformed into an An-12 at the Voronezh aircraft factory for the purpose of checking the viability of the aforementioned 'airliner-to-airlifter quick conversion' idea.

An-10A Ookraïna airliner

New versions of Antonov's *Cat* began appearing pretty soon. The first of these 'kittens' was an improved version designated An-10A, which started coming off the production line in December 1959, supplanting the original An-10 with no suffix letter (or *sans suffixe*, as we will call it from now on). Apart from appropriate nose titles, outwardly the An-10A differed from the previous model in cabin window arrangement, with 16 windows to port (2 + exit + 1 + door + 1 + 3 + exit + 2 + door + 3) and 13 to starboard (1 + exit + 1 + 1 + 6 + door + 2). Additionally, there were two smaller windows on each side in line with the fin/fillet junction, and a rectangular baggage hatch was added immediately ahead of the starboard main-gear fairing. The An-10A is often described as featuring a stretched fuselage but this is a statement open to doubt.

The first 'As were still powered by AI-20A engines, but these were replaced by 4,250 ehp AI-20Ks on later examples. The An-10A was built in two versions, which initially seated 89 and 100 passengers respectively. Later the seating capacity was increased to 117–18 and then to 132 by changing the cabin layout and reducing the seat pitch. The payload was increased to 14.5 tons (31,970 lb).

Perfecting the manufacturing technologies used at Plant No. 64 improved the external finish of the aircraft, and the surface of its skin became smoother. Coupled with some other measures taken by GSOKB-473, these improvements increased the maximum speed of production machines from 675 km/h (420 mph) to 705–10 km/h (438–41 mph), with a corresponding increase of the cruising speed.

As of 1 January 1960, only 26 machines out of the 58 An-10s and An-10As manufactured by then were operated by Aeroflot. The remainder served with the VVS as troop/assault transports, sometimes in full Aeroflot livery but usually in overt military markings.

The *Cat's* production run was rather modest, totalling 104 machines (including the Kiev-built prototype and the static test airframe; the exact proportion of An-10s and An-10As is unknown). Of these, three aircraft were built in 1957 (including one in Voronezh), 16 aircraft in 1958, 39 more in 1959 and 46 in 1960. Two An-10As were initially manufactured in a luxuriously appointed export version to be delivered to India in 1960, but the order was eventually cancelled and both machines were delivered to Aeroflot after having their passenger cabins refitted to standard configuration.

Originally the An-10A had the same tail-unit design as the initial production version. In 1962, however, the single ventral fin and endplate fins of the An-10As (and some An-10s *sans suffixe*) were replaced by two splayed ventral fins. They were mounted on the aft fuselage underside, in an area where separation of the turbulent airflow occurred. As a result, the ventral fins not only had a positive effect on the aerodynamic characteristics but also caused unpleasant vibration of the aircraft.

The effect of this, strictly speaking, minor modification was felt immediately. Flight tests conducted by GK NII VVS between 5 and 30 September 1961 showed that the onset of Mach buffet was delayed until the aircraft reached Mach 0.702. There was an improvement of longitudinal stability under high g loads during landing approach. At the same time one of the 'bugs' of the initial version was still there: deflection of the rudder to an angle of 16–18° caused vibration of the tail surfaces. The aircraft was flown by GK NII VVS test pilots A. Terentyev, A. Starikov, Bryksin and NII GVF test pilot Vozniakov.

An-10AS transport conversion

This was a civil cargo version of the An-10A intended for carrying various small cargoes with an all-up weight of 16,300 kg (35,940 lb). The meaning of the S suffix to the designation remains unknown. The freighter conversion involved removal of the passenger seats and cabin partitions and the installation of a reinforced cargo floor featuring tie-down points. The conversion was effected by Aeroflot divisions operating the An-10A.

An-10B airliner project (first use of designation?)

Operational experience accumulated by Aeroflot with the An-10, the first Soviet turboprop airliner, revealed that the aircraft had the potential for considerably improving the performance and operational characteristics (i.e. ease of operation and maintenance, direct operating costs, etc.). Several upgrade projects were developed; however, the improved versions largely remained on the drawing-board.

One of the unbuilt projects was designated An-10B. The aircraft featured a new avionics suite and an altered passenger cabin layout with up to 118 seats.

An-10B airliner prototype (second use of designation?)

A single An-10A retained by the Antonov OKB as a 'dogship' for testing new features (CCCP-11185, c/n unknown) was converted into a version seating 132 passengers without changing the fuselage dimensions or interior layout. The additional seating capacity was obtained by installing seven-abreast seating instead of the standard six-abreast arrangement and increasing the number of seat rows from seven to nine in the centre cabin. The aircraft also featured increased fuel tankage, extending the range to 2,000 km (1,240 miles) with a payload of 14,500 kg (31,970 lb). The modified aircraft sported An-10B nose titles.

THE WINGED 'UKRAINE'

This cutaway display model of the radically redesigned An-10V (alias An-16) was displayed at the Central Air Terminal at Moscow-Khodynka, the origin of shuttle buses to the city's airports, in 1967. The model shows clearly the stretched fuselage and swept tail. (Sergey Komissarov)

THE WINGED 'UKRAINE'

The Soviet Air Force operated the *Cat* in substantial numbers. Here a pre-upgrade An-10A in basic Aeroflot colours (c/n unknown) is seen on short finals to Moscow-Vnukovo in September 1964; note the exhaust stains on the flaps. (Sergey Komissarov)

Another SovAF An-10A staff transport, this time in late configuration with no endplate fins. Curiously, such aircraft wore no tactical codes and were identified only by their ATC callsigns and construction numbers which are mostly unknown. (Yefim Gordon archive)

An-10V (An-16) airliner project

One more projected version of the aircraft was designated An-10V (also known as the An-16). It had a new fuselage of increased cross-section and 6 m (19 ft 8 in) greater length accommodating 175 passengers, mostly seven-abreast, in four cabins (a 58-seat tourist-class forward cabin, a luxury compartment seating ten, and two more tourist-class cabins for 84 and 23 passengers respectively). The tail unit was revised, featuring a moderately sweptback vertical tail.

A cutaway model with An-10V nose titles and the registration CCCP-11744 was displayed in the Air Terminal building at Moscow-Khodynka in 1967 (in those days the place functioned as a heliport, with Mil Mi-4P *Hound* helicopters providing shuttle services to the city's airports). The model lacked wings and stabilisers; therefore it is not known what changes were made to these airframe components to cater for the higher all-up weight.

32

Apart from staff transports, the VVS also had numerous An-10TS troopship aircraft. These wore an overall silver finish and large tactical codes. Here a squadron of An-10TSs rests between flights in 1971; the nearest aircraft is coded 19 Blue. Other known examples include 12 Blue, 14 Blue, 18 Blue and 20 Blue. (TASS News Agency)

An-16 airliner project (first use of designation?)

Confusingly, the designation An-16 is also quoted for another proposed version of the An-10, which was intended to carry 130 passengers a distance of 2,000 km (1,240 miles). The increase in the seating capacity was to be achieved by inserting a 3 m (9 ft 10 in) cylindrical plug in the fuselage. The project developed in 1957 was not implemented.

An-10D airliner project

In January 1960 Chief Designer O.K. Antonov proposed developing a version designated An-10D; it was to incorporate a fairly large number of new features which could place the An-10 on a par with the world's best airliners in its category. Among other things, the proposal envisaged increasing the range to 3,650 km (2,270 miles) by using the empty space in the wing torsion box for extra fuel cells (D = dahl'niy – long-range). Incorporating integral fuel tanks in the detachable outer wings would further increase the range to 4,400 km (2,735 miles). Work in this direction was already under way at GSOKB-473 and the first aircraft thus modified was to be manufactured by Plant No.64 in the first quarter of 1960.

The seating capacity was to be increased to 124 (in a tourist-class layout) for flights of up three hours' duration. It was hoped to increase the speed (and thereby improve fuel efficiency) by fitting new propellers with fibreglass blades. Passenger comfort was to be enhanced (among other things, cabin noise levels would be reduced by moving the engines away from the fuselage thanks to inner wing panels of approximately 1 m (3 ft) greater span). The increased dimensions of the centre passenger cabin would allow movies to be shown in flight.

Implementation of the above-mentioned ideas increased the economic efficiency of the An-10D by some 30 per cent; however, the project did not progress further than the drawing board.

An An-10TS (18 Blue) in action, showing the standard baggage hatch used as a paratroop door, with static lines dangling from it. (Yefim Gordon archive)

Another action shot showing paratroopers leaving an An-10TS. (Sergey and Dmitriy Komissarov archive)

The An-10 was operated by several of Aeroflot's Civil Aviation Directorates. Here, An-10A CCCP-11198 (c/n 9401903) operated by the Komi CAD/Syktyvkar United Flight Detachment/75th Flight taxies out at Moscow-Sheremet'yevo in 1965. Note the leaping stag logo of the Komi CAD (which served as the inspiration for the Komiavia logo in the 1990s); also note the Central International Services Directorate Il'yushin Il-62s and Tupolev Tu-114 in the background. (Sergey Komissarov)

An-10TS military transport

To suit the needs of the Soviet Air Force's transport arm GSOKB-473 developed a version designated An-10TS (*trahnsportno-sanitarnyy* – transport and ambulance). The aircraft had a payload of 14,500 kg (31,970 lb) and was capable of paradropping personnel through the standard cargo door on the starboard side of the aft fuselage. Forty-five An-10TS aircraft were in service by July 1965; interestingly, only ten of them were operated full-time by the VTA, while the remaining 38 were loaned to the Ministry of Civil Aviation so as to ensure the most profitable use of the aircraft. Some of the An-10TSs used by Aeroflot were fitted out for passenger transportation. The passenger cabin lacked partitions, creating an unpleasant 'tunnel effect'.

The An-10's service was marred by several fatal accidents which earned the type a bad reputation. Here, Ukrainian CAD An-10A CCCP-11215 (c/n 0402502?) is seen on finals to Moscow-Vnukovo in September 1964. It was the crash of this very aircraft near Khar'kov on 18th May 1972 that put an end to the *Cat*'s airline career. (Sergey Komissarov)

An-10KP airborne command post

In response to an order from the Airborne Troops, in 1970 a single An-10A registered CCCP-11854 (possibly ex CCCP-11150; c/n unknown) was converted into an airborne command post intended for combat control and for maintaining communications with various headquarters and ground control posts. This mission could be performed with the aircraft airborne or on the ground. The passenger cabin accommodated a 'war room' and secure communications equipment operators' workstations. Outwardly the aircraft could be easily identified by the four large blade aerials mounted dorsally ahead of the wings and ventrally ahead of the main gear fairings; additionally, the first window aft of the forward entry door and two windows aft of the rear entry door were faired over.

Designated An-10KP (*komahndnyy poonkt* – command post), CCCP-11854 served with the Group of Soviet Forces in Germany, operating from the Soviet airbase at Sperenberg near Berlin, until it was withdrawn from use as time-expired. There were plans to preserve the aircraft for posterity in the open-air museum at the GSFG headquarters in Wünsdorf; eventually, however, the An-10KP was trucked to the aerial gunnery range at Rupine Heide, ending its days as a target for trigger-happy ground-attack aircraft pilots.

The shortest life (the An-10 in service)

It took only 15 months to create the first Soviet turboprop airliner (by comparison, the Lockheed Company required 28 months to develop the L-188 Electra airliner belonging to the same class). Interestingly, chief designer O.K. Antonov himself said, 'It is important to avoid the temptation to build a new product, test it and triumphantly report about the results as quickly as possible, to the detriment of quality.'[22] But let's take a look at what happened in reality.

The *Cat* possessed many strong points, yet it was plagued by poor reliability. In the course of An-10/An-10A operations up to 1961 no fewer than 670 defects were revealed and rectified. As related above, the configuration of the tail unit was revised to increase directional stability. The initial version with a small ventral fin and two endplate fins on the stabilisers gave place to another in which two big splayed ventral fins were mounted on the aft fuselage and the endplate fins were deleted. Each of the two variants had its strengths and weaknesses which affected the aircraft's longitudinal stability.

The An-10's longitudinal stability problems manifested themselves during the troublesome service introduction period. Twenty-three fatal and non-fatal accidents with the type occurred between April 1958 and February 1963 (true, not all of them resulted in total hull losses); more than 56 per cent of them were associated with airframe and powerplant defects. By July 1965 11 An-10s had been lost.

For example, the following characteristic occurrence was revealed in the course of the trials and initial service period. On short finals, when the speed was reduced to about 280–90 km/h (174–80 mph) and the aircraft was quite close to the ground,

Sic transit gloria mundi... Forty-two An-10s were struck off charge and scrapped after the 1972 crash. Here, An-10A CCCP-11183 (c/n 0401804) is stripped of usable items before facing the breaker's torch, with a sister aircraft just visible behind. Note the additional cargo door ahead of the starboard wing which was a distinguishing feature of the A model. (Yefim Gordon archive)

The tail unit of An-10A CCCP-11174. The aircraft was on display at the Economic Achievements Exhibition in Kiev. (Yefim Gordon)

The starboard main-gear unit and gear actuator fairing of CCCP-11174. Note the ground power sockets in the rear end of the fairing. (Yefim Gordon)

it would often drop its nose abruptly, going into a dive. At low altitude and given reduced elevator authority compounded by the suddenness of the phenomenon and limited time available for taking a decision, this often led to accidents.

One of the first fatal crashes with the type involved a Ukrainian CAD An-10 *sans suffixe* registered CCCP-11167 (c/n unknown). As the airliner came in for landing at Lvov airport on 16 November 1959, nothing seemed to forebode disaster. Having completed the landing pattern and performed all the necessary cockpit checks, the crew commenced final approach. The runway could be glimpsed through gaps in the clouds when the captain suddenly felt the control column move abruptly forward on its own. Within a moment the heavy aircraft entered a steep dive and crashed 1 km (3,280 ft) from the inner marker beacon (IMB), killing all 32 passengers and eight crew.

Initially all attempts to ascertain the cause of the crash were to no avail. The accident investigating commission found no deviations in the aircraft's longitudinal stability and controllability characteristics, the functioning of its systems or the actions of the crew during the landing approach. A repeated analysis of the results of the An-10's State acceptance trials conducted by the best experts of GSOKB-473, LII and the State Research Institute of Civil Aviation (GosNII GA – *Gosoodarstvennyy naoochno-issledovatel'skiy instituot grazhdahnskoy aviahtsii*, the former NII GVF) yielded no positive results either: the longitudinal stability and controllability characteristics were completely in accordance with the technical requirements in force at the time. (However, documents in the Accident Investigation Branch of the CIS Interstate Aviation Committee – the successor of the Soviet-era State Flight Safety Inspectorate (*Gosavianadzor*) – attribute the crash of CCCP-11167 to accidental use of reverse thrust on short finals; the pilots had accidentally retarded the throttles past ground idle.)

Shortly afterwards another crash occurred at the same airport. On 26 February 1960 An-10 CCCP-11180 (c/n 9401801?) dived into the ground 350 m (1,150 ft) from the IMB; again there were no survivors among the 24 passengers and eight crew. All An-10s were grounded immediately pending investigation of the disaster. The decisive word was pronounced by GosNII GA test pilots and engineers, who pointed out that the crash had occurred during a period when aircraft were susceptible to intensive icing. Icing is always a very dangerous phenomenon: ice

The port AI-20D engines and AV-68 reversible-pitch propellers of An-10A CCCP-11174. Note the generator cooling intakes on top of the engine nacelles, as well as the entry doors and the port rear emergency exit. (Yefim Gordon)

formations on the wings and propeller blades lead to deterioration of the aerodynamic qualities and controllability, causing airflow separation and decreasing lift; icing of pitot tubes puts flight instruments (notably airspeed indicators) out of action.

GosNII GA test pilots N. Karlash and O. Dmitrenko and engineers O.K. Troonov, A. Bondarenko, G. Balashov and V. Yooshkevich succeeded in solving a tough task. Using specially equipped An-10 CCCP-11133 (the only one exempt from the grounding order) to investigate the aircraft's behaviour in natural icing conditions, they established that the second crash had been caused by icing of the stabiliser leading edges, which led to a complete loss of elevator authority through airflow separation on the underside of the horizontal tail. It was established that even a small ice formation on the horizontal tail surface – just 8–10 mm (0.3–0.4 in) – dangerously affected the stability of the aircraft. This was associated with the peculiarities of high-wing turboprop aircraft equipped with powerful high-lift devices. The deterioration of longitudinal stability and controllability of these aircraft is caused by a change in the character of the airflow around the horizontal tail during landing approach and to the negative incidence of the horizontal tail approaching a critical angle when ice formed on the stabiliser leading edge.

In the final count this research led to the retrofitting of all Antonov aircraft with a stabiliser de-icing system. Antonov OKB, LII and GosNII GA specialists very quickly developed and tested a new effective de-icing system with so-called 'thermal knives' which was installed on the tail surfaces of all An-10s and An-10As. This system was later incorporated in many other Aeroflot aircraft.

During the first five years of operation the An-10 transported more than ten million passengers and more than 500,000 tons (1,102,290 lb) of cargo. By 1967 the *Cat* was operated on more than 90 routes inside the country. New routes were opened every year, and by 1971 the type had carried 35 million passengers and one million tons (2,204,585 lb) of cargo. Thus the An-10 ranked first among Aeroflot's types as far as the passenger turnover was concerned. Everything seemed to be going nicely when unexpectedly disaster struck again. On 18 May 1972 a Ukrainian CAD An-10A (CCCP-11215; c/n 0402502?) crashed near Kharkov-Sokolnikovo airport, killing all 114 passengers and eight crew. The tragedy provoked a tremendous public outcry both in the Soviet Union and abroad – not least because the victims of the crash included Nina Aleksandrova, a well-known female reporter from the *Izvestiya* daily newspaper, and Viktor Chistyakov, an actor from Leningrad who was very popular in those years. As a result, all An-10s were grounded immediately and an authoritative commission was set up to investigate the causes of the crash.

The cause was found fairly quickly. The 'tin kickers' discovered fatigue cracks in the wing centre-section stringers which had caused the wing to disintegrate. Considering that the crashed aircraft was a late-production example, a fleet-wide check was mounted and the same defect was promptly discovered on other An-10s as well. By then some 70 machines of this type were operated by Aeroflot's East Siberian, North Caucasian, Komi, Volga, Moldavian and Ukrainian CADs and the Ulyanovsk Higher Flying School. As a result, on 27 August 1973 the Ministry of Civil Aviation issued Order No. 032, withdrawing the An-10 from Aeroflot service. Forty-two high-time aircraft were struck off charge and scrapped, and another 25 An-10As in reasonably good condition were transferred to the Air Force and various MAP enterprises.

The tragic accident near Kharkov and its investigation posed dozens of questions before aircraft designers, flight and ground crews, and the top executives of Aeroflot. How come an aircraft that shouldered such a big volume of work became unsafe all of a sudden? Why, despite the fairly high total flying time and repeated service life extensions, hadn't the aircraft received even a modest upgrade? Why did its stablemate, the An-12 built just a little later than the An-10 and sharing the same layout, have a much happier fate?

No answers were ever given to these and other questions. What the authorities did was do their damnedest to obliterate every trace of the An-10 from the history of Soviet aviation. Even the designation of this aircraft was literally censored from advertising brochures, aviation reference books and any materials on aviation matters. Vigilant MAP officials expressly 'recommended' that even mentioning the An-10 in the press should be avoided, as though it had never existed. However, time has passed and now it can in all justice be stated that this aircraft left a notable trace in the Soviet aircraft design school and also became the 'forebear' of the famous An-12 transport which is the subject of this book and will be dealt with in the next chapter – an aircraft which will remain for ever inscribed in the history of world aviation.

While we are on the subject of the An-10, it deserves mention that in 1961 an unsuccessful attempt was undertaken to establish a world speed record in the An-10. The flight was performed in a closed circuit from Moscow to Melitopol and back again. At the closing stage of the flight it became clear that the remaining fuel was insufficient, and in order to bring the machine back to base the crew had to consecutively shut down the engines. GSOKB-473 test pilot Yuriy V. Koorlin shut down the No. 1 engine, then the No. 2 engine. With the portside propellers feathered, the machine continued a stable flight. Then the pilot shut down the No. 3 engine. Still the machine continued a stable cruise at the required altitude for another 45 minutes.

Nevertheless, a world speed record for turboprop-powered aircraft was established, albeit not at once. On 22 April 1961 pilot A. Mitronin performed a flight on a 500 km (310.5 mile) closed circuit, clocking an average speed of 730.6 km/h (437.3 mph). This result was quite commendable for a turboprop airliner at the time, bearing in mind that the cruising speed of aircraft in this class averaged 560–650 km/h (348–404 mph).

In the mid-1970s the Soviet Air Force Museum in Monino added an ex-Komi CAD/Syktyvkar United Flight Detachment An-10A (CCCP-11213, c/n 0402406) to its collection. Another An-10A, CCCP-11174 (c/n unknown), was preserved in Kiev and a third, CCCP-11200, became a café in Kuibyshev (now Samara).

The following brief structural description applies to the baseline An-10A.

Type: Four-engined medium-haul airliner.

Fuselage: semi-monocoque all-metal stressed-skin structure with 68 full-section frames, nine formers and 110 stringers; the maximum fuselage diameter is 4.1 m (13 ft 5.5 in). The fuselage is built in three sections: forward, centre and aft. Two doors on the port side serve for the embarkation and disembarkation of passengers, with a cargo door and a baggage hatch on the starboard side. The greater part of the fuselage is pressurised with a pressure differential of 0.5 kg/cm^2 (7.14 psi) to ensure normal conditions for the crew and passengers at altitudes up to 10,000 m (32,810 ft). The height of the passenger cabin is 2.6 m (8 ft 6 in).

Wings: cantilever shoulder-mounted wings of trapezoidal planform and all-metal two-spar construction. The wings are built in five sections, comprising a centre section integral with the fuselage, two inner wing panels (which carry the engines) and two outer wing panels. In aerodynamic layout the wings are similar to those of the An-8 but feature 3º anhedral on the outer panels. Eighteen self-sealing bag-type fuel tanks are accommodated in the inner-wing torsion boxes, plus four non-sealing fuel tanks in the centre-section torsion box. The high-lift devices comprise double-slotted flaps. The wings are equipped with two-section ailerons with balance trim tabs, assisted for roll control by mechanically linked four-section spoilers.

Tail unit: conventional cantilever tail surfaces with one-piece conventional rudder and elevators. The fixed-incidence stabilisers have zero incidence and zero dihedral. A single ventral fin under the rear fuselage, augmented by stabiliser endplate fins, was fitted originally; in 1962 these were replaced by twin outward-canted ventral fins. The elevators are 100 per cent mass-balanced and incorporate two trim tabs. The rudder is also 100 per cent mass-balanced and equipped with a trim tab and a spring-loaded balancing tab.

Landing gear: hydraulically retractable tricycle landing gear, with a retractable tail bumper to protect the rear fuselage in the event of over-rotation or a tail-down landing. The twin-wheel nose unit with non-braking 900 × 300 mm (35.43 × 11.81 in) wheels retracts aft; the inward-retracting main units have four-wheel bogies with 1,050 × 300 mm (41.33 × 11.81 in) brake wheels.

Powerplant: four 4,000 ehp Ivchenko AI-20 (AI-20A) or 4,250 ehp AI-20K turboprops in individual nacelles attached to the wing centre section underside, driving AV-68I four-blade reversible-pitch automatically feathering propellers.

Avionics and equipment: the avionics suite includes a 1-RSB-70 communications radio, an R-836 command radio, an ARK-5 ADF, an SP-50 ILS, an RV-2 low-range radio altimeter and an RBP-2 ground-mapping radar.

De-icing system: hot-air de-icing system using engine bleed air on the wing leading edges, engine air intakes and flight deck/navigator's station glazing. Electric de-icers on the fin, stabilisers, propeller blades and spinners, pitot tubes and windshields.

Basic specifications of the An-10

	An-10	An-10A
Powerplant	4 × AI-20	4 × AI-20A
Power, ehp	4 × 4,000	4 × 4,000
Length overall	31.0 m (101 ft 8.47 in)	31.0 m (101 ft 8.47 in)*
Height on ground	9.83 m (32 ft 3 in)	9.83 m (32 ft 3 in)
Wingspan	38.0 m (124 ft 8 in)	38.0 m (124 ft 8 in)
Wing area, m² (sq. ft)	121.73 (1,308.9)	121.73 (1,308.9)
Empty weight, kg (lb)	31,614 (69,695)	32,500 (71,650)
Maximum all-up weight, kg (lb)	51,000 (112,430)	54,000 (119,050)
Maximum payload, kg (lb)	12,000 (26,455)	14,500 (31,970)
Maximum fuel load, kg (lb)	10,780 (23,765)	10,780 (23,765)
Maximum speed, km/h (mph):		
at sea level	520 (323)	n.a.
at 8,000 m (26,246 ft)	675 (420)	n.a.
Climb time, min:		
to 8,000 m	17.5	n.a.
to service ceiling	45	n.a.
Service ceiling, m (ft)	10,000 (32,810)	10,300 (33,790)
Range with a 12,000 kg payload	2,000 (1,240)	2,750 (1,708)
Take-off run, m (ft)	880–1,035 (2,890–3,400)	880 (2,890)
Landing run, m (ft)	845–995 (2,770–3,265)	825 (2,700)

* Some sources stated an overall length of 34.0 m (111 ft 6.58 in).

CHAPTER THREE

Birth of an Airlifter

Except for the choice of the engine type, few major problems were encountered in designing the An-12, which received the in-house designation *izdeliye* T (meaning ***trahns**portnyy samo**lyot*** – transport aircraft; sometimes called *samo**lyot*** T – 'Aircraft T'). The general arrangement, basic structural design features and principal systems and equipment of the new Antonov 'twins' (the An-10 and An-12) had been verified on the An-8; yet, while retaining the latter's high-wing, fuselage-mounted gear layout, the An-12 was very different from the 'Whale'. The first available photos of the American counterpart – the Lockheed YC-130A Hercules – confirmed to the Antonov engineers that the choice of a four-engined layout and the upswept rear fuselage with rear loading doors had been correct.

The detail design work on the An-12 took just 11 months to complete; in contrast, prototype construction at the Irkutsk aircraft factory No. 39 lasted a year and a half. Actually the term 'production prototype' would be more appropriate in this case. The An-10 and the initial version of the An-12 had such a high degree of commonality (86 per cent for the airframe and 100 per cent for the powerplant) that production could begin right away, with no need to master new manufacturing techniques, and for all practical purposes the first An-12 prototype powered by NK-4 engines was also the first production aircraft.

Even though the airliner version enjoyed priority over the freighter, the general arrangement, overall dimensions, fuselage cross-section and the wing, tail unit and landing gear design of the An-10 were selected with military uses in mind. That is to say, from the outset the engineers had designed into the aircraft the possibility of manufacturing the airliner and transport versions on the same production line. In fact, it was even suggested that if a war became imminent the An-10 fleet could be quickly *converted into An-12s by replacing the entire aft fuselage*! This was made possible – in theory at least – by a production break aft of the wings. Paraphrasing a well-known saying, what a man has joined together another man can always set apart.

The uncoded and unpainted first production prototype An-12 (c/n 7900101) seen at Irkutsk in December 1957 soon after its maiden flight. (Yefim Gordon archive)

41

Up to fuselage frame 41 the An-12's airframe was identical to that of the production An-10 *sans suffixe*. The upswept aft fuselage was new, being similar to that of the An-8; the flat underside incorporated a large cargo hatch closed by an upward-hinged rear door segment and two forward door segments split fore and aft which opened inwards and upwards to lie flat against the sides of the freight hold. The tail surfaces were basically similar to those of the *Cat* but the vertical tail had a much deeper fin fillet, which transitioned smoothly into a 'superstructure' incorporating a glazed tail-gunner's station. The fuselage terminated in a DB-65U powered turret with two 23 mm (.90 calibre) Afanasyev/Makarov AM-23 cannon. The cabin window placement was 2 + exit + 1 + door + 3 + exit + 1 to port and 1 + exit + 1 + 5 to starboard.

The mock-up review commission concluded its work on the *izdeliye* T on 22 July 1957. Five months later, on 16 December 1957, the first production prototype An-12 (c/n 7900101; see end of chapter for explanation) took off from Irkutsk-2 airfield at 14.37 local time with many of the plant's employees watching. The uncoded aircraft was captained by LII test pilot Yakov I. Vernikov, Hero of the Soviet Union, with G.I. Lysenko (who had recently been transferred to GSOKB-473 from NII GVF) as co-pilot. The test crew also included navigator P.I. Oovarov, flight engineer I.M. Morozov, radio operator M.G. Yoorov and tail gunner V.G. Zhilkin.

In its maiden flight the aircraft became unstuck a little earlier than anticipated, and raising the flaps and throttling back to nominal power the crew put the transport into a climb. All of a sudden, vibration was felt in the forward fuselage and Vernikov chose to abort the mission and land. During the nine-minute first flight the An-12 had managed to reach an altitude of 880 m (2,890 ft) and a speed of 340 km/h (211 mph).

It was quickly established that the vibration had been caused by a nosewheel well door which had opened of its own accord (as is usually the case during a first flight, the landing gear had stayed down throughout the flight, and the An-12's wheel well doors were designed to close when the gear was down). There had been no danger for the aircraft and crew; yet Vernikov, who had been assigned captain only a few days earlier, had not had a chance to study the aircraft thoroughly, and his decision to return to base had been a prudent one. From the second test flight onwards G.I. Lysenko was assigned as project test pilot.

The strengths and weaknesses of the An-12 came to light almost immediately as the flight tests continued. Pilots who flew the new transport were impressed by the An-12's unusually high power-to-weight ratio and good aerodynamics, as well as by the sheer dimensions of the machine, which was truly a whale of an aeroplane by the standards of the day. On the other hand, the initial test flights were performed with no payload, and the unladen aircraft accelerated quickly during take-off, reaching rotation speed before the pilots knew it, which led to an over-high unstick speed. Because of the powerful gyroscopic force created by the four propellers (which turned clockwise when seen from the front) the starboard main gear bogie absorbed a higher load than the port one; this resulted in a propensity to swing to the right during the take-off run. Countering this propensity by differential braking was impossible because of the relatively narrow landing-gear track; the problem was cured by introducing nose-gear steering effected by the rudder pedals on the second prototype. This aircraft (c/n 8900102) also had no tactical code but sported large grid-shaped photo calibration markings on the rear fuselage sides.

During landing the An-12 was quite a handful: the aircraft refused to land with the engines running at flight idle, and

As this view shows, the first An-12 lacked wing anhedral. The circular section of the fuselage is also readily apparent. (Yefim Gordon archive)

A side view of the production prototype, showing to advantage the upswept rear fuselage. The perfectly parallel lines of the fin fillet and lower fuselage contour give the An-12 a very distinctive appearance. (Yefim Gordon archive)

moving the throttles to ground idle would produce a braking effect, causing the aircraft to lose altitude excessively fast. Hence the landing procedure demanded a lot of concentration and skill, and heavy landings were a common occurrence. In the sixth test flight one of the throttle levers jammed as the flight engineer retarded the throttles sharply at the moment of flareout. Banking sharply, the aircraft struck the ground with one wingtip, then banked the other way and touched down on the runway shoulder – mercifully suffering no further damage. After this incident the flight tests were suspended and a special technique developed for the An-12 which required the inner engines to be set at ground idle and the outer engines at flight idle for final approach.

Early flight tests also revealed poor lateral and longitudinal stability, which was remedied by increasing the anhedral on the outer wing panels. The rear fuselage structure proved insufficiently rigid, and when the cargo doors were opened in flight for the first time they could not be closed again because the fuselage had flexed under the aerodynamic loads, deforming the cargo hatch cutout. The An-12 landed safely with the doors open, and the rear fuselage was reinforced afterwards.

As mentioned in the preceding chapter, there is no documentary evidence to prove that 'Aircraft T' was designed around Ivchenko TV-20 (AI-20) turboprops from the start. On the contrary, test reports filed by Plant No. 39 testify that both production prototypes were powered by Kuznetsov NK-4s. Subsequent Irkutsk-built aircraft, however, switched to the definitive AI-20 powerplant.

The manufacturer's flight test programme was relatively brief, lasting eight months (in comparison, the An-8 and An-10 had taken more than a year and two years respectively to complete manufacturer's flight tests); it included never-exceed speed (V_{NE}) trials and engine failure simulations during which the aircraft landed with one or two engines shut down. A third aircraft (c/n 8900103) had joined the two prototypes by August 1958 when the tests were completed.

Aircrew training proceded in parallel, and the process was sometimes accompanied by spills. On one occasion factory test pilot Yeliferov applied the port wheel brakes sharply during the take-off run to keep the aircraft from leaving the runway centreline. With a puff of smoke and a BANG! BANG! two of the four wheels on the port main-gear bogie exploded, sending fragments of rubber flying in all directions. On landing the pilot was a bit overenthusiastic with the brakes again: two more 'shotgun blasts' resounded as the two remaining tyres disintegrated and the aircraft banked, making a tremendous racket as the wheel rims struck sparks from the concrete runway.

A rather funny episode occurred when a pilot named Petrov was the aircraft captain. The An-12 had two independent hydraulic systems, port and starboard, both of which could operate the landing gear. After retracting the landing gear on take-off, using the port system, the captain forgot to set the gear control lever to neutral. During the landing approach the very same factory test pilot Yeliferov who was the co-pilot extended the landing gear by means of the starboard hydraulic system – again neglecting to set the lever to neutral. A hardware conflict ensued, the two systems fighting each other as valves popped and hydraulic lines vibrated. The starboard system won and the gear extended normally, but no sooner had the aircraft touched down than the port system took over and the gear started retracting. Luckily the pilots realised what had happened and took corrective action in the nick of time, and the An-12 came to a standstill 'on bent knees', as one Russian author later put it.

In late August 1958 An-12 c/n 7900101 was ferried from Irkutsk to Tretyakovo airfield near the town of Lookhovitsy, Moscow Region.[23] The flight proceeded at 9,000–10,000 m (29,530–32,810 ft) and the aircraft was no more than a speck of dust when seen from the ground; yet the airport and ATC authorities along the route had somehow got wind that a new aircraft type was going their way. Consequently the crew were pestered with questions from curious ATC officers which G.I. Lysenko had to avoid answering – politely but firmly – so as not to disclose sensitive information. Near Gorkiy (now renamed back to Nizhniy Novgorod) the An-12 was even 'intercepted' by a flight of fighters whose pilots were eager to have a close look.

Six months later the first prototype was due to be transferred to GK NII VVS for State acceptance trials; yet these plans were foiled by a crash landing at Moscow's Central airfield named after Mikhail Vasilyevich Frunze (better known as Moscow-Khodynka) where the An-12 was to be demonstrated to the military top brass. The airfield is located in downtown Moscow, a mere 6 km (3.75 miles) from the Kremlin, and the approaches to the runway are a built-up area with lots of tall obstacles, which means a lot of pilot skill is required to operate into and out of Khodynka. This flight was no exception. The crew captain G.I. Lysenko maintained the minimum recommended speed during final approach. As the aircraft passed the perimeter fence at an altitude of 25 m (80 ft), he throttled back the Nos 2 and 3 engines as prescribed by the manual; however, the aircraft lost speed and landed hard with a slight right bank, undershooting by 65 m (213 ft). The starboard main gear unit collapsed, the aircraft keeled over and groundlooped, the No. 4 propeller striking the ground. Apart from the landing gear and propeller, some structural damage was also incurred. Sure enough, the accident investigation board quickly found the cause and made appropriate recommendations, but the aircraft was unairworthy for the moment.

The second production prototype had to be flown from Irlutsk to LII's airfield in Zhukovskiy so that the trials could continue. This aircraft was used, for the first time in Soviet practice, to investigate the stalling and spinning characteristics of a heavy aircraft; the tests showed that there was a delay between the stall and the onset of the spin – a few precious seconds during which the pilots could (and should) take corrective action and recover.

In late 1958 GK NII VVS took delivery of another production An-12 (tactical code unknown, c/n 8900305) which also participated in Stage A of the State acceptance trials. These were duly completed in June 1959. This aircraft was flown by project test pilots I.K. Goncharov and A.K. Degtyar, with I.V. Orlitskiy as project engineer. Interestingly, part of the trials programme was performed in Kiev at the OKB's flight test facility. The State commission's verdict was a thumbs-up and the An-12 was recommended for inclusion into the Soviet Air Force inventory.

Yet the top command of the VVS and the leaders of the Soviet Ministry of Defence were far from unanimous in their appraisal of the new airlifter. Debates as to whether the Armed Forces needed this aircraft raged among the military top brass, with the anti-An-12 lobby asserting that the cheaper An-8, which also required less metal to build, would cater for all of the Soviet Army's transport needs in the foreseeable future. Eventually, however, the sceptics were put to shame; subsequent events showed that the decision to launch large-scale production of the An-12 had been right. The aircraft could carry a much wider range of loads than the An-8 and outperformed the *Camp* by a considerable margin; besides, it had a considerable upgrade potential. Small wonder that the An-12 became the mainstay of the Soviet Air Force's military airlift component for many years to come.

Stage B of the State acceptance trials, which lasted from October 1959 to April 1960, involved paradropping of personnel and materiel near Boozovaya settlement. Apart from G.I. Lysenko, test pilots Yuriy V. Koorlin (who went on to become the Antonov OKB's chief test pilot) and I.Ye. Davydov flew as crew captains at this stage.

Various versions of the An-12 were produced by three major Soviet aircraft factories – No. 39 in Irkutsk (located at Irkutsk-2 airfield), No. 64 in Voronezh (located at Pridacha airfield) and No. 84, named after the famous test pilot Valeriy Pavlovich Chkalov, in Tashkent (located at Tashkent-Vostochnyy, i.e. Tashkent-East airfield). All in all, 1,275 examples were built in the USSR alone, not counting unlicensed Chinese production (which still continues and is described separately) – 155 aircraft in Irkutsk (December 1957 to December 1961), 290 in Voronezh (June 1961 to mid-1968) and

Three-quarters rear view, showing the tail-gunner's station and the flattened rear fuselage underside. These photos have never been published previously. (Yefim Gordon archive)

Head-on view of the second production prototype An-12 (c/n 8900102). Like the first aircraft, it originally lacked wing anhedral. (Antonov OKB)

The second production prototype paradrops a mock-up of an ASU-57 self-propelled gun during manufacturer's flight tests. Note the phototheodolite calibration markings on the fuselage. (Yefim Gordon archive)

830 in Tashkent (mid-1961 to late 1972).

A note must be made here on construction numbers (manufacturer's serial numbers). Each of the three factories had its own construction number system(s), explained as follows:

System 1: An-12A CCCP-98101 manufactured on 15 June 1961, c/n 1901706:

1 year of manufacture (1961)
9 Irkutsk Aircraft Factory No. 39 (P/O Box A-3621; the first digit is omitted for security reasons to confuse would-be spies)
017 production batch number
06 number of the aircraft in the batch (five per batch in Batches 1–5, ten per batch in Batches 6–18)

System 2: An-12A CCCP-11916 manufactured on 31 July 1962, c/n 2400901:

2 year of manufacture (1962)
4 Voronezh Aircraft Factory No. 64 (P/O Box 71, later P/O Box V-8808; the first digit is omitted for security reasons)
009 production batch number
01 number of the aircraft in the batch (six per batch in Batches 1–14, 12 per batch in Batches 15–28 and 30, and 13 per batch in Batches 29 and 31)

The year of manufacture was usually no longer indicated for Voronezh-built examples after 1962:

System 3: An-12B CCCP-11236 manufactured on 30 January 1964, c/n 402111:

4 Aircraft Factory No. 64
021 production batch number
11 number of the aircraft in the batch

System 4: An-12BP CCCP-11789 manufactured on 30 April 1966, c/n 6343905:

6 year of manufacture (1966)
34 Tashkent Aircraft Factory No. 84 (P/O Box 116, later P/O Box A-1380)
39 production batch number
05 number of the aircraft in the batch (ten per batch)

In 1970 the Tashkent aircraft factory started using two-digit year designators. For example, An-12BP CCCP-12990 manufactured on 31 July 1970 is c/n 00347304, An-12BP CCCP-11116 manufactured on 30 November 1971 is c/n 01348006 and An-12BP CCCP-11122 manufactured on 31 January 1972 is c/n 02348104.

Bird's eye perspective of a production An-12, showing the anhedral introduced on the outer wings to improve lateral stability. (Antonov OKB)

This uncoded An-12 in Soviet Air Force markings is obviously some kind of development aircraft. Despite having VVS insignia, it has no tail-gunner's station; the colour scheme with a black pinstripe running the full length of the fuselage is equally strange. (Yefim Gordon archive)

Grey-painted Soviet (CIS) Air Force An-12s have the c/n stencilled on the starboard side of the nose and tail, and sometimes under the wing leading edge at the roots. Civil and quasi-civil examples in Aeroflot colours carry the c/n on the tail only; interestingly, truly civil aircraft usually have it on the port side while quasi-civil examples often have it on the starboard side. Only the last four digits were sometimes stencilled on export An-12s (except Voronezh-built examples).

System 5 (export aircraft only): Iraqi Air Force An-12B '507', c/n 024012:

024 a code for the An-12?
012 sequential number of the exported aircraft under this system

Some Soviet aircraft intended for export received special 'Aviaexport c/ns', the Aviaexport All-Union Agency being the sole national exporter of aircraft in those days. These 'Aviaexport c/ns' were intended to conceal the batch number and the number of the aircraft in the batch so as to avoid indicating how many had been built. The above-mentioned Iraqi An-12 may be one of these aircraft. Eventually, however, only 12 examples received c/ns under this system and all other export An-12s had normal c/ns.

As noted earlier, the An-12 was formally included into the VVS inventory in 1959 after Stage A of the State acceptance trials had been completed. Much later a handful of An-12s was delivered to the air forces of two Warsaw Pact nations – Czechoslovakia and Poland (Bulgaria had a number of civil An-12s but of course these could be operated on behalf of the Air Force if the need arose).

In recognition of their part in the development of the An-12, GSOKB-473 Chief Designer (later General Designer)[24] Oleg K. Antonov and other leading engineers involved in the project – A.Ya. Belolipetskiy, V.N. Ghelprin, Ye.K. Senchuk and Ye.A. Shakhatooni – were awarded the prestigious Lenin Prize by decree of the Soviet government.

To conclude this chapter it may be said that promising theories often prove to be impracticable, and the An-12 was a case in point. The idea of converting An-10s into An-12s in times of war was thwarted by the difference in the two types' mission equipment and by the progressive improvement of the transport, which was manufactured by various plants into the bargain. As production progressed, the An-10 and An-12 drifted steadily farther apart as far as the design was concerned. For instance, after the first hundred or so aircraft had been built in Irkutsk the pressure sealing of the An-12's fuselage structure in the freight hold area was deleted, leaving only a small pressurised area at the front. As the differences added up, the conversion idea was called into question and proof had to be provided that it was feasible. To this end, as recounted in the preceding chapter, the Voronezh aircraft factory converted at least one An-10 into an An-12.

CHAPTER FOUR

Mission Variety

Originally codenamed *Cat-B*, the An-12 was soon recognised by the West as a separate design and the reporting name was changed to *Cub*. The An-12 turned out to be a truly versatile aircraft, which no doubt partly accounts for its long career. Known versions are described here.

An-12 *Cub* military transport (*izdeliye* 100, 'Aircraft T')

The initial production version which entered production in 1958 at the Irkutsk Aircraft Factory No. 39 was powered by 4,000 ehp AI-20A engines driving AV-68I propellers. Later, when new versions designated by suffix letters started appearing, the initial production aircraft became known unofficially as **an-*dvenahdsat*' '*bez bookvy*'** – 'An-12 with no [suffix] letter', or *sans suffixe*. The aircraft could carry 60 paratroopers or 91 fully equipped troops, or 20 tons (44,090 lb) of cargo. Paradropping was typically performed at 250–300 km/h (155–186 mph; 135–162 kt) with the aircraft flying at 600–1,000 m (1,970–3,280 ft).

The defensive armament consisted of a DB-65U powered turret with two 23 mm (.90 calibre) Afanasyev/Makarov AM-23 cannon having a 1,000 rpm rate of fire, with 360 rounds per gun. Bomb armament was also incorporated in the form of a DYa-SS-AT cassette in the rear fuselage holding six 10 kg (22 lb) TsOSAB-10 coloured signal flare bombs and four beam-type bomb cradles, two of which were mounted inside the rear portions of the main landing gear fairings and the other two externally beneath the forward portions of same – again for carrying flare bombs. The An-12 could be used for setting up minefields in case of need, carrying up to ten mines of similar dimensions to 1,500 kg (3,306 lb) FAB-1500 bombs or 20 mines of similar dimensions to 500 kg (1,102 lb) FAB-500 bombs.[25] NKPB-7 and AIP-32 bombsights were provided for precision paradropping and, if necessary, bomb-aiming.

There were 8 mm (0.31 in) sheets of APBL-1 steel armour installed beneath the pilots' seats on both sides of the flight deck for protection against AA shell fragments. Also, the pilots' seats featured 16 mm (0.63 in) armoured seat backs and 25 mm (0.98 in) armoured headrests. The tail gunner was protected by bullet-proof glass panels 135 mm (5.31 in) thick at the rear and 112 mm (4.41 in) thick on the sides.

The An-12 could operate from tactical dirt or grass strips with a bearing strength of 8–9 kg/cm^2 (114–128 lb/sq. in). Early production aircraft had a take-off weight of 54 tons (119,050 lb), including 10.8 tons (23,810 lb) of fuel, and could paradrop a 14.5-ton (31,970 lb) load. The aircraft was capable of sustained horizontal flight at up to 5,000 m (16,400 ft), even with two engines inoperative.

This early Irkutsk-built An-12 preserved at the Soviet Air Force Museum (now Central Russian Air Force Museum) in Monino (04 Blue, c/n 8900203) is representative of the initial production version, the An-12 *sans suffixe*. Note the flight-deck glazing design identical to that of the prototypes and the lack of an APU in the port main-gear fairing. (Yefim Gordon)

The basic military version of the *Cub* was equipped with an RBP-2 ground-mapping radar and a Proton-M radio for precise navigation to the drop zone. Vertical cameras, including those for detailed and night photography, could be installed – mostly for 'post-strike reconnaissance' (i.e. evaluating the accuracy of the drop).

Many airframe subassemblies and equipment items were borrowed from the An-10 airliner ('Aircraft U') in as-was condition.

An-12A *Cub* military transport

The first attempt to improve the baseline transport resulted in the An-12A, which entered production in Voronezh (Plant No. 64) and Tashkent (Plant No. 84) in 1961. Plant No. 64 in Voronezh eventually built 31 batches of An-12s, totalling 258 aircraft in 1961-7.

The main changes over the basic An-12 *sans suffixe* concerned the powerplant and fuel system. The An-12A was powered by 4,250 ehp AI-20K engines. Four additional fuel cells were installed in the parts of the inner wing panels adjacent to the engines, increasing the total number to 26 and the overall capacity to 15,440–16,600 litres (3,396–3,652 imp. gal) (different sources quote different figures). The result was a 600 km (370 mile) increase in range. The nose landing gear was beefed up by fitting reinforced 900 × 300 mm (35.43 × 11.81 in) K2-92/I non-braking wheels. The freight hold featured a gantry crane with a lifting capacity of 2,100 kg (4,630 lb). The existing seven 12SAM-28 DC batteries were augmented by a further ten of the same type to ensure trouble-free engine starting; the batteries were housed in the starboard main landing-gear fairing and in an underfloor bay at the rear of the freight hold. Main electric power was supplied by eight 12kW STG-12TMO starter-generators. An oxygen system with 12 permanently installed 12-litre (2.64 imp. gal) bottles was fitted, and two toilets were provided; thus, unlike the An-12 *sans suffixe*, the A model had an adequate oxygen supply for maximum-range flight at any altitude, not only for the crew, but for the 'passengers' as well.

The avionics and equipment also received an upgrade. The An-12A's avionics fit included an AP-28D1 autopilot, an ARK-11 ADF, a KS-6G automatic heading reference system (*koorsovaya sistema*), a DAK-DB-5 remote compass, an NI-50BM-1 navigation display (*navigatsionnyy indikahtor*), an RSBN-2 Svod (Dome) short-range radio navigation system (SHORAN – *rahdiosistema blizhney navigahtsii*), an RBP-2 ground-mapping radar, an SP-50 ILS, an MRP-56P marker beacon receiver, an SP-1M astrosextant (located on top of the flight deck), a 1RSB-70 HF comms radio, a Gheliy backup HF comms radio, an RSIU-5 UHF command radio, an SPU-7 intercom, an RV-2 radio altimeter, a Proton-M radio for precise navigation to the drop zone, an SRO-2M IFF transponder, an SOD-57M air traffic control (ATC) transponder, an updated Sirena-3 RWR, Kedr-S (Cedar-S) and DP-3 radios. The main gear fairings housed AFA-42/20, AFA-42/50 or AFA-42/75 day cameras or an NAFA-MK-25 camera and FotAB flare bombs for night operations.[26]

The An-12A remained in production until 1962, the Voronezh aircraft factory producing eight batches (up to and including CCCP-11804, c/n 2400806),[27] while the one in Tashkent built six batches (up to and including CCCP-12978, c/n 2340610). Early-production 'As (for Plant No. 64 it was up to and including c/n 2400806) retained the original wing centre-section torsion box, with a resulting TOW limit of 54 tons (119,050 lb) and a payload limit of 13 tons (28,660 lb). Subsequent aircraft introduced a beefed-up wing centre section, allowing the maximum TOW to be increased to 61 tons (134,480 lb) and the payload to 20 tons (44,090 lb).

An-12B *Cub* military transport

The next version which superseded the An-12A on the production lines in 1962 was the extended-range An-12B, development of which had begun in 1960. The AI-20K turboprops of the preceding model gave way to identically rated but more reliable AI-20Ms (*modernizeerovannyy* – upgraded). The detachable outer wing panels incorporated integral fuel tanks, each holding 1,390 litres (305.8 imp. gal) or, according to other sources, 1,600 litres (352 imp. gal); this increased the total tankage to 18,240 litres (4,012.8 imp. gal) or 19,500 litres (4,290 imp. gal). Thus, while the B suffix to the designation could be simply in alphabetical sequence, it might just as easily stand for [*dopolnitel'nyye*] *bahki* – extra tanks. The additional tankage required the wing centre section to be further reinforced.

A TG-16 APU was built into the aft portion of the port main gear fairing for self-contained engine starting and providing electric power up to an altitude of 1,000 m (3,280 ft). Consequently the rear pair of bomb cradles in the main gear fairings was deleted. The rudder trim tab was enlarged. A separate workstation was provided for the flight engineer. Finally, the existing BL-52 winches (*bortovaya lebyodka* – on-board winch) in the freight hold were replaced by more powerful BL-1500 units developing 1,500 kgf (3,306 lbf) each, permitting the loading of trailers and the like weighing up to 8 tons (17,640 lb).

Some sources state that An-12B production in Voronezh began with CCCP-11916 (c/n 2400901) and in Tashkent with a Soviet Air Force aircraft which received the tactical code 87 Red (c/n 2340701). Up to and including c/ns 401911 and c/n 3341510 (identity unknown) the An-12B's dry weight was 34.2 tons (75,400 lb), increasing to 34.45 tons (75,950 lb) on subsequent aircraft.

An-12P *Cub* military transport

1963 saw the appearance of the An-12P, which was basically an An-12 *sans suffixe* with two extra fuel cells under the freight hold floor. The P stood for [*dopolnitel'nyye bahki*] *pod polom* – extra tanks under the floor. The forward cells located between fuselage frames 14-24 held 5,500 litres (1,210 imp. gal) and the aft group located between frames 33 and 41 held 4,350 litres (957 imp. gal). Thus the underfloor baggage compartments (or rather storage compartments) became unusable and the various accessories carried there had to be stored in the freight hold. The earliest reported example is a quasi-civilian Soviet Air Force aircraft registered CCCP-11864 (c/n 401704); the construction number, however, suggests this is an An-12A or even an An-12B. Most An-12Ps were apparently Voronezh-built, but a Tashkent-built aircraft registered CCCP-11145 (c/n 3341605)[28] has also been referred to as an An-12P.

Two views of a later An-12A seen during trials. The unpainted aircraft (c/n unknown) carries the non-standard registration CCCP-75617 (the 75xxx registration block was normally assigned to Il'yushin Il-18 *Coot* airliners). Note the production-standard flight-deck glazing design. (Yefim Gordon archive)

An-12AP *Cub* military transport

The underfloor fuel tanks soon found their way to the An-12A as well, and the resulting combination was designated An-12AP (i.e. An-12A *s bahkami pod polom*). The total fuel load of this version rose from the original *Cub*'s 10.8 tons (23,810 lb) to 20.3 tons (44,750 lb), increasing maximum range at 9,000 m (29,530 ft) to 5,200 km (3,230 miles). No An-12APs were built as such; this version was obtained by converting An-12As – e.g. Irkutsk-built CCCP-21510 (c/n 0901404), Voronezh-built CCCP-11327 (c/n 1400104) and Tashkent-built CCCP-11382 (c/n 2340605).

An-12BP *Cub* military transport

Predictably, the An-12B underwent a similar modification, which resulted in the An-12BP (i.e. An-12B *s bahkami pod polom*). The total number of fuel tanks rose to 29 and the overall capacity to 26,980 litres (5,935.6 imp. gal) – or, according to other sources, to 29,350 litres (6,457 imp. gal). The An-12BP's fuel load has been stated variously as 22,066 kg (48,646 lb) or 22,400 kg (49,382 lb).

Changes also concerned the avionics suite, which was modernised and expanded. New equipment introduced on the An-12BP included a KS-6G compass system, an NAS-1B1-28 (or DNSS-13-12) self-contained navigation system and

MISSION VARIETY

A row of blue-coded Soviet Air Force An-12Bs ready to taxi out for take-off during an exercise. Note the TG-16 APU in the port main-gear fairing. (Sergey and Dmitriy Komissarov archive)

66 Red, a Voronezh-built An-12B, takes off. Approximately half the Soviet Air Force's *Cub* fleet wore this overall grey colour scheme. (Yefim Gordon archive)

an RSKM-2 radio coordinate monitoring system (*rahdiolokatsionnaya sistema kontrolya mesta*). The aircraft also featured an ARK-11 ADF replacing the earlier ARK-5, an RV-5M radio altimeter instead of the RV-2, an SOD-64 ATC transponder instead of the SOD-57, a PDSP-2N homing system for navigation to the drop zone instead of the earlier PDSP-21, and R-863 and R-856MA comms radios replacing the earlier 1RSB-70 and RSB-5 respectively.

Early-production An-12BPs were outwardly identical to the previous versions. From Batch 34 onwards, however, the Tashkent aircraft factory introduced cargo doors widened by 105 mm (4.13 in) at the bottom to facilitate loading and unloading. Outwardly this could be recognised by prominent bulges flanking the lower lip of the cargo hatch. The first aircraft to have the new cargo door design was an Indian Air Force example serialled L2172 (c/n 5343401).

The An-12P introduced underfloor fuel tanks. This particular example (UR-BYW, c/n unknown) seen at Kiev-Svyatoshino on 15th September 2002 even has appropriate nose titles but no reference to the operator! (Dmitriy Komissarov)

Until the late 1970s Aeroflot (and quasi-Aeroflot) An-12s wore this red/white livery with 'feathers' identical to one of the An-10's colour schemes. Illustrated here is An-12BP CCCP-11129 (c/n 02348204) of the Central Directorate of International Services/64th Flight at a foreign airport. It was extensively damaged (possibly beyond repair) at Yanina, Bulgaria, on 8th November 1991 while operating for the Bulgarian carrier SiGi Air Cargo. (RART)

17 Red (c/n 5342810), a very early Tashkent-built An-12BP, banks as it makes a high-speed pass for the spectators at the open doors day at Kubinka airbase on 29 May 1993. This aircraft still has the original narrow cargo hatch. Note the twin strake aerials on the rear fuselage (port, LORAN; starboard, ADF) replacing the single aerial atop the forward fuselage on earlier aircraft. (Sergey Komissarov)

An-12BP '15 Red' taxies at Moscow-Domodedovo airport in July 1967. Fom Batch 34 onwards the An-12BP featured a widened cargo hatch to facilitate loading and unloading, identifiable by characteristic bulges at the bottom. The unusual colour scheme with a red cheatline was applied for an airshow. (Sergey Komissarov)

The final batches of An-12BPs (built in military and civil configuration alike; see description of civil version below) have fewer cabin windows. The window arrangement is 2 + exit + 1 + door + 1 + exit to port and 1 + exit + 1 + 1 + 1 to starboard.

An-12BK *Cub* military transport

In 1963 the Antonov OKB and LII undertook a joint flight test programme aimed at increasing the *Cub*'s payload to 30 tons (66,140 lb). To this end a Tashkent-built An-12A coded 05 Blue (c/n 2340307) was retrofitted with a new avionics suite, including an Initsiativa-2 (Initiative/NATO code name *Short Horn*) panoramic ground-mapping radar, an NVU-V navigation computer and a Trassa-2 (Route, or Trail) Doppler speed/drift indicator. The OPB-1B optical bombsight and the existing NAI-1 navigation computer were deleted. In May 1963 05 Blue was turned over to GK NII VVS for State acceptance trials; Air Force pilots Platonov and Tkal flew the aircraft at this stage.

Tests revealed that the Initsiativa radar had twice the detection range of the RBP-2; at an altitude of 5,000–9,000 m (16,400–29,530 ft) the radar could detect a large city like Moscow or Gorkiy from a distance of 200–260 km (124–161 miles). However, the test protocol said that 'as regards precision paradropping the new avionics suite in its current condition offers no significant advantages over the navigation equipment of production aircraft'; besides, the new avionics were troublesome.

The results of this programme materialised three years later in the form of a Voronezh-built An-12 with the non-standard registration CCCP-83962 (c/n 402210).[29] This was the prototype of a new version designated An-12BK which underwent flight tests in August 1966; the K stood for *kompleks* [*oboroodovaniya*] – equipment suite.

Like the An-12B, the aircraft was powered by 4,250 ehp AI-20M turboprops. The APU, however, was new; the upgraded TG-16M equipped with a GS-24A starter-generator provided in-flight engine starting capability right up to 3,000 m (9,840 ft).

Other changes included the installation of a new GL-1500DP remote-controlled winch and a new overhead gantry crane capable of lifting 2,300 kg (5,070 lb) in the freight hold, the provision of vehicle loading ramps which could be converted into troop seats, and a cargo door aperture widened by 105 mm *à la* An-12BP (with associated lateral bulges at the bottom). The An-12BK featured an improved Initsiativa-4-100 radar. The new radar required a powerful air-cooling system; for want of available space this was installed in the passenger compartment aft of the flight deck, reducing its seating capacity by almost 50 per cent (to 11). The heavier equipment in the forward fuselage and the augmented load on the nose gear unit necessitated the fitment of heavy-duty K2-92/IV nosewheels – again measuring 900 × 300 mm (35.43 × 11.81 in).

Outwardly the An-12BK could be easily identified by the much-enlarged and recontoured radome of the Initsiativa radar which caught your eye immediately. The new model entered production in Tashkent in 1966 (the earliest known example is 85 Red, c/n 6343901) and was supplied exclusively to the Soviet Air Force.

(Note: CCCP-11320, a *Cub* built in 1964 (c/n 4342604), has been reported as an An-12BK, but this is wrong; photos show this aircraft had a regular-size chin radome associated with the RBP-2 radar. So have some civil aircraft reported in the Western press as An-12BKs; however, since they are ex-Air Force aircraft, it is possible they were built as 'BKs but stripped of military equipment before sale to civilian owners, which included a change of radar.)

Soviet Air Force An-12s were retrofitted *en masse* with the following mission avionics in service conditions. From 1965 onwards An-12As and 'Bs received the Klin formation-keeping system (the name translates as 'wedge' or 'Vee formation' according to the context but is also the name of a town north of Moscow). The An-12BK received several upgrades – the Yakhta (Yacht) scrambler providing secure voice communications with the ground or other aircraft (1969), the *izdeliye* 75T module for flying international air routes

The An-12BK equipped with an Initsiativa-4-100 radar (readily identifiable by the much-enlarged radome) made up a large proportion of the VTA's *Cub* fleet. (Yefim Gordon archive)

This view accentuates the size of the An-12BK's 'beard' which was painted grey on some aircraft and white on others. These three were photographed somewhere in Belorussia in March 1970 during the Warsaw Pact exercise *Dvina*. (TASS News Agency)

(1971), the Zveno (flight, as a tactical unit) system for flying in close formation (1972) and finally the Kremniy (Silicone) long-range navigation system in 1974.

Electronic support measures (ESM) equipment was incorporated later on as a result of Afghan War experience. Many VVS An-12BPs and 'BKs operating into Afghanistan were equipped with shallow strakes low on the forward fuselage sides, each housing two 30-round ASO-2 chaff/flare dispensers in tandem; these fired 26 mm (1.02 in.) PPI-26 magnesium flares to decoy infra-red homing missiles.[30] Later, some Russian Air Force *Cubs*, including a quasi-civil An-12BK registered RA-11668 (c/n unknown), were retrofitted with more capable infra-red countermeasures (IRCM) equipment comprising two streamlined fairings on the centre fuselage sides, each of which housed 12 32-round chaff/flare dispenser modules using the same type of flares.

An-12UD/An-12UD-3 military transport

The inadequate range of the early versions was one of the *Cub*'s chief shortcomings, and increasing it became a top priority for the Antonov OKB (as the reader will have guessed from the descriptions of the An-12A/B/AP/BP). One of the early attempts to crack the problem resulted in the development of the An-12UD (*oovelichennoy dahl'nosti* – with increased range). The prototype was converted from a production Irkutsk-built An-12 (c/n 9901007) by installing two extra tanks holding a total of 7,600 litres (1,672 imp. gal) in the freight hold between Frames 16 and 26. The tanks were taken straight from the Myasishchev 3M *Bison-B* strategic bomber. As a result, the fuel capacity rose to a more agreeable 21,870 litres (4,811.4 imp. gal). The engines' oil tankage and the oxygen supply had to be increased accordingly in view of the greater endurance.

Flight tests of the An-12UD held jointly by the OKB and the Air Force took place on 20–7 October 1960, with Yuriy V. Koorlin (Antonov OKB) as project test pilot. The results were encouraging: with a maximum take-off weight and a 3-ton (6,613 lb) payload the range increased by 1,900–2,000 km (1,180–1,240 miles) over the An-12 *sans suffixe*, reaching 4,900 km (3,040 miles).

Some sources state that the aircraft could be fitted with two or three auxiliary tanks holding 4,000 litres (880 imp. gal) each, and the two configurations were known as An-12UD and An-12UD-3 respectively.

An-12BP polar version

A special version based on the An-12BP was developed in 1961 for operating in the polar regions of the USSR and for supporting Soviet polar research stations in the Arctic. Three bladder tanks with a total capacity of 9,800 litres (2,156 imp. gal) were installed in the underfloor baggage compartments to obtain the required range of 6,000 km (3,725 miles).

An-12PL polar transport/support aircraft

In the same year another customised version of the *Cub* designed for off-base operation in Arctic and Antarctic regions was developed for Aeroflot's polar division. Apart from the obligatory extra fuel tanks, the aircraft featured non-retractable streamlined skis equipped with brakes, hence the designation An-12PL (*polyarnyy, lyzhnyy* – polar, ski-equipped). The V-shaped planing bottoms of the skis were skinned in abrasion-resistant OT4-1 titanium alloy and heated by hot air before taxiing to stop them from sticking to ice and snow surfaces. The front and rear ends of the main skis were connected to the fuselage by telescopic links; two more rods connecting the rear ends with a fitting on

Several An-12s operated by Aeroflot's Polar Directorate were suitably modified with additional fuel tanks and celestial navigation equipment. Illustrated here is An-12A or B CCCP-04363 (the 04xxx block was used for Polar Aviation aircraft). Note the unusual colour scheme (silver with a red cheatline), TACAN aerials under the nose and outer wings (a leftover from its Air Force days) and the astrosextant on the flight-deck roof. (Yefim Gordon archive)

Two *Cub*s were fitted out with a non-retractable ski undercarriage for polar operations and designated An-12PL; this anonymous aircraft was one. Though heavily retouched, this photo shows interesting details such as the old-style flight-deck glazing (identifying it as one of the first Irkutsk-built An-12s) and the civil-style tailcone in lieu of a tail-gunner's station. (Yefim Gordon archive)

MISSION VARIETY

The other An-12PL was converted from Voronezh-built An-12B CCCP-11381 (c/n 402807) seen here before and after conversion. Note that the aircraft has been demilitarised, with a fairing replacing the tail turret. (Yefim Gordon archive)

Close-up views of the main skis of An-12PL CCCP-11381, showing the Vee-shaped bottoms, the oleo strut fairings, the shock absorbers and connecting rods acting as torque links. (Yefim Gordon archive)

the fuselage centreline functioned as torque links. All three oleo struts were carefully faired to minimise drag.

The pressure cabin featured heavy-duty heat insulation for operating in extreme cold climates and a powerful self-contained heater for heating the cabin and warming up the engines prior to start-up. Despite the drag created by the fixed landing gear, the range was an impressive 7,500 km (4,650 miles).

Two aircraft were converted to An-12PLs in 1961. One was a natural metal aircraft in Soviet Air Force markings (identity unknown); the other was an Aeroflot aircraft registered CCCP-11381 (c/n 402807).[31]

An-12T fuel carrier aircraft

Specialised versions of the *Cub* began appearing almost immediately. The first of these was probably the An-12T (*toplivovoz* – fuel carrier) developed in 1961. The aircraft was designed to transport automotive, aviation and rocket fuels and oxidisers in special tanks installed in the freight hold.

An-12BKT refuelling tanker

Whereas the version descibed above was strictly a fuel carrier, a refuelling tanker version did not appear until much later – and then it was not a flight refuelling tanker but a 'flying petrol station' designed to refuel tactical aircraft on the ground. In 1972 the Antonov OKB brought out the An-12BKT (i.e. An-12BK – *toplivozaprahvschchik*). The aircraft could top up two fighters at a time; total transferrable fuel was 19,500 litres (4,290 imp. gal).

An-12A ballistic missile transporter version

In mid-1962 a single Irkutsk-built An-12 (92 Red, c/n 1901507) was converted for carrying ballistic missiles to the launch sites; no separate designation is known for this version. The freight hold featured a more efficient heating system, additional lighting and a heat insulation curtain installed at fuselage frame No. 43 (i.e. at the cargo door lip). In the autumn of 1962 the aircraft was turned over to GK NII VVS for State acceptance trials. These were performed by project test pilots A.Ya. Bryksin (captain), A.S. Borzov (co-pilot) and project engineer V.I. Kozlov.

The trials revealed that the missile transporter did not meet the requirements of the military in full as far as safety issues were concerned; in particular, it lacked a system for neutralising possible leaks of the missiles' oxidiser which could be corrosive and toxic. In as-was condition the An-12 could carry only Type 3R9 and 3R11 intermediate-range ballistic missiles (IRBMs) with solid-fuel rocket motors and unrefuelled R-11M and R-17 IRBMs (the latter type, alias 9K72, is known to the West as the SS-1 *Scud*). Hence the idea was not pursued further.

An-12BM satellite communications relay aircraft

In 1962 a production An-12 (identity unknown) was converted experimentally to evaluate the possibility of long-range satellite communications (SATCOM). Radio signals were relayed via the Molniya-1 (Lightning-1) communications satellite; hence the aircraft was known as the An-12BM (M for *molniya*). The four operators' workstations of the SATCOM suite were located in the passenger cabin.

An-12B communications relay aircraft (?)

At least seven Voronezh-built examples with no tail-gunner's station – An-12A CCCP-11131 (c/n 2400702) and An-12Bs CCCP-11652 (c/n 402702), CCCP-11653 (c/n 402703), CCCP-11654 (c/n 402602), CCCP-11791 (c/n 402611), CCCP-11792 (c/n 402701) and CCCP-11992 (c/n 402604) – were converted into (or possibly purpose-built as) a special mission version of unknown purpose. Despite being built in unarmed configuration, these are military aircraft operated by the Soviet, and later Russian, Air Force. The only external recognition feature is an additional TA-6 APU buried in the rear fuselage immediately ahead of the tail unit, with a prominent aft-angled exhaust on the port side. The main air intake, also to port, is closed by an aft-hinged door when not in use, with a small auxiliary intake closed by wire mesh on the starboard side.

The second APU was obviously installed because the aircraft's mission equipment requires too much power, which the engine-driven generators cannot provide. The question is, WHAT mission equipment? Since the aircraft do not have any of the prominent aerials associated with intelligence gathering or ECM rôles, the most likely explanation is that they are communications relay aircraft.

An-12BK SAR derivative

A search and rescue (SAR) version based on the An-12BK was developed in the 1960s. Little is known about this version except that it was equipped with an *Istok-Goloob'* (Source [of a river]/Dove) system for homing in on signals sent by the emergency UHF radio of a downed aircraft.

An-12PS maritime SAR aircraft

The An-12PS airborne maritime search and rescue system (PS = *poiskovo-spasahtel'nyy* – SAR, used attributively) was developed around the An-12B in 1969. The aircraft's intended mission was to support the Soviet manned space programme, locating and rescuing space crews in the unlikely event of a splashdown somewhere in the world ocean,[32] and to operate in the interests of the Soviet Navy, rescuing the occupants of ships in distress or downed aircraft.

The An-12PS carried a Yorsh (Ruff, alias Project 03447) lifeboat with a displacement of 5.2 tons (11,460 lb) or its improved derivative, the 7.4-ton (16,314 lb) Gagara (Loon, alias Project 03473). The lifeboat could be paradropped with a crew of three on sighting people in distress. The Gagara had a 500 km (270 nm) range and a top speed of 7 kt; maximum seating capacity was 20 rescuees. Additionally, the tail-gunner's station of the An-12PS was converted into a bay for a PSN-25/30 inflatable life raft (*plot spasahtel'nyy nadoovnoy*) seating another 25 or 30 persons; this raft could be jettisoned by the crew and subsequently towed by the lifeboat.

Outwardly the SAR version was readily identifiable by the boxy windowless fairing supplanting the tail-gunner's station (reminiscent of the rear-end treatment on demilitarised An-8s and some

MISSION VARIETY

CCCP-11653 (c/n 402703), one of several military An-12Bs equipped for special-mission (possibly communications relay) duties, on final approach to its home base at Kubinka. (Yefim Gordon archive)

The rear end of the same aircraft in later days as RA-11653 (c/n 402703), seen here at Kubinka AB in August 2002. The air intake and exhaust of the additional APU powering the mission equipment are visible ahead of the tail. (Dmitriy Komissarov)

CCCP-11398 was the prototype of the An-12PS maritime SAR aircraft. This view shows the faired-over tail-gunner's station modified to house a PSN-25/30 inflatable life raft, the pylons fore and aft of the main-gear fairings for carrying KAS-150 rescue gear pods, and the phototheodolite target on the rear fuselage. The object on the starboard wingtip is probably a camera. (Yefim Gordon archive)

16 Yellow (c/n 7344702?) is one of the few *Cub*s completed as An-12PS maritime SAR aircraft. This one, adorned with a red 'lightning bolt' cheatline, belongs to the Russian Navy's Black Sea Fleet and is seen here at its home base in Anapa in September 2000. Note the exceptionally long 'towel rail' aerial atop the fuselage associated with the SAR rôle, and that the pylons have been removed for some reason. (Yefim Gordon)

46 Red, an An-12PP ECM aircraft (c/n unknown), taxies out for a sortie, showing the characteristic boat-tail fairing. (Via Sergey Panov)

demilitarised An-12s) with Cyrillic 'PSN-25' stencils on the sides and by the characteristic red, blue or yellow 'lightning bolt' side flashes livening up the standard overall grey colour scheme. Also, since the An-12PS was expected to operate in the northern regions of the Soviet Union, the tops of the outer wings and of the horizontal tail tips were painted red for high definition against ice and snow (to assist in finding the aircraft in the event of a forced landing).

The An-12PS prototype was registered CCCP-11398 (c/n unknown) and featured small pylons fore and aft of the main gear fairings for carrying KAS-150 pods (*konteyner avareeyno-spasahtel'nyy*) filled with small life rafts or other rescue equipment; for some reason, however, these pylons have been removed from in-service aircraft.

A handful of An-12PSs were delivered to the Soviet Naval Air Arm (AVMF – *Aviahtshiya voyenno-morskovo flota*). Known examples are c/ns 7344702, 7344703 (coded 17 Yellow) and 7344704.

An-12B-I ECM aircraft

The electronic countermeasures (ECM) rôle is of special importance among the An-12's many applications. The first version of the *Cub* adapted for ECM duties was the An-12B-I active ECM aircraft evolved from the An-12B in 1964. It was equipped with the *Fasol'* (String bean) individual protection active jammer, and this probably explains the I suffix (for 'individual'). Only seven aircraft were built.

An-12PP (An-12B-PP, An-12BP-PP) ECM aircraft

The next electronic warfare version was the An-12PP (*postanovschchik pomekh* – ECM aircraft) developed in 1970; it was designed for group protection, operating as part of large formations of regular *Cubs*. The An-12PP had an automatic active jammer system which detected enemy air defence radars, determined their location and emitted well-aimed noise signals in their direction. The tail-gunner's station was replaced by a slab-sided ogival fairing housing ASO-24 chaff dispensers (*avtomaht sbrosa otrazhahteley* – in this case, automatic chaff dispenser) with ventral outlets.

A total of 27 aircraft were converted to An-12PP standard; depending on the original version they were sometimes referred to as An-12B-PP or An-12BP-PP respectively. Like the other ECM versions, the An-12PP was not exported, even though at least one aircraft operated in phoney Egyptian Air Force markings in the Middle East for a while. In the 1980s and 1990s at least two An-12PPs were stripped of mission equipment and sold to civil owners as CCCP-48978 (c/n 9346410) and RA-11301 (c/n 00347107). The ogival tailcone remained, indicating the original rôle of these aircraft all too clearly.

An-12BK-IS ECM aircraft

Another ECM variant which entered production in 1970 was the An-12BK-IS, based on the standard An-12BK. The mission equipment comprised Fasol' and Siren' (Lilac; pronounced *seeren'*) individual protection active jammers in four large cigar-shaped pods flanking the forward fuselage and the base of the fin. The pods were detachable; each pod had dielectric front and rear portions with lateral bulges and a dorsal cooling intake (interestingly, the intakes on the forward pods were located at the front, while those on the rear pods were located well aft). The installation of the ECM pods required some local reinforcement of the airframe.

MISSION VARIETY

Close-up of the tail end of An-12PP '68 Red' (c/n 9346303) operated by GK NII VVS. The ventral outlets of the ASO-24 chaff dispensers are easily visible. (Yefim Gordon archive)

This heavily retouched but interesting photo shows the An-12BK-IS version outfitted with four strap-on active jammer pods. Unlike the externally similar An-12BK-PPS, the aircraft has a conventional tail-gunner's station and lacks the ventral jammer arrays and crew radiation protection packs. (Yefim Gordon archive)

Front view of an An-12BK-PPS (06 Red, c/n 01347904) at Ivanovo-Severnyy AB, showing the starboard forward Siren ECM pod and some of the many cooling air intakes characteristic of this version. (Aleksandr Melikhov via Yefim Gordon)

Forty An-12BK-IS aircraft (some sources say 45) were built as such, but this was not enough by any margin. Therefore, starting in 1974, a further 105 *Cub*s were converted to this standard; they differed from the new-build aircraft in the equipment complement, being fitted with *Baryer* (Barrier) and Siren jammers and automatic infra-red jammers. The An-12BK-IS could still fulfil ordinary transport tasks. In the first years of the 21st century, however, a number of surplus An-12BK-ISs have been reconverted to transport aircraft.

An-12BK-PPS *Cub-C* ECM aircraft

The ultimate ECM variant called An-12BK-PPS appeared in 1971 as an evolution of the An-12PP. Like the latter version, the An-12BK-PPS was designed to operate as part of large formations. Its efficiency was maximised by combining the strap-on Siren jammer pods with the ogival tailcone replacing the tail-gunner's station which housed chaff dispensers. However, some aircraft also referred to as An-12BK-PPSs in available sources have a tail-gunner's station and feature twin square-section tubes with retaining braces exiting through the cargo door rear segment: these serve as chaff outlets.

Three pairs of 'elephant's ear' air intakes and outlets for the mission equipment heat exchangers were located near the forward pods, which required the forward pair of emergency exits and the windows immediately aft of them to be deleted (i.e. there were only two windows to port and one to starboard ahead of the wings instead of the usual four and three respectively). A biological protection package was also installed on the lower forward fuselage to shield the crew from the radiation generated by the mission avionics; this looked like a wide, shallow flat-bottomed bulge with two semi-cylindrical fairings side by side.

Nineteen An-12BKs were converted to this standard, and most of them remain in service with the Russian Air Force. The type was last mentioned in the official press in March 1999, when three An-12BK-PPSs, captained by Major Aleksandr Koostarev, Major Vladimir Kolgyashkin and Major Nikolay Tarlykov, took part in a major command and staff exercise held by the Russian Armed Forces.

An-12 *Cub-B* ELINT aircraft

A small number of Soviet Air Force An-12s was adapted for electronic intelligence (ELINT) duties in the early 1970s. Outwardly such aircraft could be identified by two small hemispherical dielectric fairings

A poor but interesting shot of an An-12BK-PPS in flight with the forward pair of Siren pods removed. The ventral ECM and crew protection system fairings are easily visible. (Yefim Gordon archive)

35 Blue, an An-12B equipped for electronic intelligence duties, seen from a shadowing NATO fighter over international waters. The ventral radomes are clearly visible. The tail cannon are in the fully up position to avoid incidents; it is a standing rule that neither aircraft may use the other as a practice target during such encounters. (Yefim Gordon archive)

located in tandem ahead of the mainwheel wells and by four additional blade aerials on the forward fuselage (two located dorsally in tandem and the other two ventrally in line with them). No separate designation is known but the most likely one is An-12R ([samolyot] rahdiotekhnicheskoy razvedki – ELINT aircraft). The ELINT version is sometimes misidentified in Western publications as the An-12PS maritime SAR aircraft (see above).

ELINT Cubs flew patrol missions over international waters and over Central Europe on a regular basis, monitoring radio traffic in Western Europe and shadowing NATO warships. One such aircraft converted from an An-12A (c/n 2340709) wore the civil registration CCCP-11038 and Aeroflot titles but standard Soviet Air Force grey colours. Two other examples wore VVS insignia and the tactical codes 07 Red and 35 Blue (c/ns unknown).

A later version featured smaller teardrop-shaped ventral radomes and lacked the additional blade aerials. Two aircraft in this configuration – An-12B '84 Red' (c/n 4341905) and An-12BP CCCP-11875 in full 1973-standard blue/white Aeroflot livery (c/n unknown) have been identified to date; both were stationed outside the USSR. The NATO code name was *Cub-B*.

An-12BL experimental transport/SEAD aircraft

Suppression of enemy air defences (SEAD) was recognised as a separate rôle for combat aircraft during the Vietnam War, when surface-to-air missile (SAM) systems started posing a major threat. Specialised SEAD aircraft (known in US Air Force slang as 'Wild Weasels') were developed from fighter-bombers or attack aircraft. But have you ever heard of a 'Wild Weasel' transport? In 1970 the Antonov OKB decided to give the *Cub* an offensive capability, adapting it to a secondary SEAD rôle in order to ensure mission success; simply jamming the enemy radars was not enough.

The result was the An-12BL – a version of the An-12B armed with four Kh-28 anti-radiation missiles (ARMs) for destroying AD radars. Two of these bulky weapons were carried on pylons flanking the forward fuselage and the other two on pylons under the outer wings. A guidance antenna in a thimble radome was installed in the extreme nose ahead of the navigator's glazing. The An-12BL was tested but the modification did not find its way into service.

An-12RR NBC reconnaissance aircraft

Since it was generally assumed that future wars would be fought in a nuclear/biological/chemical contamination (NBC) environment, in 1968–9 the Soviet Air Force converted a handful of An-12Bs for NBC reconnaissance duties. Designated An-12RR ([*samolyot*] *rahdiatsionnoy razvedki* – NBC reconnaissance aircraft; sometimes mis-spelled as 'An-12RKR' or 'An-12RCh' in Western publications), these aircraft had special cradles on the forward fuselage sides for carrying two RR8311-100 standardised air-sampling pods. A small cigar-shaped pod with air intakes was installed on two tandem horizontal pylons on the starboard side of the nose; this housed air-sampling sensors for detecting toxic agents. Only two aircraft, coded 11 Red (c/n 4342604) and 21 Red (c/n 3341404), have been identified so far. Additionally, an An-12BK coded 07 Red (c/n 8345709) has been fitted out with RR8311-100 pods.

An-12BKV bomber and minelayer aircraft

In 1969 GK NII VVS investigated the possibility of using the *Cub* as an auxiliary bomber. This was because the Soviet Air Force's General Operational Requirements (OTTT VVS – *Obschchiye taktiko-tekhnicheskiye trebovaniya Voyenno-vozdooshnykh sil*) insisted that a military transport aircraft absolutely had to be capable of dropping bombs – just in case there would be no other aircraft left to drop them, as some observers caustically commented! The An-12's large payload made it all the more attractive for this rôle.

Designated An-12BKV (the meaning of the V remains unknown), the 'bomber' featured a permanently installed conveyor belt in the freight hold for propelling bombs towards the cargo doors. Several aircraft were converted in this fashion and delivered to the VVS; however, tests revealed that the bombing accuracy was appallingly low and the idea was dropped.

An-12BSh navigator trainer

A special version of the An-12B, designated An-12BSh (*shtoormanskiy* – for navigators), was developed for training navigators for the VTA. Little is known about this version, except that it had ten trainee workstations in the freight hold.

An-12BKSh navigator trainer

A similar navigator trainer version, designated An-12BKSh, was evolved from the An-12BK in 1970. As was the case with the An-12BSh, this version was obtained by converting standard An-12BKs at the Tashkent aircraft factory.

An-12BKK *Kapsoola* VIP aircraft

A single An-12BK transport was converted into a VIP/executive aircraft for the commander of the Soviet Air Force's transport arm (VTA) in 1975. The aircraft was known as An-12BKK *Kapsoola* because a pressurised passenger module ('capsule') with all appropriate furnishings was installed in the normally unpressurised freight hold. Unfortunately the identity of the An-12BKK is unknown.

An-12VKP (An-12B-VKP) *Zebra* airborne command post

A single Irkutsk-built An-12A (19 Red, c/n 9900902) was converted into an airborne command post (ABCP) version designated An-12VKP *Zebra*. The aircraft could be immediately recognised by three cigar-shaped fairings at the wingtips and atop the fin which housed antennas associated with the secure HF communications suite. Additionally, long 'towel rail' aerials ran along the upper and lower fuselage sides from the wing trailing edge to a point in line with the front end of the fin fillet. Obviously a pressurised compartment used as a 'war room' by Army commanders was provided in the freight hold, as was a communications and encoding/decoding equipment bay.

No longer wearing a tactical code or a civil registration, the An-12VKP was tested at LII in Zhukovskiy. The aircraft remained a one-off because the Ilyushin Il-18D *Coot* airliner with its completely pressurised fuselage was far better suited for conversion to the ABCP rôle – a fact which led to the development of the Il-22 *Coot-B* which entered production and service with the Soviet Air Force in substantial numbers. Interestingly, the initial version of the Il-22 (aka Il-18D-36) bore the same Soviet codename, *Zebra*; the later Il-22M, however, was coded *Bizon* (Bison)

Later the An-12VKP put in an appearance in East Germany, operating for the Soviet 16th Air Army. According to press reports, in the winter of 1991–2 the aircraft was damaged beyond repair in a hard landing at Mahlwinkel AB, one of the East German airfields where 16th Air Army units were stationed. The outwardly intact aircraft languished at Mahlwinkel until finally scrapped in the spring of 1995.

An-12M development aircraft

In 1972 a standard production *Cub* (identity unknown) was re-engined with 5,180 ehp AI-20DM turboprops driving AV-68DM propellers of 4.7 m (15 ft 0.42 in) diameter. Despite an improvement of performance, the aircraft, designated An-12BM (*modifitseerovannyy* – modified) remained a one-off because the AI-20DM did not enter quantity production.

An-12A/B/BP/BK demilitarised version

Starting in 1959, considerable numbers of An-12As, An-12Bs, An-12BPs and

MISSION VARIETY

An An-12RR radiation reconnaissance aircraft (21 Red, c/n 3341404) immediately after completing its landing run. (Yefim Gordon archive)

Close-up of the same aircraft's forward fuselage, showing the starboard RR8311-100 air sampling pod and the pylon-mounted sensor pod on the starboard side.
(Yefim Gordon archive)

The sole An-12VKP airborne command post on final approach to Zhukovskiy during trials, showing the characteristic antenna pods on the wings and tail and traces of two 'towel rail' aerials on the rear fuselage side. The type was outclassed by the Il-22 which had much the same mission equipment but offered far better working conditions. (Viktor Drushlyakov)

Many 'military' An-12s were transferred to Aeroflot and demilitarised, which meant removing the tail turret and fitting a fairing instead. Here, An-12B CCCP-11366 (c/n 402808) of the Magadan CAD/1st Magadan UFD/181st Flight taxies out at Moscow-Sheremet'yevo past an Austrian Airlines Sud Aviation SE210 Caravelle VIR (OE-LCI). This aircraft has even had the gunner's station windows faired over. (Yefim Gordon archive)

CCCP-11367 (c/n 402901), another demilitarised An-12B and the first *Cub* to carry this registration, in standard pre-1973 red/white livery as applied to the An-10 at one time. (Antonov OKB)

An-12BKs were transferred from the VTA to the Soviet airline Aeroflot and various industry organisations to fill the need for carrying civil cargoes with speed and efficiency. Of course, such aircraft had to be adapted to their new career in 'civvy street'. First of all the cannon were removed from the tail turret; as often as not the DB-65U turret itself was removed and replaced by a hemispherical fairing (e.g. on An-12B CCCP-11991, c/n 402006) or the aperture was simply faired over with sheet metal in a similar manner to ex-VVS An-8s (e.g. on An-12BP RA-11962, c/n 5343007). Sometimes even the tail-gunner's station glazing was overpainted in order to dispel any doubts about the aircraft's civil status. Such aircraft with the turret deleted or the rear glazing overpainted are from now on described as **demilitarised**.

The paradropping equipment which the airline had no use for was also removed. Finally, some sensitive avionics items had to be replaced; for example, the military communications radios were replaced with civilian ones using a different frequency grid, and the RBP-2 ground-mapping radar gave way to the civil ROZ-1 Lotsiya (Navigational directions; NATO codename *Toad Stool*) weather/navigation radar[33] in an identical radome. Curiously, some ex-VVS An-12BKs had the ROZ-1 fitted as well, becoming outwardly identical to An-12BPs, while others retained the bulbous radome of the Initsiativa-4-100 radar.

An-12B/BP commercial transport version ('An-12V', 'An-12MGA')

From approximately March 1964 onwards the Voronezh aircraft factory started building a dedicated civil version of the An-12B lacking armament. The tail-gunner's station was replaced by a neat narrow slab-sided fairing which was semicircular in side view; the ventral doors of the flare bomb compartment were still there but now they provided access to a bay housing 16 additional DC batteries. The civil version was formally unveiled in 1965 when an Aeroflot aircraft registered CCCP-11359 (c/n 402804) took part in the 25th Paris Air Show. From then on the civil version was often erroneously referred to in the West as either 'An-12V' or 'An-12MGA' (for M*in*iste*r*stvo gr*azh*d*ahn*sk*oy* avi*ahtsii* – Ministry of Civil Aviation), but neither of these designations is found in Soviet/Russian documents. Also, some authors have used the designation An-12BK for the unarmed commercial version in the mistaken belief that the K stood for *kommehrcheskiy*, while others erroneously called CCCP-11359 'An-12D' (see below).

The Tashkent aircraft factory joined in about January 1966 with a similar unarmed version of the An-12BP, the earliest known example being LZ-BAC (ex CCCP-1100..., c/n 6343708). Production continued until the type was finally phased out of production in 1972. No separate batches were set aside for the civil version – the aircraft were completed with or without tail-gunner's station as per customer demand.

Ironically, not all *Cub*s built in unarmed configuration were civil! The communications relay version described earlier is a prime example. Likewise, An-12BP CCCP-12990 (c/n 00347304) belonged to the Soviet Air Force before being transferred to MAP's general transport department, and the two Yugoslav Air Force examples – 73311/YU-AIC (c/n 01348007) and 73312/YU-AID (c/n 01348010) – had no tail-gunner's station either.

An-12TB/TBK

A number of civil-operated An-12s with a tail gunner's station and a small radome (i.e. an ROZ-1 radar) have been reported both in official documents and in the press as An-12TBs, the T standing for **trahnsportnyy** [*samolyot*] – (civil) transport aircraft. Such aircraft include RA-11025 (c/n 6344103) of Kosmos Air Company, RA-11532 (c/n 402007) and RA-11851 (c/n 402003) of Aviaobschchemash and RA-11100 (c/n 01347702) of Norilsk Avia – though the latter aircraft has also been reported as an An-12BP with no tail-gunner's station, which seems far more likely! Possibly An-12TB is the designation allocated to ex-military An-12BPs.

An-12B CCCP-11359 (c/n 402804), the demonstrator of the unarmed civil version which was displayed at the 25th Paris Air Show in 1965. (Yefim Gordon archive)

Similarly, ex-Russian Air Force An-12BK RA-12108 (c/n 9346308)[34] was referred to as an An-12TBK after sale to a civil owner and refitment with an ROZ-1 radar. Surprisingly, however, this designation has also been used with reference to a Russian Air Force example coded 26 Red (c/n 9346305) which is apparently a standard An-12BK.

An-12BSM commercial transport

In 1973 the Antonov OKB developed another commercial transport version called An-12BSM (the meaning of the suffix is unknown). Unlike the basic *Cub*, the An-12BSM was designed with containerised and palletised goods in mind. The freight hold was equipped with two gantry cranes each capable of lifting 2,500 kg (5,511 lb), guide rails and roller conveyors for container/pallet handling; special panels were installed between fuselage Frames 34 and 43 to provide a smooth freight hold floor, eliminating the step at Frame 34.

The aircraft could carry eight UAK-2,5 air freight containers measuring 1,456 × 2,438 × 1,900 mm (4 ft 9.31 in × 8 ft 0 in × 6 ft 2.81 in) or PA-2,5 rigid pallets measuring 1,456 × 2,438 mm (4 ft 9.31 in × 8 ft 0 in), each weighing 2,500 kg (5,511 lb) fully loaded. An alternative payload was four 5,000 kg (11,023 lb) UAK-5A containers measuring 2,991 × 2,438 × 1,900 mm (9 ft 9.75 in × 8 ft 0 in × 6 ft 2.81 in) or four PA-5,6 pallets measuring 2,991 × 2,438 mm (9 ft 9.75 in × 8 ft 0 in), each weighing 5,670 kg (12,500 lb).

An-12BP flight refuelling tanker conversion

One of the An-12BP transports delivered to the Iraqi Air Force was reportedly converted *in situ* into a single-point hose-and-drogue flight refuelling tanker. Unfortunately no details are known, except that the aircraft was used operationally during the Iran–Iraq war. Later the aircraft was replaced in IrAF service by a similar one-off conversion of an Il-76M.

The An-12 has been extensively used for test and research purposes, civil as well as military, and a few testbeds based on the *Cub* are still around. The high payload and spacious (albeit unpressurised) freight hold which could accommodate bulky and heavy test equipment made the An-12 a capable test platform.

Known aircraft converted to testbeds are listed below.

Engine testbeds

Soviet testbed

In 1959 an An-12 (identity unknown) was used as a testbed for the Ivchenko AI-24 turboprop (initially rated at 2,500 ehp) driving an AV-72 four-bladed reversible-pitch propeller of 3.9 m (12 ft 9.5 in) diameter developed by the Stoopino Machinery Design Bureau. The new powerplant had been developed for the An-24 *Coke* twin-turboprop regional airliner which entered flight test on 20 October 1959. The An-24 turned out to be highly successful and became the progenitor of a whole family of twin-turboprop aircraft which lies outside the scope of this book; suffice it to say that most of them were powered by the same engine, which in its ultimate form (AI-24VT) was uprated to 2,820 ehp.

Egyptian testbed

In 1962 an Egyptian Air Force An-12B serialled 1223 (c/n 402309) was converted for testing the 4,800 kgp (10,580 lb st) E-300 afterburning turbojet developed by the German engineer Dr Ferdinand Brandner for the Egyptian Helwan HA-300 light fighter. The development engine was mounted in place of the No. 2 AI-20 turboprop in a compact nacelle attached to a suitably modified engine bearer. However, the flight-cleared engine was never installed in the real thing; the two HA-300 prototypes (300-001 and 300-002), the first of which made its maiden flight on 7 March 1964, were powered by 2,200 kgp (4,850 lb st) Bristol Orpheus BOr 12 turbojets.

Eventually, however, Egypt's attempt to create an indigenous combat aircraft was cut short by financial problems; the programme was closed down in 1968 and the HA-300 did not progress beyond the prototype stage. As for the An-12, it was reconverted to standard configuration, serving on with the EAF as 1223/SU-AOS until finally retired and scrapped.

Avionics testbeds

By far the greatest proportion of An-12 testbeds were used to test new avionics and equipment – mostly for military applications, the exact nature of which remains unknown.

a) From 1964 to 1998 a Soviet/Russian Air Force An-12B (c/n 402207) was used for testing ELINT and optoelectronic reconnaissance systems. Wearing standard overall grey camouflage and VVS star insignia but sporting the non-standard registration 08256 (originally the aircraft's ATC callsign) in lieu of a tactical code, this *Cub* sported numerous tell-tale 'bumps and bulges'. Long slab-sided fairings with streamlined front and rear ends and dielectric panels housing a side-looking airborne radar (SLAR) were mounted high on the rear fuselage sides; the panels were flat, except for an elliptical bulge at the front, and inclined slightly outward (not vertical).

The DB-65U tail turret was supplanted by a long ogival dielectric fairing looking like a supersonic fighter's radome; the tail-gunner's station probably accommodated one of the test engineers. Additional boxy fairings were located low on the starboard side of the forward fuselage and beneath the starboard SLAR fairing; the rear 'box' was much larger and incorporated what appears to be two rows of eight four-round flare launchers. Two oblong square-section boxes with unidentified equipment could be extended aft through the open cargo doors. Finally, a bulged observation blister was built into the forward starboard emergency exit. The aircraft was, and still is, based at the LII airfield in Zhukovskiy.

b) A quasi-civil grey-painted An-12A or B registered CCCP-11417 (c/n unknown) was used with anti-submarine warfare (ASW) or ELINT equipment – most probably by the All-Union Electronics Research Institute (VNIIRA – V*sesoyooznyy* n*aoochno-iss*l*ed*ov*atel'skiy* inst*itoot* rah*dioelektroniki*), alias LNPO Leninets (Leninist), in Leningrad. This establishment, a division of the Ministry of Electronic Industry (MRP – M*inisterstvo* rah*dioelektronnoy promyshlennosti*), was one of the Soviet Union's leading avionics houses.[35]

Originally large cylindric pods with cropped conical ends were mounted on the forward fuselage sides beneath the cabin windows; these housed a *Sahblya* (Sabre) monobloc SLAR, alias *izdeliye* 122, of the type fitted to the Mikoyan/Gurevich MiG-25RBS *Foxbat* reconnaissance/strike aircraft. A smaller rectangular box located ventrally on the centreline in line with their aft ends accommodated a Bulat (Damask steel, pronounced *boolaht*) radar. A fairly large rounded radome mounted on a hinged frame was installed at the rear of the freight hold, protruding through a cutout in the starboard cargo door segment; it was semi-recessed in the fuselage for take-off and landing and fully extended in flight. A small angular fairing – probably a camera housing – projected downwards from the rear cargo-door segment.

The first test flights performed by NII VVS crews gave disappointing results. The lateral pods generated powerful vortices and the turbulent airflow from the port pod was caught by the propeller of No. 2 engine, striking the entry door. As a

Egyptian Air Force An-12B '1223' (c/n 402309) was used as a testbed for the Brandner E-300 afterburning turbojet developed for the Helwan HA-300 fighter. This view clearly shows the turbojet installed in place of the No. 2 turboprop. (RART)

Two views of An-12B 08256 (c/n 402207) used for testing ELINT and optoelectronic reconnaissance systems by the Flight Research Institute. The combination of a civil registration with VVS star insignia is unusual. (Yefim Gordon archive)

Close-up of the tail end of c/n 402207; the callsign-turned-registration has yet to be applied. The photo clearly shows the rear radome, lateral SLAR fairings and the square-section boxes with unidentified equipment extended aft through the open cargo doors. (Yefim Gordon archive)

CCCP-11417, a bizarre ASW/ELINT equipment testbed operated by LNPO Leninets, photographed over the Barents Sea from a Royal Norwegian Air Force F-104 in the summer of 1984. This photo shows the aircraft in late configuration; originally the lateral fairings were cylindrical, causing intensive vibration. (Jane's All the World's Aircraft)

result, the door would vibrate, creating a deafening roar which made life unbearable for the crew. As well as this, the frame of the rear radome was not rigid enough and the radome started swaying dangerously. To remedy the situation the SLAR antennas were attached directly to the fuselage sides slightly lower than before and enclosed by huge teardrop fairings, and the said frame was stiffened.

Later CCCP-11417 received an update which involved the addition of an *Oospekh* (Success) radar in a large quasi-spherical radome installed beneath the tail-gunner's station; this radar had been developed for the Kamov Ka-25Ts *Hormone-B* shipboard over-the-horizon (OTH) targeting helicopter. The aircraft became known to the West in the summer of 1984, when it was intercepted over the Barents Sea by Royal Norwegian Air Force Lockheed F-104 Starfighters.

c) Another quasi-civil overall grey An-12A, CCCP-11790 (c/n 1400302), served as an ECM or ELINT testbed with the Yermolino flight-test centre southeast of Moscow in the early 1980s. It featured a large boxy structure incorporating five dielectric panels of different sizes attached to the aft fuselage underside, thereby rendering the rear cargo door segment inoperative, and a fairly long square-section 'stinger' fairing extending aft from the tail-gunner's station in lieu of a turret. The aircraft was later stripped of all non-standard appendages, serving as an ordinary transport with the Yermolino Flight Test & Research Enterprise as RA-11790 (the DB-65U turret was reinstated).

d) Yet another avionics testbed operated by the Yermolino flight test centre was An-12AP CCCP-11916 (c/n 2400901). In its days as a testbed it also wore grey Air Force colours, featuring an identical 'stinger' fairing replacing the tail turret and a large cylindrical 'proboscis' extending forward from the navigator's station, which required most of the glazing to be removed. Like CCCP-11790, the aircraft was reconverted to standard configuration by 1993 and operated by the Yermolino Flight Test & Research Enterprise as RA-11916.

e) A grey-painted An-12A with the non-standard registration CCCP-13321 (c/n 2340301) had been used by NPO Vzlyot (Take-off) as an SLAR testbed at one time. When first noted at Zhukovskiy in August 1992 the aircraft appeared perfectly standard at first glance, but careful inspection of the rear fuselage sides revealed that fairings similar to those of An-12B 08256 had been installed there previously.

f) 'Military' An-12BP CCCP-13402 (c/n unknown) was probably another LNPO Leninets testbed. Painted in 1973-standard blue/white Aeroflot colours, this aircraft had a huge quasi-spherical radome housing an Oospekh radar instead of the normal chin-mounted RBP-2, and again a camera fairing on the rear cargo door segment.

g) In 1969 a Soviet Air Force An-12A or B coded 77 Red (c/n unknown) was one of the most bizarre *Cub* testbeds. Designated An-12 **Koobrik** (crew quarters, a nautical term), the aircraft served for testing thermal imaging systems and IR sensors designed for detecting targets on water and land and in the air. The greater part of the navigator's station glazing was supplanted by a cylindrical metal adapter mounting a conical radome at the front and a small teardrop radome underneath and incorporating two small air intakes. A

An-12A CCCP-11790 (c/n 1400302), an ECM or ELINT testbed operated by the Yermolino flight test centre, showing the large antenna fairings supplanting the rear cargo door segment and the tail turret. The aircraft was later reconverted to standard configuration. (*Jane's All the World's Aircraft*)

MISSION VARIETY

An-12AP CCCP-11916 (c/n 2400901), one more *Cub* operated by the Yermolino test centre in a similar capacity. (*Jane's All the World's Aircraft*)

The rear end of An-12A '15 Red' (c/n 1340105), showing the radiometric and spectrometric equipment sensors replacing the tail turret. (LII archive)

large boxy dorsal canoe fairing ran nearly the full length of the forward fuselage from just aft of the flight deck to the wing leading edge; a large cylindrical 'smokestack' was installed near its aft end. A small bullet-shaped pod was carried on a short forward-swept pylon installed under the port forward emergency exit.

The rear end was non-standard as well. The tail-gunner's station was moved aft appreciably by fitting a 'plug' between it and the rest of the airframe; a PRS-4 Krypton gun ranging radar with a distinctive boxy radome (hence the NATO codename *Box Tail*)[36] was fitted above it and the cannon were replaced by some kind of sensor. Finally, a camera fairing protruded from the rear cargo door segment.

h) The An-12BK prototype (CCCP-83962 No. 2) was used in 1966–9 to test the Polyot-1 (Flight-1) navigation system and the Koopol (cupola – or rather, in this context, parachute canopy) precision paradropping system developed for the An-22 Antey (Antheus; NATO *Cock*) heavy transport aircraft.

i) Another *Cub* served as a testbed for the *Prostor* (Wide expanse, or Ample space) thermal imager in 1968–70. The unit was designed for infra-red mapping and locating fires.

j) One more An-12 was a testbed for long-range radio navigation (LORAN) systems in 1977–82; the results were used in the design of the Alpha LORAN system fitted to some Soviet combat aircraft. The aircraft was referred to as 'An-12 No. 3108' – i.e. either An-12B c/n 403108 or An-12BP '15 Red' (c/n 5343108) which was later transferred to the airlift regiment at Kubinka AB.

An-12B instrumentation calibration laboratory (*izdeliye* 93T)

In 1972 a single An-12 (identity unknown) was equipped as 'a flying laboratory for running metrological checks on a range of measuring instruments used by Soviet Air Force regiments' (*sic*). The aircraft was known as *izdeliye* 93T. The nature of the equipment to be checked is unclear but one might suppose that the aircraft was in reality a navaids calibrator. If that was indeed the case, it is clear why the aircraft remained a one-off: navaids calibration duties were far better performed by the smaller and less thirsty An-26ASLK *Curl* (alias An-26KPA, alias An-26 Standart).[37]

An-12B (LIAT) air accident investigation laboratory

Again in 1972, another Soviet Air Force *Cub* (identity unknown) was converted into a mobile air accident investigation laboratory, designated An-12B (LIAT), which could travel to the airbase where a crash had taken place. The LIAT suffix in parentheses stood for *laboratoriya issledovaniya aviatsionnoy tekhniki* – aviation hardware examination laboratory. The freight hold housed specialised equipment for deciphering the 'black boxes' (flight data recorder and cockpit voice recorder) of the crashed aircraft and featured an additional crew rest area, galley and toilet facilities.

An-12BPTs *Tsiklon* weather research aircraft

By the mid-1970s radar technologies of weather and atmospheric research had gained wide use. The use of radar made it possible to study the distribution of clouds and precipitation over wide areas and follow the development of storm nuclei. Therefore a special equipment suite called *Tsiklon* (Cyclone) was developed to meet an order placed by the Soviet Union's State Committee for Hydrometeorology and Environmental Control (*Goskomghidromet*). In 1976–9 two Tashkent-built An-12BPs, CCCP-11530 (c/n 6344503) and CCCP-11531 (c/n 6344506), were converted into weather research aircraft designated An-12BPTs *Tsiklon* (often referred to as An-12BP *Tsiklon* or An-12 *Tsiklon* – and sometimes erroneously called An-12BKTs).

The technologies employed by the *Tsiklon* system allowed stand-off research of clouds – i.e. without actually entering them, which could change their shape and structure (and could be dangerous for the aircraft itself, considering that severe turbulence is often encountered in clouds, not to mention lightning!). Apart from studying the principal thermodynamic and electric parameters of the atmosphere and cloud formations, the aircraft were designed to perform cloud-seeding missions in order to make rain – e.g. when it

The An-12BP 'Kubrik' avionics testbed was probably the most bizarre *Cub* ever. (Yefim Gordon archive)

CCCP-11530 (c/n 6344503), the first of two An-12BPTs *Tsiklon* weather research aircraft, showing the nose-mounted sensor boom, the rear radome housing a Groza-26 radar and two of the four pylons for carrying rainmaking chemical dispensers. (Goskomghidromet)

Front view of the An-12BPTs with chemical dispenser pods attached. This view shows the BMR-1 weather research radar at the base of the sensor boom and the *Tsiklon* badge below the flight-deck windows. (Yefim Gordon archive)

was necessary to prevent an impending hailstorm which could destroy crops (or to scatter rain clouds which could ruin a public holiday).

Outwardly the An-12BPTs *Tsiklon* bore a strong resemblance to the unique Lockheed C-130K-140-LM Hercules W.2 (XV208) operated by the Royal Air Force's Weather Research Flight and nicknamed 'Snoopy'. The navigator's station glazing was reduced to a single window on each side. Instead, the nose terminated in a long pointed boom tipped with sensors and painted in black and white zebra stripes to avoid damage by ground vehicles. A specialised BMR-1 weather research radar was installed in a rounded radome at the base of the boom (the standard ROZ-1 chin-mounted radar was retained). More sensors were located dorsally and ventrally on the forward fuselage centreline.

The tail-gunner's station was modified for installing an RPSN-3S[38] Groza-26 (Thunderstorm, pronounced *grozah*) weather radar borrowed from the An-26 transport, and this was closed by a fairly large rounded radome. Two large pylons were installed on each side of the lower fuselage fore and aft of the main gear fairings for carrying cloud-seeding chemical pods. Finally, three observation blisters were provided on each side for filming purposes. The aircraft wore full blue/white Aeroflot colours but the cheatline was broken beneath the flight deck by the eye-catching *Tsiklon* emblem.

Two research equipment consoles were located in the pressurised forward cabin, with two more in the freight hold. The mission equipment comprised a measurement suite, data recording/processing equipment and cloud-seeding equipment. The **measurement suite** included, first of all, a *thermodynamic measurement system* comprising a TsSV-3M-1KM central air data system, an EM TsAO electric meteorograph developed by the Central Aerological Observatory, a PK G-load-measuring kit, an SAMB-70 airborne automatic weather research module, an ASTA-74

View inside the freight hold of the An-12BPTs, showing part of the research and data recording equipment. The roller conveyor to the left was presumably used for dumping packs of chemicals through the open doors. Note also the standard overhead gantry crane. (Goskomghidromet)

airborne automatic thermoanemometer, an RV-18Zh radio altimeter and an SG-1 airborne humidity meter. It recorded the outside air temperature and its fluctuations, the aircraft's speed and heading, the wind speed and direction, airflow pulsations, static and dynamic air pressure, barometric and true altitude, vertical gusts and G loads acting on the aircraft.

The second major component was the *cloud and precipitation microstructure measurement system* comprising an IRCh water/ice particle size meter and an SEIV-3 airborne electric cloud water content meter. The third component was the *meteorological radar system* – the aforementioned BMR-1 in the nose for vertical scanning of the atmosphere and the Groza-26 radar in the tail. Finally, there was a PNP meter for measuring electric fields and the aircraft's electric charge.

The **data recording/processing equipment** consisted of a K60-42 magnetic recorder, an AKS-2 ciné camera and an SYeO common time indication system. The K60-42 automatically recorded signals generated by the thermodynamic and cloud measurement systems for future computer analysis. The ciné and photo cameras were used to film the outside conditions, using the observation blisters.

The **cloud-seeding equipment** designed to generate rain from cumulus and stratus clouds included seven KDS-155 dispensers and four ASO-2I dispensers mounted on the cargo doors, an ITU solid carbon dioxide atomiser and, as an option, four pods for dispensing powdered rainmaking agents. The most widely used among the latter is silver iodide. The KDS-155 and ASO-2I were adapted from stock chaff/flare dispensers used on Soviet military aircraft for passive ECM and IRCM. Instead of bundles of chaff, aluminium-coated glass needles or PPI-26 IRCM flares, they fire special PV-26 cartridges with chemicals which trigger the formation of ice crystals. The latter become too heavy to be supported by the air currents inside the cloud and start falling as hailstones; however, these melt and turn into rain before reaching the ground.

Since the An-12BPTs was intended to operate over vast stretches of water if necessary when chasing storms, it was provided with appropriate long-range radio navigation (LORAN) equipment.

The aircraft had a flight crew of five plus a 14-man team of researchers. In fully equipped configuration with four external pods the TOW amounted to 61 tons (134,480 lb); top speed was 550–600 km/h (340–372 mph) and the service ceiling was 8,700 m (28,540 ft). The An-12BPTs could stay airborne for up to eight hours, with a maximum range of 5,000 km (3,105 miles). The nose-mounted instrumentation boom and rear radome increased the overall length from 33.1 m (108 ft 7.16 in) to 38 m (124 ft 8 in).

The two weather research *Cubs* were operated by the State Civil Aviation Research Institute (GosNII GA – *Gosoodarstvennyy naoochno-issledovatel'skiy institoot grazhdahnskoy aviahtsii*) and home-based at Moscow-Sheremetyevo, but they were seldom seen there, travelling far and wide in pursuit of their mission. Among other things, they were periodically deployed to Cuba because the region offered plenty of material for research, being regularly hit by typhoons. The aircraft were quite efficient economically in their designated rôle because of the high accuracy of measurements and the ability to track changes in the meteorological processes in real time, influence them quickly and check the results immediately. Incidentally, CCCP-11530 and CCCP-11531 were but two of a range of assorted weather research aircraft bearing the *Tsiklon* name. These included an Ilyushin Il-18D *Coot* four-turboprop airliner (CCCP-75442), a Tupolev Tu-104A *Camel* twinjet airliner (CCCP-42454), a pair of demilitarised Tu-16K-26 *Badger G Mod* naval missile strike aircraft (CCCP-42355 No. 1[39] and CCCP-42484) and an as-yet unidentified An-26.

Regrettably, in the general chaos that followed the demise of the Soviet Union these aircraft found themselves unwanted. The Tupolev jets were withdrawn from use as time-expired, while the turboprops, including both An-12s, were stripped of their special equipment and used as cargo aircraft. Interestingly, the navigator's station glazing was never fully reinstated (there was a solid panel replacing the two upper windows in the second row) and the tail radomes on both aircraft remained, though they were empty now. The aircraft served on with GosNII GA as RA-11530 and RA-11531 for a while; the latter aircraft was then sold to Angola as D2-FVG No. 1[40] and was eventually lost in a crash.

TWA testbed

In 1975 the former An-12VKP ABCP (c/n 9900902) operated by the Flight Research Institute served as a testbed for the mighty BLT-5 winch, driven by a ram-air turbine; the winch was used to deploy a 2,500 m (8,200 ft) trailing wire aerial (TWA) with a stabilising drogue at the end. The unit had been specially developed for the Tu-142MR *Bear-J* communications relay aircraft whose mission was to maintain very low frequency (VLF) communications between submerged nuclear missile submarines and land-based or airborne command posts in the event of a nuclear attack (in this case R stands for *retranslyator* – communications relay installation). The aircraft also featured a whole network of VLF wire aerials stretched from the tail unit to the wings, looking almost like a spider's web. The tests were filmed from a Tu-124 *Cookpot* chase plane.

An-12BK ejection seat/APU/ recovery systems testbed (An-12M LL)

In 1989 An-12BK '43 Red' (c/n 8345902) was converted into a multipurpose testbed to be used in the interests of LII and the Parachute Systems Design Institute (*Naoochno-issledovatel'skiy institoot parashootostroyeniya*). In some sources this aircraft has been called An-12M LL (*letayuschchaya laboratoriya* – lit. 'flying laboratory').[41]

One of its functions was to test a recovery system intended for picking up film capsules ejected by surveillance satellites. The system was patterned on the Fulton STAR recovery gear fitted to the US Air Force version of the Lockheed HC-130H. Two long hinged booms were attached to the aft fuselage underside; these could be swung down to snag the cassette's parachute as the cassette floated earthwards. A similar system had been used in the USA, where a specially modified JC-130 picked up film cassettes ejected by Lockheed GTD-21 high-speed reconnaissance drones.

The second mission fulfilled by '43 Red' at this stage was the testing of new models of ejection seats. To this end the tail turret was removed and replaced by a detachable elongated pod emulating the cockpit of a combat aircraft. The 'cockpit' was attached by multiple bolts and could be installed at any angle from upright to inverted (0° to 180°) at 30° increments to emulate different attitudes of the stricken aircraft at the moment of ejection. This was because state-of-the-art ejection seats, such as the famous Zvezda K-36, were designed to ensure safe ejection even in inverted flight at low altitude – the worst possible combination. Two video cameras in orange egg-shaped pods were mounted under the wingtips to capture the ejection sequence; test equipment heat exchangers in characteristic white-painted teardrop fairings were installed high on the fuselage sides immediately aft of the wings.

The first photos of An-12BK '43 Red' as an ejection seat testbed were displayed at the Konversiya '91[42] trade fair held at the VDNKh exhibition centre in December 1991. At that time the aircraft still had the 'grabbing booms' left over from the previous programme, but these were later removed as unnecessary. The testbed was

Two views of the former An-12VKP following conversion into a VLF communications equipment testbed, showing the plethora of wire aerials stretching from the fin to the wings and the stabilising drogue of the trailing wire aerial protruding under the rear fuselage. (LII archive)

shown in action at the MosAeroShow'92 (11–16 August 1992) and MAKS-97 (19–24 August 1997) airshows in Zhukovskiy, performing live ejections of a seat with a dummy. On the former occasion (15 August) a standard K-36DM was fired from an inverted position, while at MAKS-97 the latest K-36DM-3.5 (featuring a reduced 3.5 G load limit to prevent pilot injuries) was fired with the cockpit set at 60° right bank.

As an alternative to the ejection cockpit a module with an auxiliary power unit could be installed. Thus by May 1994 An-12BK '43 Red' was fitted with the tailcone of an Il-114 twin-turboprop regional airliner housing a VD-100M APU. In this guise the aircraft was displayed statically at the MAKS-95 airshow (22–27 August 1995). With the APU bay in place the An-12 could still be used for testing parachutes by simply jumping out of the cargo door.

Geophysical survey aircraft

a) An-12TP-2

A single An-12B with the non-standard Polar Aviation registration CCCP 04366 (unusually, the registration was painted on with no dash; c/n unknown) was custombuilt for long-range transport and geophysical survey duties in the Antarctic. The RBP-2 radar was replaced by a different one in a much longer and deeper radome extending all the way aft to the nosewheel well (the flight deck ventral escape hatch was thus blocked). There was no tail-gunner's station, but a long slender magnetic anomaly detector (MAD) boom protruded from the 'civil' tailcone. The pre-1973 red/white colour scheme worn by Aeroflot *Cub*s was modified: the lower fuselage was white instead of grey, the vertical tail and propeller spinners were painted orange and the tops of the outer wings and stabilisers were red for high definition against white backgrounds. To make its mission patently clear the aircraft wore additional 'Polyarnaya aviatsiya' titles and penguin tail art.

Designated An-12TP-2, the aircraft took part in an expedition to the Antarctic in December 1961. On arrival in the Antarctic CCCP 04366 was re-equipped with a non-retractable ski undercarriage as fitted to the An-12PL. Interestingly, the *Cub* was referred to as an An-10 in Soviet press reports of the expedition because the designation An-12 was still classified at the time; this misinformation found its way into Western publications as well.

b) An-12AP CCCP-12186 (c/n unknown) was another geophysical survey aircraft developed in 1982 for the Leningrad branch of the Earth Magnetism Institute (a division of the Soviet Academy of Sciences). The design and conversion work was performed by the Soviet Navy's 20th Aircraft Overhaul Plant in Pushkin near Leningrad.

The aircraft, which wore full 1973-standard Aeroflot blue/white livery, was fitted with an 8 m (26 ft 2.95 in) tapered MAD boom supplanting the tail turret. A small 'superstructure' housing an L-14MA astro-inertial navigation system was mounted on top of the boom near the front, making it look like a submarine *en miniature*. As with CCCP-11417, a camera fairing protruded from the rear cargo door segment. There were three researchers' workstations in the pressure cabin, with most of the equipment being installed in the freight hold.

Originally the aircraft bore the codename 'Magnitometr'. In 1990 CCCP-12186 was upgraded by installing new scientific instrumentation and the codename was changed to 'Relikt'. The aircraft was used for studying the structure of the earth's magnetic field and for making gravimetric measurements as requested by various government agencies and ministries.

De-icing systems test aircraft (An-12 'Tanker')

LII's large fleet of test and research aircraft included an An-12BK in ex-VVS grey colours which initially wore the non-standard civil registration CCCP-48974 No. 2 (c/n 6344510).[43] At first this machine was used as a 'spray tanker' for testing the de-icing systems of other aircraft. Developed

An-12BK '43 Red' (c/n 8345902), sometimes called An-12M LL, was used by LII in several programmes, including ejection seat trials held jointly with the Parachute Systems Design Institute and NPP Zvezda. This view shows a seat towed by a rocket motor on a line (probably the Zvezda K-37 seat designed for the Kamov Ka-50 *Hokum* attack helicopter) leaving the special cockpit installed in lieu of the tail turret. Visible under the fuselage are two striped booms for picking up objects, a leftover from an earlier test programme. (Yefim Gordon archive)

The test cockpit could be installed at various angles to emulate different aircraft attitudes. Here, ejection takes place from an inverted position. (Yefim Gordon archive)

in 1981, the modification involved the fitment of an 8,000-litre (1,760 imp. gal) water tank and a drum from which a 47 m (154 ft) hose terminating in a circular sprinkler grid was deployed through the cargo door, the grid acting as a stabilising drogue. The water was presumably fed by gravity; the delivery rate could vary up to 4 litres (0.88 imp. gal) per second; the aircraft created a cloud of water mist measuring 3–5 m (10–16 ft) in diameter. Depending on the flight speed and delivery rate, the mission time could be anything from 30 minutes to six hours.

The whole thing looked so much like a single-point hose-and-drogue refuelling tanker that the aircraft was immediately dubbed 'Tanker'. This fairly complex arrangement was needed to keep the grid and the aircraft being tested out of the tanker's wake vortex.

CCCP-48974 No. 2 is known to have been used in the trials of the An-72 *Coaler* short take-off and landing (STOL) transport. Using the 'tanker' allowed the time required for verifying a new aircraft's de-icing system to be reduced by a factor of four; it also enhanced flight safety and allowed icing tests to be performed at realistic speeds (i.e. the ones at which the aircraft would be likely to operate). Incidentally, the An-12/An-72 combination was displayed in model form at the 1983 Paris Air Show; the *Cub* featured its actual registration but was painted in 1973-standard blue/white Aeroflot livery. This puzzled Western observers completely, leading to the misconception that the model represented a flight refuelling tanker akin to the RAF's C-130K Hercules C.1K and that *the new tanker was perhaps intended to have some kind of civilian role!!!*

Later the An-12 was extensively modified. A section of a wing with a symmetrical airfoil and a leading-edge de-icer was installed vertically aft of the wing centre section, requiring the fin fillet to be cropped slightly. A large circular sprinkler grid with bracing struts was mounted ahead of the wing centre section. The freight hold accommodated test equipment consoles and a water tank; a big 'elephant's ear' air intake was provided on each side in line with the wing trailing edge for pressurising this tank and feeding water to the nozzles. The first cabin window to port was blanked off with sheet metal; a large blister located high on each side of the forward fuselage provided a view of the grid and the test article, allowing the icing process to be filmed.

By 1987 the aircraft had lost its civil identity for some reason, gaining Air Force insignia and the tactical code 10 Red – presumably to match the last digits of the c/n, which was common practice at LII.[44] In early 1992 the An-12 testbed was stripped of all non-standard features except the blisters and the abbreviated fin

MISSION VARIETY

The test cockpit of the An-12M LL displayed separately at the MAKS-95 airshow, featuring a Zvezda K-36D seat with a dummy. Note the LII logo and photo-calibration markings. (Dmitriy Komissarov)

In 1994 An-12BK '43 Red' was refitted for testing the VD-100M APU designed for the Il-114 airliner. This close-up of the APU installation was taken in the static park at MAKS-95; note the video camera mounted over the gunner's station window. (Dmitriy Komissarov)

CCCP 04366, the highly modified An-12TP-2 transport/geophysical survey aircraft. (Antonov OKB)

Close-up of the An-12TP-2's nose, showing the non-standard radome. Note the additional *Polyarnaya Aviatsiya* (Polar Aviation) titles and the nose of Il-18V CCCP-75743; the two aircraft participated in a celebrated expedition to the Antarctic in December 1961/February 1962. Unfortunately the *Cub* was written off in an accident five years later. (Boris Vdovenko)

Rear view of CCCP 04366, showing the extensible MAD boom protruding from the 'civil' tailcone. The objects in the foreground are propane-butane bottles; the vehicles are a GAZ-63 4 × 4 lorry and a TZ-22 articulated refuelling bowser. (Boris Vdovenko)

For operations from snow strips in the Antarctic the An-12TP-2 was temporarily refitted with skis. (Boris Vdovenko)

An-12AP CCCP-12186, the geophysical survey aircraft developed in 1982 for the Leningrad branch of the Earth Magnetism Institute and used in the Magnitometr and Relikt programmes. (Sergey and Dmitriy Komissarov archive)

fillet, receiving the non-standard registration RA-13331 (though the Initsiativa radar and grey colour scheme still remained). Later it was sold to a Russian airline called Start and repainted in basic Aeroflot colours; an ROZ-1 radar in a small radome was installed at the same time.

Miscellaneous testbeds

a) One of the genuine Soviet-built An-12BPs supplied to China (B-3151, c/n 6344402) – misidentified by some Western observers as 'an early [Shaanxi] Y8 with a short nose glazing' (see next chapter) – was converted into a testbed of some sort with a simple conical fairing supplanting the tail turret. There have been speculations this might be an MAD fairing or even a 'cable guide for an in-flight refuelling hose'.

b) An-12BP c/n 6344204 (tactical code unknown) was used by LII in 1972-4 to investigate refuelling system parameters. Little is known, except that the results were used to develop the hose-and-drogue IFR system fitted as standard to some Soviet types.

An-12s were also used for other research and development tasks, such as:
- test drops of the spherical re-entry capsule of the first Soviet manned spacecraft, *Vostok* (East), in 1960 and the re-entry capsule of the *Voskhod* (Sunrise) and *Soyooz* (Union) manned spacecraft in 1967-72; the aircraft in question has been referred to as 'An-12 No. 902' in the Russian press, but it is an An-12A or 'B (**not** An-12BK '43 Red' (c/n 8345902) which was built in 1968!)
- tests of optical and optoelectronic airborne surveillance/reconnaissance systems (1963-65)
- investigating the integral and spectral properties of the heat signature of various aircraft types
- testing the UPAZ-1A Sakhalin refuelling pod[45] developed by the Zvezda (Star; pronounced *zvezdah*) design bureau (formerly OKB-918) under Guy Ilyich Severin – the same house that is responsible for the K-36 ejection seat.

Unfortunately some versions of the An-12 never reached the hardware stage. It's a shame, because, while some of the proposed versions admittedly called for radical changes in the design (sometimes to the point where the aircraft was no longer an An-12), they would have expanded the *Cub*'s capabilities considerably, making it more on a par with its American counterpart, the Hercules.

An-12U military transport

This project developed in 1962 envisaged the use of boundary layer control (BLC) on the wings and tail unit, hence the designation An-12U (for *oopravleniye* [*pogranichnym sloyem*] – BLC). Simple flaps equipped with boundary layer control ducting were to be fitted instead of double-slotted Fowler flaps and the air for the BLC system was to be supplied by two DK1-26 compressors in underwing pods. The use of BLC, coupled with jet-assisted take-off (JATO) solid-fuel rocket boosters, was expected to radically improve the aircraft's field performance.

Seen from the flight deck of an aircraft undergoing icing tests (probably an An-72 prototype), An-12BK CCCP-48974 No. 2 (c/n 6344510) sprays water from a sprinkler drogue deployed on a 47-m hose. This arrangement gave rise to the nickname 'Tanker'. (LII archive)

MISSION VARIETY

LII's extensively modified An-12BK icing testbed (c/n 6344510) in later configuration and military markings as '10 Red'. This picture taken at Zhukovskiy shows the port observation blister, the additional spraybar and sensors on the fuselage side, and the cine cameras for filming the test article mounted on top of the wings aft of the inboard engines. (LII archive)

Close-up of the dorsal sprinkler grid and the test airfoil on An-12BK '10 Red'. (LII archive)

MISSION VARIETY

In 1972 An-12BP CCCP-11101 (c/n 01347703) was used by the State Civil Aviation Research Institute (GosNII GA) to investigate the *Cub*'s handling in heavy icing conditions. Hence black stripes were applied to all leading edges for icing visualisation and cine cameras were installed on the fuselage and wings to capture the ice buildup. The aircraft is seen here at Moscow-Sheremet'yevo, its home base. (RART)

A heavily retouched photo showing an An-12 test-dropping the reentry capsule of the Voskhod manned spacecraft. (LII archive)

An-12 military transport with underwing tanks and IFR capability

One more projected version, also developed in 1962, was to feature two 6,000-litre (1,320 imp. gal) external tanks carried on pylons between the inner and outer engines, as on the C-130E and later versions. It was also to be equipped with an in-flight refuelling (IFR) probe in the manner of the RAF's C-130K Hercules C.1P.

An-12RU military transport

Yet another project of 1962, the An-12RU (s *raketnymi ooskoritelyami* – with rocket boosters), envisaged the installation of two PRD-63 solid-propellant rocket boosters on the aft fuselage sides to improve take-off performance, in a manner similar to the wheel/ski-equipped LC-130. The boosters were to be jettisoned after burnout.

An-12B-30 military transport

In 1963 the Antonov OKB proposed increasing the An-12B's load-carrying capacity over a 1,500 km (930 mile) range to 30 tons (66,140 lb). Designated An-12B-30 to reflect the increased payload, the aircraft was to be powered by 5,180 ehp AI-20DK engines driving new propellers of increased diameter (5.1 m; 16 ft 8.78 in). The projected maximum take-off weight and cruising speed were 75,650 kg (166,780 lb) and 600 km/h (372 mph) respectively. Some flight-test work under the An-12B-30 programme was reportedly undertaken jointly with LII in 1964, but eventually the aircraft was never built.

An-12D military transport

On 23 May 1964 the Council of Ministers issued a directive ordering the development to begin production of a radically redesigned aircraft designated An-12D, development of which had been initiated in 1963. The design objective was to increase the payload to 20 tons (44,090 lb) and the range to 1,600–1,800 km (993–1,118 miles).

Like the project described above, the An-12D was to have AI-20DK engines driving propellers of 5.1 m diameter. The wing span was increased to 44.2 m (145 ft 0.15 in) and the wing area to 170 m² (1,828 sq. ft); the overall length was 35.5 m (116 ft 5.63 in) and the height on the ground was 12.5 m (41 ft). The new tail unit was superficially similar to that of the An-24 *Coke* airliner, featuring slight sweepback on all surfaces, except that the stabilisers had no dihedral and the fin fillet was much deeper.

The main landing gear was all-new, too, comprising four separate levered-suspension units with large single wheels which retracted inwards into reshaped fairings; the whole arrangement would later be repeated on the An-72/An-74 *Coaler* STOL transport. The fat low-pressure tyres were to permit operations from airfields with a bearing capacity of no more than 4–5 kg/cm² (57–71 psi).

The An-12D featured a fully pressurised freight hold of increased length (13.9 m; 45 ft 7.24 in) and width (3.45 m; 11 ft 0.83 in), and the pressure differential was 0.25 kg/cm² (3.57 psi). The rear fuselage was more sharply upswept and the size of the cargo hatch enlarged to facilitate loading and unloading of bulky cargo. A new gantry crane was envisaged which could move out beyond the freight hold floor lip for straight-in loading from a truck bed. Remarkably, there was no defensive armament, the tail-gunner's station being eliminated.

With an MTOW of 75 tons (165,340 lb), the An-12D was expected to have a cruising speed of 500–600 km/h (310–372 mph), a service ceiling of 10,000 m (32,810 ft) and a ferry range of 7,500 km (4,658 miles). The project was not proceeded with as such but further developed into the An-40, which is described separately.

An-12D-UPS military transport

A version of the An-12D developed in parallel featured a boundary layer control system, hence the designation An-12D UPS (*oopravleniye pogranichnym sloyem* – BLC). The BLC system comprised three turbocompressors, two of which were housed in fairings atop the wing centre section close to the trailing edge, and the third, serving the tail surfaces, was buried in the fin fillet. The system was to reduce the take-off run to 550–600 m (1,800–1,970 ft) and the landing run to 650–700 km (2,130–2,300 ft).

An-12DK military transport

This was the designation of a projected version re-engined with 5,500 ehp Ivchenko AI-30 turboprops in order to improve performance. Unfortunately little else is known.

An-12SN military transport

This version (SN stood for [*samolyot*] *spetsiahl'novo naznacheniya* – special-mission aircraft) was a derivative of the An-12B designed in 1965 for transporting the T-54 main battle tank, weighing 37.2 tons (82,010 lb), which was the principal tank type operated by the Soviet Army and the armies of the Warsaw Pact nations. The fuselage diameter was increased, thereby increasing the freight hold width from 3.0 m (9 ft 10.11 in) to 3.45 m (11 ft 0.83 in), and the cargo doors were redesigned accordingly. The powerplant consisted of 5,180 ehp AI-20DK engines augmented by a 3,800 kgp (8,377 lb st) Mikulin RD-9 turbojet of the type fitted to the Mikoyan/Gurevich MiG-19 *Farmer* fighter. The booster engine was installed at the base of the fin, supplanting the tail-gunner's station. A brake parachute was provided for shortening the landing run. Part of the standard *Cub*'s equipment was deleted to save weight.

An-12R military transport

This was a redesign so radical that the resulting aircraft was not an An-12 any more. Designated An-12R (*reaktivnyy* – jet-powered), this project, completed in 1969, envisaged the use of four Lotarev D-36 turbofans rated at 6,500 kgp (14,330 lb st), swept wings and a T-tail. The freight hold was fully pressurised, being 15 m (49 ft 2.55 in) long, 3.45 m (11 ft 0.83 in) wide and 2.5 m (8 ft 2.42 in) high. The tail-gunner's station was replaced by a remote-controlled barbette.

With a 90-ton (198,410 lb) MTOW the An-12R was to carry a 25-ton (55,115 lb) payload over a distance of 2,500 km

(1,550 miles). The design maximum speed was 850 km/h (528 mph). The An-12R was not built but the project evolved into the An-112 transport (the designation speaks for itself), which lies outside the scope of this book – and also remains a 'paper aeroplane' at the time of writing.

An-12BZ-1 military transport and An-12BZ-2 flight refuelling tanker

Also in 1969 the Antonov OKB proposed giving the *Cub* in-flight refuelling capability. Two versions were envisaged which would work together. One, called An-12BZ-2, was a single-point hose-and-drogue tanker similar to the RAF's Lockheed C-130K Hercules C.1K, except that the hose drum unit was podded, not built in. The receiver aircraft designated An-12BZ-1 was analogous to the C-130K Hercules C.1P, featuring a fixed IFR probe atop the nose (the Z stood for *zaprahvka* – refuelling). The upgrade, which was to be effected in service conditions, was expected to boost the *Cub*'s range to 3,800 km (2,360 miles) with a 20-ton (44,090 lb) payload and 6,900 km (4,285 miles) with a 7-ton (1,540 lb) payload.

An-40 military STOL transport

Of all the projects aimed at improving the *Cub*, this one reached the highest degree of completion, and the redesign was extensive enough to warrant a new designation, An-40. Design work started in 1964 as a further development of the An-12D project. Looking at first glance like a 'stretched' An-12BK, the aircraft was powered by four 5,500 ehp AI-30 turboprops driving four-bladed propellers of 5 m (16 ft 4.86 in) diameter. These were augmented by four 2,550 kgp (5,620 lb st) Kolesov RD36-35 booster/brake jets fitted with thrust reversers installed in twin nacelles between the inner and outer engines.

The nose gear unit was similar to that of the An-12, while the main gear consisted of four independent inward-retracting levered-suspension struts with a single large wheel on each unit; all five landing-gear struts were equipped with small skids to permit operations from dirt or snow strips with a bearing strength of 4–6 kg/cm^2 (57–85 lb/sq. in).

The tail-gunner's station was deleted. Instead, the An-40 featured a DB-75 remote-controlled tail turret mounting two 23 mm (.90 calibre) Gryazev/Shipoonov GSh-23 (alias AO-9) double-barrelled cannon. A PRS-4 Krypton radar (*izdeliye* 4DK) and a VB-257A-5 computer were mounted at the base of the rudder above the turret. The cannon were aimed and fired by a gunner sitting in the pressure cabin aft of the flight deck under a large observation/sighting blister.

The cargo door design was changed completely. The upward-opening rear segment was still there but the two inward-opening doors were supplanted by a cargo ramp of unique design which had been developed and patented by the Antonov OKB. First used on the An-26 transport (and later on the An-32, An-72/An-74 and An-38), the ramp could be either lowered conventionally for loading/

A model of the proposed Sever air cushion vehicle based on a time-expired An-12 airframe. Despite holding considerable promise, the project never came to fruition. (TASS News Agency)

unloading troops and vehicles or slid forward under the aft fuselage for straight-in loading from a truck bed – or paradropping. The cargo hatch was flanked by large ventral fins similar to those of the An-32, which were meant to optimise the airflow around the aft fuselage, reducing vibrations and ensuring acceptable paradropping conditions.

The forward pressure cabin accommodated 17 persons. In troopship configuration the An-40 could carry 125 fully equipped troops; alternatively, 82 stretchers could be installed for casualty evacuation duties.

A full-scale mock-up was built and approved by the mock-up review commission in 1965, but all further work on the project was halted because the Soviet military did not believe in turboprops any more. Jet aircraft were deemed to be more promising, and eventually the larger and faster Ilyushin Il-76 *Candid* was selected as the successor of the *Cub*. (Well, 'successor' is not exactly true; the two types were destined to serve side by side for quite some time yet.)

An-42 military STOL transport

This was a version of the An-40 featuring a BLC system similar to that of the An-12D UPS, with three turbocompressors based on Kolesov RD36-35 turbojets atop the wing centre section and in the fin root. Structurally the An-42 was almost identical to the An-40, except for the airframe changes associated with the turbocompressor installation and the provision of simple hinged flaps instead of double-slotted flaps.

An-40PLO ASW aircraft

The Antonov OKB also envisaged an anti-submarine warfare version of the An-40 designated An-40PLO (*protivolodochnaya oborona* – ASW). An unusual feature of this aircraft was its powerplant, which was to run on both kerosene and hydrogen; to this end the freight hold was to accommodate high-pressure tanks holding 134.5 m^3 (4,750 cu. ft) of compressed hydrogen. The 10-ton (22,045 lb) weapons load, comprising ASW torpedoes and depth-charges, was to be housed in the suitably lengthened forward portions of the main gear fairings.

According to preliminary design documents the An-40PLO was to have a 90-ton (198,410 lb) maximum TOW. In maximum-range mode the aircraft would have a cruising speed of 550 km/h (341 mph); the maximum range was 15,500 km (9,627 miles). Maximum on-station loiter time when cruising at 500 m (1,640 ft) and 350 km/h (217 mph) was 22 hours at a distance of up to 7,750 km (4,813 miles) from the base; maximum endurance in cruise at 9,000 m (29,530 ft) was 27 hours.

Sever ACV

Though not an aircraft, this project deserves mention because it was based on the An-12. In 1983 Professor V. Ignatyev, a department head at the Kuibyshev Aviation Institute (KuAI),[46] proposed converting time-expired turboprop transports, including the An-12, into air cushion vehicles (ACVs) for use in the northern regions of the USSR; hence the family bore the generic name Sever (North). The conversion included cropping the wings so that only the inboard engines were left, fitting a large platform with flexible 'skirts' to the centre fuselage underside and installing ducts on the existing propellers to maximise their thrust. The latter was an absolute necessity because the ducts incorporated air scoops diverting part of the prop wash under the platform to create the air cushion. The standard landing gear was retained but the radar was removed and a hemispherical fairing was fitted instead of the navigator's glazing.

The idea won support from the director of KuAI and several scientists, including Academician A. Trofimook, who headed the Sibir (Siberia) multi-aspect regional development programme. Ignatyev started development work in 1983 with a small group of fellow enthusiasts. In 1987 a model of the Sever ACV based on the An-12 with a tail-gunner's station was displayed at the international trade fair in Leipzig in the former East Germany. (Apart from the An-12, Ignatyev proposed similar conversions of the An-22 and An-26.) However, by 1987 the team still hadn't succeeded in obtaining a surplus airframe for conversion purposes and the project came to naught.

CHAPTER FIVE

Cloning the *Cub*: Chinese Versions

Apart from the Soviet Union, the An-12 was manufactured in the People's Republic of China to suit a heavy transport aircraft requirement formulated by the People's Liberation Army Air Force (PLAAF). The Chinese aircraft industry had been established with Soviet assistance and had been building mostly Soviet aircraft under licence – or, after the break between Moscow and Peking on ideological grounds in 1960, *without* the benefit of a licence. Designated Y8 (Yunshuji-8 – transport aircraft, Type 8), the *Cub* is still in limited production on the other side of the Great Wall and new versions still keep appearing! The Chinese variants are dealt with in this chapter.

Shaanxi Y8 military transport

China started gearing up for An-12 production in 1960 – that is, immediately before the rift in Sino-Soviet relations. The latter – or rather the events which led to it – came at a most inopportune time. According to Prime Minister Chou En-Lai's plan the Chinese aircraft industry was to proceed from copying Soviet designs to developing and manufacturing indigenous aircraft. However, this plan suffered a serious setback because of the notorious Cultural Revolution and the equally notorious plan of accelerated industrial development known as the Great Leap Forward. On reflection, this plan deserves to be called the Great Leap Backward, as it had a huge negative effect on the national economy, including the aircraft industry. Like everywhere else, quantity was considered the prime target, to the detriment of quality, and the industry was completely disorganised.

Originally the aircraft factory in Xian (sometimes spelled Xi'an or Sian), the capital of Shensi (Shaanxi) Province, was chosen to build the *Cub*, but the Cultural Revolution put these plans on hold, and it was not until 1972 that the work was resumed. A year later, however, the Chinese aircraft industry changed its mind and all the jigs and tooling for Y8 production, together with all components manufactured so far, were transferred to the brand-new Shaanxi aircraft factory in Hanchung, also in Shensi Province.

The first prototype Y8 (c/n 000801)[47] assembled from Xian-manufactured and Soviet-supplied components took to the air on 25 December 1974, the first locally manufactured example following almost exactly a year later on 29 December 1975. Destructive testing of a static test airframe was completed on 29 September 1976 and the Y8 received its type certificate in February 1980.

The 4,250 ehp AI-20K engine was also reverse-engineered and put into production by the Zhuzhou factory in Shanghai[48] as the WJ-6 (Wojiang-6 – turboprop engine, Type 6), while the Chinese copy of the AV-68 propeller was designated J17-G13 (J for *Jiang* – propeller). Chinese efforts to improve the reliability of the engine paralleled those in the USSR, and in due course the TBO of the WJ-6 was increased from 300 to 2,000 hours. The

Though externally identical to a late-production 'military' An-12BP, 1053 might actually be an early-production Shaanxi Y8 retaining the original short nose. (RART)

People's Liberation Army Air Force '181 Red' is a typical Y8 with a Tu-16-style pointed nose and a tail turret likewise borrowed from the *Badger*. (*China Aircraft*)

TG-16 APU was likewise copied and put into production at Xian.

Initial production aircraft assembled from Soviet-made components and on Soviet-supplied jigs were almost identical to genuine Soviet-built An-12Bs with a tail-gunner's station, having the same nose contour. Soon, however, a longer and more pointed nose borrowed from the Tupolev Tu-16 *Badger-A* twinjet medium bomber was grafted on ahead of the flight deck glazing, giving the Y8 a distinctive 'Pinocchio look'. It is not known whether this was meant to improve the navigator's working conditions or to provide commonality with the Tu-16 which was in production – again without the benefit of a licence – in Xian as the H-6 (Hongzhaji-6 – bomber, Type 6). Also, the DB-65U tail turret was original replaced by a DK-7 turret mounting two AM-23 cannon with 500 rpg – likewise borrowed from the Tu-16; it was of basically cylindrical shape, not spherical. The aircraft incorporated the wide cargo hatch characteristic of the An-12BP/BK, with the associated bulges on the lower aft fuselage sides.

The Y8 is 34.02 m (111 ft 7.37 in) long, with a 38.0 m (124 ft 8.06 in) wingspan, and stands 11.16 m (36 ft 7.37 in) high on the ground. The empty weight is 35.5 tons (78,260 lb), the maximum take-off weight 61 tons (134,480 lb), the maximum landing weight 58 tons (127,865 lb) and the payload 20 tons (44,090 lb). The aircraft could clock a top speed of 662 km/h (411 mph), with a 550 km/h (341 mph) cruising speed; the service ceiling was 10,400 m (34,120 ft) and the ferry range was 5,615 km (3,487 miles). In a nutshell, the performance of the Y8 broadly matched that of the An-12B, except for the slightly longer take-off run and the slightly shorter landing run.

Y8A military transport

One of the PLAAF's most valuable assets consisted of 24 Sikorsky S-70C helicopters (despite the 'civilian' designation, they were effectively UH-60L Black Hawk military utility helicopters but equipped with a chin-mounted search radar as fitted to the MH-60G combat SAR version). To ensure rapid deployment of these helicopters to remote locations the Shaanxi Transport Aircraft Factory developed a specialised version of the Y8 in 1987. Designated Y8A, it had a C-130-style cargo door design with a one-piece downward-hinged cargo ramp replacing the two inward-opening doors hinged at the sides, thus obviating the need for separate vehicle loading ramps. Since loading and unloading the choppers was basically a roll-on/roll-off operation, the overhead gantry crane was deleted to increase available 'headroom' by 120 mm (4.72 in). The rear fuselage was supported by a hydraulic jack during loading/unloading to prevent the aircraft from falling over on its tail.

Oddly enough, at least one Y8A was demilitarised – the DK-7 tail turret was replaced by a fairing similar to that of most demilitarised Soviet-built *Cub*s and the gunner's station glazing faired over (except for the side windows). The deletion of the armament may have been a weight-saving measure.

Y8B commercial transport

Development of a civilianised version for the Civil Aviation Administration of China (CAAC) – the 'Chinese Aeroflot', so to say, since it was the nation's sole air carrier at the time – began in 1986. The aircraft's empty weight was reduced by 1,720 kg (3,792 lb) by deleting the paradropping equipment and other military equipment items. Surprisingly, the Chinese chose not to delete the tail-gunner's station on the commercial variant – the Y8B featured the 'demilitarised' rear-end treatment described above.

The prototype Y8B made its maiden flight on 17 December 1990. Testing was quite protracted and the type certificate was issued only in 1993, by which time CAAC was no longer extant, having been deregulated into numerous independent airlines back in 1987.

Y8C experimental military transport

This upgraded version was developed with assistance from the Lockheed Company in the late 1980s. The Y8C featured a C-130-style cargo ramp as fitted to the Y8A. Unlike earlier versions, the freight hold was fully pressurised, increasing the volume of the pressurised area from 31 m^3 (1,095 cu. ft) to 212 m^3 (7,847 cu. ft). Additional emergency exits were incorporated and the pressurisation/air conditioning and oxygen systems improved. Aircraft intended for the civil market were to have the tail-gunner's station finally deleted.

There were plans to re-engine the aircraft with General Electric CT7 turboprops driving Western propellers (various versions of this engine are rated at 1,600–1,870 ehp). However, the brutal suppression of student unrest in Beijing's Tiananmen Square in 1989 caused a rift in Sino-American relations and the 'westernisation' plan was shelved for the time being.

Two prototypes were built – or possibly converted from standard Y8s. At any rate, the second prototype (c/n 001802)[49] wore the serial 182 Black, but the same serial had been reported on a Y8 *sans suffixe* back in 1988! On 5–10 November 1996 Y8C '182 Black' was displayed at Airshow China '96 in Zhuhai (Sanzao airport), wearing Aviation Industry Corporation (AVIC) demonstrator colours.

Y8D export version

The Y8D designation applies to an export version of the military transport equipped with Litton and Collins avionics. The first flight took place in 1987 and deliveries started in 1992 but scant success has been achieved. At the time of writing, four Y8Ds have been delivered to the Myanmar Air Force, three to the Sri Lankan Air Force (though at least one of these appears to be an ex-Air Changan Airlines Y8B!) and two to the Sudanese Air Force.

Interestingly, all known examples except Sri Lankan Air Force CP-701 (later reserialled CR-871, c/n 060801) were demilitarised. Even so, the Sri Lankan examples were used as makeshift bombers in a manner similar to the An-12BKV. CR-871, which had a fully equipped tail turret, was shot down by Tamil Tiger separatists on 18 November 1995.

Y8E drone launcher aircraft

A drone launcher version of the Y8 was developed in 1989 to meet an Air Force requirement. Until then the PLAAF had operated ten Tupolev Tu-4 *Bull* long-range bombers which had been modified locally by substituting the Shvetsov ASh-73TK radials and V3B-A5 propellers with locally made WJ-6 turboprops and J17-G13 propellers. These 'Turbo-Bulls' had been adapted to carry two Chang Hong-1 (Long Rainbow-1) jet-propelled target drones – an adaptation of the Ryan AQM-34N Firebee reconnaissance drone which had been reverse-engineered by the Beijing University of Aeronautics and Astronautics (BUAA) after several examples had been shot down over Chinese territory during the Vietnam War. By the end of the 1980s the elderly Tu-4s had run out of service life and a replacement was urgently required.

Designated Y8E, the new version of the *Cub* was the Chinese counterpart of the Lockheed DC-130E, except that it had no underwing tanks and no guidance antenna in an undernose radome. Two pylons were fitted between the inner and outer engines for carrying a pair of Chang Hong-1 drones. The pylons were of lattice-like construction and similar to

The Y8C demonstrator, 182 Black, in flight. (*China Aircraft*)

The forward fuselage of the Y8E drone launcher prototype (4139 Red) with a Chang Hong-1 drone under the starboard wing. (*China Aircraft*)

those of the Tu-4 drone launchers but rather longer because of the Y8's high-wing layout.

The Y8E prototype presumably had full PLAAF markings and the serial 4139 Red. Interestingly, it was demilitarised. There have been suggestions that the standard RBP-2 radar might be replaced with a drone guidance antenna in the future.

Y8F livestock carrier

One of the most unusual versions of the *Cub* created in China was the Y8F developed in early 1990 – a dedicated livestock-carrier aircraft. The freight hold was equipped with two rows of cages installed three deep which could accommodate up to 350 sheep or goats. The Y8F's *raison d'être* was the need to carry livestock to and from pastures in remote areas of the country which were inaccessible (or required too much time to reach) by other kinds of transport.

Y8F-100

A number of civil Y8s, including B-3101 (c/n 1001), B-3102 (c/n 1002), B-3103 (c/n 1005), B-3109 (c/n 1303) and B-3110, have been reported as Y8F-100s. The aircraft listed here are operated by China Postal Airlines as 'freighters with a 16-ton (35,270 lb) payload'; hence there is a possibility they might be specialised mailplanes.

Y8F-201

A single demilitarised example with no civil registration or military insignia is known to have worn Y8F-201 titles on the forward fuselage. The role and distinguishing features of this version are unknown.

Y8F-300

This is an upgraded civil version equipped with Western avionics, including a conventionally mounted weather radar in a new, shorter but more streamlined 'solid' nose, and an advanced cargo-handling system. The new version was announced by the China Aircraft Technology & Industry Corporation (CATIC) at Airshow China 2000, which took place in Zhuhai on 6–12 November 2000.

Y8F-400

This is another upgraded civil version reportedly differing from the Y8F-300 only in the design of the freight hold; however, a desktop model displayed at Airshow China 2000 created the impression of a new and much fatter fuselage.

China Postal Airlines are the launch customer for this version, with a single example to be leased from AVIC II in 2002.

Y8F-600

Time heals old wounds, they say. Ten years after the Tiananmen massacre the idea of 'westernising' the venerable *Cub* has been resuscitated. At Airshow China 2000 CATIC unveiled a much-modernised version designated Y8F-600. Basically similar to the 'solid-nosed' Y8F-300, the aircraft is to be powered by Western turboprops driving six-bladed low-noise propellers with scimitar-shaped blades. Unfortunately little else is known.

Y8G development aircraft

a) Turboprop conversions of Tu-4s were used for various purposes by the Chinese; a few were operated by the People's Liberation Army Naval Air Force (PLANAF) until the early 1990s as maritime ELINT aircraft. As the need to replace the ageing *Bulls* grew increasingly acute, the Chinese aircraft industry started work on an ELINT version of the *Cub* provisionally designated Y8G. The aircraft was to feature a powerful radar and a mix of Western and indigenous mission avionics. GEC Marconi assisted with the development of the Y8G but pulled out after Tiananmen and the project was shelved before a prototype could be built. (That was not the end of it, though – see next entry.)

b) According to some sources, it was decided to use the Y8G airframe, which never received its mission avionics and was sitting idle, for conversion into a flight refuelling tanker prototype with the same designation. Other sources, though, claim there was never a Y8G ELINT airframe and the designation was merely reallocated after the demise of the former programme.

Work on a tanker version had been under way in China since the mid-1980s. The first evidence came in 1986 when a model of a tanker-configured Y8 was

The Y8F-100 was a mailplane version developed for the Chinese Ministry of Posts & Telecommunications. (*China Aircraft*)

displayed at an aviation trade fair in Beijing. The British company Flight Refuelling Ltd must have rendered assistance with the project because the aircraft was equipped with two compact refuelling pods under the outer wings similar to the FR Mk 32 hose drum units (HDUs) fitted to the Vickers VC.10 C.1K tanker/transport. The Y8 tanker was to work primarily with Nanchang Q-5 (A-5) *Fantan* fighter-bombers retrofitted with fixed refuelling probes ahead of the cockpit windshield, as was illustrated by the accompanying models of two such aircraft.

Once again, however, British aid was withdrawn after the 1989 events and the project was shelved. As a result, the PLAAF's tactical aircraft still lack IFR capability.

Y8 AEW aircraft

In May 2000 the *Air Forces Monthly* magazine reported that an airborne early warning (AEW) version of the Y8 (no separate designation has been stated) had been developed for the PLANAF. The aircraft had a rather bizarre appearance, since the usual glazed nose was replaced by a large drooped radome housing a Racal Skymaster search radar; the shape of the nose was designed to give the radar a full 360° field of view. A similar arrangement had been used earlier on the Britten-Norman Searchmaster – an experimental AEW version of the Britten-Norman BN-2 Defender equipped with a Racal Searchwater radar.

The Skymaster is actually based on the Searchwater model and is equally suited for overwater operations (as regards clutter resistance) but has enhanced capabilities against ground targets. The detection range was still classified at the time of the report, but *AFM* cited a provisional figure of more than 200 km (124 miles) at high altitude, which rendered the AEW version of the Y8 suitable for monitoring the Strait of Taiwan. It was reported that the aircraft would serve alongside the Ilyushin/Beriyev A-50I *Mainstay* airborne early warning and control (AEW&C) aircraft ordered by China, tackling tactical tasks while the *Mainstay* took care of the strategic ones.

Y8MPA (Y8X) maritime patrol/ASW aircraft

In 1984 the Shaanxi Transport Aircraft Factory began development of a maritime patrol version of the *Cub* which initially received the Western-style designation Y8MPA. The all-Western mission equipment suite included a dual Litton LTN-72 inertial navigation system (INS), a Litton LTN-211 Omega navigation aid and a Litton Canada AN/APS-504(V)3 360° search radar in a deeper, flat-bottomed chin radome which gave the Y8MPA a certain degree of similarity to the An-12BK. The equipment also included sonobuoys and a mission computer for processing data generated by the buoys.

The prototype Y8MPA was reportedly quasi-civil and registered B-4101; a photo of the aircraft, however, shows full PLANAF markings and the serial appears to be 8711 Red. It is doubtful if the aircraft eventually entered service because deliveries of some of the avionics were embargoed after the events in Tiananmen Square and in view of the mounting tensions with Taiwan (which mainland China purportedly still aims to recapture by military force). However, in 1993 the Y8MPA was redesignated Y8X, which indicates that the programme was still alive then.

The cheatline and Aeroflot titles on grey-painted civil An-8s soon became so faded as to be almost invisible, as illustrated by CCCP-13323 (c/n 0E 3430). Originally a MAP/Moscow UFD/201st Flight aircraft, it was later transferred to another MAP division, the Kaluga Engine Factory (Kadvi). CCCP-13323 was damaged beyond repair in a landing accident at Yerevan-Erebuni on 12 December 1993. (Yefim Gorfon)

CCCP-11213, one of the last An-10As built (c/n 0402406), in the Central Russian Air Force Museum, Monino, in the 1990s. Do not believe the yellow-tipped spinners – this aircraft was never military-operated (in reality it belonged to the Komi CAD/Syktyvkar UFD/75th Flight). Unfortunately the Komi Directorate's leaping stag tail logo and the c/n were obliterated soon after arrival at the museum in the early 1970s, and the bogus 'squadron markings' added. (Yefim Gordon)

An-12B CCCP-11359 (c/n 402804) wore this unusual demonstrator colour scheme. It is seen here at Paris-Le Bourget in 1965. (RART)

The now-familiar 1973-standard Aeroflot livery was progressively applied to the civil-registered fleet from the mid-1970s onwards. An-12BP CCCP-12990 (c/n 00347304) has red-tipped spinners which may indicate military ownership (despite the 'civil' rear end), though the aircraft quite probably belonged to MAP/Moscow UFD/201st Flight when this picture was taken. (Sergey and Dmitriy Komissarov)

As before, many Soviet Air Force *Cubs* received the latest Aeroflot livery, and many still wear it. This is An-12B CCCP-12126 (c/n 402507), a 223rd OSAP aircraft based at Chkalovskaya AB near Moscow. Incredibly, this aircraft is fully demilitarised, with the tail gunner's station windows faired over!

Lit by the rising sun, immaculate An-12PS '17 Yellow' (c/n 7344703) of the Russian Navy's North Fleet Air Arm sits at Novofyodorovka AB, Saki, the Ukraine, in July 2000. The aircraft has brought ground personnel and spares to support a training session by 279th KIAP (Carrier-Based Fighter Regiment) Sukhoi Su-33 *Flanker-D* fighters at the 'Nitka' carrier training complex located in Saki. Note the polar bear nose art, the tail raft compartment and the 'bald patch' where a pylon for KAS-150 rescue pods used to be. (Yefim Gordon)

An-12PP '68 Red' (callsign RA-10440?, c/n 9346303) in the static park during the open doors day at Chkalovskaya AB on 15 August 1999, with an Il'yushin Il-22M *Coot-B* airborne command post in the background. (Mikhail Yevdokimov)

Levashovo-based An-12RR '11 Red' (c/n 4342604) on display at Pushkin during the Business Aviation-2001 airshow (5–8 August 2001). The RR8311-100 air sampling pods have been removed but their shackles and the sensor pod on the starboard side are well visible. Note the very 1950s-style 'feathers' aft of the flight-deck windows. (Dmitriy Komissarov)

Some An-12BK-PPS ECM aircraft, including 52 Red (c/n 02348109) seen at Ivanovo-Severnyy in July 2002, have been stripped of all mission equipment and reconverted to freighters. Note the patches on the forward fuselage where the heat exchanger intakes and outlets are faired over, traces from a wiring conduit above them and the empty platform where jammer antennae and biological protection packs used to be. (Aleksandr Melikhov)

The An-12BP 'Kubrik' avionics testbed was probably the most bizarre *Cub* ever. (Yefim Gordon)

LII's An-12M-LL ejection seat testbed (An-12BK '43 Red', c/n 8345902) fires a Zvezda K-36DM seat during a demonstration flight at MosAeroShow '92 on 15 August 1992. (Yefim Gordon)

A rare colour photo of the An-12TP-2 geophysical survey aircraft (CCCP 04362) taken during a refuelling stop somewhere en route to Antarctica in December 1961. The red-tailed Il-18V CCCP-75743 is just visible in the background. (RART)

Resplendent in the colours of cargo carrier Avial, An-12B RA-11324 (c/n 2340802) makes a typically smoky take-off from Moscow-Domodedovo; this aircraft is now operated by Avial-NV. Note how the soot picks out rivet lines, showing the location of the fuselage frames. (Dmitriy Petrochenko)

Russian Air Force An-12B '93 Red' (c/n 3341102) operated by the 226th OSAP at Sperenberg AB, East Germany, received this unusual dark gloss grey finish after an overhaul. The aircraft relocated to Kubinka AB near Moscow after the Russian pullout from Germany.

This Russian Naval Aviation An-12B based at Ostaf'yevo just south of Moscow ('70 Black', c/n 3341402) is unusual in combining basic Aeroflot colours with Air Force insignia. (Yefim Gordon)

An-12BP '661 Black' (c/n 5343208) belonging to the 978th VTAP at Klin-5 AB has a non-standard three-digit tactical code matching the last three of its former civil registration, CCCP-11661. (Sergey Panov)

Lit by the setting sun, An-12BP RA-11768 (c/n 5343103) of the Yermolino Flight Test & Research Enterprise (YeLIIP) awaits the next flight at Moscow-Domodedovo on 25 December 1998. (Dmitriy Komissarov)

An-12BP UR-11315 (c/n 4342307) in the house colours of the Antonov Design Bureau is seen at Kiev-Gostomel', the OKB's flight test facility, during the Aviasvit-2000 airshow. (Yefim Gordon)

Ukrainian Air Force An-12BK '86 Red' (c/n 9346607?) still has a red code, although most Ukrainian military aircraft wear blue, yellow or white codes. The darker grey area aft of the flight deck glazing reveals that a blue 'wing' trim worn by some Ukrainian *Cubs* has been removed. (Sergey Popsuyevich).

A magnificent shot of An-12BP UR-LTG (c/n 00347201) with appropriate nose titles in the smart colour scheme of Volare Aircompany. (Yefim Gordon)

An-12BP LZ-BAF *River of Maritza* (c/n 402408) looks splendid in Balkan Bulgarian Airlines' penultimate livery. (Yefim Gordon archive)

People's Liberation Army Air Force Y8 '94001 Red' in a typical colour scheme. As can be seen, PLAAF transports also perform some civil tasks, calling at airports when required. (Sebastian Zacharias via RART)

Ill-starred An-12B CU-T827 (c/n 401504) of Cubana de Aviacion is the only confirmed *Cub* to have been delivered to Freedom Island, as Cuba was commonly referred to in the Soviet press. (Yefim Gordon archive)

Czech Air Force An-12BP '2105 Black' (c/n 4342105) at RAF Fairford during one of the Royal International Air Tattoos. (RART)

(*Above left*) An-12B SU-AOJ (c/n 402302) was the first *Cub* to be delivered to Egypt. (RART)

(*Above right*) Most Iraqi Air Force An-12s, including An-12BP I.A.F.806 (c/n 8345910), wore this grey/white colour scheme. This aircraft later received Iraqi Airways markings and the registration YI-AFJ. (RART)

(*Left*) Even though it now has an ROZ-1 radar in a small radome, EL-ALJ of Santa Cruz Imperial (c/n 8346202) was originally built as an An-12BK. (Nikolay Ionkin)

(*Below*) YU-AIC (c/n 01348007) was one of two An-12BPs delivered to the Yugoslav Air Force. (RART)

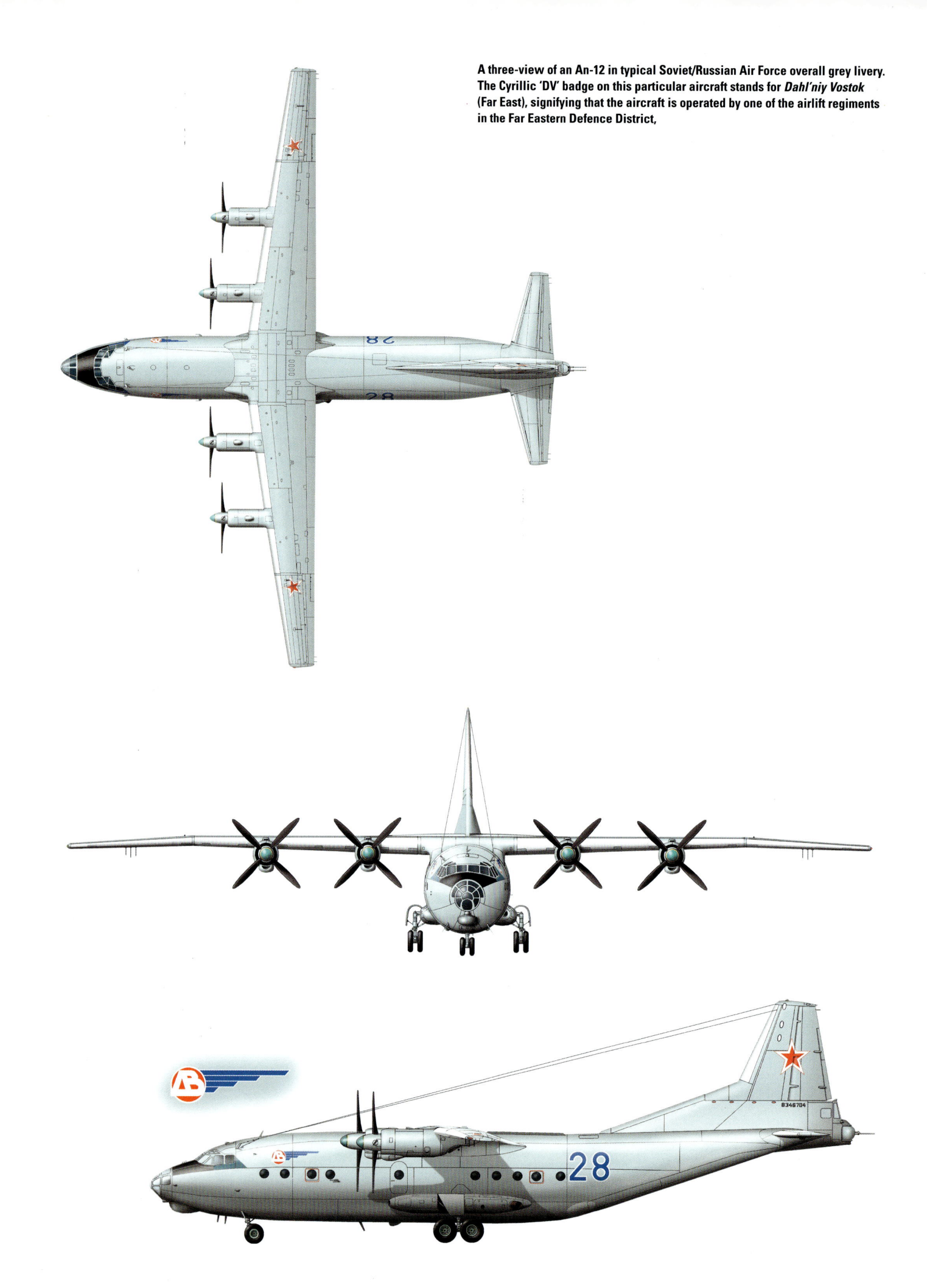

A three-view of an An-12 in typical Soviet/Russian Air Force overall grey livery. The Cyrillic 'DV' badge on this particular aircraft stands for *Dahl'niy Vostok* (Far East), signifying that the aircraft is operated by one of the airlift regiments in the Far Eastern Defence District.

CHAPTER SIX

An-12 Anatomy

The following structural description applies to the basic An-12BP. Details of other versions are indicated as appropriate.

Type

Four-engined medium military and commercial transport. The military transport version was originally intended to transport and paradrop personnel, as well as BTR-152 and BTR-40 armoured personnel carriers, ASU-57 self-propelled guns (specially designed to be paradropped), ZiL-157 6×6 lorries, etc., and gradually the range of typical cargoes was expanded. The airframe is of all-metal construction.

Fuselage

Semi-monocoque stressed-skin structure of beam-and-stringer construction with 68 frames and 110 stringers; the skin thickness is 1–2 mm (0.04–0.08 in). Chemical milling is used on some panels. The riveted fuselage structure is made mainly of D16 duralumin; some structural components are made of MD8 and ML5-T4 magnesium alloy. Attachment bolts and fittings are made of 30KhGSA- and 40KhNMA-grade steel.

Structurally the fuselage is made up of four sections: the forward fuselage (Frames 1–13), the centre fuselage (Frames 13–41), the aft fuselage (Frames 41–65) and the rear fuselage or tail section (Frames 65–68). The last is a flattened fairing on the commercial version (with a semicircular contour in side view) or the tailgunner's station on the military version. All four sections are joined by flanges. On production aircraft the last two sections effectively form a single whole. The fuselage cross-section is basically circular up to Frame 41; further aft it is progressively flattened from below. Maximum fuselage diameter is 4.1 m (13 ft 5.5 in).

The pressurised *forward fuselage (Section F1)* includes the crew section (the flight deck plus the navigator's station) and a compartment for persons accompanying the cargo or vehicle crews. The flight deck accommodates the pilots, flight engineer and radio operator; the navigator sits slightly below them in the extreme nose. The volume of the pressure cabin is 18.5 m^3 (653.32 cu. ft). Section F1 terminates in a flat rear pressure bulkhead.

The navigator's station features extensive glazing (Frames 0–2) with curved Plexiglass panels and an optically flat elliptical lower panel. The flight deck glazing frame is located between Frames 4 and 8, with optically flat birdproof triplex panes at the front, and the side panes and eyebrow windows are made of Plexiglass. The flight deck features two triangular sliding windows which can be used as emergency exits on the ground. An inward-opening dorsal escape hatch is located in the same area between Frames 7 and 8 to be used in the event of ditching; there is also a ventral entry/escape hatch between Frames 6 and 8 (the hatch cover is hinged at the front, acting as a slipstream deflector when the crew bale out.

An unpressurised bay for the radar antenna is located beneath the navigator's compartment between Frames 2 and 4; the nosewheel well is located behind it between Frames 9 and 13. Sheets of APBL-1 armour 8 mm (0.31 in) thick are installed beneath the pilots' seats and along the flight deck sides; the seats themselves have 16 mm (0.63 in) armoured backs made of AB-548 steel.

The *centre fuselage (Section F2)* accommodates the unpressurised freight hold, which is 13.5 m (44 ft 3.49 in) long, 3.0–3.5 m (9 ft 10.11 in) wide and 2.4–2.9 m (7 ft 10.48 in to 9 ft 6.17 in) high; the height and width vary. The freight hold volume is 123.3 m^3 (4,354 cu. ft).

Fuselage Mainframes 25 and 30 serve as attachment points for the wing centre section's front and rear spars respectively. The wing/fuselage joint is enclosed by a fairing.

The freight hold floor is an important structural component of the fuselage. It consists of a load-bearing framework and a skin with stiffening ribs. Parts of the fuselage frames act as transverse members of the framework, which is also formed by beams, stamped profiles and channels (U-sections) supporting the skin.

Two luggage compartments used for storing engine covers, wheel chocks and the like (except on the An-12P/ AP/ BP/BK, where they house underfloor fuel cells) are located under the freight hold floor between Frames 13 and 25 and 33 and 41. They are accessed via downward-opening ventral doors offset to starboard (between Frames 16 and 19 and 35 and 37 respectively) and hatches in the freight hold floor. The volume of the forward and aft luggage compartments is 11.4 m^3 (402.58 cu. ft) and 5.3 m^3 (187.16 cu. ft) respectively. The space between the compartments (Frames 27–30) is occupied by the mainwheel wells separated by the fuselage keel beam.

A quasi-oval rearward-hinged entry door with a window opening inwards is located on the port side between Frames 22 and 24. Three square-shaped emergency exits with windows are provided in the hold (on both sides between Frames 14 and 16 and on the port side between Frames 37 and 39). The cabin features 15 circular windows of 384 mm (1 ft 3.11 in) diameter – 2 + exit + 1 + door + 3 + exit + 1 to port and 1 + exit + 1 + 5 to starboard.

Two elongated fairings of semicircular cross section are located on the centre fuselage sides between Frames 22 and 38, enclosing the main-gear attachment points and actuators. These fairings accommodate the APU (in the rear section of the port fairing), as well as components of the pressurization, hydraulic, electric and fuel systems.

The unpressurised *aft fuselage (Section*

The forward fuselage of a civil-operated An-12B, showing the flight deck and navigator's station glazing and the chin radome of the ROZ-1 radar. This particular aircraft (CCCP-11381) was operated by the Polar Aviation, hence the astrosextant on the flight-deck roof. (TASS News Agency)

AN-12 ANATOMY

The An-12 has no integral cargo ramp, so detachable ramps normally stowed in the hold have to be fitted for loading vehicles. During loading and unloading a detachable support is installed under the aft fuselage to prevent the aircraft from falling on its tail. (Yefim Gordon archive)

F3) incorporates attachment points for the vertical tail (at Mainframes 59 and 62) and horizontal tail (at Mainframes 62 and 65). A cargo floor of similar design to the one in Section F2 is fitted between Frames 41 and 43. A dorsal escape hatch for troopers (used in the event of ditching) is provided between Frames 42 and 44 immediately to the right of the fuselage centreline.

Section F3 features a large cargo hatch between Frames 43 and 59 which is closed by three cargo door segments; the two forward segments (Frames 43–51) open inwards and upwards to lie flat against the sides of the freight hold and the rear segment upwards. The hatch is flanked by beams serving as attachment points for the doors. The doors incorporate steps used for access to the tail-gunner's station on armed military versions; the outer skin of the doors (and the aft fuselage between Frames 59 and 61) is protected by titanium sheets to prevent damage by parachute static lines during paradropping.

As already mentioned, the **rear fuselage** or **tail section (Section F4)** is just an unpressurised fairing on the commercial version or a tail-gunner's station on the basic military transport. The An-12PP electronic countermeasures aircraft and the initial version of the An-12BK-PPS have an elongated ogival fairing housing chaff dispensers and ESM equipment; on the An-12PS search and rescue aircraft the tail-gunner's station is converted into a bay housing a rescue raft.

On military versions the tail-gunner's station is a pressure compartment accessed from the freight hold by walking up the inside of the cargo doors and through a pressure door in the front wall (Frame 65). A ventral escape hatch is provided, the cover opening forwards hydraulically to act as a slipstream deflector for baling out. The gunner's station features three rear windows made of bulletproof glass 110–135 mm (4.33–5.31 in) thick and two side windows made of 14 mm (0.55 in) Plexiglass. The gunner is also protected by a removable 20 mm (0.78 in) armour shield.

Wings

Cantilever shoulder-mounted monoplane of basically trapezoidal planform, mounted above the fuselage to leave the interior unobstructed. The wings are all-metal, stressed-skin two-spar structures made of V95T aluminium alloy. Structurally they are made up of five pieces: the centre

99

section (which is integral with the fuselage), inner wing panels (which carry the engine nacelles) and outer wing panels. The sweepback at quarter-chord is 9° 56', with 1° dihedral on inner wing panels and 3° anhedral on outer wing panels, incidence 4°, no camber, aspect ratio 11.85, taper 2.8. The wings utilise TsAGI S-5-18, S-3-16 and S-3-14 airfoils. Wingspan is 38.015 m (124 ft 8.63 in); wing area is 121.73 m^2 (1,308.9 sq. ft) overall or 119.5 m^2 (1,284.9 sq. ft) less the wing centre section.

The wing panels are joined by attachment fittings and splice plates; the wing skins incorporate numerous removable panels for access to the control runs, hydraulic and electric system components, fuel tank filler caps and fuel meters. The wing/fuselage joint is covered by a fairing (see above).

The inner wings are equipped with three-section double-slotted flaps; there are two-section ailerons on the outer wings and twin spoilers on the inner wings (see Control system). Flap settings are 5° for take-off and 25° for landing.

Tail unit

This is a conventional tail unit of all-metal stressed-skin construction. The *vertical tail* consists of a fin with a prominent fillet and a one-piece rudder (see Control system). The fin is a two-spar structure built in two sections (the upper portion is detachable); the lower portion built integrally with the aft fuselage features a large root fillet and incorporates a passage to the tail-gunner's station. The fin spars are attached to aft fuselage Mainframes 59 and 62. There are three rudder mounting brackets. Vertical tail area, including fin fillet, is 21.534 m^2 (231.5 sq. ft).

The cantilever *horizontal tail* of similar two-spar construction consists of two stabilisers and one-piece elevators (see Control system); it utilises a NACA-0012M symmetrical airfoil and has no dihedral. Horizontal tail span is 12.196 m (40 ft 0.15 in), horizontal tail area 26.95 m^2 (289.78 sq. ft). There are three elevator mounting brackets on each stabiliser.

Landing gear

This is a hydraulically retractable tricycle type, with free-fall extension in emergency. The twin-wheel nose unit retracts aft, the main units with four-wheel bogies retract inwards. Early versions have 900 × 300 mm (35.43 × 11.81 in) K2-92/I wheels on the nose-gear unit; on the An-12BP/An-12BK they were replaced by K2-92/IV wheels of the same size. The mainwheel bogies have 1,050 × 300 mm (41.33 × 11.81 in) KT-77M wheels (KT = *koleso tormoznoye* – brake wheel) replaced by KT-77U wheels of the same size on the An-12BP/An12BK.

The nosewheel well is closed by two lateral doors and a small forward door segment hinged to the oleo strut. Each main unit has a large main door attached to the fuselage keel beam and a curved door segment hinged to the oleo which closes the cutout in the main gear fairing. All doors open only when the gear is in transit; this prevents mud, water and slush from entering the wheel wells.

The aft fuselage and tail unit of An-12BP '30 Red' (c/n 5343508), showing the tail-gunner's station and AM-23 cannon. (Sergey and Dmitriy Komissarov archive)

This rear view of An-12AP UR-21510 (c/n 0901404) shows clearly the cargo-door design; the forward door segments are folded agaìnt the cabin walls. Note the dark steel plates protecting the doors against damage by parachute static lines and the strike camera doors to the right of the rear plate on the aft segment.
(Dmitriy Komissarov)

Many An-12s built with a tail-gunner's station and transferred to the Soviet airline Aeroflot were demilitarised by fitting a dished fairing instead of the tail barbette. (TASS News Agency)

All landing-gear struts have oleo-pneumatic shock absorbers; the steerable nose unit can turn ±35° for taxiing and is equipped with a shimmy damper. Tyre pressure is 6–6.5 bars (86–93 psi) for the mainwheels and 5 bars (71 psi) for the nosewheels. The landing-gear wheelbase is 9.576 m (31 ft 5 in); the landing gear track is 4.92 m (16 ft 1.7 in) if measured by the oleos or 5.412 m (17 ft 9.07 in) if measured by the outer mainwheels.

Powerplant

The An-12 *sans suffixe* is powered by four Ivchenko AI-20A turboprop engines rated at 4,000 ehp for take-off and 2,300 ehp for cruise; these are substituted by AI-20K engines with a take-off rating of 4,250 ehp and a cruise rating of 2,700 ehp on the An-12A or identically rated AI-20Ms (also called AI-20 Srs VI) on the An-12B/BP/BK. The engine was manufactured by the Zaporozhye Engine Factory (ZMZ) in 1958–63; in 1966 production switched to the Perm Engine Production Association (PPOM).

The AI-20 is a single-shaft turboprop with an annular air intake, a ten-stage axial compressor, an annular combustion chamber, a three-stage uncooled turbine and a fixed-area jetpipe with a conical centrebody; power is transmitted via a planetary gearbox with a reduction ratio of 0.087. Engine pressure ratio is 8.5 (AI-20A) or 9.2 (AI-20M); mass flow at take-off rating 20.9 kg/sec (46 lb/sec) for the AI-20A or 20.7 kg/sec (45.6 lb/sec) for the AI-20M. Turbine temperature is 1,080 °K for the AI-20A and 1,173 °K for the AI-20M. Engine speed is 10,400 rpm at ground idle and 12,300 rpm 9 kg/sec (46 lb/sec) for the AI-20A or 20.7 kg/sec (45.6 lb/sec) for the AI-20M. Turbine temperature is 1, at full throttle.

Specific fuel consumption (SFC) at take-off rating is 0.259 kg/hp · h (0.57 lb/hp · h) for the AI-20A and 0.243 kg/hp · h (0.53 lb/hp · h) for the AI-20M; cruise SFC 0.21 kg/hp · h (0.46 lb/hp · h) for the

The nose-gear unit with a towbar attached. The axle is hollow, allowing the forked fitting of the towbar to be locked into position at the ends. (RART)

The starboard main-gear unit, showing the side-mounted scissor link and forward drag strut. Unusually, this aircraft has both the original type of mainwheels with cooling vents and the later heavy-duty solid wheels on a single bogie. (RART)

AI-20A and 0.197 kg/hp · h (0.43 lb/hp · h) for the AI-20M.

Length overall is 3,097 mm (10 ft 1.93 in), width 842 mm (2 ft 9.15 in), height 1,180 mm (3 ft 10.45 in); dry weight 1,080 kg (2,381 lb) for the AI-20A and 1,040 kg (2,292 lb) for the AI-20M. The AI-20M has a 24,000-hour service life and a 7,000-hour time between overhauls.

Construction is of steel and magnesium alloy. The spool rotates in three bearings: a roller bearing in the air intake assembly (with an extension shaft to the reduction gear), and a ball thrust bearing and a roller bearing in the combustion chamber casing. The air intake assembly has inner and outer cones connected by six radial struts and is de-iced by engine bleed air. The combustion chamber has ten burner cones, with igniters and pilot burners at the top. The outer casing is split horizontally for access to the burner cones.

Two accessory gearboxes (dorsal and ventral) are provided, the accessories proper being mounted on the forward casing. The pressure-feed lubrication system uses a 75/25 mixture of MK-8 oil and MS-20 or MK-22 oil. The AI-20 is started by twin STG-12TMO-1000 starter-generators using DC power from the APU or a ground power source; the engine starting sequence is 1-4-3-2. Operational ambient temperature limits are −60/+50°C (−76/+122°F).

The engines are mounted in individual nacelles attached to the underside of the inner wings and carried in truss-type bearers; the engine attachment lugs are mounted on the forward and centre casings. Each nacelle consists of a one-piece annular forward fairing incorporating a ventral oil cooler (with air intake and rear airflow adjustment flap), two hinged cowling panels and a fixed rear fairing incorporating a jetpipe angled slightly downward.

The engines drive AV-68I four-blade reversible-pitch automatically feathering propellers with spinners turning clockwise when seen from the front, diameter 4.5 m (14 ft 9.16 in), weight 370 kg (815 lb). Blade pitch is adjusted hydraulically. The propeller features electric de-icer cuffs. The AV-68 is developed and manufactured by the Stoopino Machinery Design Bureau.

A Kazan Machinery Design Bureau TG-16M auxiliary power unit is installed in the rear portion of the port main-gear fairing for self-contained engine starting and ground power supply (except on the An-12 *sans suffixe* and An-12A/AP). Maximum continuous power is 81.6 hp and rotor speed is 24,000 rpm. The APU has an upward-opening rear-hinged dorsal intake door, a one-piece upward-hinged cowling and a lateral exhaust.

An-12B RA-11654, a communications relay aircraft serving with the 226th OSAP at Kubinka AB, takes off past the demonstration facility hangars at Kubinka, with An-26 RA-26696 in the background. Note the lack of the tail gunner's station and the exhaust of the extra APU powering the mission equipment. (Yefim Gordon)

Control system

Conventional mechanical dual control system with push-pull rods, control cranks and levers. An AP-28D1 autopilot is fitted.

Roll control is provided by two-section ailerons on the outer wings assisted by two-section spoilers/lift dumpers on the inner wings. The ailerons have geared trim tabs on the inner sections; each section is hinged on two brackets.

Pitch control is provided by one-piece elevators. Each elevator is hinged on one root support and three brackets and incorporates a trim tab. The elevators are mass-balanced; the balancing may be changed on the ground by means of movable counterweights.

Directional control is provided by a one-piece rudder of single-spar construction with an auxiliary spar. The rudder is likewise mass-balanced and features a spring-loaded servo tab at the root, with a trim tab above it. On early-production aircraft the trim tab terminated some way short of the top but was later extended all the way to the top. The rudder is hinged on three brackets plus upper and lower supports located aft of the fin torsion box.

Fuel system

On all versions the fuel system is divided into port and starboard subsystems, each of which is split into two groups, one for each engine. The two subsystems are connected by means of a cross-feed valve, enabling each engine to draw fuel from any group of tanks.

The An-12 *sans suffixe* has 22 flexible fuel tanks (fuel cells) in the inner wing and centre-section torsion box; the inner-wing fuel cells are self-sealing for better protection against battle damage, while those in the wing centre-section are not. On the An-12A the number of fuel cells was increased to 26 by adding four self-sealing tanks in the portions of the inner wings adjacent to the engine nacelles, while the An-12B introduced two integral fuel tanks in the outer wings.

The An-12P has 24 fuel cells (22 in the wings and two in the former underfloor baggage compartments); similarly, the An-12AP features underfloor fuel cells in addition to the 26 wing tanks, while the An-12BP/An-12BK has 26 flexible tanks in the wings, two more under the floor and two outer-wing integral tanks. Total fuel capacity is 15,440 or 16,600 litres (3,396 or 3,652 imp. gal) on the An-12A; 18,240 or 19,500 litres (4,012.8 or 4,290 imp. gal) on the An-12B; 25,290 or 26,450 litres (5,536.8 or 5,819 imp. gal) on the An-12AP; and 28,090 or 29,350 litres (6,179.8 or 6,457 imp. gal) on the An-12BP/BK.[50]

The An-12 has single-point pressure refuelling. Fuel grades used are Russian T-1, TS-1 or T-2 jet fuel, Western Jet A-1,

DERD.2494 and DERD.2498 (NATO F35 and F43) or equivalent.

An inert gas pressurisation system is provided on military versions to pressurise the fuel tanks and reduce the hazard of explosion if hit by enemy fire.

Ancillary Systems

Hydraulics

There are two separate hydraulic systems (port and starboard) which power the landing gear, wheel brakes, spoilers, cargo doors and windshield wipers. Nominal hydraulic pressure is 150 kg/cm^2 (2,140 psi).

Electrics

The electric system serves for engine starting and operates part of the de-icing system, fuel system components (pumps and cocks), avionics, cargo handling equipment, defensive and offensive armament and reconnaissance cameras. There are three subsystems: 28.5 V DC, 115 V/400 Hz single-phase AC and 36 V/400 Hz three-phase AC.

Main DC power is supplied by eight engine-driven STG-12TM or STG-12TMO-1000 starter-generators, four SGO-12 generators and the APU. The electric system includes two PT-500Ts three-phase AC converters (*preobrazovahtel' tryokhfahznyy*), one PAG-1FP AC converter and one PO-750A backup single-phase AC converter (*preobrazovahtel' odnofahznyy*). Backup DC power is provided by seven 12SAM-28 batteries on the An-12 *sans suffixe* (17 on subsequent versions). A ground power receptacle is provided.

Oxygen system

Liquid oxygen (LOX) bottles and a KPZh-30 LOX converter (*kislorodnyy preebor zhidkosnyy*) are installed in one of the main gear fairings to provide breathing oxygen for the crew and troops in the freight hold. Six sets of KP-23 breathing apparatus are provided for the crew to ensure survival in the event of baling out.

De-icing system

The wing leading edge, engine air intakes, oil coolers and flight deck/navigator's station side windows are de-iced by engine bleed air. Electric de-icing is provided on the fin and stabiliser leading edges, propeller blades and spinners, pitot heads, static ports, windscreens and navigator's station forward glazing panel.

Fire suppression system

Three groups of fire extinguisher bottles charged with carbon dioxide are available for each engine. The first shot is triggered automatically by flame sensors in the engine nacelles; the second and third shots are fired manually. A separate fire extinguisher is provided for the APU bay.

Air conditioning and pressurisation system

The crew section, 'passenger cabin' immediately aft of it and, on armed versions, the tail-gunner's station are pressurised by engine bleed air. Pressurisation air is cooled by a heat exchanger located in the forward portion of the port main-gear fairing, with a small air intake at the front and efflux gills on the underside. A mobile air conditioning unit may be connected to the aircraft on the ground, using a connector in the nosewheel well; alternatively, hot-air supply trunks may be passed directly into the freight hold through the emergency exits.

Accommodation/cargo handling equipment

The standard An-12 is equipped for transporting personnel, combat vehicles (complete with crews and a supply of ordnance), engineering troops' vehicles and other loads and delivering them by landing or paradropping. There are seats along the freight-hold walls. In troopship/paradrop configuration tip-up seats along the freight-hold walls and quickly removable seats along the centreline permit the carriage of up to 96 fully equipped troops or 58 paratroopers. Vehicles and other loads are paradropped, using PDMM-47 sacks, PDUR-47 energy-absorbing straps and PDTZh-120 rigid containers.

A siren and illuminated signs are provided for initiating the drop sequence.

Self-propelled wheeled and tracked vehicles are driven onto/off the aircraft, using two detachable vehicle loading ramps stowed in the freight hold when not in use. In this case an adjustable circular telescopic support is installed immediately ahead of the cargo door lip to stop the aircraft from falling over on its tail; the An-12BP (An-12BK) has two such supports side by side. Two BL-52 winches (An-12 *sans suffixe*/An-12A/P/AP), BL-1500 winches (An-12B/BP) or GL-1500DP winches (An-12BK) are installed in the freight hold for loading unpowered vehicles weighing up to 8 tons (17,640 lb). A gantry crane with a lifting capacity of 2,100 kg (4,630 lb) on most versions or 2,300 kg (5,070 lb) on the An-12BK is used for handling other heavy cargoes.

The freight-hold floor features numerous threaded holes into which cargo tie-down lugs can be screwed; these are otherwise stored in special canvas bags attached to the walls and the holes closed by screw-in plugs. The cargo is secured by nets, chains and turnbuckles. If the mission requires paradropping heavy equipment on PGS-500 pallets, a hydraulically powered TG-12 conveyor (*transportyor groozov* – cargo transporter) can be installed on the freight-hold floor to propel the pallets towards the cargo hatch where they are whisked away by drogue parachutes.

The floor also incorporates fittings for installing stretcher supports, allowing the aircraft to be configured for the casualty evacuation (CASEVAC) rôle. In this case the An-12 can carry up to 60 patients on standardised army stretchers plus a medical attendant.

Armament

Most military versions feature a PV-23U or PV-23US defensive armament system (*pushechnoye vo'oroozheniye* – cannon armament) comprising a DB-65U powered tail turret with two 23 mm (.90-calibre) Afanasyev/Maliasrov AM-23 cannon, an electric remote control system and a ballistic computer. The AM-23's rate of fire is 1,250–1,350 rounds per minute. The cannon are belt-fed; the ammunition supply is 350 rounds per gun. The ammunition boxes are located in the unpressurised aft fuselage between Frames 60 and 61 and accessed from the freight hold.

Ranging and aiming is by means of a Gamma-547 gun-ranging radar installed at the base of the rudder above the gunner's station, a KPS-53N or KPS-53A gunsight and a VB-155 computer (replaced by a VB-257-1 unit from An-12A c/n 9900902 onwards).

Two bomb cradles can be fitted under the forward portions of the main-gear fairings at fuselage Frames 24–25 for carrying 100 kg (220 lb) FotAB-100-80 flare bombs, NOSAB-100 night marker bombs or DOSAB-100 day marker bombs. Additionally, six 10 kg (22 lb) TsOSAB-10 coloured marker bombs, OMAB-5-8N maritime marker bombs or paradroppable radio beacons can be carried vertically on a DYa-SS-AT rack enclosed by clamshell doors between Frames 62 and 64 to designate the drop zone for oncoming aircraft in a large formation.

The An-12 has an offensive capability as well, operating as an auxiliary bomber. Up to 70 100 kg (220 lb) HE or incendiary bombs, or up to 32 250 kg (551 lb) HE/fragmentation, incendiary, armour-piercing or cluster bombs, or up to 22 500 kg (1,102 lb) HE, incendiary, HE/incendiary or cluster bombs, or up to 18 UDM-500 anti-shipping mines can be carried in the freight hold; these are propelled towards the cargo doors by a TG-12MB conveyor belt. An NKPB-7 night-capable collimator bombsight and an AIP-32 optical bombsight (an OPB-1R with an infra-red imaging adapter) are installed at the navigator's station for bomb-aiming and precision paradropping.

Avionics and equipment

The An-12 is fully equipped for all-weather day/night operation, including automatic flight assisted by an autopilot.

Navigation and piloting equipment

Military An-12s *sans suffixe*, An-12As, 'Bs, 'Ps, 'APs and 'BPs are equipped with an RBP-2 panoramic navigation/ ground-mapping radar in a chin radome. Alternatively, civil examples have an ROZ-1 Lotsiya panoramic navigation/ weather radar in an identical radome, while the An-12BK has an Initsiativa-4-100 panoramic navigation/ground-mapping radar in a much larger radome.

The navigation suite also includes an RSBN-2S Svod (Dome) short-range radio navigation (SHORAN) system with flush antennas built into the fin, an SP-50 Materik instrument-landing system and a KS-6G compass system. The aircraft is equipped with an RV-2 Kristall radio altimeter with dipole aerials under the stabiliser tips, an ARK-5 Amur automatic direction finder (replaced by the ARK-11 from the An-12A onwards) with a dorsal strake aerial on the forward or aft fuselage, an MRP-56P Dyatel marker beacon receiver, SOD-57M distance-measuring equipment (***stahnt**siya opre**de**leniya **dahl**'nosti* – DME), an SPI-1M receiver/indicator unit and an NI-50BM-1 navigation display.

Military An-12s also have a long-range radio navigation (LORAN) system with an additional dorsal strake aerial offset to starboard aft of the wings and a PDSP-2S Proton-M receiver for homing in on the drop zone. Some aircraft feature an SP-1M astrosextant in the flight-deck roof escape hatch.

Communications equipment

A 1-RSB-70 HF communications radio with an RPS receiver, a Gheliy (Helium) or Neon or RSB HF comms radio, an RSIU-4V UHF command radio (replaced by the RSIU-5V from the An-12A onwards), are served by dorsal and ventral blade aerials on the forward fuselage. An AVRA-45 emergency radio (*ava**ree**ynaya **rah**diostahntsiya*) for sending distress signals is also fitted. An SPU-6 or SPU-7 intercom (*samo**lyot**noye perego**vor**noye oo**stroy**stvo*) is provided for communication between crew members.

IFF system

SRO-2 Khrom (Chromium; NATO *Odd Rods*) IFF transponder (*samo**lyot**nyy **rah**diolokatsee**on**nyy ot**vet**chik* – lit. aircraft-mounted radar responder), was replaced by the SRO-2M from the An-12A onwards. The characteristic triple IFF aerials are located ahead of the flight-deck glazing and under fuselage section F4.

Electronic support measures (ESM) equipment

An S-3M Sirena-2P radar homing and warning system (RHAWS) with aerials on the forward/aft fuselage sides and wingtips, was replaced by the Sirena-3 from the An-12A onwards. Some Soviet/CIS aircraft have four 30-round ASO-2 dispensers mounted in tandem pairs low on the forward fuselage sides, firing 26 mm (1.02 in) PPI-26 magnesium flares or bundles of chaff to provide a passive ECM/IRCM capability. Alternatively, two streamlined fairings housing 12 32-round chaff/flare dispenser modules can be permanently installed on the centre fuselage sides.

Specialised ECM versions feature additional active/passive ECM equipment mounted internally and in removable pods. For example, the An-12PP has an APP-22 active jammer; the An-12BK-IS is equipped with active jammers and ASO-24-E7R chaff dispensers.

Photographic equipment

An AFA-42/20, AFA-42/75 or AFA-42/50 vertical camera for day photography or an NAFA-MK/25 camera for night photography can be installed in the aft portion of the starboard main-gear fairing or in the aft fuselage between Frames 57 and 58, shooting through a hatch offset to starboard in the rear cargo door segment.

Data recording equipment

Standard Soviet MSRP-12-96 primary flight data recorder (FDR), K-3-63 backup FDR and MS-61B cockpit voice recorder (CVR) are fitted.

Exterior lighting

Port (red) and starboard (green) navigation lights are fitted at the wingtips, with a white tail navigation light on the tailcone (civil version) or under the tail-gunner's station (military version) and three retractable landing/taxi lights on the flight-deck ventral entry/escape hatch and under the front ends of the main gear fairings. Red SIM-1VM rotating anti-collision beacons were fitted in teardrop-shaped Perspex fairings ahead of the cargo door lip and at the top of the fin (replaced by SMI-2KM red strobe lights on late-production An-12Bs, 'BPs and 'BKs). Three EKSR-46 electric flare launchers (*elek**trich**eskaya kas**se**ta sig**nahl**'nykh raket*) are fitted on the starboard side of the aft fuselage between Frames 43 and 46; each launcher fires four 26 mm (1.02 in) signal flares (red, green, yellow and white).

An-12 family specifications

	An-12 *sans suffixe*	An-12A	An-12B	An-12BP
Crew	7	7	7	7
Powerplant	4 × AI-20A	4 × AI-20K	4 × AI-20M	4 × AI-20M
Power, ehp	4 × 4,000	4 × 4,250	4 × 4,250	4 × 4,250
Length overall	33.1095 m	33.1095 m	33.1095 m	33.1095 m
	(108 ft 7.52 in)	(108 ft 7.52 in)	(108 ft 7.52 in)	(108 ft 7.52 in)
Height on ground*	11.44 m	11.44 m	11.44 m	11.44 m
	(37 ft 6.39 in)	(37 ft 6.39 in)	(37 ft 6.39 in)	(37 ft 6.39 in)
Wingspan	38.015 m	38.015 m	38.015 m	38.015 m
	(124 ft 8.65 in)	(124 ft 8.65 in)	(124 ft 8.65 in)	(124 ft 8.65 in)
Wing area, m^2 (sq. ft)	121.73 (1,308.9)	121.73 (1,308.9)	121.73 (1,308.9)	121.73 (1,308.9)
Empty weight, kg (lb)	36,000 (79,365)	36,500 (80,467)	37,000 (81,570)	37,000 (81,570)
Take-off weight, kg (lb):				
normal	56,000 (123,456)	56,000 (123,456)	56,000 (123,456)	56,000 (123,456)
maximum	61,000 (134,480)	61,000 (134,480)	61,000 (134,480)	61,000 (134,480)
Maximum fuel load, kg (lb)	11,000 (24,250)	12,500 (27,557)	14,500 (31,966)	23,200 (51,146)
Paradroppable load, kg (lb):				
normal	10,000 (22,045)	10,000 (22,045)	10,000 (22,045)	10,000 (22,045)
maximum	20,000 (44,090)	20,000 (44,090)	20,000 (44,090)	20,000 (44,090)
Personnel capacity:				
troops	91	91	96	96
paratroopers	60	60	58	58
casualties	85	85	85	85
Maximum speed, km/h (mph)	n.a.	650 (403)	656 (407)	656 (407)
Service ceiling (at normal TOW), m (ft)	10,500 (34,450)	10,500 (34,450)	9,600 (31,500)	9,600 (31,500)
Range, km (miles):				
at 1,000 m (3,280 ft)	1,300 (807)	1,580 (981)	1,940 (1,205)	3,290 (2,043)
at 9,000 m (29,530 ft)	2,120 (1,316)	2,690 (1,670)	3,290 (2,043)	5,910 (3,670)

* Some documents quote the height on ground as 10.53 m (34 ft 6.56 in.).

Weights of some An-12 versions

	An-12 *sans suffixe*	An-12A	An-12B	An-12P	An-12AP	An-12BP
TOW, kg (lb)	61,000 (134,480)	61,000 (134,480)	61,000 (134,480)	61,000 (134,480)	61,000 (134,480)	61,000 (134,480)
Dry weight, kg (lb)	33,500 (73,853)	35,000 (77,160)	35,500 (78,260)	35,000 (77,160)	35,500 (78,260)	35,500 (78,260)
Fuel load, kg (lb)	11,000 (24,250)	12,500 (27,557)	14,500 (31,966)	18,700 (41,225)	20,300 (44,753)	22,400 (49,382)
Payload, kg (lb)*	15,000 (33,068)	11,500 (25,352)	9,500 (20,943)	5,800 (12,786)	3,700 (8,157)	1,600 (3,527)

* **Not** the maximum payload!

Take-off performance

Take-off weight, kg (lb)	Take-off run, m (ft)	Take-off distance, m (ft)	Unstick speed, km/h (mph)
61,000 (134,480)	1,230 (4,035)	2,520 (8,270)	230–240 (143–149)
58,000 (127,865)	1,160 (3,805)	2,420 (7,940)	228 (141)
56,000 (123,456)	900 (2,950)	2,100 (6,890)	221 (137)
54,000 (119,047)	835 (2,740)	2,050 (6,725)	219 (136)
52,000 (114,638)	750 (2,460)	1,800 (5,900)	215 (133)
50,000 (110,229)	675 (2,215)	1,650 (5,410)	211 (131)
48,000 (105,820)	625 (2,050)	1,580 (5,180)	207 (128)
46,000 (101,410)	560 (1,840)	1,490 (4,890)	203 (126)
41,000 (403,880)	460 (1,510)	1,100 (3,610)	190 (118)

Range of some An-12 versions

	Fuel load, kg (lb)	Payload, kg (lb)*	Range, km (miles): at 500 m (1,640 ft)	at 1,000 m (3,280 ft)	at 5,000 m (16,400 ft)	at 9,000 m (29,530 ft)
An-12 *sans suffixe*	5,000 (11,020)	20,000 (44,090)	300 (186)	320 (198)	400 (248)	n.a.
An-12 *sans suffixe*	11,000 (24,250)	14,000 (30,864)	1,210 (751)	1,300 (807)	1,780 (1,105)	(2,120 1,316)
An-12A	12,500 (27,557)	11,500 (25,352)	1,470 (913)	1,580 (981)	2,160 (1,341)	2,590 (1,608)
An-12B	14,500 (31,966)	9,500 (20,943)	1,810 (1,124)	1,940 (1,205)	2,680 (1,664)	3,290 (2,043)
An-12UD	16,800 (37,037)	7,700 (16,975)	2,160 (1,341)	2,310 (1,434)	3,240 (2,012)	4,030 (2,503)
An-12P	18,700 (41,225)	5,800 (12,786)	2,460 (1,528)	2,640 (1,639)	3,710 (2,304)	4,640 (2,882)
An-12AP	20,300 (44,753)	3,700 (8,157)	2,730 (1,695)	2,920 (1,813)	4,090 (2,540)	5,200 (3,230)
An-12BP	22,400 (49,382)	1,600 (3,527)	3,700 (2,298)	3,290 (2,043)	4,630 (2,875)	5,910 (3,670)

* **Not** the maximum payload!

All-up weight, kg (lb)	Service ceiling, m (ft)
45,000 (99,206)	11,950 (39,200)
48,000 (105,820)	11,300 (37,070)
51,000 (112,433)	10,500 (34,450)
54,000 (119,047)	10,000 (32,810)
56,000 (123,456)	9,600 (31,500)
58,000 (127,865)	9,300 (30,510)
61,000 (134,480)	9,000 (29,530)

Landing performance

Landing weight, kg (lb)	Landing run, m (ft)	Landing distance, m (ft)	Touchdown speed, km/h (mph)
38,000 (83,774)	620 (2,030)	1,370 (4,490)	186 (115)
40,000 (88,183)	650 (2,130)	1,430 (4,690)	191 (118)
43,000 (94,797)	700 (2,300)	1,500 (4,920)	198 (123)
46,000 (101,410)	760 (2,490)	1,610 (5,280)	205 (127)
48,000 (105,820)	810 (2,660)	1,740 (5,710)	208 (129)
50,000 (110,229)	860 (2,820)	1,880 (6,170)	218 (135)
51,000 (112,433)	890 (2,920)	1,990 (6,530)	220 (136)
52,000 (114,638)	960 (3,150)	2,080 (6,820)	223 (138)
53,000 (116,843)	965 (3,165)	2,200 (7,220)	225 (139)
58,000 (127,865)	1,125 (3,690)	2,260 (7,415)	230–240 (143–149)

Climb time, minutes

	TOW 51,000 kg (112,433 lb)	TOW 54,000 kg (119,047 lb)	TOW 56,000 kg (123,456 lb)	TOW 58,000 kg (127,865 lb)	TOW 61,000 kg (134,480 lb)
to 2,000 m (6,560 ft)	3.2	3.7	4.0	4.7	4.9
to 4,000 m (13,120 ft)	7.0	8.0	8.3	9.7	10.2
to 6,000 m (19,685 ft)	11.8	13.5	14.1	15.5	16.8
to 8,000 m (26,250 ft)	19.0	22.1	23.6	25.7	29.4
to 9,000 m (29,530 ft)	n.a.	n.a.	n.a.	n.a.	45.7
to 9,300 m (30,510 ft)	n.a.	n.a.	n.a.	44.2	–
to 9,600 m (31,500 ft)	n.a.	n.a.	43.5	–	–
to 10,000 m (32,810 ft)	34.0	46.5	–	–	–

Note: Forward speed in climb to 6,000 m is 350 km/h (217 mph) for a 54-ton all-up weight, 360 km/h (223 mph) for an AUW of 55–56 tons and 370 km/h (229 mph) for an AUW of 57–61 tons.

CHAPTER SEVEN

In Times of War and Times of Peace, or Forty Years of Service

Unlike its civilian look-alike, the An-12 was destined to have a long and varied career both in its home country and just about in every other part of the globe. Deliveries of the *Cub* to the Soviet Air Force began in 1959. Two airlift regiments of the 12th M*ginskaya* GvVTAD headquartered in Tula were the first to re-equip with the new type; they were tasked with holding service trials and developing operational tactics.

Working in close contact with the Antonov OKB, the regiment commanders Col. N.G. Tarasov and Col. A.Ye. Yeriomenko coped with the challenge *par excellence*. During the evaluation period large groups of An-12s commanded by Tarasov and Yeriomenko flew from Krechevitsy AB near Novgorod and Seschcha AB near Bryansk to various regions of the USSR with widely different climates (Moldavia, the Central Asian republics, the Arctic regions and the Far East). These flights included landings on semi-prepared tactical airstrips and training in the techniques of paradropping and tactical offloading of personnel and materiel.

About the same time the 3rd GvVTAD headquartered in Vitebsk (Belorussian Defence District) began converting to the An-12, followed by other VTA formations and units. Soviet Air Force units equipped with the type included the 3rd GvVTAD comprising the 103rd *Krasnoselskiy* GvVTAP in Smolensk, 196th *Minskiy* GvVTAP at Migalovo AB near the city of Kalinin[51] (May 1966) and 334th *Berlinskiy* VTAP at Kresty AB near Pskov (May 1963); 6th *Zaporozhskaya* GvVTAD headquartered in Krivoy Rog (1960) including the 37th VTAP, 338th VTAP and 363rd *Cherkasskiy* VTAP; 12th GvVTAD/566th *Solnechnogorskiy* GvVTAP in Rakveri, Lithuanian SSR (1959–1970); 14th *Zaporozhskaya* GvVTAD headquartered in Zavitinsk, Amur Region, comprising the 192nd VTAP in Ukurey and the 930th VTAP (1967); 11th *Taganrogskaya* GvVTAD (Baltic DD) comprising the 128th VTAP in Panevezhis, Lithuania (later moved to Orenburg, Russia) and the 600th VTAP in Kedainiai, Lithuania (1964; later moved to Shadrinsk, Russia), 978th VTAP at Klin-5 AB in Klin near Moscow, 223rd OSAP at Chkalovskaya AB near Moscow, and 517th VTAP of the 610th TsBP i PLS (*Tsentr boye****voy*** *podgo****tovki*** *i pereoochivanita* **lyot***novo so****stahva*** – combat and conversion training centre) at Ivanovo Severnyy AB.

VTA crews quickly took a liking to the *Cub* and came to trust the machine. Rugged dependability even in the harshest of environments and the ability to make do with an absolute minimum of maintenance became indelible traits of the An-12's character for many decades. (Everything has a limit, though, and 'an absolute minimum of maintenance' taken too literally (i.e. neglect) is bound to end in trouble sooner or later – but that's another story!)

Unfortunately, as with most new types, the An-12's service introduction was not trouble-free and took its toll of human lives. The first fatal crash occurred on 31 January 1959 when a 3rd GvVTAD/339th VTAP aircraft (tactical code unknown, c/n 8900202) lost control on take-off from its home base in Vitebsk after suffering a simultaneous uncommanded rudder trim tab deflection and uncommanded propeller feathering on one of the engines. On 21 November 1959 another An-12 was lost near Belaya AB; the cause of the crash was never found out for certain but the investigation focused on two possible areas – an in-flight fire or disconnection of the aileron control linkage causing loss of roll control. In each case only the tail gunner survived.

These are but two of the many accidents and incidents which marred the

A Soviet Air Force An-12B at one of the many VTA airbases. The BRDM-1 scout vehicle carrying the Airborne Troops (VDV) badge waits its turn to be loaded. (Yefim Gordon archive)

Soviet paratroopers board a grey-painted An-12B coded 01 Red. (Yefim Gordon archive)

beginning of the *Cub*'s career. Alarmed by these developments, Soviet Air Force Commander-in-Chief Air Marshal Konstantin A. Vershinin, GKAT Chairman Pyotr V. Dementyev and V. Balandin, who headed one of GKAT's directorates, wrote to the Communist Party Central Committee in 1959: 'State acceptance trials and static tests, as well as operational use of An-12 aircraft, have revealed numerous design flaws and manufacturing defects, some of which are serious enough to endanger flight safety . . .'.

As a result, in December 1959 all An-12s were grounded until further notice – that is, until all major defects had been rectified. The deadline for these modifications was set at 1 June 1960, and in the summer of 1961 the new airlifter was publicly unveiled at the annual Tushino flypast, whereupon the An-12 received the NATO codename *Cub*.

Gradually, as VTA crews mastered the type, Soviet Air Force An-12s were used on an increasingly wide scale for tackling both military and civil transport tasks. (Using the VTA fleet in the interests of the national economy was common practice in the USSR, and it still is in Russia; after all, it doesn't matter a hoot for the recipient if the aircraft which brings him the much-needed goods is civil or military.) For instance, in the late 1960s a task force of 35 An-12s commanded by M.M. Gamaris flew to the polar regions of the Soviet Union for several months, redeploying troops as part of the effort to repair the damage done by the infamous traitor Oleg Penkovskiy.[52] Notable missions of a more peaceful nature included a case when mobile compressor units weighing 8 tons (17,640 lb) apiece had to be urgently delivered from Krasnodar in the south to Norilsk in the north, half-way across the country, for some major construction work. The An-12's payload was then officially limited to 12 tons (26,455 lb); yet Lt. Col. Sharafutdinov, the commander of the airlift task force, took a risk, ordering that two compressor units be loaded into each aircraft. The *Cub* coped admirably with the augmented load and the official payload limit was subsequently increased to 16 tons (35,270 lb).

The An-12 was a key factor in turning the Soviet Airborne troops into a powerful geopolitical instrument which the Soviet leaders could use at will (as was the case in Czechoslovakia in 1968). By providing strategic airlift capability the *Cub* enabled the Soviet Union to promptly react to changes in the world situation – for instance, provide disaster relief at home and abroad, support national liberation movements (from a Soviet point of view, that is; the Western world would have said 'Marxist guerrillas'!), etc. Being the main transport aircraft of the Warsaw Pact until the late 1970s (though far from all of the bloc's member nations operated the type), the An-12 fulfilled an important mission during several major WarPac military exercises. For example, in 1970 a swarm of nearly 200 *Cubs* paradropped 8,000 personnel and a large number of combat vehicles in just 22 minutes during the *Dvina* exercise (the name of two rivers in north-western Russia, pronounced *Dvinah*). Impressed by the capabilities of the An-12, Soviet Air Force C-in-C Army General V.F. Marghelov even solicited the Soviet government in 1977 to confer the Communist Labour Collective title – no mean award in Soviet times – on the Antonov design bureau.

The might of the Soviet Airborne troops (VDV – *vozdooshno-desahntnyye voyskah*) was bolstered considerably when the VTA mastered the technique of paradropping combat vehicles (primarily ASU-57 SP guns) on lightweight PGS-500 pallets equipped with a five-canopy parachute system.[53] For safety reasons the crews parachuted separately from the vehicles; this meant a certain amount of time was lost while the crews got to the vehicles after landing, which the VVS C-in-C was quite unhappy about. V.F. Marghelov, who was enchanted by the An-12 and convinced of the parachute system's reliability, urged that the vehicles be paradropped with the crews already inside so that they could join the action as soon as the platforms hit the ground. Wishing to prove the feasibility of his concept, he volunteered to perform a test drop personally; when Defence Minister Marshal Rodion Ya. Malinovskiy vetoed the idea (one can hardly blame him for not wishing to lose his Air Force C-in-C!), the general's son, A.V. Marghelov, successfully performed the mission.

Predictably, the An-12's service introduction period was accompanied by a few teething troubles. The Antonov OKB persistently worked on eliminating these problems, at the same time trying to meet the customer's demands while creating new versions of the *Cub*. The main efforts were directed at increasing the range, reducing dependence on ground support equipment and developing special-mission versions of the basic transport. The OKB also went to great lengths to improve the An-12's operational reliability, and these efforts bore fruit: gradually the proportion of accidents and incidents attributable to design flaws and manufacturing defects was reduced to 10–12 per cent.

True, even when the hardware let the people down it was often still possible to make it back to base and land normally. In 1961 a test crew captained by M.M. Gamaris was making a pre-delivery test flight on an An-12 destined for the Indian Air Force. As the aircraft came in to land the crew got 'two greens, one red' – the

View inside the freight hold of a fully loaded *Cub*, looking aft; static lines hooked up, the paratroopers are ready for action. Note how detachable seats were installed along the middle. (Yefim Gordon archive)

The An-12 could swallow quite bulky vehicles, including ASU-57 SP guns. (Yefim Gordon archive)

A major airborne operation is brewing! This photo shows how vehicles (in this case, two ASU-57s) were secured on PGS-500 pallets for paradropping; the wheels were attached to the pallets for ground handling only. Interestingly, this grey-painted An-12B has a civil registration, CCCP-11880 (c/n 2340807), though traces of the former tactical code are still discernible underneath. Visible in the background is CCCP-11890 (c/n 3340909) which was later transferred to Aeroflot (specifically, the Yakutian CAD/Yakutsk UFD/139th Flight). (Yefim Gordon archive)

starboard main gear unit would not extend. The malfunction occurred at night, so the captain was told to make a low pass over the control tower for a look-see. As the aircraft was caught by the searchlights on the tower it was immediately apparent that the starboard main gear unit was jammed half-way through extension. Climbing to 3,000 m (9,840 ft) and entering a holding pattern, the crew initiated the emergency procedure prescribed by the flight manual. Meanwhile, on the ground all hell was let loose as the technical staff at various levels tried to find a solution. Within an hour the matter – still unresolved – had been reported to the Air Force's chief engineer V.V. Filippov, who was at one of Moscow's theatres, watching a play. Filippov made a phone call to Kiev, contacting chief designer Oleg K. Antonov, and together they decided that the crew should make a belly landing on a dirt strip beside the runway if the gear still refused to extend.

The crew, however, had different ideas. As already mentioned, the aircraft was intended for export and hence built with special attention to quality. Fully realising the damage that would be incurred in a wheels-up landing, the crew were determined to avoid this outcome if at all possible. Cutting through the freight hold floor with an axe and a crowbar, the airmen gained access to the starboard mainwheel well; then the loadmaster tied a safety rope around his waist and climbed down into the wheel well, tying another rope to the jammed strut. Using the on-board winch, the crew managed to wrench the stubborn strut into fully extended position and land safely. For this deed the brave young officer was awarded the Order of the Red Banner of Combat. Another result of this incident was that the crowbar became standard equipment on the An-12 – albeit unofficially.

There were also cases in the *Cub*'s service career when the human component failed but the aircraft stood up to the abuse and all ended well. In November 1988 the flight deck of a Soviet Air Force An-12 decompressed at 8,000 m (26,250 ft) between Chelyabinsk and Ufa because an escape hatch had not been closed properly before flight. The entire crew except the tail gunner passed out through hypoxia. For 90 minutes the aircraft flew on, out of control, changing altitude and heading on its own accord; only the greatest good luck prevented the runaway freighter from causing a disastrous mid-air collision. Unbelievably, none of the three civil ATC centres and three PVO radar pickets monitoring the area reacted in any way to the aircraft's erratic movements; the first reaction came only when the co-pilot regained consciousness and called out in despair over the radio, 'Where ARE we?!'.

VTA units equipped with An-12s and staffed with highly skilled crews were regularly used by the Soviet government for delivering humanitarian aid and other cargoes to various corners of the world. Usually such aircraft ostensibly wore civil registrations and Aeroflot colours – the same red/white livery with 'feathers' aft of the flight deck as originally worn by the An-10, which was standard for Aeroflot *Cub*s until the mid-1970s (though some examples had civil markings applied over the overall medium-grey military colour scheme). The reason is obvious; imagine red-starred An-12s landing somewhere in Europe in the Cold War days! It would be pretty hard to convince everyone World War III had not begun yet! For the same reason VTA crews were issued Aeroflot uniforms when flying abroad – but, of course, the undisguised tail turret told too plain a tale.

One of the earliest known operations of this kind was in July 1970 when a devastating earthquake hit Peru, causing massive destruction and a large loss of life. When the 3rd GvVTAD received orders to urgently prepare a humanitarian airlift task force, the ground personnel had to spend all night repainting the aircraft in civil markings under heavy rain. Among other Soviet aircraft[54] a group of 35 An-12s commanded by the division's CO, Maj.-Gen. N.F. Zaïtsev, flew from Moscow to Lima with a load of medicines and foodstuffs, staging through several airports and airbases in Iceland, Canada, Cuba and Colombia. Still, the new paint job was a waste of effort and the Aeroflot colours did not fool anyone. A Peruvian newspaper published a picture of Zaïtsev in VVS uniform. It should be noted that the general's face was disfigured by burns; compounded by the poor printing quality, the result was positively hair-raising. The

A PGS-500 pallet with a wheeled vehicle (possibly a BTR-64 light armoured personnel carrier) is whisked from the freight hold of An-12B '67 Blue'. (Sergey and Dmitriy Komissarov archive)

GERONIMO!! An-12s were widely used for airborne assault operations during Warsaw Pact exercises; this involved flying in close formations and required considerable skill on the part of the crews. (Yefim Gordon archive)

caption read: 'The most bloodthirsty Soviet general has come to Peru'.

(Speaking of registrations, Soviet/CIS civil and quasi-civil An-12s are normally registered in the 110xx to 119xx, 121xx, 123xx, 124xx, 125xx, 127xx, 128xx and 129xx blocks. Unlike many other Soviet types (where registrations were allocated in large batches), An-12s were usually registered haphazardly, though some civil-configured aircraft built consecutively for Aeroflot **did** have registrations running in sequence. To complicate matters further, many registrations were reused two or three times as aircraft shifted from military to civil identities and vice versa; thus, the An-12 is something of a registration spotter's nightmare!

Apart from the 'standard' registration blocks, quite a few *Cub*s operated by MAP and other industries had non-standard registrations in blocks which were a 'mixed bag' of assorted types. Aeroflot's polar division used the 04xxx block for a long time, and known An-12s in this block were registered CCCP-04331, -04341, -04343, -04346, -04362, -04363, -04366 and -04373. Other examples are CCCP-06105, 08256 (no prefix), CCCP-10212, -10222, -10231, -10232, -13320, -13321, RA-13331, UR-13332, CCCP-13340, RA-13341, -13357, CCCP-13391, -13392, -13402, UR-21510, CCCP-29110, -29312, -31120, -33688, -46741, -48970 to -48972, -48974, -48975, -48977, -48978, -48984, -58644, -69314, -69321, -75617, -75622, -75625, -86721, -93912, -93913, -93915, -93919, -93920, -93922, -98101 to -98103, -98105 and -98116 to -98119.

Additionally, Soviet/Russian Air Force An-12s (and some other aircraft as well) used phoney registrations as ATC callsigns. Known examples are RA-08332, RA-08658 (An-12B '35 Blue', c/n 3341601), CCCP-08952 (An-12BP CCCP-11339) CCCP-09370 (An-12BK CCCP-46741), CCCP-09524 (An-12A CCCP-11874), RA-10440 (very probably An-12PP '68 Red', c/n 9346303), CCCP-10563, CCCP-10622 (An-12B CCCP-11765), CCCP-10785, RA-10861 (An-12BPTs RA-11531), and CCCP-86580 (actually this registration belonged to Il-62M c/n 2343554).

As for colour schemes, VTA aircraft masquerading in full Aeroflot colours were given away by the characteristic triple rod aerials projecting downwards from the outer wings and flight-deck entry/escape hatch, as well as by the tips of the propeller spinners which were painted black, blue or red to designate the regiment within a division (or squadron within the regiment?) – the same as on grey-painted *Cub*s in full military markings. Please note, however, that such coloured spinner tips are not a totally reliable indication of quasi-civil status. Some ex-military An-12s retained these markings long after being transferred to civil operators; also, nowadays many *Cub*s registered outside the CIS have similar-coloured spinner tips, though they are definitely **not** military-operated!

In 1974 VTA units and formations began re-equipping with the latest Soviet airlifter, the Ilyushin Il-76 *Candid-B*, and again the 3rd GvVTAD in Vitebsk led the way for the introduction of new hardware. In the process many An-12s were transferred to Aeroflot as surplus. Nevertheless, the *Cub* continued to constitute an important element of the Soviet military airlift force, to say nothing of the various specialised versions which the *Candid* could not replace.

In addition to the numerous VTA bases in the USSR, Soviet Air Force An-12s were permanently deployed in some of the Warsaw Pact nations, including Czechoslovakia (TsGV – *Tsentrahl'naya grooppa voysk*, Central Group of Forces), East Germany (ZGV – *Zahpadnaya grooppa voysk*, Western Group of Forces)[55] and Poland (SGV – *Severnaya grooppa voysk*, Northern Group of Forces). The ones stationed in Czechoslovakia (including grey-painted An-12A CCCP-11961 and An-12B CCCP-11934) operated from Mladá-Milovice AB near Mladá Boleslav. The SGV *Cub*s served with the 245th OSAP (*otdel'nyy smeshannyy aviapolk* – independent composite air regiment) at Legnica AB which was part of the 4th VA (*vozdooshnaya armiya* – air army).

In East Germany the type was operated by the 226th OSAP and 39th ORAO (*otdel'nyy razvedyvatelnyy aviaotryad* – independent reconnaissance air detachment) at Sperenberg AB near Berlin, plus another unit (number unknown) at Oranienburg, Potsdam District/Brandenburg, which were part of the 16th VA. Most aircraft wore VVS insignia, although two were originally quasi-civil. Most 226th OSAP An-12s were standard transports which flew resupply missions for the Soviet forces stationed in East Germany and were used for troop rotation (assisted by quasi-civil *Cub*s from other units, including the 223rd OSAP at Chkalovskaya AB near Moscow, and miscellaneous airliners chartered from Aeroflot). A few, however, were fitted out for special missions, including An-12R '11 Red' (c/n 4342604) and

ELINT-configured An-12B '84 Red' (c/n 4341905). VVS An-12s, including ECM variants, also operated occasionally from Köthen AB (Halle District/Sachsen-Anhalt) and the so-called 'Netzeband highway strip', a stretch of motorway 5 km (3.1 miles) north-west of Neuruppin AB (Potsdam District/Brandenburg).

Later, An-12s were used, along with An-22s, An-124 Ruslan (*Condor*) heavy transports, Il-76s and freighter-configured Il-78 *Midas-A* tanker/transports, to carry personnel and materiel during the Russian withdrawal from Germany in 1991–4. One of the 226th OSAP *Cubs*, An-12B '96 Red' (c/n 4341708) was the last Russian Air Force (ZGV) aircraft based in Germany to leave German soil. (The distinction of being the very last transport to leave belongs to Il-76M RA-86833 which took off from Berlin-Schönefeld airport on 9 September 1994, but it was not **based** in Germany.)

Military An-12s were regular participants of various airshows. The first of these was probably the show held at Moscow-Domodedovo airport on 9 July 1967 when about a dozen An-12BPs landed on Runway 14R, staging a simulated landing assault for the spectators. The transports had been adorned for the occasion by adding a smart Day-Glo orange cheatline outlined in red and white to the standard overall grey colour scheme. The static display at several open doors days at Kubinka AB near Moscow featured An-12BP '15 Red' (c/n 5343103) on 11 April 1992, An-12P CCCP-11415 (c/n 401708) on 29 May 1993, An-12BP '17 Red' (c/n 5342810) on 14 May 1994, An-12B RA-11791 (c/n 402611) on 7 August 1998 and An-12B RA-11653 (c/n 402703) on 5 August 2002. The freight hold and flight deck were wide open for inspection on all occasions. Foreign *Cubs* had their share of airshow performances, too; e.g. impeccably finished Slovak Air Force An-12BP '2209 Black' (c/n 4342209) participated in the 1999 Royal International Air Tattoo at RAF Fairford, Gloucestershire.

On 26 October 1988 a group of Czech sportsmen used the An-12 for setting two national records in group skydiving. The Czechoslovak Air Force had operated the *Cub* since 1964; however, the aircraft in question was not one of their own two examples but a quasi-civil grey-painted Soviet Air Force An-12A registered CCCP-11833 (c/n 3341008). Of course, the parachutists were equipped with heavy fur-lined wind-proof clothing to protect them from the slipstream and the killing cold of the stratosphere (-50 °C/-58 °F), ZSh-7B 'bone dome' helmets of the type worn by Soviet combat aircraft pilots, oxygen masks and the all-important altimeters, barographs and chronometers.

Taking off from Mladá-Milovice AB, the An-12 climbed initially to 10,100 m (33,140 ft), where four female skydivers (Lída Cejpová, Helena Machulová, Marie Nahodilová and Vlasta Pospíšilová) left the aircraft. Next, skydivers Bretislav Brodský, Jaroslav Hladík, Ivan Hoššo, Miroslav Kruliš, Miloš Netoušek, Oldrich Soucek, Jiří Studený and Josef Zíbar performed a jump at 10,500 m (34,450 ft). The way up had lasted approximately an hour; in contrast, the way down took just 2.4 minutes.

First blood

Like its US counterpart, the Hercules, the An-12 has fully proved its worth in combat, participating in numerous armed conflicts around the world – including some in which the Soviet Union was not formally involved. The first real-life combat operations involved delivering Soviet military aid to the numerous 'friendly nations' which were habitually torn apart by internal strife or embroiled in border conflicts. As often as not the materiel and Soviet military advisers had to be delivered directly to the war zone, which meant considerable risks for the An-12 crews; the ostensibly civil colour scheme obviously would not deter the enemy from shooting at the planes!

The first major operation of this kind was the military airlift in North Yemen (the Yemen Arab Republic) launched in 1963 when Soviet Air Force *Cubs* carried Yemeni troops and materiel during the civil war. Brand-new An-12s were accepted and test-flown by the personnel of the 6th GvVTAD/363rd VTAP and put into action straight away. After accumulating about 250 flight hours in Yemen the aircraft were returned to the Soviet Union, yielding their place to fresh ones. The operation continued until 28 November 1967; Egyptian Air Force An-12Bs replaced the Soviet aircraft at the closing stage of the airlift.

After the third Arab–Israeli War, better known as the Six-Day War (5–11 June 1967), Soviet An-12s and An-22s flew to Egypt and Syria in the late summer and autumn of that year, delivering Mikoyan/Gurevich MiG-17F *Fresco-C* fighters, MiG-21F-13 *Fishbed-B* fighters and Sukhoi Su-7BMK *Fitter-A* fighter-bombers to replace combat losses. A

As this photo shows, major airborne operations also meant very small horizontal separation minima so that a large number of troops could be disgorged within a short time. (Yefim Gordon archive)

IN TIMES OF WAR AND TIMES OF PEACE, OR FORTY YEARS OF SERVICE

The An-12BK made up a large proportion of the VTA's *Cub* fleet. Illustrated here is 33 Blue (c/n 9346207), one of the many An-12s taking part in Exercise *Dvina* in March 1970. (TASS News Agency)

Apart from the USSR, Soviet Air Force An-12s were stationed in several WarPac nations. This 226th OSAP An-12B (16 Red, c/n 3340910) was caught by the camera at Sperenberg AB near Berlin. It is now based at Levashovo AB near St. Petersburg. The coloured spinner tips which were typical of Soviet/Russian AF turboprop transports marked the squadron operating the aircraft.

Military An-12s often participate in various airshows. These red-coded An-12BPs wearing an unusual colour scheme with a Dayglo orange cheatline (applied for the occasion) put on a show of force during the grand air fest at Moscow-Domodedovo airport on 9th July 1967. (Yefim Gordon archive)

similar air bridge was organised in 1973 immediately before the Holy Day War, or Yom Kippur War (6–24 October), when more aircraft and T-54 tanks were delivered. These missions were risky because Israeli fighters were active in the area. On one occasion a Soviet Air Force *Cub* taking off from Hodeidah, Syria, was actually attacked by four Israeli Defence Force/Air Force (*Heyl Ha'avir*) McDonnell Douglas F-4E Phantom IIs. Doing the only possible thing, the aircraft's captain, Vladimir Akimov, performed a violent evasive manoeuvre and flew over the sea at ultra-low level, causing the Israelis to lose their prey.

A squadron of An-12BK-PPS ECM aircraft (with ogival tailcone but minus strap-on jammer pods) was also detached to Syria from Siauliai (Lithuanian SSR) to disrupt the operation of Israeli air defences, protecting Syrian strike aircraft which attacked Israeli HAWK surface-to-air missile batteries. For appearance's sake the *Cub*-Cs wore Syrian Air Force roundels and fin flashes but were flown by Soviet crews; of course they reverted to red stars after completing their Middle Eastern tour of duty.

Now we have to travel back in time a bit. In April 1967 a coup d'état occurred in Nigeria and the corrupt government was toppled by Gen. Irons, C-in-C of the Nigerian Armed Forces. A month later, however, Irons was killed in a new coup organised by Col. Ojukwu, governor of the Eastern province and one of the leaders of the Ibo tribe. The rebels declared their intention to secede, forming the so-called State of Biafra, named after a bight in the Gulf of Guinea. This immediately sparked a bitter three-year civil war between the separatists and the federal government.

At first the Federal Nigerian Air Force (FNAF) had to make do with six impressed Nigeria Airways DC-3s (ex 5N-AAN, 5N-AAP, etc.) and 12 Czech-supplied Aero L-29 Delfin advanced trainers in the bomber and strike rôles respectively. Pretty soon, however, it obtained real combat aircraft. According to some sources, the Nigerians approached the Soviet Union and purchased 41 MiG-17Fs, four UTI-MiG-15 *Midget* fighter trainers and a suitable stock of spares. The MiGs were delivered to Nigeria by Soviet Air Force An-12s, which made a total of 86 flights. (Other sources, however, say the fighters and Il-28 *Beagle* tactical bombers were supplied by Arab nations supporting the Islamic government in Lagos in its struggle against the Christian Ibo separatists and that the MiGs were in fact ex-Egyptian machines!)

A shameful page in the *Cub*'s service career was opened in 1968 when a large group of Soviet and East German forces was deployed to Czechoslovakia to squash an incipient anti-communist uprising in that country. On 20 August 1968, spearheaded by a quasi-Aeroflot An-24B acting as a command post, a steady stream of VVS An-12s landed at Prague-Ruzyne airport, disgorging troops, vehicles and heavy armament. Taking over control of the airport in a few minutes, the troops rolled on towards the capital to seize key points and prevent armed opposition. Unlike the Hungarian uprising of 1956, there was no armed opposition and the Soviet Air Force suffered no losses.

Between 7 November and 31 December 1977 quasi-civil An-12s (still in pre-1973 red/white livery) were used alongside Il-76Ms to airlift supplies to Ethiopia when the Soviet Union supported the regime of Mengistu Haile Mariam in its losing struggle against separatists in the Eritrea and Ogaden provinces. The transports flew from Tashkent (Uzbek SSR) and Tbilisi (Georgian SSR) to the town of Masawa[56] near Addis Ababa, flying over Afghanistan, Iran and the People's Democratic Republic of Yemen (the South Yemeni capital Aden served as a staging point). Apart from military hardware and ammunition, 20,000 Cuban troops were airlifted to Ethiopia.

The Afghan experience

The best-known armed conflict in which the An-12 took part was arguably the Afghan War of 1979-91 – the first major conflict in which the Soviet Union openly participated after the Second World War. This war was also marked by the largest-scale An-12 operations during the type's combat career.

Soviet forces entered Afghanistan at 18.00 local time on 25 December 1979 when the Soviet government decided to cement its influence in this country. Much has been said and written about the reasons of this war and the fallacy of the Soviet involvement therein but this lies outside the scope of this book; we'd better leave this issue to the politologists. During the 47-hour airlift operation on 25–28 December the VTA made 343 flights into the country, transporting the personnel and materiel of the 103rd Airborne Division and an unnumbered Airborne Regiment; the total amounted to 7,700 servicemen, 894 vehicles and 1,062 tons (2,341,270 lb) of assorted cargoes. The An-12 bore the brunt of this opening operation, making 200 flights; in contrast, 77 flights were performed by Il-76 *sans suffixe*/Il-76M *Candid-B*s and another 66 by An-22s.

The An-12 was heavily involved in this war from beginning to end. Quasi-civilian grey-painted *Cub*s (mostly An-12BPs and 'BKs) were mostly used for resupply and in-country troop redeployment missions in the interests of the 40th Army (or, as it was called in the official press, the limited contingent of Soviet troops in Afghanistan). A squadron of ten An-12s commanded by Col. Ishmuratov was stationed at Bagram. The unit reported directly to the Chief Soviet military adviser in Afghanistan and occasionally operated for the Afghan government troops loyal to President Najibullah; the aircraft were flown by both Soviet and Afghan crews. Later the aviation element of the 40th Army was augmented by several more units, including the 50th OSAP. As the name implies, the regiment operated a 'mixed bag' of aircraft and helicopters; besides 16 MiG-21PFM *Fishbed-F* fighters, 12 Mil Mi-24 *Hind* attack helicopters, 12 Mi-8MT *Hip-H* assault/transport helicopters and four An-26 transports, the complement included four An-12BPs and 'BKs.

In Afghanistan the *Cub* quickly proved its worth as an indispensable workhorse. True enough, the Il-76MD could lug twice the payload, but the An-12 could do what the *Candid* could not – it could operate into and out of mountain airfields with short dirt strips. Another virtue much appreciated in Afghanistan was the *Cub*'s sturdiness and high combat survivability. More than once the An-12s managed to get away from an airfield under attack by the Mujahidin rebels and make it safely back to base, despite having hundreds of holes blown in their airframes, dead systems and wounded crew members on board.

Unfortunately, the An-12 suffered combat losses, as did most Soviet aircraft used in the Afghan War. Most of these losses were attributed to man-portable air defence systems (MANPADS) – General Dynamics FIM-43A Redeye, FIM-92A Stinger and Shorts Blowpipe missiles supplied to the Mujahideen by the USA and, ironically, captured 9K32 Strela-2 (Arrow-2, pronounced *strelah*; NATO SA-7 *Grail*) missiles. The first *Cub* was shot down on 30 September 1980; there were no survivors among the 45 persons on board. Other shootdowns occurred on 25 April 1983, in May 1983 and on 11 November 1984. On 29 November 1986 a 50th OSAP/1st Sqn An-12 bound for Jalalabad was hit by a Stinger 24 km (15 miles) from Kabul airport as it climbed to 6,400 m (21,000 ft). The aircraft was carrying a load of ammunition and the resulting explosion blew it apart, leaving no chances of survival for the crew, commanded by Capt. Khomootov, and the 27 passengers.

In Kandahar there was a case when a *Cub* came under fire during final approach; apparently the captain was killed and the co-pilot couldn't cope with the aircraft for some reason. The An-12 overran, crashing into a parked Mi-6 *Hook* heavy transport helicopter, and both aircraft were destroyed by the ensuing fire. In 1987 another An-12 had a narrow escape when a Stinger scored a direct hit but failed to detonate as the aircraft was cruising above 9,000 m (29,530 ft) near Gardez. The unexploded missile tore away more than a third of the lower skin on one of the stabilisers and ripped away the oxygen bottles in the aft fuselage; nevertheless the aircraft pressed on towards Kabul, making a safe emergency landing.

Of course, due credit has to be given to the crews who managed to keep their heads cool in such situations and did their best to bring the aircraft home. One such incident occurred at Farah, the capital of the province of the same name, in 1983. As a *Cub* captained by Maj. Zalyotinskiy was offloading supplies the Mujahidin launched a mortar attack on the airfield. Mortar shells began exploding all over the hardstand, and shell fragments struck down the aircraft's navigator and punctured the rear underfloor fuel tank. Zalyotinskiy immediately ordered the crew to start the engines and take off. As soon as No. 1 engine had reached ground idling rpm the crew opened the throttle and started taxiing, starting Nos 4 and 3 engines en route. Before the last engine could be started another mortar round exploded right next to the runway; it became clear that the next one would fall squarely on the runway and there was no choice but to get out of there immediately. Even though every single man aboard was wounded, the crew managed to take off on three engines and escape to Kabul; the aircraft and the crew were saved.

On another occasion a Stinger knocked out the No. 1 engine, causing a massive fire. Showing considerable bravery and skill, the crew managed a safe landing with much of the port flap consumed by the fire. Yet the joy of making it back in one piece was killed by the tragic death of the youngest member of the crew – the tail gunner who, unable to bear the immense stress, baled out immediately after touchdown.

Of course the commanders of the 40th Army were not going to put up with these losses, especially since other Soviet aircraft also fell victim to the Stingers. Previous combat experience was carefully analysed and countermeasures were developed. First, in the case of the An-12, tandem 30-round ASO-2 chaff/flare dispensers were installed on the forward fuselage for protection against heat-seeking missiles, which required some local reinforcement of the airframe. If you see a *Cub* with what looks like shallow strakes low on the forward fuselage sides, you can be sure this one is an Afghan veteran. The tail gunner acted as an observer, activating the chaff/flare dispensers after spotting the tell-tale flash on the ground and the characteristic smoke trail of an incoming missile; the flares were fired at preset intervals. Aircraft updated in this fashion included An-12BPs CCCP-11302 (c/n 5343705), CCCP-11756 (c/n 4342208), CCCP-11844, An-12BKs CCCP-11724, CCCP-11868 (c/n 9346310) and 11 Yellow (c/n 7345410).

Secondly, the Stingers brought about a change in tactics. From then on the crews of Soviet military transports used a new piloting technique similar to the 'Khe Sanh tactical approach' introduced by the USAF in Vietnam. The aircraft would stay at about 5,400 m (17,700 ft) above ground level until it entered the airfield's security zone, measuring approximately 4 ×6 km (2.5×3.75 miles), then descend in a tight spiral to minimise the danger of being fired upon. The sink rate during this manoeuvre reached 20–25 m/sec (3,940–4,920 ft/min), which was about three times the normal rate. The climbout on the return trip was also in a tight spiral.

Of course, such fighter-style approaches required the flight manual to be disregarded in certain areas – but then, the crews would rather bend the rules than bend the aircraft! For instance, the standard operational procedure was to set the throttles to flight idle for descent; however, during the 'Afghan tactical approach' An-12 pilots were forced to retard the throttles past the flight idle stop (all the way to ground idle), otherwise the aircraft would descend all too fast. As it was, approach speeds were 40–50 km/h (25–31 mph) higher than normal because of the rarefied air in the mountainous regions of Afghanistan; reverse thrust was ineffective for the same reason.

Avenues of approach were changed for each single flight, as the rebels were avid mountain-climbers who could lug heavy armament to vantage points, and even using the same route twice involved a considerable risk of being ambushed. For the same reason the general rule was to fly as high as possible, staying out of range of Mujahidin air defences.

Finally, extra attention was paid to crew training, including the psychological aspect; crew coordination was crucial during such manoeuvres with extreme pitch and bank angles in mountainous terrain. This is well illustrated by the minor accident which occurred in Kabul on 25 September 1986 when a newly arrived crew were making a familiarisation flight in a 50th OSAP/1st Sqn An-12 registered CCCP-11408. The four-minute flight included the 'Afghan tactical approach'... and ended in an unceremonious belly landing because the crew had simply *forgotten to extend the landing gear* owing to the excessively high psychological stress![57] Nevertheless, this tactic proved effective enough, saving many crews from being shot down.

As an extra safety measure, take-offs and landings of heavy transport aircraft were always covered by a pair of Mi-24 gunship helicopters – especially during the pullout phase when personnel was airlifted out of the country. The Mi-24s also fired IRCM flares and could promptly take out a Mujahidin ambush on the outskirts of the airport. Sometimes the choppers got hit by a Stinger missile intended for the transports.

An-12 operations in the hot and dusty climate of the mountainous regions of Afghanistan were a sore trial for the crews, considering that, unlike the smaller An-26, the *Cub* did not have a cooling turbine in the cabin ventilation/pressurisation system. The control wheels and electric switches got hot enough to burn the fingers, while the headsets *dribbled molten fat all over your ears*, as the pilots in Afghanistan used to say.

As already mentioned, the An-12s brought fresh personnel, heavy equipment, ammunition, fuel, etc. to the Soviet bases in Afghanistan. One of the most common loads on the return trip was wounded personnel going to 'Unionside'

The An-12 was extensively used in the Afghan War from beginning to end. For appearance's sake the aircraft usually wore civil registrations (but still had grey Air Force colours). Here a line-up of five An-12BKs, with CCCP-11724 foremost, is seen at an Afghan airfield in 1988. (Novosti Press Agency)

Many of the An-12s operating into Afghanistan, including this An-12BK, were retrofitted with ASO-2 flare dispensers on the forward fuselage sides for protection against the heat-seeking missiles fired by the Mujahidin. (Novosti Press Agency)

hospitals. The An-12 also had to fill the hated rôle known in Soviet Army Afghan contingent slang as '**Chornyy tyul'pahn**' (Black Tulip). This appellation, the origin of which is unknown, applied to any aircraft carrying the bodies of servicemen killed in action back to Soviet territory for burial. The bodies themselves were euphemistically called *grooz dvesti* ('cargo 200'), while wounded personnel was referred to as *grooz trista* ('cargo 300').

Aircraft designers also learned a thing or two from the Afghan experience. First of all, all Soviet Air Force transport aircraft operating into Afghanistan (and many others as well) were equipped with either permanently installed IRCM flare dispensers or provisions for removable flare packs. Secondly, inert gas pressurisation systems were retrofitted (or upgraded where already present) to pressurise the fuel tanks, reducing the hazard of explosion if hit by enemy fire. Also, the An-12's flap tracks and carriages had to be reinforced to withstand the augmented loads during the famous tactical approaches.

Of course, the VTA top command drew some important conclusions as well. Changes were made to the VTA crews' combat training programme to include the 'Afghan tactical approach' and IRCM techniques. Most of the Soviet Air Force's transport aircraft pilots – first and foremost the highly skilled ones – had a tour of duty in Afghanistan. All of this allowed the VTA's combat potential to be improved dramatically by the late 1980s.

Internal strife

Sadly enough, the An-12 has also participated in several wars in its own country – or, to be precise, the Commonwealth of Independent States (CIS). Shortly before and immediately after the breakup of the Soviet Union, a spate of ethnic conflicts erupted in the southern republics, one of them being the Georgian–Abkhazi civil war of 1992-4. In the course of this conflict a pair of Ukrainian Air Force An-12s delivered humanitarian aid and evacuated ethnic Georgian refugees from the war zone in October 1993. In so doing the aircraft were repeatedly fired upon by the Abkhazi side but got away unharmed. They were lucky to do so; within just three days of the previous month (21–3 September) the Abkhazi separatists had atrociously destroyed three civil jets operated by the Georgian airline Transair Georgia (Tu-134A-3 65893, Tu-154B 85163 and Tu-134A CCCP-65001), causing a large loss of civilian life.

The An-12 was actively used in the First Chechen War (1994–6) as the Russian federal government strove to restore law and order in this republic which had turned into a loose cannon. Together with Russian Air Force Il-76MDs and An-124s, the *Cubs* delivered troops, equipment and ammunition to Groznyy-Severnyy airport[58] and Mozdok (Ingushetia) from all over Russia.

***

As with other types in the VVS inventory, the collapse of the Soviet Union had its adverse effect on An-12 operations. First, the bases in the former Baltic Defence District had to be abandoned and the units redeployed to Russia as Estonia, Latvia and Lithuania strove to gain independence – and, as Russian popular wisdom says, one removal to a new home is equivalent to two fires. Then, many units operating the *Cub* found themselves in other CIS republics – mostly in the Ukraine which was at odds with Russia over the Black Sea Fleet issue and other problems. In the general political and economic chaos of the early 1990s, fuel and spares procurement became a problem. Hence many *Cubs* had to be grounded and cannibalised for spares in order to keep others flyable. In Russian aviation slang such aircraft are called 'Avrora' (Aurora) – an allusion to the famous Russian Navy cruiser which signalled the beginning of the 1917 October Revolution by firing its nose cannon and was later permanently moored on the Neva River in Leningrad as a museum.

As a result, the An-12 is actively moving into the civil air transport market (where, true enough, it has been present for many years now); quite a few *Cubs* with considerable airframe life remaining are stripped of military equipment and sold to airlines big and small, including some rather obscure ones. The Ukraine has taken a different approach: the Air Force has spawned numerous commercial divisions which generate revenue, helping to solve financing and serviceability problems. (Known An-12 operators in and outside the CIS are dealt with in separate chapters.)

Cubs at war elsewhere

The An-12s supplied to various 'friendly nations' (and even the Chinese Y8 clone) had their share of combat, too. After pulling out its troops from Afghanistan in 1989 the Soviet Union left a lot of military hardware behind (including a few An-12Bs) which it donated to

Najibullah's government. Najibullah immediately put the Cubs to good use against the 'irreconcilable opposition' (i.e. the Mujahidin): flying high and out of range of the Stingers, the An-12s performed carpet bombing of Mujahidin positions. After the opposition seized Kabul in May 1992, the various warlords scrambling for power (Gulbuddin Hekmatyar, Burhanuddin Rabbani, Ahmad Shah Masoud and Gen. Abdul Rashid Dostum) tore the Afghan Air Force apart and started using the aircraft against each other.

Later, several An-12s were appropriated by the new opposition – the fundamentalist Taliban movement which gained notoriety for the destruction of 'non-Islamic' culture and its affiliations with the al-Qa'eda terrorist group. Little is known about the operations of Taliban Cubs, except that one such aircraft crashed near Quetta, Pakistan, on 13 January 1998.

Starting in 1977, Ethiopia obtained 16 second-hand An-12s from the Soviet Union, and in the same year the aircraft were used in repelling an aggression from neighbouring Somalia. The Cubs were also actively used against the separatists in Eritrea and Ogaden – again both as transports and as auxiliary bombers. One of them, an An-12B serialled 1506 (c/n 402002), was blown up by Eritrean guerillas who overran the airfield at Tesenni on the night of 15 January 1984; another Cub reportedly crashed while taking off from the Eritrean capital Asmara in 1987. Still another was damaged beyond repair prior to May 1984, overshooting the runway at Addis Ababa during an attempted hijack.

In 1962–7 Egypt was involved in the civil war in Yemen, supporting the Republicans who had overthrown the king. Egyptian Air Force An-12Bs took part in the closing stage of the aforementioned airlift operation initiated by the Soviet Union; this may account for the addition of civil registrations at some stage of their service career. At least eight EAF Cubs were destroyed on the ground at Cairo-West by Israeli air strikes on 6 June 1967, the second day of the Six-Day War; these reportedly included An-12Bs 1217 (c/n 402303) and 1218 (c/n 402304). Egyptian An-12s were active during the Yom Kippur War, deploying troops and flying to the Soviet Union to deliver fresh consignments of weaponry. Later, they shouldered the main burden of bringing United Nations Peace Force troops to the Middle East (except for the Polish UNPF contingent which arrived in a Polish Cub).

The Indian Air Force holds the distinction of being the world's first air arm to use the An-12 in actual combat. Frictions between India and China had started in 1959 after the Khampa rebellion against the Chinese occupation of Tibet, when the Dalai Lama fled to the Indian town of Tawang. On 20 October 1962 the tension escalated into outright military conflict when Chinese People's Liberation Army (PLA) troops infiltrated Indian territory, attacking and encircling several Indian Army outposts along the Himalayan border. India's newly delivered An-12As were used to deliver food and ammunition to the besieged garrisons – usually by paradropping. Remarkably, only 5 per cent of the cargo was lost, despite the fact that the drop zones lay in difficult mountainous terrain. Part of the cargo was offloaded at nearby airbases for further delivery by smaller planes.

Besides resupply missions, the An-12s were used alongside IAF Fairchild C-119G Flying Boxcars to deploy the 114th Infantry Brigade to the area, flying from Chandigarh to Chushul. The latter airfield had a perforated steel plate (PSP) runway which could not stand up to six An-12 and eight C-119 flights a day, becoming unserviceable every now and then. By 13 November more than 150 sorties had been flown to Chushul; even so, the 114th Infantry Brigade was outnumbered four times and would have been defeated, had it not been for a troop of French-made AMX-13 light tanks and field guns which the Cubs airlifted to the area. The PLA Air Force did not put up any opposition to these operations, and no An-12s were lost. Finally, on 20 November China called a ceasefire.

More action came in December 1965 and January 1966 during the Indo-Pakistani conflict over the State of Kashmir. Again, the Cubs carried replenishments to the war zone and evacuated casualties. During the next war with Pakistan which broke out on 3 December 1971 (and ended in a complete victory for India) the IAF An-12s performed a much wider range of tasks. For instance, on 12 January a group of An-12s and C-119s paradropped a battalion of assault troopers

Egyptian Air Force Cubs, including An-12BP 1242/SU-ARD (c/n 9346710), took part both in the Yemeni civil war of 1962–7 and in two Arab–Israeli wars. (RART)

The Indian Air Force *Cub*s were the first to see actual combat, participating in the repulsion of the Chinese aggression of 1962. Here a pair of An-12As (BL533, foreground, and BL729) fly along the Himalayas, the area where the conflict took place. This view illustrates the two different liveries worn by IAF *Cub*s. (Yefim Gordon archive)

near Dacca which cut off the supply routes for the Pakistani garrison stationed there.

This was also the first time the An-12 was used as a bomber, dropping up to 40 450 kg (992 lb) bombs or 200-litre (44 imp. gal) napalm tanks; during several successful night raids against targets in western Pakistan the bomb load reached 16 tons (35,270 lb)! On one occasion a *Cub* bomber was intercepted by a Pakistani Air Force Dassault Mirage III but managed to get away. It was probably the Indian experience that prompted the Antonov OKB to develop the An-12BKV bomber version.

The Indian An-12s were also used operationally in northern Sri Lanka in the late 1980s and early 1990s alongside other IAF assets against the Tamil separatists known as the Liberation Tigers of Tamil Eelam (LTTE). This was the Indian Peacekeeping Force operation in Sri Lanka, a determined but fruitless attempt to stop the prolonged civil war in that country. LTTE air defences were still weak then (until the Tigers obtained some shoulder-launched SAMs from North Korea) and the *Cub*s suffered no losses. Their Sri Lankan brethren were far less lucky.

Iraqi Air Force An-12BPs saw a lot of action both during the incessant war which Saddam Hussein waged against the Kurdish minority in the northern regions of the country and during the Iran–Iraq war of 1980–8. Their missions included flights abroad to pick up weapons, maritime reconnaissance over the Persian Gulf and the Red Sea and even in-flight refuelling of IrAF Dassault Mirage F1EQ-200 fighter-bombers, as well as Mikoyan MiG-23BN *Flogger-D* attack aircraft retrofitted locally with Mirage F1 fixed refuelling probes. In this case 'maritime reconnaissance' means simply spotting Iranian ships and reporting their position to attack aircraft. For instance, on 12 August 1986 a flight of Mirage F1EQ-200s attacked three Iranian ships and several oil rigs after being topped up by the An-12 tanker.

IrAF An-12s presumably also participated in the Iraqi invasion of Kuwait in early August 1990. What is certain is that two of the *Cub*s were destroyed on the ground by Royal Air Force Blackburn Buccaneer S.2 strike aircraft toting 'smart bombs' on 27 February 1992 during the Gulf War (Operation *Desert Storm*).

The Cuban Air Force reportedly had a few An-12s and used them alongside Soviet *Cub*s to extend military help to the pro-Communist Angolan government of José Eduardo dos Santos between 1975 and the late 1980s. It is indeed known that in the crucial autumn days of 1975, when the South African Defence Force (SADF) supporting the opposition was advancing on Luanda, two An-12s brought urgently needed ammunition and military advisers, enabling the government troops to stem the assault. Operating into Angolan airfields, the An-12s were frequently fired upon by UNITA rebels but suffered no losses – as yet.

Now we have to focus our attention on Sri Lanka again. In 1991 the government in Colombo struck close ties with mainland China, which at the time was the only nation willing to extend any tangible support – including military support. Arms deliveries began same year; these included two Shaanxi Y8D transports for the Sri Lankan Air Force (SLAF), followed by a second-hand Y8B in 1994. The second aircraft, serialled CR-872, exploded in mid-air shortly after take-off on 5 July 1992, killing all 20 persons on board; there are speculations that the aircraft was carrying a load of ammunition which became dislodged and detonated. The first aircraft (CR-871) sat unserviceable for a while.

In 1995 the LTTE called a ceasefire – only to regroup forces and acquire additional weapons, as it turned out. In April 1995 the hostilities resumed with renewed fury, now that the rebels had North Korean-built 9M319 Igla-1E (Needle-1E, pronounced *iglah*; NATO SA-18 *Grouse*) MANPADS at their disposal. The SLAF's 1st Transport Wing (especially the 2nd Heavy Transport Sqn) was the hardest hit, losing five aircraft to the shoulder-launched missiles that year, including Y8D CR-871 which was shot down on approach to Palaly AB on 18 November. The stricken aircraft ditched in the Gulf of Mannar and sank; only one of the four crew members survived.

Sudanese *Cub*s were used in the struggle against the National Liberation Army (NLA) rebels terrorising the southern regions of Sudan (El Istwâ'ya province) in the 1970s. Algerian Air Force An-12Bs also took part in a civil war – this time in neighbouring Morocco, supporting the anti-government Polisario Front. Finally, the two Yugoslav Air Force An-12BPs played an important part in evacuating federal government troops from Bosnia, Slovenia and Croatia into Serbian territory as the country disintegrated into a collection of belligerent states.

In civil service

The An-12's career with Aeroflot, the Soviet flag carrier, started with several celebrated missions to the Arctic regions and Antarctica to support Soviet polar research stations. Reliable aircraft were required to fulfil these demanding missions, and the four-engined *Cub* fitted in ideally here.

Regular flights to the drifting research stations in the Arctic Ocean began on 5 April 1960 when an early-production *Cub* carrying a load of more than 8,500 kg (18,740 lb) departed from one of the Arctic airfields to the research station SP-8 (*Severnyy polyus* – North Pole). In press reports the aircraft was referred to as 'a cargo-configured An-10' because the true designation was still classified then. The airstrip was prepared on a stretch of icefield 1,300 m (4,260 ft) long; the heavy An-12 performed the landing flawlessly. Interestingly, the aircraft was unloaded within just 15 minutes. If the same load had been delivered by the piston-engined Il-14G, six such aircraft would have been required.

As already mentioned, on 15 December 1961 the unique An-12TP-2 transport/geophysical survey aircraft (CCCP 04366) departed from Moscow to Ice Station Mirnyy in the Antarctic in company with suitably modified Il-18V CCCP-75743 (c/n 181002901). The mission was led by Mikhail I. Shevelyov (Hero of the Soviet Union), head of Aeroflot's polar division. The An-12's crew comprised captain Boris S. Osipov, first officer P. Rogov, navigator V. Steshkin, flight engineer I. Naïkin, technician V. Sergeyev and radio operator N. Starkov – all airmen with a large experience of flying in polar regions.

The route, which was 26,423 km (16,411 miles) long,[59] took the aircraft across four continents and two oceans. The An-12 covered this distance in 48 hours 7 minutes,[60] clocking an average speed of 532 km/h (330 mph).[61] Refuelling stops were made in Tashkent, Delhi, Rangoon, Darwin, Sydney, Christchurch and at the US Antarctic research station McMurdo. The last-but-one leg of the journey (from Christchurch to McMurdo) turned out to be the hardest because the American radio officer would not answer the radio calls of the Soviet crews who needed meteorological and navigation information. Still, despite lacking the all-important weather report, the crews of both aircraft maintained the planned route without deviating. Having nothing but their weather radars and astrosextants to rely on, they circumnavigated tall mountains obscured by clouds, including the 3,743 m (12,280 ft) Mt Erebus, and made a precision approach to McMurdo's airstrip.

The two aircraft spent a full month on the glacial continent. On arrival at Mirnyy the *Cub* was re-equipped with non-retractable skis, which had been stored in the freight hold, and went on to make several survey flights over unexplored areas of Antarctica, measuring the earth's magnetic field. Several landings were made on suitable clearings spotted from the air. CCCP 04366 also made a dozen take-offs and landings specifically to determine the suitability of the skis for operation from airfields covered by deep snow (no small matter, since preparing the hard-packed runways in Antarctica is a back-breaking job).

On 2 February 1962 the An-12TP-2 returned to Moscow, spending a total of 90 hours in the air during the expedition. The success of the mission proved that aircraft could resupply the Antarctic research stations much quicker and at less cost as compared to the traditional delivery by sea. All participants of the expedition were awarded government orders; additionally, B.S. Osipov and A.S. Polyakov (the captain of the Il-18) received the coveted Hero of Socialist Labour title.

Gradually, as the needs of the Soviet Air Force were met, Aeroflot started taking delivery of its own *Cubs* (augmented by second-hand examples transferred from the VTA). All in all the An-12 was operated by 14 of the Soviet Union's Civil Aviation Directorates (UGA – *Oopravleniye grazhdahnskoy aviahtsii*). These included the Central Directorate of International Services (TsUMVS – *Tsentrahl'noye oopravleniye mezhdunarodnykh vozdooshnykh so'obschcheniy*)/64th Flight, Komi Civil Aviation Directorate/Syktyvkar United Flight Detachment (OAO – *obyedinyonnyy*

The An-12 served with many of the Soviet Union's Civil Aviation Directorates. Here, civil-configured An-12BP CCCP-11031 (c/n 7345003) of the Tyumen CAD/2nd Tyumen UFD/435th Flight is being unloaded at an airport somewhere in Siberia, judging by the caterpillar tractor used to tow the cargo trailer. Unfortunately this particular aircraft was lost in a fatal crash at Mys Kamennyy on 1 October 1970. (Yefim Gordon archive)

Aeroflot aircraft were tasked with resupplying Soviet drifting research stations in the Arctic Ocean; when the Polar Directorate was disbanded in the late 1960s, the other CADs took over the job. Special missions required special equipment. An-12BP CCCP-12962 (c/n 9346406) of the Krasnoyarsk CAD/Noril'sk UFD/434th Flight is seen here offloading fuel cisterns at Ice Station SP-26 (North Pole-26) in April 1974. Due to their appearance the cisterns were promptly dubbed *parovoziki* ('Li'l Steam Engines')! The one in the foreground holds B-95 petrol. (TASS News Agency)

aviaotryad)/318th Flight, Komi CAD/Vorkuta UFD/366th Flight, Krasnoyarsk CAD/1st Krasnoyarsk UFD/214th Flight, Krasnoyarsk CAD/Norilsk UFD/329th and 434th Flights, Leningrad CAD/Leningrad UFD, Leningrad CAD/Penza UFD, Magadan CAD/1st Magadan UFD/181st Flight (1st and 2nd Squadrons), Moscow Territorial CAD, North Caucasian CAD/Rostov UFD, Siberian (later East Siberian) CAD/Irkutsk UFD/134th Flight, Tyumen CAD/2nd Tyumen UFD/435th Flight, Urals CAD/Chelyabinsk UFD, Urals CAD/Sverdlovsk UFD, Volga CAD/Kuibyshev 1st UFD/368th Flight and Yakutian CAD/Yakutsk UFD/139th Flight. Aeroflot *Cubs* carried all manner of civilian cargoes. These included heavy construction and earth-moving equipment, livestock, foodstuffs (including tangerines and oranges for the workers of Siberian oil and gas fields, which gave rise to the slang phrase *mandarinovyy reys* – 'tangerine flight'), money and other valuables, and humanitarian aid.

Until the mid-1970s every type of aircraft operated by Aeroflot had a colour scheme of its own, and sometimes several. As already noted, the An-12 shared the livery of early An-10s featuring a white top, a grey belly and a bright red cheatline with 'feathers' aft of the flight-deck glazing. In March 1973 the Ministry of Civil Aviation approved the familiar standard livery featuring a blue cheatline with blue pinstripe (on which the aircraft type was painted on the nose), Aeroflot titles in bold rounded type and heavily outlined exits as required by ICAO rules. In practice, however, the new standard was not introduced until a couple of years later, and Aeroflot *Cubs* retained the old livery until the end of the 1970s. Once again, nearly half the VTA's An-12 fleet sported 1973-standard Aeroflot colours in the 1980s, but the coloured spinner tips gave them away.

Aircraft operated in the northern regions received the so-called polar colours with a red cheatline, red vertical tail on which the Soviet flag was superimposed on a broad white band, red outer wings and horizontal tail (for high definition against white backgrounds in the event of a forced landing) and black titles. Many Aeroflot An-12s wore this smart colour scheme.

Then, in the early 1980s someone decided that the standard livery could use some livening up. Hence an experimental version of it was developed and tested on several types operated by Aeroflot and the VTA; this was basically a blue/white spin-off of the polar scheme. Over the years it was worn by such varied types as the An-3T, An-8, An-24B/An-24RV, An-26, An-72S, An-124, Il-76T/Il-76TD, Tu-134A-3/Tu-134AK/Tu-134 *Balkany*[62]/ Tu-134B, Tu-154B-2 and Yak-42 – and the An-12, too. At least five *Cubs* operated by MAP and MOM enterprises – 'military' An-12B CCCP-11408 (c/n 4341209), 'military' An-12BPs CCCP-11789 (c/n 6343905) and CCCP-11819 (c/n 6344009), 'civil' An-12BP CCCP-12995 (c/n 00347402) and An-12BK CCCP-83962 No. 2 (c/n 402210) – sported blue/white tails and blue outer wings. Unfortunately, this livery did not gain wide use and is mostly worn by quasi-civil An-72S VIP transports.

Originally the cargoes were carried in bulk or at best in their own packaging. In October 1977, however, the An-12 introduced containerised cargo transport on Aeroflot's routes, which was much more convenient and civilised, reducing the risk of damage – or theft. The cost of such ttransport was an all-time low in the airline's practice – 10 kopecks per tonne-kilometre (one kopeck is 1/100th of a rouble).

Speaking of humanitarian missions, the An-12's robust airframe, high payload and ability to operate into semi-prepared fields made it an ideal aircraft for such tasks. The *Cub* was much used in this capacity in different parts of the world. For example, in 1993 Tyumen Airlines An-12BPs RA-11112 (c/n 01347907) and RA-12976 (c/n 9346510) were operated by the United Nations World Food Programme (WFP) in Angola and Ethiopia, wearing the all-white UN colours and appropriate titles; An-12A UR-11833 was also used in a similar capacity in Angola in January 1994. In October 1994 Russian Air Force An-12s delivered medicines, food, tents and diesel-powered generators to Iturup Island in the Kuriles, which had been hit by a powerful earthquake.

As already mentioned, in 1965 An-12B CCCP-11359 was displayed at the 25th Paris Air Show, together with the An-22 prototype (CCCP-46191). On 3 February 1966 a TsUMVS *Cub* captained by Ovsyannikov inaugurated Aeroflot's first international cargo service from Moscow-Sheremetyevo to Paris via Riga; the flight time was 5 hours 30 minutes. A second route – the first transcontinental route from Vladivostok in the Far East to Amsterdam, with several staging points – was opened in July 1969. Others followed quickly.

Apart from Aeroflot units, the An-12 was operated by various enterprises within the frameworks of the Ministry of Aircraft Industry, the Ministry of General Machinery, the Ministry of Shipbuilding and the Ministry of Electronic Industry. MAP *Cubs* belonged to the aircraft factories in Arsenyev, Irkutsk, Kazan (No. 22), Komsomolsk-on-Amur, Kuibyshev, Kumertau, Omsk, Tashkent, Ulan-Ude, Ulyanovsk and Voronezh, the Zaporozhye Engine Factory (now Motor-Sich), the Transport Aviation Production Association and the Antonov OKB itself.

An-12 operators in the MOM system were the Kirov Machinery Production Association and Zlatoust Machinery Plants (divisions of NPO Energiya), the Kuibyshev Engine Production Association named after Mikhail V. Frunze, the Omsk Engine Production Association and the Orenburg 'Strela' Production Association. Known MRP divisions operating the type were the Kamensk-Uralskiy Radiotechnical Plant (a division of Moscow-based NPO Vzlyot (Take-off)), NPO Vega-M in Moscow and LNPO Leninets. MSP An-12 operators included the Amur Shipbuilding Plant in Komsomolsk-on-Amur.

According to Soviet practice one or two aircraft overhaul plants (ARZ – *aviaremontnyy zavod*) would repair all aircraft of a given type, regardless of where they were based – including export aircraft. Thus, ARZ No. 412 in Rostov-on-Don traditionally handles civil An-12s. Military *Cubs* are dealt with by two Russian Air Force plants – ARZ No. 123 in Staraya Roossa near Velikiy Novgorod and ARZ No. 325 in Novocherkassk; some repair and conversion work is also done by ARZ No. 308 at Ivanovo-Severnyy AB. What's more, the Air Force plants are now moving into the civil overhaul market, undertaking, among other things, demilitarisation work on ex-VVS aircraft (see the previous chapter). AI-20 engines are likewise repaired by the Air Force's ARZ No. 123. In post-Soviet days the Aviant aircraft factory at Kiev-Svyatoshino started refurbishing An-12s, notably ex-military machines being sold to civil operators. Also, in Soviet times the Fergana Mechanical Plant in Uzbekistan did some upgrade work on An-12s.

In due course the An-12 was supplemented in Aeroflot service by the larger Il-76, just as had been the case in the Soviet Air Force. Yet even at the time of writing the *Cub* is still going strong, serving with a multitude of new airlines which have sprung up in the CIS following the demise of the 'one-size-fits-all' Soviet-era Aeroflot giant. The An-12 is cheap on the used aircraft market, which means pretty high revenues for the operator, and stocks are reasonably large. Moreover, the An-12 is enjoying a revival these days; old it may be, but it conforms to ICAO Annex 16 Chapter 3 noise regulations enacted on 1 April 2002, which the Il-76TD *Candid-A* – the most popular Russian commercial airlifter – does not.

The biggest problem associated with An-12 operations nowadays is the maintenance and overhaul issue. All major overhaul plants dealing with the type are situated in Russia, which makes it pretty hard for foreign operators – especially military ones – to keep their *Cubs* fit and healthy. One of the opportunities is at Sharjah in the United Arab Emirates; this

The Antarctic expedition of the unique An-12TP-2 (CCCP 04366) in December 1961/February 1962 marked the beginning of the *Cub*'s civil service. (Boris Vdovenko)

is a major cargo hub frequented by Soviet types (including the An-12), and a special maintenance base for these has been set up at Sharjah. One of the most important aspects of the problem is service life extension, considering the aircraft's advanced age (who said 'geriatric airliners'?!). In the mid-1990s the Antonov OKB subjected one of the high-time airframes to fatigue tests; as a result, the type's service life is currently set at 43,000 hours, 16,000 cycles and 40 years.

Most aircraft find their way into museums sooner or later. The Central Russian Air Force Museum in Monino boasts an early-production Irkutsk-built An-12A coded 04 Blue (c/n 8900203); the Kaunas Technical & Aviation Museum has the last-but-one Voronezh-built An-12B, 34 Red (c/n 403112). An Indian Air Force example serialled BL727 (c/n unknown) is preserved in the IAF Museum at Palam AFB. Additionally, demilitarised An-12B CCCP-11355 (c/n 402712) was preserved on a plinth at Magadan's Sokol airport in the later 1970s as a tribute to the sterling service rendered by the type.

Other *Cubs* serve as ground instructional airframes (GIAs) at various educational and training establishments, but these are mostly inaccessible to the aviation enthusiast. For example, the military technical school at Chortkov airbase in the Ukraine had no fewer than five An-12As – CCCP-04363/'01 Blue' (c/n 0901309), '41 Red' (c/n 1901702), '81 Red' (c/n 1901809), '84 Red' (c/n 1901709?) and '85 Red' (c/n 1901804); all of these have now been scrapped. A Tashkent-built An-12A (c/n 2340404) serves as a classroom at the Kiev Civil Aviation Engineers Institute (KIIGA – *Kiyevskiy instritoot inzhenehrov grazhdahnskoy aviahtsii*), while An-12Bs CCCP-11344 No. 1 (c/n 401707) and CCCP-11357 No. 1 (c/n 402802)[63] are GIAs in Krivoy Rog, the Ukraine.

The Irkutsk Military Aviation Technical School (IVATU) has a locally built An-12A coded 23 Blue (c/n 8900404). Another ex Soviet Air Force An-12A, CCCP-11339 No. 1 (c/n 2400505), serves the same purpose at the Samara State Aviation University (SGAU); An-12B CCCP-11351 No. 1 (c/n 401809)[64] is a GIA at the Slavyansk Technical School, Russia.

Thirty years after the beginning of its service career the An-12 still suffered from a fairly high accident rate – for various reasons. Powerplant failures were one; this also accounted for the crashes of several Il-18 airliners which, as the reader remembers, were powered by the same AI-20 engines driving the same AV-68 propellers whose feathering mechanism proved particularly troublesome at first. Between June 1958 and April 1963 alone there were ten major accidents involving Aeroflot An-12s, 30 per cent of which were caused by hardware defects. Percentagewise, though, the number of accidents and total hull losses was far smaller than for the An-8 and An-10. Besides, as the reader will see in Appendix 1, in many cases the aircraft was not to blame – a large proportion of the accidents were caused by human error or simply negligence.

Even though largely supplanted by more modern types, the perennial An-12 still enjoys well-earned respect from the people who fly it. This was clearly demonstrated in 1999 when the Russian peacekeeping forces contingent in Kosovo used *Cubs* along with Il-76MDs.

Cubs on the tabletop

As a point of interest, it may be said that, whereas Soviet combat aircraft are popular with scale modellers (and hence model kit manufacturers), Soviet civil aircraft have never enjoyed the same popularity. Fortunately the tide is beginning to turn and the model kit manufacturers are finally doing justice to Soviet airliners, transports and light aircraft. Thus, after all these years, the *Cub* is fairly well represented on the model kit scene.

The first-ever An-12 kit (to 1/100th scale) was released by the East German company VEB Plastikart (long since dead) in the 1970s. This appallingly inaccurate model has been an out-of-stock item for ages, and though Plastikart has been reborn recently under the ADP Master-Modell brand, the An-12 is unlikely to be reissued.

Available products are: a 1/72nd scale vacuform kit by the Ukrainian company Vacuum Lion (!), though it is pretty hard to find; a fine die-cast model of the An-12BK to the same scale from Roden, another Ukrainian manufacturer; and a reasonably high-quality 1/144th scale die-cast model of the An-12BP (even though the box-top art depicts an An-12BK) from the Chinese company Trumpeter. Another 1/144th scale kit by the Russian company Eastern Express was due to appear at the time of writing.

As for the progenitors of the An-12, a Soviet toy manufacturer used to make a very basic kit of the An-10A to no exact scale in the 1970s; more recently, Vacuum Lion has released a 1/72nd scale version of the An-8.

CHAPTER EIGHT

*Cub*s at Home . . . (CIS Operators)

After the break-up of the Soviet Union and the sole national carrier, Aeroflot An-12s found themselves in several of the new CIS republics, finding new owners. For each republic, operators are listed in alphabetical order, with each airline's two-letter IATA designator (where applicable) and three-letter ICAO designator. Aircraft no longer operated by the respective carrier are shown in italic script in the fleet lists (except in cases when the airline itself no longer exists and *all* of its aircraft have been sold or retired). In the fleet lists, aircraft built in military configuration (with a tail gunner's station) are marked with a (+); those built in commercial configuration are marked with a (−).

Armenia

- An An-12BK with the non-standard registration EK-46741 (c/n 8345408)[65] was operated by an airline called **Aviatek** at an unspecified date.

- In 1998 the same An An-12BK EK-46741 was operated by **Armenian Airlines [R3/RME]**. By 2001 the aircraft had been sold to UAE-based Phoenix Airways, retaining the Armenian registration (see the next chapter).

- **Dvin-Avia Cargo [–/DVN]** based at Yerevan-Erebuni operated seven An-12s.

Registration	Version	C/n	Notes
EK-11028	An-12BK	7345310?	C/n should be 8345310! Bought ?-00
EK-11029	An-12BP (+)	7344908	Demilitarised; ex-RA-11029, bought ?-98
EK-11030	*An-12BP(+)?*	*9346208*	*Reported as An-12BP but may be An-12BK. Ex-Ukrainian Air Force 22 Blue*
EK-11304	An-12A (+)	0901304	Ex-Lasare Air 4L-11304; resold to original owner???
EK-11351	*An-12BP(+)*	*4341910*	*Ex-Ukrainian AF UR-11351, ex CCCP-11351 No. 2*; sold to Ararat-Avia ?-98*
EK-11660	An-12BP (+)	5343209	Bought ?-00
RA-48984	*An-12B(+)*	*402913*	*Leased from Voronezh aircraft factory (VASO) ?-97 to ?-??*

* CCCP-11351 No. 1 was a Voronezh-built An-12B (c/n 401809).

- **Ararat-Avia** purchased An-12BP EK-11351 in mid-1998.

Azerbaijan

- **Azerbaijan Airlines** (AZAL, or Azerbaijan Hava Yollari) **[J2/AHY]** based at Baku-Bina airport operated An-12A 4K-48971 (ex Volga Dnepr Airlines RA-48971, c/n 1340107) around 1995.

- **AZAL Cargo [–/AHC]**, the specialised cargo division of Azerbaijan Airlines established in 1998, briefly leased a demilitarised An-12BK, UK 11418 (ex CCCP-11418 No. 2, c/n 7344705),[66] from Avialeasing in 2000. In September 2001 the airline purchased a single An-12BP (RA-12108, c/n 9346308) from Gromov Air; the aircraft was duly reregistered 4K-AZ18. This aircraft was originally reported (probably in error) as operated by CAC Azerbaijan.

- The Baku-based airline **Imair [IK/ITX]**, a division of the Improtex trading company, operates pasenger and cargo aircraft, mostly leased in other CIS republics as required. These included 'civil' An-12BP 4K-12999 leased from Ural Airlines from December 1995 to 1997 (ex RA-12999, c/n 01347701); the aircraft wore basic Ural Airlines colours with an Azeri flag and Imair titles.

- **Silk Way Airlines** operated two demilitarised An-12BKs registered 4K-AZ21 and 4K-AZ23 (version and c/ns unknown) in August 2002; the registrations were incorrectly painted on as 4KAZ-21 and 4KAZ-23!

- The **Azerbaijan Air Force** operated at least one ex-VTA An-12 registered 4K-12425 (c/n 2401103) and based at Nasosnaya AB near Baku.

Belarus (Belorussia)

- The **Belorussian Air Force** had seven An-12s on strength, operated by the 2nd Squadron of the 50th OSAP; six have been identified so far. Originally based at Lipki AB near Minsk, the unit moved to Machoolischchi AB (also near Minsk) in 1994 and was transformed into the 50th Air Force Base; a second reorganisation took place on 26 March 1996 when the unit became the 50th Transport Air Base. By then only a single *Cub* (12 Yellow) remained with the unit. The aircraft wears the overall grey finish standard for Soviet Air Force An-12s, with faded VVS star insignia and the red/green Belorussian flag (strongly reminiscent of the flag of the former Belorussian Soviet Socialist Republic) aft of the flight deck.

C/n	Version	Tactical code	Notes
4342010	An-12BP (+)	07 Yellow	Code removed by 5-96; sold to Techaviaservice as EW-11368
4342108	An-12BP (+)	08 Yellow	Code removed by 5-96; sold to Techaviaservice as EW-11371
5343109	An-12BP (+)	09 Yellow?	Sold to Techaviaservice as EW-11365
7345210	An-12BP (+)	10 Yellow	Transferred or sold, fate unknown
7345410	An-12BK	11 Yellow	Transferred or sold, fate unknown
00347107	An-12BK	12 Yellow	

- In 1996 the airline **Techaviaservice [–/BTS]** based in Vitebsk acquired three Belorussian Air Force An-12BPs which were registered EW-11365, EW-11368 and EW-11371 (see above). The aircraft were operated for the Russian petroleum company **LUKoil**. EW-11368 crashed near Kalomboloka, Angola, on 26 August 1998.

- An airline called **Wings [–/VGS]** had at least one An-12A, EW-11322 (c/n 0901409).

Georgia

Lasare Air [–/LRE] flew demilitarised An-12A 4L-11304 (c/n 0901304) in 1995–7 before selling it to Dvin Air Cargo as EK-11304. (However, the 2002/03 edition of the JP Airline-Fleets yearbook lists 4L-11304 for Lasare Air as ex-EK-11304!) Later the airline acquired 'military' An-12B 4L-11241 (ex-Russian Air Force RA-11241, c/n 402102); this aircraft was subsequently reregistered 4L-CAA and then leased to Sarit Airlines in October 2000 as ST-SAR.

Kazakstan

- **Avia-Pusk [–/GFR]**, an airline based in Almaty, has a demilitarised An-12BP registered UN 11001 (c/n 5343408).

- **Ak-Kanat [–/KAN],** another airline from Almaty, operated ex-Kazakstan Air Force An-12BP UN 11373 (c/n 02348304) and An-12B UN 11374 (c/n 3341501) in 1999.

- **GST Aero** (Gulf Sand Tours Cargo) **[–/BMK]** owns An-12BP UN-11002 (ex Magadanaerogrooz RA-11002, c/n 5343703).

- The **Kazakstan Air Force** operated a number of *Cubs*. Known aircraft are listed below.

Registration/ tactical code	Version	C/n	Notes
UN 11367	An-12B (+)	3341201	Ex-Soviet Air Force '11 Blue'; basic Aeroflot c/s with Kazakstan titles
UN 11373	An-12BP (+)	02348304	Sold or leased to Ak-Kanat in 1999
UN 11374	An-12B (+)	3341501	Sold or leased to Ak-Kanat in 1999
CCCP-11377	An-12B (+)	?	
UN 11395	An-12B (+)	402508	Basic Aeroflot c/s with Kazakstan titles
08 Blue	An-12A (+)	1340209	
12 Red	An-12B (+)	402212	
19 Red	An-12B (+)	3340905	
79 Red	An-12BP (+)	5342909	

- **Varty Pacific Airlines [–/MDO]** based in Almaty and Karaganda operated two An-12s – 'military' An-12BP UN 11005 (c/n unknown) and 'civil' An-12BP UN 11006 (ex Tyumen' Airlines RA-12960, c/n 9346602).[67] The latter aircraft was sold to Inter Trans Avia in December 2001, becoming EX-12960

- Yet another An-12 registered UN 11006 (c/n unknown) appeared in August 2002; its operator was likewise unknown at the time of writing.

Kyrghyzstan

- **Inter Trans Avia Ltd [YS/ITD]** based at Bishkek-Manas operates a single 'civil' An-12BP, EX-12960 (ex-Varty Pacific Airlines UN 11006, c/n 9346602).

- The fleet of **KAS Air Company [KW/KSD]**, also based at Manas airport, likewise consists of just one *Cub* – 'military' An-12BP EX-11001 (c/n 6344104).[68]

- An-12BK EX-46741 belonging to an unknown airline was seen at Nairobi-Jomo Kenyatta airport on 29 March 2002. This is in all probability ex-Phoenix Airways EK-46741 (c/n 8345408).

Moldova

- **Aerocom [–/MCC]**, an airline based in Kishinyov (Chişiňau), operated five An-12s.

Registration	Version	C/n	Notes
ER-ACI	An-12BP (+)	6343707	Ex-ICAR Airlines UR-PWH, bought ?-99
ER-ACP	An-12B (+)	3341108	Ex-DQ-FBS, bought ?-01, named 'July Morning'
ER-ADE	An-12A (+)	2340503	Ex-D2-FCU, bought ?-00
ER-ADT	An-12A (+)	2340605	Ex-Renan, bought ?-98. Crashed Honiara 16-10-01
ER-AXA	An-12BP (–)	01347907	Ex-Avial-NV RA-11112 (or ex-Bright Aviation Services LZ-BRW?), bought 2-02. Operated for Air Bridge Group

- **Mikma [–/ITL]**, the flying division of an electronics industry enterprise, operated ten An-12s. In 2000 the airline changed its name to **Tiramavia [–/TVI]**.

Looking very weathered, Varty Pacific Airlines 'military' An-12B UN 11005 is seen at Sharjah, UAE, in March 2002. The AI-20 turboprops are characterised by a very smoky efflux, and the An-12's rear fuselage soon gets covered in soot, rendering the registration all but illegible (the problem is especially acute on the port side). For this reason some An-12 operators have taken to painting the registration on the tail. (Nikolay Ionkin)

Registration	Version	C/n	Notes
ER-ACA	An-12BP (+?)	00347102	Ex-Soviet Air Force? Bought ?-00
ER-ACB	An-12A (+)	2340608	Ex-Soviet Air Force, code unknown
ER-ACD*	An-12B (+)	402605	Ex-Algerian Air Force 7T-WAC/514, bought ?-95. Sold to ALADA by 1998 as D2-FAW
ER-ACE*	An-12B (+)	402812	Ex-Algerian Air Force 7T-WAG/591, bought ?-95. Lst Aerotropical, Lda; shot down Lukapa, Angola, 27-2-96
ER-ACG	An-12BP (−)	9346504	Ex-Special Cargo Airlines RA-12972. Sold to Congo Brazzaville as TN-AGK No. 1
ER-ACH	An-12BP (+)	4342209	Ex-Slovak Air Force 2209 Black. Sold to unknown operator by 9-01
ER-ACJ	An-12BP (−)	01347909	Ex-National Commuter Airlines D2-FDC, bought by 5-01. Sold to Space Cargo, Inc ?-01 as 3C-QRI
ER-ADL	An-12BP (+)	4342610	Ex-D2-FBD. Crashed Monrovia 15-2-02
ER-ADM	An-12BP (+)	5343405	Ex-NAPO-Aviatrans RA-12388. Sold or retired by 1-01
ER-ADN	An-12B (+)	3341606	Ex-NAPO-Aviatrans RA-11328, bought ?-99

* ER-ACD and ER-ACE were reported for Velocity Airlines in some sources.

- **Renan [–/RAN]** had three An-12s.

Registration	Version	C/n	Notes
ER-ACK	An-12BP (−)	8345503	Ex-Ural Airlines RA-12952. Sold to Burundi ?-00 as 9U-BHO

| ER-ADD | An-12A (+) | 2340403 | Ex-CCCP-11961. Also reported as An-12B (+) c/n 2340803! |
| ER-ADT | An-12AP (+) | 2340605 | Ex-RA-11382. Also reported as ER-ADI; opf Air Bridge Group. Sold to Aerocom |

- **Valan Internatinal Cargo Charter Ltd [–/VLN]** acquired a single An-12BK, ER-AXC (former tactical code unknown, c/n 7345209), in 2001.

- A *Cub* registered ER-ACT (version and c/n unknown) was reported for an unidentified operator in 1999.

Russia

- **Aerofreight Airlines** (alias **Aerofrakht**) **[–/FRT]** founded in 1998 operated seven An-12s.

Registration	Version	C/n	Notes
RA-11115	An-12BP (−)	01348003	Lsf Aeroflot-Don; basic Aeroflot c/s, Aeroflot-Don logo/Aerofreight Airlines titles
RA-11116	An-12BP (−)	01348006	Ex-Baikal Airlines
RA-11124	An-12BP (−)	02348106	Ex-Baikal Airlines
RA-11408	An-12B (+)	3341209	Ex-Aviaobschchemash, full c/s
RA-11529	An-12BP (+)	6344109	Leased from Aviastar, basic Aviastar c/s
RA-12974	An-12BP (−)	9346506	Leased from Aeroflot-Don
RA-12992	An-12BP (−)	00347306	Ex-Avial-NV, bought ?-02
RA-12994	An-12BP (−)	00347401	Leased from Aeroflot-Don by 8-01
RA-48984	An-12B (+)	402913	Ex-Ukraine Air Alliance UR-48984

CUBS AT HOME... (CIS OPERATORS)

Anonymous-looking 'civil' An-12BP ER-ACJ of Tiramavia (c/n 01347909) sits under threatening skies at Sharjah in company with at least two sister ships on 2 March 2002; Sharjah is a regular watering hole for CIS types. The aircraft retains the basic colours of its previous owner, the Angolan carrier National Commuter Airlines, with which it flew as D2-FDC. (Nikolay Ionkin)

Aerofreight Airlines had quite a large fleet of An-12s but only one of them, An-12B RA-11408 (c/n 3341209), wore this smart blue/white colour scheme. (Dmitriy Petrochenko)

- **Aero-Nika** leased 'military' An-12A RA-11790 (c/n 1400302) from the Yermolino Flight Test & Research Enterprise on 11 September 1994. Unfortunately the aircraft crashed in Ust-Ilimsk on 29 October that year.

- An airline called **Airstars** (or, in Russian, **Aerostars**) [–/ASE] leased An-12BK RA-13392 (c/n 00347210) from KAPO-Avia (see below) in June 2001. The aircraft was in basic KAPO-Avia colours with Airstars (to port)/Aerostars (to starboard) titles.

- An airline called **Alfa 92** operated An-12BP RA-11311 (c/n unknown) in 1996.

- **Amuraviatrans** [–/AAX], the flying division of the Amur Shipbuilding Plant in Komsomolsk-on-Amur operated five An-12s.

Registration	Version	C/n	Notes
RA-11813	An-12B (+)	3340908	
RA-11831	An-12B (+)	3341206	Sold to Southern Cross ?-97 as 3D-ASC
RA-11886	An-12A (+)	2340302	
RA-11890	An-12B (+)	3340909	Sold to Special Cargo Airlines 16-8-97
RA-13341	An-12BP (+)	9346904	Demilitarised. Sold to Solis Aviation ?-01 as LZ-SAA

- **Antares Air** [–/ANH] bought demilitarised An-12BP RA-11013 (c/n 6344002) from KiT in 1995, operating it in basic Aeroflot colours with no titles or logo. On 14 August 1996 the aircraft was cancelled from the Russian register and sold to São Tomé & Principe, becoming S9-CAN on 13 October 1997.

- **Antey** [–/**TEY**], the flying division of the Omsk 'Polyot' Aircraft Production Association (OAPO – **Om**skoye aviatsionnoye proizvodstvennoye obyedineniye 'Po**lyot**', ex MAP Aircraft Factory No. 166), had seven An-12s. The plant performs An-2 to An-3 conversions, manufactures the An-74 Coaler STOL transport and is to build the An-70 heavy STOL transport.

Registration	Version	C/n	Notes
RA-11301	An-12PP	00347107	Ex-Ukrainian AF '71 Red', converted to freighter. Sold to Inter Trans Air as LZ-ITD
RA-11302	An-12BP (+)	8346004	Demilitarised. Crashed Colombo 24-3-00
RA-11303	An-12BK	00347604	Sold to Veteran Airlines
RA-11367*	An-12BP (+)	8345607	
RA-11368**	An-12BP (+)	8346006	Sold to Inter Trans Air ?-00 as LZ-ITB
RA-11369***	An-12BP (+)	00346909	
RA-11665	An-12BP (+)	6343903	

* The registration was originally worn by demilitarised An-12B CCCP-11367 (c/n 402901) and – concurrently with RA-11367 – by 'military' An-12B UN 11367 (c/n 3341201)!

** The registration was previously worn by An-12B CCCP-11368 with unknown c/n and An-12BP EW-11368 (c/n 4342010).

*** The registration was concurrently worn by demilitarised An-12BP UK 11369 (c/n 6343810)!

- The **Arsenyev 'Progress' Aircraft Production Association** (AAPO – **A**rsen'yevskoye aviatsionnoye proizvodstvennoye obyedineniye '**P**rogress', ex MAP Aircraft Factory No. 116), had two 'military' An-12BPs – RA-11650 (ex-CCCP-11650 No. 2, ex-Iraqi Air Force I.A.F.685, c/n 6344305) and RA-98102 (ex-CCCP-98102 No. 2, c/n 5343005).[69] Both were eventually sold to Gromov Air (see below). The plant manufactured the Mil Mi-24 Hind attack helicopter; now it builds the Mi-34 Hermit light utility helicopter and the Kamov Ka-50 Black Shark (Hokum-A) attack helicopter.

An-12BP RA-69314 (c/n 5343004), one of two to wear the full colours of Aviastar, resting between flights at Moscow-Domodedovo on 3 November 1998. Note the aircraft type painted boldly on the tail. (Dmitriy Komissarov)

- **Atlant-Soyuz Airlines [3G/AYZ]**, established on 8 June 1993, operate scheduled and charter passenger and cargo services from Moscow (Sheremetyevo-2 and Domodedovo) and Chkalovskaya AB, mostly with aircraft leased from other carriers and the Russian, Belorussian and Ukrainian air forces as required. These include numerous *Cubs* which come and go, so to say.

Atlant-Soyuz is known as 'the Moscow Government airline' (!) – for more than one reason. Firstly, the Moscow government has a stake in the airline; secondly, Moscow Mayor Yuriy M. Luzhkov and other government officials, including then State Duma Chairman Ghennadiy N. Seleznyov, often made use of the airline's aircraft during trips in Russia and abroad. Hence some Atlant-Soyuz aircraft wear additional Cyrillic *Aviakompahniya pravitel'stva Moskvy* titles, much to the amusement of spotters.

Registration	Version	C/n	Notes
RA-11049	An-12BP (+)	8346109	Demilitarised. Lsf Yermolino Flight Test & Research Enterprise
RA-11113	An-12BP (−)	01347908	Ex-CCCP-11113 No. 2.* Derelict Moscow-Vnukovo by 8-01
RA-11125	An-12B (+)	3341006	Demilitarised, Aeroflot polar c/s. Lsf Komsomolsk-on-Amur Aviation Production Association 1996
RA-11356	An-12BP (+)	7345206	Lsf Yermolino Flight Test & Research Enterprise 3-99
RA-11516	An-12BP (+)	4341909	Lsf Yermolino Flight Test & Research Enterprise 1997
RA-11666?	An-12BP (+)	?	Seen Luxembourg 9-01; registration confirmed but operator unconfirmed!
RA-11916	An-12AP (+)	2400901	Lsf Yermolino Flight Test & Research Enterprise 1997. Basic Aeroflot colours, no titles
RA-12984	An-12BP (−)	00347109	Lsf Magadanavialeasing 1998. Ex-Magadanaerogrooz; white overall, MAG Cargo Services (Magadanaerogrooz) stickers

* CCCP-11113 No. 1 was a grey-painted 'military' An-12BP.

- **Avia (Yuriy Petrov's Airline) [–/AWL]** based at Novosibirsk-Tolmachovo operated 'civil' An-12BP RA-11122 (c/n 02348104) and 'civil' An-12A RA-11131 (c/n 2400702) purchased from Klyuch-Avia. Despite lacking a tail-gunner's station, the latter aircraft was originally a military communications relay version with an extra APU in the aft fuselage.

- **Aviacor [–/VCR]**, the flying division of the Samara aircraft factory of the same name, operated two 'civil' *Cubs* – An-12BP RA-11110 (ex CCCP-11110 No. 2, c/n 01347902)[70] and An-12B RA-11117 (c/n 5402707) from Samara-Bezymyanka airfield. The former aircraft was written off in a landing accident at El Fasmer, Sudan, on 7 August 1993; the other one was sold to Etele Air by October 1998.

- Starting in 1992, the Moscow cargo airline **Avial Aviation Company Ltd [–/RLC]** operating from Domodedovo, Sheremetyevo-1 and Zhukovskiy operated eight An-12s. In 2000 the name was changed to **Avial-NV**.

Registration	Version	C/n	Notes
RA-11112	An-12BP (−)	01347907	Ex-Tyumen Airlines. White overall, no titles. Sold to Aerocom 2-02 as ER-AXA
RA-11128*	An-12BP (−)	02348203	Ex-Tyumen Airlines; full c/s
RA-11324*	An-12B (+)	2340805	Demilitarised, full c/s. Leased to Eurasia Airlines ?-02
RA-11339	An-12BP (+)	6344310	Ex-Penza Air Enterprise; ex-CCCP-11339 No. 2.** Demilitarised, full c/s. Leased to Eurasia Airlines ?-02
RA-11345	An-12B (+)	401801	Ex-Sakha Avia. Demilitarised, full c/s
RA-11766	An-12B (+)	401605	Lst/jointly operated with East Line (1998); basic Aeroflot colours, large East Line titles; sold to Etele Air ?-00
RA-11899*	An-12B (−)	402601	Full c/s; sold or retired by 2002
RA-12992	An-12BP (−)	00347306	Lst/jointly operated with East Line (1998); basic Aeroflot colours, no titles; sold to Aerofreight Airlines by 2002

* Aircraft thus marked originally wore full livery with Avial titles (without the 'NV' suffix).
** CCCP-11339 No. 1 was a Voronezh-built An-12A (c/n 2400505).

- The Troitsk-based cargo carrier **Aviaobschchemash [–/OBM]**, also referred to as **AOM Air Company** (not to be confused with the French AOM – Air Outre Mer), operated eight An-12s in Aeroflot colours. As the name implies, Aviaobschchemash is the flying division of the former Ministry of General Machinery (Minobschchemash).

Registration	Version	C/n	Notes
RA-11327	An-12A (+)	1400104	Ex-Russian Air Force. Damaged Bryansk 8-11-97
RA-11408	An-12B (+)	4341209	Blue/white tail. Sold to Aerofreight Airlines ?-00
RA-11532	An-12B (+)	402007	
RA-11756	An-12BP (+)	4342208	Sold to Aviast
RA-11795	An-12A (+)	8900704	Ex-CCCP-11795 No. 2*
RA-11830	An-12B (+)	4342210	
RA-11851	An-12TB (+)	402003	Crashed Nizhnevartovsk 2-11-96
RA-98116	An-12A (+)	9901101	

* CCCP-11795 No. 1 was a demilitarised An-12A (c/n 1400103) which crashed on 25 March 1986.

- **Aviaprima Sochi Airlines [J5/PRL]** briefly leased 'civil' An-12BP RA-11959 from Samara Airlines in May 1994.

- An airline called **Aviast [–/VVA]** owns two 'military' An 12BPs – RA-11756 (ex-Aviaobschchemash, c/n 4342208) and RA-11962 (ex-Trans Aero Samara, c/n 5343007). The latter aircraft is demilitarised and wears full Aviast livery, while RA-11756 has a grey/white colour scheme. In 2001 they were joined by An-12BP RA-69314 leased from Aviastar (see below).

- The fleet of the **Aviastar Joint-Stock Company [–/FUE]** includes two 'military' An-12BPs – RA-11529 (c/n 6344109) and RA-69314 (c/n 5343004); the former aircraft is leased to Aerofreight Airlines. Aviastar is the post-Soviet name of the Ulyanovsk Aircraft Production Complex (UAPK – *Ool'yahnovskiy aviatsionnyy proizvodstvennyy kompleks*) building the An-124 Ruslan (*Condor*) heavy transport and the Tu-204 medium-range airliner.

- **Aviatrans Cargo Airlines [V8/VAS]** established in 1992 (formerly the 201st Flight of MAP's Moscow UFD) operated eight *Cubs* from Moscow-Domodedovo and Moscow-Myachkovo. On 1 January 1997 the airline was renamed **Atran – Aviatrans Cargo Airlines**.

Registration	Version	C/n	Notes
RA-11868	An-12BK	9346310	Full c/s
RA-11901	An-12A (+)	1340103	Basic Aeroflot c/s; WFU Myachkovo by 8-98, used for spares
RA-12990	An-12BP (−)	003437304	Full c/s
RA-93912	An-12B (+)	4341709	Full c/s
RA-93913	An-12BP (+)	4342609	Full c/s, c/n falsely painted on as 3442609!!!; lst Miras Air by 8-02
RA-93915	An-12B (+)	4342103	Full c/s, c/n falsely painted on as 4132103!!!; lst Miras Air by 8-02
RA-98117	An-12B (+)	402301	Leased to Sakhaviatrans
RA-98118	An-12BP (+)	6344304	Demilitarised. Basic Aeroflot c/s. Leased to Sakhaviatrans

- **Baikal Airlines [X3/BKL]**, alias Baikalavia, was the successor of the East Siberian CAD's Irkutsk UFD. Its fleet included six An-12s. The airline's financial position was shaky in the late 1990s and plans of a merger with Chita-Avia in the hope of improving things were announced in April 1998. However, the 17 August 1998 bank crisis ruined these plans and Baikal Airlines filed for bankruptcy in September. Operations were restarted on a small scale in the spring of 1999 but the company terminally vanished soon afterwards; the fate of its aircraft is mostly unknown.

Registration	Version	C/n	Notes
RA-11032	An-12BP (−)	7345004	
RA-11034	An-12BP (−)	7345010	
RA-11116	An-12BP (−)	01348006	Sold to Aerofreight Airlines
RA-11124	An-12BP (−)	02348106	Sold to Aerofreight Airlines
RA-11996	An-12B (+)	402504	
RA-12988	An-12BP (−)	00347206	Basic Aeroflot colours, no titles. Sold to Flight JSC

- **CNG Transavia [–/CGT]** based in Voronezh has An-12BK RA-98103 (c/n 00347003) and 'military' An-12BP RA-98119 (c/n 7344801). Both have been leased to Sharjah-based subsidiary KNG Transavia Cargo as 3C-AAL and 3C-AAG respectively.

- The **Chelyabinsk Air Enterprise** (*Chelyabinskoye aviapredpriyahtiye*) **[H6/CHB]**, formerly Chelal (Chelyabinsk Airlines), operated a single 'civil' An-12BP (RA-12987, c/n 00347202) in basic Aeroflot polar colours without titles but with the old Chelal 'bird' nose logo. The aircraft was sold to ALADA as D2-FRG in July 1998.

- What's in a name? Moscow-based **Dobrolyot [–/DOB]** is an airline with a famous name. The original Dobrolyot was a passenger carrier, the precursor of Aeroflot, and ceased operations in 1922. Reborn 70 years later as a cargo airline, the new Dobrolyot was the flying division of the Soyuz Production Association (NSA Soyuz), an aerospace industry company. Its fleet included An-12B RA-11240 (c/n 402706).

- **Donavia Joint-Stock Company** (*Donskiye avialinii* – Don Airlines) **[D9/DNV]** was established in August 1993 as the successor of the North Caucasian CAD/Rostov-on-Don UFD. Its fleet included five late-production 'civil' An-12BPs. In 1998 the debt-ridden airline came under outside management and, after a period of negotiations with Aeroflot Russian Airlines, was absorbed as the Rostov division, changing its name to **Aeroflot-Don** in 2000.

Registration	C/n	Notes
RA-11115	01348003	Full colour scheme. Leased to Aerofreight Airlines
RA-12960	9346602	*Full colour scheme. Sold to Varty Pacific as UN 11006*
RA-12965	9346409	Leased to Fresh Air Cargo 5-01 as 5N-BCN
RA-12974	9346506	
RA-12994	00347401	

- **East Line [P7/ESL]** was established at Moscow-Domodedovo in 1993, initially operating cargo charters with a single Il-76TD. Since then it has grown into a major airline with cargo services to Belgium, China, Greece, India, Italy, South Korea, Pakistan, Turkey and the UAE; passenger services were added later. Until recently the carrier had no fleet of its own, and the An-12s it operates are leased from other airlines as required – often in the owner's colours with East Line titles.

Registration	Version	C/n	Notes
RA-11112	An-12BP(−)	01347907	Lsf/jointly operated with Avial (1998); white overall, partial UN titles
RA-11766	An-12B (+)	401605	Lsf/jointly operated with Avial (1998); basic Aeroflot c/s, large East Line titles
RA-12992	An-12BP(−)	00347306	Leased from/jointly operated with Avial (1998); basic Aeroflot colours, no titles
RA-13392	An-12BK	00347210	Leased from KAPO-Avia, basic KAPO colours, East Line titles
UR-BWM	An-12BK	00347004	Demilitarised. Leased from Volare Aviation Enterprise, returned by 5-02
UR-LAI	An-12BP(−)	8345505	Lsf Volare Aviation Enterprise by 11-99; basic Volare colours, East Line titles

East Line operated Cubs on short-term leases as required. This is An-12B RA-11766 (c/n 401605) leased from Tyumen' Airlines, also pictured at Moscow-Domodedovo on 3 November 1998. (Dmitriy Komissarov)

UR-LIP	An-12BK	9346405	Lsf Volare Aviation Enterprise by 11-99; basic Volare colours, East Line titles
UR-SVG	An-12BP(+)	4342309	Demilitarised. Leased from Volare Aviation Enterprise by 11-99, returned by 10-01; basic Volare colours, East Line titles, Russian flag

- **Elf Air [E6/EFR]**,[71] the commercial flying division of avionics designer NPO Vzlyot, operates a mixed bag of passenger and cargo aircraft from Zhukovskiy, including grey-painted 'military' An-12A RA-13321 (c/n 2340301), a former avionics testbed. The aircraft retained the overall grey finish and Aeroflot titles it had worn when operated by the Soviet Air Force. It was retired in 1997.

- **Etele Air [–/ETO]** bought 'civil' An-12B RA-11117 (c/n 5402707) from the defunct Aviacor in 1998. In 2000 it was joined by demilitarised An-12B RA-11766 (c/n 401605) purchased from Avial-NV; unlike RA-11117 which retains the basic Aviacor colour scheme, this aircraft wears all-white UN World Food Programme colours.

- **Eurasia Airlines [UH/EUS]** based at Moscow-Vnukovo leased An-12BPs RA-11324 and RA-11339 from Avial-NV in the spring of 2002.

- The **Exparc [–/EPA]** 'airline' was formed in 1992 for providing logistical support of the Russian polar research stations under the EksPArk programme (*Ekspeditsiya "Parashooty nad Arktikoy"* – 'Parachutes over the Arctic' Expedition) so as not to depend on the Air Force or GosNII GA from which aircraft had to be leased. Apart from two Il-76TDs of its own, it briefly leased 'military' An-12A RA-11734 (c/n 2340809) from the Russian Air Force and An-12B RA-11892 (c/n 402501) from Sakha Avia in 1994.

- **Far Eastern Cargo Airlines** (*Dahl'nevostochnyye groozovyye avialinii*) [–/FEW] based in Khabarovsk leased An-12s from other carriers as required.

- **Flight Joint-Stock Co.** (*Aviakompahniya Flaït*) [–/FLV] based at Astrakhan-Narimanovo had two Cubs – ex-SPAir demilitarised An-12BP RA-11003 (c/n 5343704) and ex-Baikalavia 'civil' An-12BP RA-12988 (c/n 00347206). The former aircraft was sold to Air West in 1998 as ST-AWM.

- The **Flight Research Institute named after M.M. Gromov (LII)** in Zhukovskiy operated a variety of Cubs – both as testbeds and for regular transport duties. The transport-configured aircraft were operated by LII's own airline, **Volare Air Transport Company** (*Aviatrahnsportnaya kompahniya Volare*) [OP/VLR] founded in 1992.[72] In 1997 this ceased operations[73] and the aircraft were transferred to LII's new airline, **Gromov Air [–/LII, later –/GAI]**.

An-12B RA-11117 (c/n 5402707), one of two owned by Etele Air, shortly after arriving at Moscow-Domodedovo on 18 November 1998. The blue/white colour scheme was inherited from Aviacor which previously operated the aircraft. (Dmitriy Komissarov)

Registration	Version	C/n	Notes
RA-11650	An-12BP (+)	6344305	Ex-BF Cargo LG-BFG, ex-LZ-BAG, ex-RA-11650, ex-CCCP-11650 No. 2, ex-Iraqi Air Force I.A.F.685; all-white c/s
RA-11813	An-12B (+)	3340908	Basic Aeroflot polar c/s
RA-12108	An-12TBK	9346308	Ex-BF Cargo LZ-BFE, all-white c/s; sold to AZAL Cargo 9-01 as 4K-AZ18
RA-13331	An-12BK	6344510	Ex-10 Red, ex-CCCP-48974 No. 2, former de-icing systems testbed; grey c/s, no titles. Sold to Start in 1994
RA-98102	An-12BP (+)	5343005	Demilitarised. Ex-BF Cargo LZ-BFD, ex-CCCP-98102 No. 2, ex-Soviet AF '29 Blue'; basic Aeroflot polar c/s
43 Red	An-12BK	8345902	An-12M-LL ejection seat/APU testbed

• **GosNII GA** (the State Civil Aviation Research Institute at Moscow/Sheremetyevo-1) [–/ISP] had one 'civil' An-12BP (RA-11101, c/n 01347703) and two demilitarised 'BPs – RA-11530 (c/n 6344503) and RA-11531 (c/n 6344506) which were former An-12 Tsiklon 'storm chasers'. The aircraft were operated jointly with the **Flight-Chernobyl Association** (*Polyot-Chernobyl'*) [–/FCH] in Aeroflot colours. RA-11101 crashed in Lukapa, Angola, on 6 October 1996; RA-11531 was sold to Air Nacoia as D2-FVG No. 1 in the same year; the fate of the third aircraft is unknown.

• **Impulse-Aero** [–/IMR] based at Moscow/Vnukovo-3 had a single An-12BK with the non-standard registration RA-13357 (c/n 8345604). The aircraft was sold to Air Ukraine in 1996 to become UR-11314.

• **Irkut-Avia** [–/UTK], the flying division of the Irkutsk Aircraft Production Association (IAPO – *Irkootskoye aviatsionnoye proizvodstvennoye obyedineniye*), had four ex-VTA *Cubs* – An-12BP RA-11309 (c/n 00347510), An-12BP RA-11310 (c/n 4342601), An-12B RA-12162 (ex CCCP-12162 No. 2, c/n 3341509)[74] and An-12BP RA-13391 (c/n 5342805). At least one of them wears an eye-catching three-tone blue/white livery.

• **KAPO** [–/KAO] (*Kazahnskoye aviatsionnoye proizvodstvennoye obyedineniye imeni S. P. Gorboonova* – Kazan Aircraft Production Association named after Sergey Petrovich Gorboonov (MAP Aircraft Factory No. 22) which builds the Tupolev Tu-22M *Backfire* and Tu-160 *Blackjack* bombers, the Tu-214 medium-haul airliner and is set to build the Tu-324 short-haul airliner and Tu-330 civil/military medium transport), has a single demilitarised An-12BK re-equipped with an ROZ-1 radar. Registered RA-13392 (c/n 00347210), the aircraft wears the smart house colours of blue and white; it was leased to Aerostars at the time of writing.

- The fleet of **KiT Air** (*Kosmos i Trahnsport* – Space & Transport), a division of the Omsk 'Polyot' (Flight) Production Association (in the days when it was an MOM enterprise before resuming aircraft production), included demilitarised An-12BP RA-11013 (c/n 6344002). 'Kit' is Russian for 'whale', and the airline's logo depicted exactly that. The aircraft was sold to Antares Air in 1995.

- The Samara-based airline **Klyuch-Avia** ('Key-Avia') had a single 'civil' An-12A, RA-11131 (c/n 2400702) which was operated for the Samara Metal Works. It was sold to Yuriy Petrov's Airline in 1996.

- **KnAAPO [–/KNM]** (*Koms mol'skoye-na-Amoore aviatsionnoye proizvodstvennoye obyedineniye imeni Yu. A. Gagarina* – Komsomolsk-on-Amur Aircraft Production Association named after Yuriy Alekseyevich Gagarin), which produces single-seat versions of the Su-27 *Flanker* tactical fighter, the Beriyev Be-103 six-seat general-purpose amphibian and the Sukhoi Su-80 utility aircraft, has four An-12s.

Registration	Version	C/n	Notes
RA-11125	An-12B (+)	3341006	Demilitarised
RA-11230	An-12BP (+)	5342708	Ex-BF Cargo LZ-BFA
RA-11789	An-12BP (+)	6343905	Ex-BF Cargo LZ-BFB. Demilitarised, blue/white tail, KnAAPO badge on nose, no titles
RA-48978	An-12PP	9346410	Converted to freighter. Basic Aeroflot colours, KnAAPO badge on nose, no titles

- **Komiavia [–/KMA]** (to be specific, the airline's main division in Syktyvkar), later renamed **Komiaviatrans**, operated a number of An-12s. After the reorganisation of the airline in 1998 these were transferred to the Syktyvkar-based **Komiinteravia [8J/KMV]**, a sister company established in 1996, along with all other heavy fixed-wing aircraft. At the time of writing, all the *Cubs* have been sold off.

Registration	Version	C/n	Notes
RA-11114	An-12B (–)	01347909	Sold to Special Cargo Airlines ?-99
RA-11375	An-12TB (+)	402405	Demilitarised. Crashed Slavgorod 20-8-93
RA-11526	An-12B (–)	02348207	Sold to Angola as D2-FDB
RA-12972	An-12BP (–)	9346504	Sold to Special Cargo Airlines

- The charter airline **Korsar [6K/KRS]** based at Moscow/Vnukovo-3 operated two demilitarised *Cubs* – An-12B RA-11008 (c/n 402612) and An-12TB RA-11025 (c/n 6344103) – on lease from NPO Energiya, the corporation responsible, among other things, for the Buran (Snowstorm) space shuttle. The aircraft flew in Aeroflot colours – which was probably just as well, because Korsar's own livery was singularly uninspiring. *Korsar* means 'corsair' in Russian, but the airline's name has nothing to do with pirates; it is derived from the names of its founders, Korovin and Sarzhveladze. RA-11008 was written off in a landing accident at Huambo, Angola, on 22 November 1995.

- By mid-1996 RA-11025 had been transferred to **Kosmos Aircompany [–/KSM]**, a division of NPO Energiya based at Vnukovo-3, and received a stylish livery with a red/white/blue cheatline and a blue tail featuring a Planet-Earth-cum-orbiting-satellite tail logo. (Some observers have dubbed this colour scheme 'Milky Way', though the 'candy bar' allusion is rather questionable!) By September 2001 it was joined by 'civil' An-12BP RA-12957 (c/n 8345508) which combines a red Aeroflot 'polar' cheatline with Kosmos tail colours and titles.

- **Kumertau Express**, the flying division of the Kumertau Aircraft Production Enterprise (KumAPP) manufacturing the Kamov Ka-27/Ka-32 *Helix* and Ka-226 helicopters, owned demilitarised An-12A RA-48970 (c/n 2400502). The aircraft was leased to BF Cargo in 1994-96, wearing the Bulgarian registration LZ-BFC for most of this period; later it was returned and operated by Kumertau Express until sold to the Yermolino Flight Test and Research Enterprise in 1998.

- **Magadanaerogrooz** (=Magadan Air Cargo, or Magadan Cargo Airlines) **[–/MGG]** operated seven An-12s until it went out of business in 1998.

Registration	Version	C/n	Notes
RA-11002	An-12BP (+?)	5343703	Sold to GST-Aero ?-01 as UN 11002
RA-11102	An-12BP (–)	01347704	Sold to British Gulf International Airlines 12-00 as S9-BOS
RA-11106	An-12BP (–)	01347808	C/n also reported as 01347802
RA-11113	An-12BP (–)	01347908	
RA-11366	An-12B (+)	402808	Demilitarised. Leased to CAT Cargo as TC-KET 3-8-94, never returned
RA-11986	An-12B (+)	401901	Sold to Angola as D2-FCV
RA-12984	An-12BP (–)	00347109	Sold to Magadanavialeasing

- The leasing company **Magadanavialeasing [–/MLZ]** took over the fleet of the bankrupt Magadanaerogrooz, including RA-12984 which it leased to Atlant-Soyuz.

- **Moscow Airways** (*Moskovskiye avialinii*) **[M8/MSC]**, established in 1991 and based at Sheremetyevo-2, owned a single demilitarised An-12A, RA-11318 (c/n 401908). In 1996 the airline had its licence revoked because of unsatisfactory operational standards.[75] The *Cub* was sold to the Angolan carrier von Haaf Air as D2-FVG No. 2 (see the next chapter) and the flight code was reallocated to start up Med Airlines, SpA [M8/MDS] of Palermo, Italy.

- **Mostransgaz**, one of the natural gas industry's (initially) many flying divisions, operated demilitarised An-12AP RA-12188 (c/n 1400106) in a striking blue/white colour scheme. In 1997 the airline was absorbed by **Gazpromavia Ltd [–/GZP]**, the flying division of the powerful Gazprom corporation; two years later the *Cub* was sold to United Arabian Co., Sudan, as ST-AQE.

- **NAPO-Aviatrans** [–/NPO], the flying division of NAPO (*Novosibeerskoye aviatsionnoye proizvodstvennoye obyedineniye imeni V. P. Chkalova* – Novosibisk Aircraft Production Association named after Valeriy Pavlovich Chkalov) which produces the Su-34 fighter, the An-38 regional airliner and is set to build the Su-49 new-generation primary trainer, had six *Cubs*.

Registration	Version	C/n	Notes
RA-11328	An-12B (+)	3341606	Ex-Soviet Air Force '23 Red'. Sold to Mikma ?-99 as ER-ADN
RA-12192	An-12BP (+)	5343305	
RA-12193	An-12BK	9346805	
RA-12194	An-12BK	00347203	
RA-12195	An-12BK	00347410	
RA-12388	An-12BP (+)	5343405	Sold to Mikma ?-99 as ER-ADM

- The **Norilsk Air Enterprise** (*Noril'skoye aviapredpriyahtiye*), the successor of the Krasnoyarsk CAD/Norilsk UFD, has five An-12s.

Registration	Version	C/n	Notes
RA-11100	An-12BP (–)	01347702	Also reported as an An-12TB
RA-11816	An-12B (+)	3341003	
RA-11906	An-12AP (+)	2340802	
RA-11989	An-12B (+)	401910	
RA-12981	An-12BP (–?)	00347104	

- **Petrolada**, an airline based in Petrozavodsk, had a single 'military' An-12A registered RA-12187 (c/n 1340201). The aircraft was damaged in a landing accident in Lensk on 19 December 1993.

- **Aviakompaniya Pilot** ('Pilot Airlines') [–/PIL] based in Krasnodar operated three An-12s.

Registration	Version	C/n	Notes
RA-11038	An-12B (+)	2340709	Demilitarised. Ex-ELINT aircraft. Leased to AntonAir International ?-97 as 7P-ANA
RA-11760	An-12BP	4342404	Leased to AntonAir International ?-97 as 7P-ANB
RA-11658	An-12BP	9346608	Leased to AntonAir International ?-97 as 7P-ANC

- The **Penza Air Enterprise** [–/PNZ] had three 'military' *Cubs* – An-12Bs RA-11337 (c/n 3341204), RA-11338 (c/n 3341506) and An-12BP RA-11339 (c/n 6344310). The former aircraft crashed on approach to Baku on 14 March 1995. In 2000 RA-11338 was sold to Angola as D2-FRC, while RA-11339 was sold to Avial-NV.

- **Polyot Russian Airlines** (*Rosseeyskaya aviakompahniya 'Polyot'*) [–/POT] operated two 'military' An-12BPs – RA-11320 (c/n 4342409) and RA-11325 (ex CCCP-11325 No. 2, c/n 5342801).[76] The former aircraft was sold to Hellier International in 1999 as TN-AGE, while the other aircraft went to Ariana Afghan Airlines as YA-DAB.

- **Pulkovo Avia** (originally known as the **St Petersburg Air Enterprise**) [Z8/PLK], another cargo airline, operated seven 'civil' An-12BPs. For years the entire fleet wore Aeroflot colours with or without titles; it was not until 1997 that Pulkovo introduced its own livery. However, the freighters did not last that long – all of the An-12s had been sold or retired before any of them could be repainted.

Registration	C/n	Notes
RA-11105	01347801	Aeroflot blue/white (later polar) colour scheme. Sold or retired 1997
RA-11108	01347810	Ex-CCCP-11108 No. 2.* Lst Global Air 9-92 to 7-93 as LZ-PVK. Sold or retired 1997
RA-11109	01347901	Ex-CCCP-11109 No. 2.* Aeroflot polar c/s. Lst UNPF in Bosnia 11-92 as 11109. Sold or retired 1997
RA-11127	02348202	Aeroflot c/s. Lst Global Air 9-92 to 7-93 as LZ-PVL. Damaged Lucapa (Angola) 9-5-95 and repaired
RA-11527	02348208	Aeroflot blue/white (later polar) colours. Sold or retired 1997
RA-12983	00347106	Aeroflot polar c/s. Sold or retired 1997
RA-12995	00347402	Aeroflot polar c/s. Leased to HeavyLift Cargo Airlines 12-96

* The registrations CCCP-11108 and -11109 previously belonged to grey-painted military An-12Bs.

- The **Russian Air Force** (VVS RF) continues to operate the An-12 in substantial numbers; about 600 were reportedly in service in the mid-1990s, though this number has now dwindled because of both 'natural deaths' and sales of surplus aircraft to civil operators. The remaining aircraft are in service with the 61st VA (*vozdooshnaya armiya* – air army, ≅ air force) into which the former VTA has been reorganised. This consists of two airlift divisions, each with four or five airlift regiments. Known An-12 units were based in Ivanovo (517th VTAP and 610th TsBP i PLS, Severnyy AB), Klin (978th VTAP, Klin-5 AB), Ostafyevo, Shadrinsk, Tver, Ulyanovsk, etc.

A substantial part of the fleet is still quasi-civil, wearing full 1973-standard Aeroflot colours; known aircraft are listed in the first part of the table.

Registration	Version	C/n	Notes
RA-11139	An-12B (+)	3341001	Based Ostafyevo
RA-11178	An-12B (+)	?	Grey c/s
RA-11227	An-12B (+)	?	
RA-11240	An-12B (+)	402706	Based Ulyanovsk-Vostochnyy
RA-11241	An-12B (+)	402102	Sold to Lasare Air as 4L-11241
RA-11265	An-12B (+)	402107	
RA-11266	An-12B (+)	?	
RA-11275	An-12B (+)	?	Based Ostafyevo
RA-11286	An-12B (+)	?	610th TsBPiPLS, Ivanovo-Severnyy; derelict by 6-99
RA-11290	An-12B (+)	?	
RA-11327	An-12A (+)	1400104	Sold to Aviaobschchemash
RA-11358	An-12B (+)	?	Russian Navy
RA-11364	An-12B (+)	?	Based Ostafyevo

Many Russian Air Force *Cub*s, like 226th OSAP An-12B RA-11653 (c/n 402703) pictured at Kubinka AB on 8 August 2002, still wear full Aeroflot colours. Note the blue-tipped spinners and the false emergency exit outlines suggesting the exits are much larger than they actually are. (Dmitriy Komissarov)

RA-11393	An-12B (+)	?	Based Ulan-Ude/Vostochnyy	RA-11791	An-12B (−)	402611	226th OSAP, Kubinka AB;
RA-11400	An-12BP (+)	?					communications relay version
RA-11401	An-12BP (+)	5343402		RA-11792	An-12B (−)	402701	226th OSAP, Kubinka AB;
RA-11406	An-12BP (+)	?	Grey c/s				communications relay version
RA-11408	*An-12B (+)*	*3341209*	*Sold to Aviaobschchemash*	RA-11803	An-12BP (+)	4342204	
			before 1995	RA-11835	An-12BP (+)	?	
RA-11412	An-12BP (+)	?		RA-11844	An-12BP (+)	?	
RA-11420	An-12BP (+)	?		RA-11861	An-12BP (+)	?	
CCCP-11425	An-12B (+)	401807	Based Ostafyevo 1994; see next	RA-11894	An-12B (+)	402708	226th OSAP, Kubinka AB
			line!	RA-11924	An-12BP (+)	6344508	226th OSAP, Kubinka AB
RA-11425	An-12BP (+)?	9346802	Grey c/s; may be An-12BK	RA-11931	An-12B (+)	?	
RA-11426	An-12BP (+)	4342204	Grey c/s	RA-11936	An-12A (+)	2340507	Based Ostafyevo
RA-11428	An-12BP (+)	?	Grey c/s	RA-11943	An-12BP (+)	5343609	978th VTAP, Klin-5 AB
RA-11432	An-12BP (+)	?		RA-11945	An-12BP (+)	?	Based Ulan-Ude/Vostochnyy
RA-11652	An-12B (−)	402702	226th OSAP, Kubinka AB;	RA-11965	An-12BP (+)	?	Grey c/s
			communications relay version	RA-11969	An-12BP (+)	?	
RA-11653	An-12B (−)	402703	226th OSAP, Kubinka AB;	RA-11995	An-12BP (+)	?	
			communications relay version	RA-12101	An-12B (+)	402509	Based Ivanovo-Severnyy
RA-11654	An-12B (−)	402602	226th OSAP, Kubinka AB;	RA-12103	An-12B (+)	?	610th TsBPiPLS; derelict
			communications relay version				Ivanovo-Severnyy by 6-99
RA-11660	An-12BP (+)	?		RA-12105	An-12BP (+)	5343404	Leased to NPO Vzlyot; W/O
RA-11666	An-12BP (+)	?					Nar'yan-Mar 11-12-97 in ground
RA-11668	An-12BK	?	Grey c/s				collision with Mi-8T RA-24247
RA-11680	An-12A (+)	9900805		*RA-12108*	*An-12BK*	*9346308*	*Polar c/s; sold to civil operator*
RA-11719 No. 1	An-12BP (+)	6344601	WFU Chkalovskaya AB by 8-99,				*by 1995*
			c/n painted on as 4601; see next	RA-12115	An-12BP (+)	?	
			line!	RA-12122	An-12BK	?	Based Ostafyevo
RA-11719 No. 2	An-12BK	02348110	Ex-Soviet AF '48 Red', seen	RA-12124 No. 1	An-12B	402505	In service 7-93; see next line!
			Chkalovskaya AB 8-02!	RA-12124 No. 2	An-12BK?	00347507	Based Chkalovskaya AB 2000-
RA-11732	An-12BP (+)	?					01; Aeroflot c/s, no titles
RA-11740	An-12BP (+)	?	Based Ulan-Ude/Vostochnyy	RA-12131	An-12BP (+)	?	
RA-11742	An-12BP (+)	?		RA-12132	An-12BP (+)	?	
RA-11786	An-12BP (+)	?		RA-12133	An-12BP (+)	?	

RA-12135	An-12BP (−)	00347002	226th OSAP, Kubinka AB. Crashed nr Rzhev 22-5-01
RA-12137	An-12BP (+)	?	
RA-12143	An-12BP (+)	?	
RA-12187	An-12BP (+)	?	
RA-12330	An-12BP (+)	?	
RA-12574	An-12BP (+)	5343504	978th VTAP, Klin-5 AB

The remainder of the fleet wears the familiar red star insignia and, with a few exceptions, an overall grey colour scheme (of varying degrees of greyness). Lately it has been enlivened by colourful nose art on some aircraft. Since the tactical codes do not tell much, the list is in c/n sequence.

C/n	Version	Tactical code	Notes
2400602	An-12A (+)	47 Red	Based Ostafyevo
402009	An-12B (+)	28 Yellow	Based Ostafyevo
402409	An-12B (+)	28 Red	Based Ulyanovsk-Vostcochnyy
2340708	An-12A (+)	94 Red	16th VA/226th OSAP, Sperenberg AB; ex-4th VA/245th OSAP '18 Blue'
2340710	An-12A (+)	89 Red	16th VA/226th OSAP, Sperenberg AB; to 4th VA/535th OSAP, Rostov-on-Don
3341102	An-12B (+)	93 Red	16th VA/226th OSAP; Sperenberg AB, later Kubinka AB
3341203	An-12B (+)	92 Red	Ex-CCCP-11407. 16th VA/226th OSAP, Sperenberg AB
3341207	An-12B (+)	90 Red	Ex-CCCP-1218...; 16th VA/226th OSAP, Sperenberg AB
3341402	An-12B (+)	70 Black	Basic Aeroflot c/s, based Ostafyevo
3341503	An-12B (+)	08 Red	226th OSAP, WFU/stored Kubinka; Russian flag on tail instead of star
3341507	An-12B (+)	98 Red	16th VA/226th OSAP; Sperenberg AB, later Kubinka AB
3341601	An-12B (+)	85 Red	16th VA/226th OSAP, Sperenberg AB; ex 4th VA/245th OSAP '16 Blue'. To 4th VA/535th OSAP, Rostov-on-Don, as 35 Red
3341602	An-12B (+)	50 Red	978th VTAP, Klin?
4341708	An-12B (+)	98 Red	16th VA/226th OSAP, Sperenberg AB
4341905	An-12B (+)	84 Red	Ex-CCCP-11537; 16th VA/226th OSAP, Sperenberg AB
4342203	An-12BP (+)	91 Red	Ex-CCCP-12182; 16th VA/226th OSAP, Sperenberg AB
4342407	An-12BP (+)	99 Red	16th VA/226th OSAP; Sperenberg AB, later Kubinka AB
4342410	An-12BP (+)	95 Red	16th VA/226th OSAP; Sperenberg AB, later Kubinka AB
4342604	An-12RKhR	11 Red	
4342703	An-12BP (+)	86 Red	16th VA/226th OSAP, Sperenberg AB
5342810	An-12BP (+)	17 Red	
5343108	An-12BP (+)	15 Red	
5343207	An-12BP (+)	97 Red	16th VA/226th OSAP; Sperenberg AB, later Kubinka AB
5343208	An-12BP (+)	661 Black	Ex-CCCP-11661, basic Aeroflot c/s. 978th VTAP, Klin-5 AB
5343310	An-12BP (+)	34 Red	Based Ostafyevo, Woolly Mammoth nose art
6343802	An-12BP (+)	02 Red	Based Tver
5343901	An-12PP	85 Red	16th VA/226th OSAP, Sperenberg AB; to 4th VA/535th OSAP, Rostov-on-Don
7344702	An-12PS	not known	
7344703	An-12PS	17 Yellow	North Fleet Air Arm, Severomorsk-1 AB, blue side flash
7344704	An-12PS	not known	
7345104	An-12BP (+)?	34 Red	Could be An-12BK
7345203	An-12BK	09 Red	257th OSAP, leaping tiger nose art
8345907	An-12BP (+)?	not known	Could be An-12BK
9346303	An-12PP	68 Red	Callsign RA-10440? Based Chkalovskaya AB
9346305	An-12BK	26 Red	Reported as An-12TBK; based Ostafyevo
00346908	An-12BK?	42 Red	Based Ivanovo? Russian flag on tail instead of star
00347007	An-12BK	18 Red	Damaged, stored Chkalovskaya AB
02348206	An-12BK-PPS	02 Red	
02348303	An-12BK-PPS	24 Red	

- The Russian Air Force has commercial divisions. The 223rd OSAP, one of the units making up the 8th ADON (*otdel'naya aviadiveeziya osobovo naznacheniya* – independent special mission air division) at Chkalovskaya AB, was transformed into an 'airline' called **223rd Flight Unit State Airline [–/CHD]**. Among other things it operated An-12B RA-12126 (c/n 402507) and An-12BP RA-12137 (c/n 6344410) in Aeroflot markings.

- **RVPP Rostvertol [–/RUZ]**,[77] the Rostov helicopter factory, operated at least two 'military' *Cub*s – An-12A RA-11976 (c/n 1340106) and An-12B 13387 (no prefix; c/n 402902?). The latter aircraft crashed on approach to Tyumen on 25 September 1993; RA-11976 remained in service until 1999 when it was sold to Vega Airlines as LZ-VEA.

- **Sakha Avia [K7/IKT]**, formerly Yakutavia, is the national airline of the Republic of Yakutia (Sakha) and one of the biggest Russian air carriers. It is headquartered in Yakutsk and consists of several branches (air enterprises), more than one of which operated An-12s; there were 13 aircraft in all. In the late 1990s Sakha Avia suffered from excessive capacity, and much of its enormous fleet was put in storage or leased to other carriers. Only a single An-12 remained in 2002.

Registration	Version	C/n	Notes
RA-11130	An-12BP(−)	02348205	Batagai A.E. Sold to Sir Aero ?-00
RA-11234	An-12B(+?)	401907	Retired by 1997
RA-11236	An-12B(+)	402111	Yakutsk A.E. Basic Aeroflot polar colours, Sakha Avia logo, no titles; registration painted on as RA 11Z36. Sold to Natalco ?-99 as S9-BAN
RA-11345	An-12B(+)	401801	Yakutsk A.E. Demilitarised; sold to Avial-NV
RA-11354	An-12B(+?)	401812	Yakutsk A.E. Sold or retired by 2002
RA-11403	An-12B	401906	Crashed near Lyudino 24-2-96
RA-11767	An-12B(+)	401909	Yakutsk A.E.
RA-11884	An-12B(+)	401710	Yakutsk A.E.
RA-11892	An-12B(+)	402501	Yakutsk A.E. Sold to Sir Aero ?-96
RA-11991	An-12B(+)	402006	Yakutsk A.E. Demilitarised, basic Aeroflot polar colours, Sakha Avia titles/logo. Sold to Aviostart by 2-00 as LZ-ASY
RA-12953	An-12BP(−)	8345504	Yakutsk A.E. Sold to Coptrade Air Transport by 10-99 as ST-AQF
RA-12955	An-12BP(−)	8345506	Nyurba A.E. Reported for Viliuy Aircompany; crashed near Krasnoyarsk 11-11-98
RA-12959	An-12BP(−)	8345510	Aeroflot polar colours. Sold to Hellier International 1999 as D2-FBY

• **Sakhaviatrans [–/SVT]**, the Far Eastern sister company of Atran (ex Aviatrans) based in Yuzhno-Sakhalinsk, leases aircraft from Atran as required; these included two 'military' *Cubs* – An-12B RA-98117 and An-12BP RA-98118 leased in 1994. The former aircraft now wears full Sakhaviatrans colours while the other An-12 was returned in 1998 but reportedly was leased again the following year.

• **Samara Airlines [E5/BRZ]**, one of the biggest Russian regional carriers based at Samara-Kurumoch airport, operated four *Cubs*, all of which have been disposed of.

Registration	Version	C/n	Notes
RA-11959	An-12B(+)	402410	Demilitarised. Sold to Rila Airlines ?-98 as LZ-RAA
RA-12954	An-12BP(−)	8345505	Sold to Volare Aviation Enterprise 1999 as UR-LAI
RA-12956	An-12BP(−)	8345507	Sold to Expo Aviation 1998 as 4R-EXC
RA-12986	An-12BP(−)	00347201	Sold to Volare Aviation Enterprise 1999 as UR-12986

• **Sir Aero Joint-Stock Co. [–/SRN]** based in Yakutsk owned two ex-Sakha Avia *Cubs* – 'civil' An-12BP RA-11130 (c/n 02348205) bought in 2000 and 'military' An-12B RA-11892 (c/n 402501) bought in 1996.

• **SPAIR Air Transport Corporation [–/PAR]** (*Aviatrahnsportnaya korporahtsiya Spaer*)[78] based at Yekaterinburg-Koltsovo airport and mainly concerned with cargo carriage operated four An-12s. The letters SP in the carrier's name are derived from the name of its director, Valeriy Spoornov.

Registration	Version	C/n	Notes
RA-11003	An-12BP(+)	5343704	Demilitarised. Sold to Flight Air Company
RA-11049	An-12BP(+)	8346109	Demilitarised. Sold to Yermolino Flight Test & Research Enterprise
RA-11356	An-12BP(+)	7345206	Sold to Yermolino Flight Test & Research Enterprise
RA-11415	An-12P(+)	401708	Fate unknown

• **Special Cargo Airlines** (*Spetsiahl'nyye groozovyye avialinii*) [–/SCI] based at Yermolino south of Moscow operated ten *Cubs*.

Registration	Version	C/n	Notes
RA-11114	An-12B(−)	01347909	Sold to National Commuter Airlines as D2-FDC
RA-11301	An-12PP	00347107	Demilitarised (converted to transport). Sold to Bulgaria as LZ-LTD
RA-11321	An-12BP(+)	9346801	Sold to Air Cess 1-96 as EL-AKR
RA-11329	An-12BK	8346010	Ex-CCCP-11329 No. 2*; demilitarised and re-equipped with small ROZ-1 radar. Sold to Hellier International ?-98 as D2-FBZ
RA-11863	An-12BP(+)	401905	Basic Aeroflot c/s, no titles
RA-11890	An-12B(+)	3340909	Ex-Amuraviatrans, bought 16-8-97; sold to Santa Cruz Imperial 8-10-97 as EL-ASA
RA-12116	An-12BP(+)	402108	Sold to Santa Cruz Imperial as EL-ALB
RA-12191	An-12BK	401905	Refitted with ROZ-1 radar. Sold to Air Cess as EL-AKW
CCCP-13320	An-12BP(+)	8345407	Demilitarised. Crashed Khatanga 23-9-91
RA-12972	An-12BP(−)	9346504	Ex-Komiavia. Sold to Mikma as ER-ACG

* CCCP-11329 No. 1 was a Mi-6 (c/n 4681705V).
Note: 'Civil' An-12BP RA-12959 (c/n 8345510; sold to Savanair as D2-FBY) was also reported for Special Cargo Airlines but this is doubtful (see Komiavia)!

• **Start Air Transport Co.** based in Zhukovskiy had a single An-12BK, RA-13331 (c/n 6344510) bought from LII in 1994. This was a highly non-standard aircraft retaining traces of earlier use as a de-icing systems testbed. Interestingly, the titles were an attempt to combine the Roman (START) and Cyrillic (СТАРТ) rendering, and the result was something in between.

• **SVGAL** (*Severo-vostochnyye groozovyye avialinii* – North-Eastern Cargo Airlines) [–/MGD] based at Magadan-Sokol (Russia) and Kent International (UK) operated three 'military' An-12Bs until its demise in 1999, whereupon most of the aircraft went to Magadanavialeasing.

Registration	C/n	Notes
RA-11242	3341406	
RA-11421	401711	Ex-avionics testbed. Sold to ALADA as D2-FBJ
RA-12119	402109	

- Cargo carrier **Trans Aero Samara** [–/TSL] based at Samara-Bezymyanka had two demilitarised An-12BPs, RA-11363 (c/n unknown) and RA-11962 (c/n 5343007). In 1999 the airline ceased operations; RA-11962 was sold to Aviast, but the fate of the other aircraft is unknown.

- The now defunct **Tyumen' Airlines** (*Tyumenskiye avialinii*) [7M/TYM] based at Tyumen-Roschchino airport had nine An-12s; only one remained in service by 2002.

Registration	Version	C/n	Notes
RA-11112	An-12BP(–)	01347907	White overall, partial UN titles. Sold to Avial ?-98
RA-11128	An-12BP(–)	02348203	White overall, no titles. Sold to Avial by 8-99
RA-11766	An-12B(+)	401605	Basic Aeroflot colours, no titles. Sold to Avial 1998
RA-11973	An-12B(+)	401606	Retired Tyumen-Roschchino by 8-95
RA-12973	An-12BP(–)	9346505	Full colour scheme. Crashed 11-5-98, circumstances unknown (written off)
RA-12976	An-12BP(–?)	9346510	White overall, no titles
RA-12980	An-12BP(–?)	00347103	WFU Tyumen-Roschchino by 2000
RA-12992	An-12BP(–)	00347306	Basic Aeroflot colours, no titles. Sold to Avial 1998
RA-12998	An-12BP(–)	01347610	Not in fleet list 2002, fate unknown

- The **Ulan-Ude Aircraft Production Association** (U-UAPO) had a demilitarised An-12B registered RA-12174 (c/n 3341505). The aircraft was sold to Skycabs as 4R-SKL in May 1998.

- **Ural Airlines** (*Oorahl'skiye avialinii*) [–/URW, later U6/SVR] operated six An-12s. This airline based in Yekaterinburg (formerly Sverdlovsk) came into being in 1993 when the Sverdlovsk Aviation Enterprise was organisationally separated from Koltsovo airport. All the *Cubs* have been sold off now.

Registration	Version	C/n	Notes
RA-11017	An-12BP(+)	6344008	Retired by 1999
RA-11019	An-12BP(+)	6344202	Demilitarised. Aeroflot colours. Retired by 1999
RA-11036	An-12BP(+)	7344810?*	Full colour scheme. Retired by 1999
RA-12952	An-12BP(–)	8345503	Sold to Renan ?-99 as ER-ACK
RA-12975	An-12BP(–)	9346509	Sold ?-00 as 3C-OOZ
RA-12999	An-12BP(–)	01347701	Sold to Vega Airlines ?-99 as LZ-VEB

* There is some confusion concerning RA-11036. Some sources report this aircraft as c/n 7345310 and c/n 7344810 as CCCP-11086.

- **Velocity** [–/VKT] (formerly VIA Viktor Airlines) operated a single Ukrainian-registered 'military' An-12A, UR-11961 (c/n 2340403), leased from the Antonov OKB in 1995.

- Zhukovskiy-based **Veteran Airlines** [–/VTN], a sister company of the Ukrainian airline of the same name (see below), reportedly operated ex-Antey An-12BK RA-11303 (c/n 00347604). The airline suspended operations in 1997 and the aircraft went to the *other* Veteran Airlines as UR-11303.

- Established in 1990 as the first non-Aeroflot specialised cargo carrier in the Soviet Union and later Russia, **Volga-Dnepr Airlines** [VI/VDA] operated ten An12s – mostly on short-term leases.

Registration	Version	C/n	Notes
CCCP-11341 No. 2*	An-12BK?	00347606	Leased from Soviet Air Force
CCCP-11342	An-12BK	00347607	Ex-Soviet Air Force. Crashed near Skopje 23-7-92
CCCP-11343 No. 2*	An-12BK?	00347503	Leased from Soviet Air Force
CCCP-11344 No. 2*	An-12BK?	00347409	Lsf Soviet Air Force, grey c/s; became RA-11344 while on lease
RA-11529	An-12BP(+)	6344109	Leased from Aviastar 10-95 to ?-97
CCCP-11746	An-12BP(+)	7345007	Lsf Soviet Air Force 1-92 to ?-??; full c/s
RA-11814	An-12BP(+)	7345008	Leased from Aviastar 10-95 to ?-97
CCCP-11908 No. 2*	An-12BP(+)?	6344501	Leased from Soviet Air Force
CCCP-11922	An-12B P(+)	7345005	Leased from Soviet Air Force 8-92 to ?-??
RA-48971	An-12A(+).	1340107	To Azerbaijan Airlines as 4K-48971 c.1995

* CCCP-11341 No. 1 was a Voronezh-built An-12B (c/n 401702) which crashed on 17 February 1973; CCCP-11343 No. 1 was another An-12B (c/n and fate unknown); CCCP-11344 No. 1 was An-12B c/n 401707 (written off as time-expired); CCCP-11908 No. 1 was another Tashkent-built An-12BP (c/n 4342101) which was sold as LZ-SFL.

- The **Voronezh Aircraft Production Joint-Stock Company** (VASO – *Voronezhskoye aktsionernoye samolyotostroitel'noye obschchestvo*, ex MAP aircraft factory No. 64) [DN/VSO] which produces the Il-96-300 long-range airliner operated An-12B RA-48984 (c/n 402913). The aircraft was sold to Ukraine Air Alliance as UR-48984 in 1997.

- The **Yermolino Flight Test & Research Enterprise** (YeLIIP – *Yermolinskoye lyotno-ispytahtel'noye issledovatel'skoye predproyahtiye*) [–/EFE], later renamed **Yermolino Airlines**, operated seven *Cubs* from Yermolino. The airline ceased operations in 2002.

Registration	Version	C/n	Notes
RA-11049	An-12TB(+)	8346109	Ex-SPAIR; demilitarised
RA-11356	An-12BP(+)	7345206	Ex-SPAIR; reported as an An-12BK
RA-11516	An-12B(+)	4341909	
RA-11768	An-12BP(+)	5343103	Ex-Russian AF '36 Blue', ex-CCCP-11436. Full c/s

Registration	Version	C/n	Notes
RA-11790	An-12A (+)	1400302	Ex-avionics testbed. Crashed Ust'-Ilimsk 29-10-94 while opf Aero-Nika
RA-11916	An-12B (+)	2400901	Basic Aeroflot c/s, titles; ex-avionics testbed
RA-48970	An-12A (+)	2400502	Demilitarised. Ex-Kumertau Express, bought ?-98

- **Zenit [–/EZT]** based in Zhukovskiy operated 'military' An-12B RA-11312 (ex Soviet AF '87 Red', c/n 3340903) and 'civil' An-12B RA-11992 (c/n 402604, a former Soviet Air Force communications relay aircraft). RA-11312 was retired in 2001.

- The operator of 'military' An-12B RA-11010 (c/n 3341110?) is unknown; the aircraft was in basic Aeroflot colours without titles.

The Ukraine

- **Air Ukraine/Avialinii Ukraïny [6U/UKR]**, the Ukrainian flag carrier, leased at least one An-12BK (54 Red, c/n 8345702) from the Ukrainian Air Force in December 1996; the aircraft was reregistered UR-11346 for the duration. In 1996 the airline acquired An-12BK RA-13357 (c/n 8345604) from Impulse-Aero; the aircraft was reregistered UR-11314.

- The Antonov Design Bureau operates a large fleet of assorted aircraft of its own make, including four An-12s. These are operated by **Antonov Airlines [–/ADB]** and wear a smart blue/white colour scheme with the ADB logo and titles.

Registration	Version	C/n	Notes
UR-11315	An-12BP (+)	4342307	Demilitarised. Basic Aeroflot c/s with large 'Antonov 12' titles, later full c/s
UR-11322	An-12A (+)	0901409	Ex-EW-11322, leased from Wings ?-96
UR-11765	An-12B (+)	401705	Was leased to Air Sofia 1993–98 as LZ-SFM
UR-21510	An-12AP (+)	0901404	Ex-CCCP-21510, ex-Soviet Air Force '88 Red'. Grey c/s with large 'Antonov 12' titles, repainted in full c/s by 12-96; retrofitted with non-standard radar (bigger than ROZ-1 but smaller than Initsiativa-4-100)

- **Antonov Airtrack [–/UAP]** operated 'military' An-12BP UR-UAA (previous identity unknown, c/n 6344701) in 1996–8, eventually selling it to Khors Aircompany. There were also plans to add one ex-Soviet Air Force An-12BP and three An-12BKs to the fleet, but the aircraft were unserviceable and the reconditioning job dragged on so long that the airline ceased operations before taking delivery.

- Simferopol-based **Atlant-SV [L4/ATG]** had at least four 'military' Cubs. The airline ceased operations in 1997; the L4 flight code was subsequently transferred to Lauda Air, SpA [L4/LDI], the Italian subsidiary of the Austrian carrier of the same name.

A former Atlant-SV Airlines An-12BP (ex UR-11302, c/n 5343705) sits forlorn at Kiev-Svyatoshino on 15 September 2002, five years after the airline has ceased to exist; the titles on the forward fuselage are all that remains. In the 1980s the aircraft participated in the Afghan War and was fitted with ASO-2 flare dispensers which have since been removed. (Dmitriy Komissarov)

Registration	Version	C/n	Notes
UR-11300	An-12B (+)	402211	Ex-Polissyaaviatrans
UR-11302*	An-12BP (+)	5343705	Ex-tactical code unknown; ASO-2 flare packs; seen WFU Kiev-Svyatoshino 9-02 with the registration and Atlant logo scrubbed out
UR-11357	An-12BP (+)	5343203	Ex-Polissyaaviatrans; ex-CCCP-11357 No. 2*
UR-11501	An-12A (+)	1340206	

* The registration CCCP-11302 was used before by An-12BP c/n 8346004; CCCP-11357 No. 1 was an An-12B (c/n 402802).

- The Russian-Ukrainian joint venture **Avirciti [–/VTI]** based at Odessa-Central airport operates 'miitary' An-12B UR-11961 (c/n 2340403).

- Kiev-based **Busol Airline [–/BUA]** (the name, pronounced *boosol*, is Ukrainian for 'stork') operated a pair of Cubs. They retained the standard Air Force overall grey colours but had Busol Airline titles and a stork superimposed on a Ukrainian flag on the tail. This airline vanished in 1998.

Registration	Version	C/n	Notes
UR-11348	An-12BK	7345208	Ex-Ukrainian AF '21 Blue'. Transferred to Volare Aviation Enterprise 3-00 as UR-SMA
UR-11349	An-12BK	9346302	Former tactical code unknown; ASO-2 flare packs. Registration CCCP-11349 used before by An-12B c/n 401807. Transferred to Veteran Airlines ?-00 as UR-YMR

- Kharkov-based **ICAR Airlines (Independent Carrier) [C3/IPR]** owned a single 'military' An-12BP registered UR-PWH (previous identity unknown, c/n 6343707). The aircraft was sold to Aerocom in 1999 as ER-ACI. Previously it leased An-12BP UR-11819 from the Kharkov aircraft factory (see next entry).

- The aircraft fleet of the **Kharkov State Aircraft Manufacturing Co.** (KSAMC, or KhDAVP – *Kharkovs'ke derzhavne aviatseeyne vyrobniche pidpreeyemstvo*) included a demilitarised An-12BP, UR-11819 (c/n 6344009), and a 'military' An-12B, UR-11833 (c/n 3341008). The latter aircraft had been retired by 2002.

- **Khors Aircompany [X6/KHO, later X9/KHO]**[79] (named after the sun god of the ancient pagan Slavic peoples) operated four An-12s.

Registration	Version	C/n	Notes
UR-11319	An-12BP (–)	4342510	Shot down near Cuito-Cuanavale, Angola, 14-12-99
UR-11326	An-12AP (+)	2400802	
UR-11332	An-12BP (+)	4342202	Ex-Ukrainian AF '84 Blue', transferred ?-97. Lst BIO Air Company ?-00 as T9-CAD
UR-TSI	An-12BP (+)	6344701	Ex-Antonov Airtrack UR-UAA; operated with this registration until mid-1998

- **Motor-Sich [M9/MSI]**, the flying division of the Zaporozhye-based aero-engine factory of the same name, operated four Cubs.

Registration	Version	C/n	Notes
UR-11316	An-12BK	9346810	Ex-RA-11316 (ex-owner unknown); re-equipped with ROZ-1 radar
UR-13332	An-12B (+)	4341707	Ex-Soviet Air Force '82 Red'
UR-11528	An-12B (+)	3341005	Retired by 1999
UR-48975	An-12A (+)	1400101	

- **Polissyaaviatrans** (Polesye Air Transport) **[–/POS]** of Zhitomir operated An-12B UR-11300 (c/n 402211) and An-12BP UR-11357 (c/n 5343203). Both were transferred to Atlant-SV in 1997.

- **Ukraine Air Alliance** (*Ookrayina-Aeroal'yans*) **[–/UKL]** owned three 'military' An-12Bs – UR-11813 (c/n 3340908), UR-UAF (c/n 3341108)[80] and UR-48984 (ex Voronezh Aircraft Factory RA-48984, c/n 402913, bought in 1997). The first aircraft was sold to Amuraviatrans, becoming RA-11813; UR-UAF was sold to an unknown operator in Fiji as DQ-FBS, while UR-48984 (which reportedly carried the c/n at one time as 402603) was sold to Aerofreight, Russia, regaining its previous identity.

- The **Ukrainian Air Force** (UAF, or VPS – *Voyenno-povitryany seely*) inherited a substantial number of An-12s from the VTA when the Soviet Union collapsed. They are based in Kiev, Krivoy Rog, Lvov, Saki and Vinnitsa. However, as mentioned earlier, funding problems and political complications following the breakup of the Soviet Union and the resulting spares shortage have caused many UAF Cubs to be cannibalised for spares.

Most Ukrainian An-12s are operated by numerous 'airlines' under UAF management which help the Air Force generate urgently needed cash (though at times it is hard to tell which airline is civil and which is not!).

C/n	Version	Tactical code/ registration	Notes
1400301	An-12A (+)	83 Blue	Based Sknilov AB, Lvov?
1400304	An-12A (+)	23 Blue	
3341610	An-12B (+)	69 Red	Based Novofyodorovka AB, Saki?
4342007	An-12BP (+)	77 Red	Based Novofyodorovka AB, Saki? Ex-Soviet Air Force '70'
4342106	An-12BP (+)	79 Red	Based Novofyodorovka AB, Saki?
4342110	An-12BP (+)	83 Red	Based Novofyodorovka AB, Saki?
4342202	An-12BP (+)	84 Blue	Based Sknilov AB, Lvov. Transferred to Khors Aircompany ?-97 as UR-11332

c/n	Type	Code	Notes
4342306	An-12BP (+)	50 Red	Based Vinnitsa?
4342308	An-12BP (+)	61 Red	Based Novofyodorovka AB, Saki? Ex-Soviet Air Force '72'. Transferred to Veteran Airlines by 8-02 as UR-PLV
4342610	An-12BP (+)	86 Blue	Based Sknilov AB, Lvov. Transferred to civil register as UR-12423 (see below)
6344603	An-12BP (+)	?	Based Sknilov AB, Lvov?
6344605	An-12BK	73 Blue	Based Sknilov AB, Lvov? Transferred to Volare Aviation Enterprise 3-00 as UR-LMI
6344607	An-12BP (+)	87 Blue	
7345208	An-12BK	21 Blue	Ex-Soviet AF '84 Blue'. Transferred to Busol Airline ?-94 as UR-11348
8345702	An-12BK	54 Red	Based Sknilov AB, Lvov? Leased to Air Ukraine 12-96 as UR-11346
8346106	An-12BP (+)?	03 Blue	Based Sknilov AB, Lvov? Reported as An-12BP but may be An-12BK
9346208	An-12BP (+)?	22 Blue	Reported as An-12BP but may be An-12BK. Sold to Dvin Air Cargo as EK-11030
9346309	An-12BK	68 Red	Also still carrying ex registration CCCP-12113 and Aeroflot titles in 2002!!!
9346405	An-12BK	24 Blue	Transferred to Volare Aviation Enterprise as UR-LIP
9346607	An-12BP (+)?	86 Red	Reported as An-12BP but may be An-12BK
9346802	*An-12BP(+)?*	*?*	*Based Sknilov AB, Lvov? Reported as An-12BP but may be An-12BK. Sold to a Russian operator by 8-01 as RA-11425*
9346809	An-12BP (+)?	87 Red	Based Sknilov AB, Lvov? Reported as An-12BP but may be An-12BK
00346907	An-12BK	05 Red	Based Melitopol
00347004	An-12BK	20 Blue	Transferred to Volare Aviation Enterprise 5-98 as UR-BWM
00347006	An-12BK	57 Blue	Based Vinnitsa?
?	An-12BP (+)?	11259	WFU Odessa by 5-02
4341910	An-12BP (+)	UR-11351	Former tactical code unknown. Sold to Dvin Air Cargo ?-97 as EK-11351
401810?	An-12B (+)	UR-11352	ELINT aircraft? Based Vinnitsa?
4342610	An-12BP (1)	UR-12423	Ex-86 Blue. Sold to Angola as D2-FBD

Note: Many An-12s were transferred from one commercial division of the UAF to another. When the ultimate fate of aircraft no longer listed by a given airline is unknown these are assumed returned to the UAF.

Ukrainian Air Force An-12A '83 Blue' (c/n 1400301) makes a smoky final approach. (Sergey Popsuyevich)

'I pass'd by his garden and saw the wild briar, The thorn and the thistle grow broader and higher...'. An-12BK UR-LMI of Volare Aircompany taxies across a rain-lashed (and very weed-overgrown) hardstand somewhere in the Ukraine. Interestingly, the type is accurately marked on the nose, a rare occurrence for the type. (Sergey Popsuyevich)

- **Ukrainian Cargo Airways** (UCA, or UATK – *Ookrayins'ka aviatseeyna trahnsportna kompahniya*) [–/UKS] based in Zaporozhye operated three An-12BKs – UR-UCK (ex Veteran Airlines UR-11304, c/n 9346905), UR-UCM (c/n unknown, demilitarised) and UR-UCN (ex Veteran Airlines UR-11303, c/n 01347604). UR-UCM was no longer in the fleet in 2002; its fate is unknown.

- **Veteran Airlines** [–/VPB] based in Dzhankoy had eight An-12s.

Registration	Version	C/n	Notes
UR-11303	An-12BK	00347604	Transferred to Ukrainian Cargo Airways as UR-UCN; see six lines down!
UR-11304	An-12BK	9346905	Transferred to Ukrainian Cargo Airways as UR-UCK
UR-11305	An-12BK	00347803	
UR-11306	An-12BK	9346205	
UR-PAS	An-12AP (+)	2401105	Named 'Andrey'
UR-PLV	An-12BP (+)	4342308	Ex-Ukrainian Air Force '61 Red'
UR-UCN	An-12BK	01347604	Leased from UCA Ukrainian Cargo Airways; ex-UR-11303!
UR-YMR	An-12BK	9346302	Ex-Busol Airline UR-11349, transferred ?-00

- Kiev-based **Vitair** [–/VIT] operated An-12BP UR-11819 (c/n 6344009) in 1995.

- **Volare Aviation Enterprise Joint-Stock Company** [F7/VRE] based in Krivoy Rog operated seven An-12s.

Registration	Version	C/n	Notes
UR-BWM	An-12BK	00347004	Ex-Ukrainian Air Force '20 Blue', transferred 4-99
UR-LAI	An-12BP (–)	8345505	Ex-Samara Airlines RA-12954, bought ?-99. Leased to East Line Enterprise by 11-99
UR-LIP	An-12BK	9346405	Ex-Ukrainian AF '24 Blue'; grey c/s, later full c/s, named 'The Spirit of Cornwall 2'. Crashed near Agadir 7-2-02
UR-LMI	An-12BK	6344605	Ex-Ukrainian AF '73 Blue'
UR-LTG	An-12BP (–)	00347201	Ex-UR-12986, ex-Samara Airlines RA-12986, bought by 9-99. Leased to ACS Air Charter Sevices
UR-SMA	An-12BK	7345208	Demilitarised. Ex-Busol Airline UR-11348
UR-SVG	An-12BP (+)	4342309	Demilitarised. Ex-TN-AGE, ex-RA-11320

- An **unidentified Ukrainian airline** operates An-12P UR-BYW (c/n unknown). First seen at Kiev-Svyatoshino in September 2002, the aircraft caries only 'Cargo' titles. There are indications that previously it wore another Ukrainian registration (the letters 'BYW' were applied over a patch of fresher paint, whereas the UR- prefix was painted on a quite weathered background); possibly this is ex-UR-BWY which was painted on in error (the registration actually belongs to an ARP 410 Airlines An-26).

Uzbekistan

• **Avialeasing Aviation Company [AD/TWN]**, an Uzbek/US joint venture based at Tashkent-International (Sergheli) airport, operated An-12BP UK 11109 (civil/military version and previous identity unknown, c/n 01348009)[81] and a demilitarised An-12BK, UK 11418 (c/n 7344705), which it leased to various airlines, including Uzbekistan Airways and AZAL Cargo. UK 11109 was probably sold to Imtrec Aviation Cambodia as XU-365 in 2002. (Note: Uzbek aircraft usually have the registration painted on with no dash after the country prefix.)

• 'Military' An-12BPs UK 06105, UK 11109 and An-12BK UK 11418 were operated by **Simurg [–/JRP]**, the flying division of the Tashkent Electronics Plant, in 1997 (the name refers to a Bird of Happiness in Oriental fairy tales).

• Over the years **TAPO-Avia [PQ/CTP, later 4C/TPR]**,[82] the flying division of the Tashkent Aircraft Production Corporation based at Tashkent-Vostochnyy airfield, operated seven An-12s. Besides acting as support aircraft and generating additional revenue by carrying commercial cargo, they help advertise the factory and the aircraft it builds, being painted in the Tashkent Aircraft Production Corporation's smart livery.

Registration	Version	C/n	Notes
UK 06105	An-12BP(+)	5343606	Sold or retired by 2002
UK 11109	An-12BP	01348005	Full c/s. Sold to Avialeasing?
UK 11418	An-12BK	7344705	Full c/s. Sold to Avialeasing?
UK-11804	An-12A (+)	2400406	Demilitarised. Ex-Uzbekistan Airways
UK 11807	An-12BK	00346910	Full c/s
UK 58644	An-12A (+)	1013409287	Full c/s
UK 93920	An-12BP(+)	6344610	Sold to Vega Airlines ?-00 as LZ-VEC

• The **Uzbekistan Air Force** operated a number of *Cubs*, including An-12BPs UK 11369, UK 11372 (which were leased to Uzbekistan Airways, see below) and 11513 (c/n unknown). It is not known if they ever wore 'Uz AIR FORCE' titles (which, in the light of Uzbekistan's recent affiliations with the USA during Operation *Enduring Freedom*, have been mockingly deciphered as '**United Ztatez** Air Force'!).

• **Uzbekistan Airways** (Uzbekiston Havo Yullari) **[HY/UZB]**, the Uzbek flag carrier based at Tashkent-International and Samarkand, operated four An-12s. The airline has a penchant for changing its livery, and the *Cubs* have worn several colour schemes.

Registration	Version	C/n	Notes
UK 11109	An-12BP	01348005	Leased from Avialieasing in 1998, returned by 2002
UK 11369	An-12BP (+)	6343810	Demilitarised; leased from Uzbekistan Air Force
UK 11372	An-12BP (+)	5343204	Leased from Uzbekistan Air Force
UK 11418	An-12BK	7344705	Demilitarised; leased from Avialeasing ?-00, returned by 2002
UK-11804	An-12A (+)	2400406	Demilitarised. Sold to TAPO-Avia after 1996

CHAPTER NINE

... and Abroad (Non-CIS Operators)

Over the years the An-12 has seen service in more than 40 nations in Europe, Asia, the Middle East, Africa, Central and South America (not counting the new CIS republics) – an impressive figure by any standards. Of these, 17 countries took delivery of new (or, more rarely, used) *Cubs* directly from the Soviet Union. Of course, some nations have obscure operators flying well-used aircraft – many of which change their country of registry again and again and again (a case of the notorious 'flag of convenience' registrations).

Afghanistan

• The **Afghan Republican Air Force** (*Afghan Hanai Qurah*) operated at least 11 ex-VVS 'military' An-12Bs and 'BPs, apparently serialled consecutively 380 Black to 390 Black. Some of these later passed to the anti-Taliban coalition headed by Gen. Abdul Rashid Dostum known as the **Northern Alliance**. To date only one example (An-12BP '387 Black', c/n 4342205) has been identified by construction number. An-12BP '390 Black' was written off in an accident near Termez, Uzbekistan, on the night of 10 February 1993.

• The Afghan flag carrier **Ariana Afghan Airlines [FG/AFG]** had two *Cubs* – 'civil' An-12B YA-DAA (c/n unknown) in full Ariana livery and 'military' An-12BP YA-DAB (ex-Polyot Airlines RA-11325, c/n 5342801) in ex-Polyot colours bought in late 1997. In addition to hauling cargo the aircraft were reportedly used on passenger services because of the scarcity of true airliners, for which purpose seats were installed in the hold.

The aircraft were locked inside the country when the UN imposed a ban on Ariana's international flights in 2000 owing to the activities of the Taliban militia; both were eventually destroyed at Kabul International Airport by US bombing strikes in November 2001 during Operation *Enduring Freedom* (a massive military operation against the Taliban and al-Qa'eda in the wake of the 11 September 2001 terrorist attacks against New York and Washington, DC).

• **Pamir Airlines** operated An-12BP YA-PAA (ex-Special Cargo Airlines RA-11321, c/n 9346801?) and YA-PAB, a demilitarised An-12BK re-equipped with an ROZ-1 radar (ex-Air Cess EL-AKW, ex-RA-12191, c/n 8346202), in 1996. Both aircraft retained basic Special Cargo Airlines colours. In 1996 YA-PAA was sold to Santa Cruz Imperial as EL-ALF, while YA-PAB followed suit in 1997 as EL-ALJ.

• The **Taliban militia** had at least one ex-Afghan Republican AF *Cub* (identity unknown); the aircraft crashed near Quetta, Pakistan, on the night of 13 January 1998.

• A *Cub* serialled 00406 belonged to an **unknown Afghan operator** in April 2002; it has been reported as ex-YA-PAA, as the basic colour scheme is that of Special Cargo Airlines.

Algeria

The Soviet Union began providing military assistance to Algeria in 1962 when the country gained independence from France. In early 1966 the **Algerian Air Force** (*Force Aérienne Algérienne/al Quwwat al Jawwiya al Jaza'eriya*) took delivery of eight Voronezh-built armed An-12Bs. The aircraft were operated by the 35th Transport Squadron at Boufarik AB.[83] Interestingly, the *Cubs* wore civil registrations along with Algerian Air Force insignia and military serials.

In the early 1970s, however, President Col. Houari Boumedienne switched allegiance to the West and the Algerian Air Force started re-equipping with Western hardware. The An-12s were placed in storage and supplanted by 'short' Lockheed C-130H and 'stretched' C-130H-30 Hercules transports. Three of the aircraft remained airworthy and were ultimately resold (see table).[84]

Registration	Serial	C/n	Notes
7T-WAA	560	402607	
7T-WAB	566	402606	
7T-WAC	514	402605	Sold to Mikma as ER-ACD by 5-95
7T-WAD	?	?	No roundels and no c/n on. C/n sometimes reported in error as 402608 which is CCCP-11378!
7T-WAE	550	402810	Sold to an unknown Russian operator as RA-11119 by 12-95??? *
7T-WAF	?	402811	
7T-WAG	591	402812	Sold to Mikma as ER-ACE by 6-95
7T-WAH	516	402809?	

* The registration was re-used; the original An-12B CCCP-11119 (c/n 02348101), a Tashkent-built aircraft completed as a civil version with no gunner's station, was still operational at the same time! Other sources say, however, that 7T-WAE was sold to the Angolan airline ALADA to become D2-FAR.

Angola

• The **Angolan government** operated three An-12s registered D2-EAC, D2-EAD and D2-EAE (c/ns unknown). In reality the aircraft almost certainly belonged to the **Angolan Air Force** (FAA – *Força Aérea Angolana*). Unfortunately, D2-EAD crashed on 19 September 1984. At least one An-12 had full

Algerian Air Force An-12B 7T-WAC/514 resting between flights in company with assorted general aviation aircraft. (*Air Forces of the World*)

FAA markings and the serial T-304; this aircraft was lost in a landing accident at Kanyengue on 27 January 2002.

• An airline called **Aerotropical, Lda** leased 'military' An-12B ER-ACE (c/n 402812) from Mikma in 1996. Sadly, the aircraft was shot down on finals to Lukapa on 27 February 1996 while operating for Aerotropical.

• **Air Nacoia Exploração de Aeronaves [–/ANL]** based in Luanda leased 'military' An-12BP RA-11531 (c/n 6344506), a former weather research aircraft, from GosNII GA in June 1994. In 1996 the aircraft was sold to Air Nacoia and transferred to the Angolan register as D2-FVG No. 1. Unfortunately, on 12 March 1997 it crashed in Lukapa, Angola, whereupon its registration was reused (see below).

• **ALADA – Sociedade de Transportes Aéreos [–/RAD]**, also based in Luanda, had eight *Cubs*.

Registration	Version	C/n	Notes
D2-FAJ		?	
D2-FAO	An-12B (+)	?	Bought ?-96. Reported as ex-Algerian Air Force 7T-WAG/591 (c/n 402812) but this cannot be true (see previous chapter/Moldavia/Mikma)
D2-FAR	An-12B (+)	402810	Ex-RA-11119 No. 2????, ex-Algerian Air Force 7T-WAE/550, bought ?-96
D2-FAW	An-12 (+)	?	
D2-FAY	An-12BP (+)	8345810	Ex-Russian Air Force '37 Red'
D2-FAZ		?	*Damaged beyond repair Saurimo 11-8-98*
D2-FBJ	An-12B (+)	401711	Ex-SVGAL (North-East Cargo Airlines) RA-11421, bought ?-99
D2-FRG	An-12BP (–)	00347202	Ex-Chelyabinsk Air Enterprise RA-12987, bought 7-98

• In 1999 an airline called **Hellier International** acquired a demilitarised An-12BK re-equipped with an ROZ-1 radar (D2-FBZ, ex-Special Cargo Airlines RA-11329, c/n 8346010); in 2001 the aircraft was sold to Space Cargo as 3C-QRD. Earlier Hellier International had leased D2-FBY from Savanair (see below).

• **Loex Air Cargo** leased An-12BP RA-11531 from GosNII GA in November 1993, returning it to the lessor in May 1994.

• **National Commuter Airlines** bought 'civil' An-12BP RA-11114 (c/n 01347909) from Special Cargo Airlines; the aircraft was reregistered D2-FDC. By May 2001 it had been sold to the Moldovan airline Tiramavia as ER-ACJ.

• **Savanair, Lda [–/SVN]** owned two *Cubs* – 'civil' An-12BP D2-FBY (ex-Komiinteravia RA-12959, c/n 8345510) and 'military' An-12B D2-FRT (ex-Russian Air Force '10 Red', c/n 3341408). In 2000 the former aircraft was sold to the Moldovan carrier Airwest, becoming ER-ACW, while D2-FRT was sold to São Tomé & Principe as S9-CAQ. Additionally, Savanair leased 'military' An-12A EL-ASA (c/n 3340909) from Santa Cruz Imperial in early 1999; on 2 February 1999 the aircraft crashed fatally in Luanda. 'Civil' An-12BP TN-AFR (c/n 8345502) leased from an unidentified airline was just as unlucky – it was shot down near Luzamba on 1 July 1999.

• **Voar Airlines** ('voar' means 'to fly' in Portuguese) leased 'civil' An-12B RA-11527 (c/n 02348208) from Pulkovo Avia in 1994.

• In 1995 **Von Haaf Air** acquired 'military' An-12A D2-FVD (ex-RA-98101, c/n 1901706) from NPO Energiya; the aircraft was grey overall with a blue cheatline. The following year it was sold to Air Cess as EL-AKN and a new *Cub* was bought instead, namely ex-Moscow Airways 'military' An-12B RA-11318 (c/n 401908) which became D2-FVG No. 2. However, in 1998 this aircraft was also sold, going to Congo as TN-AFJ.

National Commuter Airlines An-12BP D2-FDB (c/n 02348207) at Sharjah in March 2002. (Nikolay Ionkin)

- Sixteen more Angolan Cubs – D2-FBB, D2-FBC, 'military' An-12BP D2-FBD (ex-Ukraine AF UR-12423, c/n 4342610), D2-FBG, D2-FBK, An-12AP D2-FBM, D2-FBS, D2-FBT, 'military' An-12A D2-FCU (c/n 2340503), 'military' An-12B D2-FCV (ex-Magadan-Aerogrooz RA-11986, c/n 401901), 'civil' An-12BP D2-FDB (ex-Komiinteravia RA-11526, c/n 02348207), 'military' An-12BP D2-FDT (ex-NAPO-Aviatrans RA-12192, c/n 5343305), 'military' An-12B D2-FRC (ex-Penza Air Enterprise RA-11338, c/n 3341506), D2-FRI, D2-FRK and D2-MAZ – were operated by unidentified Angolan carriers, lacking any insignia other than the registration. (This sure says a thing or two; if the operator is so reluctant to reveal its identity it is more than probable that the aircraft are involved in some illegal operations, such as arms trafficking.)

Two of these aircraft returned to the CIS: D2-FBD was sold to Mikma by May 1998 as ER-ADL, while D2-FCU became ER-ADE with Aerocom. D2-FDB was acquired by Vega Airlines as LZ-VED in 2001; D2-FCV and D2-FDT went to São Tomé & Principe in 2001 as S9-CDB and S9-BOT respectively.

Bangladesh

Bismillah Airlines [–/BML] leases An-12s from other airlines as required. For example, from January 1999 to March 2000 it operated 'civil' An-12BP RA-12988 (c/n 00347206) leased from the now-defunct Baikalavia.

Bosnia-Herzegovina

In 2000 the Bosnia-Herzegovenian cargo airline **BIO Air Company [–/BIO]**, a division of the Bosnian Investment Organisation, leased An-12BP UR-11332 (c/n 4342202) from Khors Aircompany; the aircraft was reregistered T9-CAD.

Bulgaria

- The cargo airline **Air Sofia [CT/SFB]** operated 12 An-12s, often wet-leasing them to other airlines.

Registration	Version	C/n	Notes
LZ-SFA	An-12BP (−)	02348007	Ex-SiGi Air Cargo LZ-SGA, ex-YU-AIC, basic SiGi Air Cargo blue/white c/s
LZ-SFC	An-12B (+)	402913	Ex-SiGi Air Cargo LZ-SGC, ex-CCCP-48984; D/D 15-2-92. To RA-48984. C/n also reported in error as 402513
LZ-SFE	An-12BP (+)	5342708	Demilitarised. Ex-Soviet AF CCCP-11230, bought 6-92. Sold to Bulgarian Flying Cargo ?-93 as LZ-BFA
LZ-SFG	An-12P (+)	3341605	Demilitarised. Ex-Soviet AF CCCP-11145 No. 2 (CCCP-11145 No. 1 was an An-10), D/D 16-6-92. Crashed Lajes, Azores, 4-2-98 while operating in own colours
LZ-SFJ	An-12BP (+)	4342105	Ex-Czech Air Force 2105 Black, D/D 10-9-97; not in 2002 fleet list, fate unknown
LZ-SFK	An-12B (+)	2341901	Demilitarised. Ex-Soviet AF CCCP-11511, D/D 16-6-92.
LZ-SFL	An-12BP (+)	4342101	Demilitarised. Ex-Soviet AF CCCP-11908 No. 1, D/D 16-6-92. Was lst Avioimpex Macedonia 6-95 to 7-96 as Z3-AFA
LZ-SFM	An-12P (+)	401705	Demilitarised. Ex-/to UR-11765, leased from Antonov Design Bureau 1993–8
LZ-SFN	An-12B (+)	2340806	Demilitarised. Ex-Phoenix Air Cargo LZ-FEA/LZ-PHA, ex-RA-11307, bought 13-10-94.
LZ-SFS	An-12BP (+)	6344308	Demilitarised. Ex-Polish Air Force SP-LZB/51 Red, bought 2-95
LZ-SFT	An-12BP (+)	9346904	Demilitarised. Ex-Solis Aviation LZ-SAA, bought ?-01
RA-12108	An-12BP (+)	9346308	Demilitarised. Leased from Aeroflot in 1994

(**Note:** The registrations LZ-SFB, LZ-SFF, LZ-SFI, LZ-SFO, LZ-SFQ and LZ-SFR have not been noted; LZ-SFD was an An-22 sans suffixe, LZ-SFH is an An-26 and LZ-SFP is an An-24B.)

With the exception of LZ-SFA which retained the basic blue/white colours of ex-owner SiGi Air Cargo, the aircraft were painted white overall. Not infrequently, however, Air Sofia An-12s leased abroad were repainted in the colours of the lessor. Also, in August 1997 LZ-SFK received a 'Noah's Ark look' with various animals painted on the aft fuselage and a black-striped fin fillet.

A curious feature of Air Sofia's An-12s is that most of them had the radar removed and the radar bay faired over. One can only guess why, and how the crews managed to do without weather radar!

• A Sofia-based airline called **Aviostart** [–/VSR] acquired a single demilitarised An-12B registered LZ-ASY (ex-Sakha Avia RA-11991, c/n 402006) in early 2000. The aircraft wore basic Aeroflot red/white polar colours without titles or logo. By 2002 it had been sold to Congo-Brazzaville as TN-AGK No. 2.

• **Balkan Bulgarian Airlines [LZ/LAZ]** was the first An-12 operator in Bulgaria, operating 12 of the type.

Registration	Version	C/n	Notes
LZ-BAA	An-12BP (−)	8346001	Crashed somewhere in Egypt in 1975
LZ-BAB	An-12BP (−)	8346002	WFU Bourgas 6-6-89, to local museum 10-98
LZ-BAC	An-12BP (−)	6343708	Ex-CCCP-1100..., bought by 7-80. Sold to Bulgarian Air Cargo by 4-02
LZ-BAD	An-12BP	6344001	Ex-CCCP-11012?, bought by 3-84. Crashed Addis Ababa 24-8-84
LZ-BAE	An-12B (−)	402001	Ex-CCCP-1100..., bought by 12-87; leased to HeavyLift Cargo Airlines
LZ-BAF	An-12B (+)	402408	Demilitarised. Ex-CCCP-113xx
LZ-BAG	An-12BP (+)	6344305	Ex-RA-11650; to Bulgarian Flying Cargo by 8-97 as LZ-BFG
LZ-BAH	An-12BP (+)	9346807	Demilitarised. Ex-RA-11317, bought by 2-00; named 'River of Iskar'
RA-11650	An-12BP (+)	6344305	Leased from Arsenyev Aircraft Production Association 9-93; bought and reregistered LZ-BAG by 4-96, see two lines up!
RA-12108	An-12BP (+)	9346308	Demilitarised. Leased from Aeroflot in 1993; later to Air Sofia
CCCP-12975	An-12BP (−)	9346509	Leased from Ural Airlines 6-92 to ?-??
12999	An-12BP (−)	01347701	Lsf Ural Airlines 10-90 to ?-??, Aeroflot colours with additional Balkan titles

• An-12BPs LZ-BAA and LZ-BAB were originally operated by **Bulair**, a sister company of TABSO (an acronym for Bulgarian-Soviet Aviation Co.). TABSO was renamed Balkan on 1 April 1968.

• **Bright Aviation Services** [–/BRW] has three An-12s.

Registration	Version	C/n	Notes
LZ-BRA	An-12BP (+)	8346006	Ex-Inter Trans Air LZ-ITB, bought 10-01
LZ-BRC	An-12BP (−)	8345510	Ex-Airwest ER-ACW, bought ?-02
LZ-BRW	An-12BP (−)	01347907?	Ex-Avial-NV RA-11112? Sold to Aerocom 2-02 as ER-AXA???

• A new airline called **Bulgarian Air Cargo** bought An-12BP LZ-BAC from Balkan in the spring of 2002.

• Sofia-based **Bulgarian Flying Cargo** or **BF Cargo** [FN/BFB] leases An-12s in Bulgaria, operating ten of the type.

An-12BP LZ-BAC (c/n 6343708) of Balkan Cargo, a subsidiary of Balkan Bulgarian Airlines, wore an unusual colour scheme with the green stripes absent from the cheatline and fin flash. (Yefim Gordon archive)

Registration	Version	C/n	Notes
LZ-BFA	An-12BP (+)	5342708	Demilitarised. Ex-Air Sofia LZ-SFE, ex-Soviet AF CCCP-11230, leased 1993; to unknown Russian airline 1996 as RA-11230
LZ-BFB	An-12BP (+)	6343905	Ex-Soviet AF CCCP-11789, leased 1993; to Komsomolsk-Avia ?-96 as RA-11789
LZ-BFC	An-12BP (+)	2400502	Demilitarised. Ex-/to RA-48970, leased from Kumertau Express 1994–6 (originally with Russian registration)
LZ-BFD	An-12BP (+)	5343005	Demilitarised. Ex-RA-98102, lsf Arsenyev Aircraft Production Association ?-95; to Gromov Air by 8-01 as RA-98102
LZ-BFE	An-12TBK (+)	9346308	Demilitarised. Ex-RA-12108, leased by 1999; to Gromov Air by 10-00 as RA-12108
LZ-BFG	An-12BP (+)	6344305	Ex-Balkan LZ-BAG, ex-RA-11650, leased by 8-97; to Gromov Air by 8-00 as RA-11650

Registration	Version	C/n	Notes
LZ-ITA	An-12B (+)	3341004	Demilitarised; previous identity unknown
LZ-ITB	An-12BP (+)	8346006	Ex-Antey RA-11368, bought ?-00. Sold to Bright Aviation Services 10-01 as LZ-BRA
LZ-ITD	An-12PP	00347107	Converted to freighter. Ex-Antey RA-11301, ex-UAF '71 Red'; sold to President Airlines 9-00 as XU-355
LZ-ITS	An-12B (+)	3341505	Ex-Skycabs 4R-SKL, bought ?-00

- **Phoenix Air Cargo** leased 'military' An-12A RA-11307 from the Russian Air Force in 1993. The aircraft was bought in the same year to become LZ-PHA, but then was reregistered LZ-FEA for some reason in 1994. Finally, on 13 October 1994 it was resold to Air Sofia, becoming LZ-SFN.

- In 1999 **Rila Airlines [–/RAB]** of Sofia acquired a single demilitarised An-12BP registered LZ-RAA; the all-white aircraft (c/n 402410) is ex-Samara Airlines RA-11959.

- In 2002 **Scorpion Air [–/SPN]** bought 'civil' An-12BP LZ-VEB (c/n 01347701) from Vega Air.

- In 1990 **SiGi Air Cargo** leased 'civil' An-12BP CCCP-11129 (c/n 02348204) from Aeroflot, repainting it in its smart blue/white colour scheme. Unfortunately the aircraft was damaged beyond repair in a landing accident at Janina, Bulgaria, on 8 November 1991. A while earlier the airline bought the

- In September 1992 – July 1993 **Global Air** operated two 'civil' An-12BPs leased from Pulkovo Avia. These were temporarily registered LZ-PVK (ex/to RA-11108, c/n 01347810) and LZ-PVL (ex/to RA-11127, c/n 02348202).

- **Inter Trans Air [–/ITT]** operated four An-12s.

Yugoslav Air Force's sole surviving 'civil' An-12BP (73311/YU-AIC, c/n 02348007) in 1991; the aircraft was registered LZ-SGA. On 16 March 1992 it was leased to Air Sofia and reregistered LZ-SFA; however, SiGi Air Cargo ceased operations the same year and the aircraft was finally sold to Air Sofia on 23 February 1998.

- **Solis Aviation [–/SOF]** of Sofia leases An-12s from other carriers as required. In 2001 it operated a demilitarised An-12BP, LZ-SAA, bought from Amuraviatrans (ex-RA-13341, c/n 9346304); that very year, however, the aircraft was sold to Air Sofia as LZ-SFT.

- Plovdiv-based **Vega Airlines [–/VEA]** owns four *Cubs*.

Registration	Version	C/n	Notes
LZ-VEA	An-12A (+)	1340106	Ex-Rostvertol RA-11976, bought ?-99
LZ-VEB	An-12BP (–)	01347701	Ex-Ural Airlines RA-12999, bought ?-99; red/blue/white c/s
LZ-VEC	An-12BP (+)	6344610	Demilitarised. Ex-TAPO-Avia UK 93920, bought ?-00; black/white c/s, named 'Tsar Simeon Veliki' (Czar Simeon the Great)
LZ-VED	An-12BP (–)	02348207	Ex-D2-FDB, bought ?-01

Burundi

Four *Cubs* with Burundi registrations – two different aircraft registered 9U-BHN (c/ns unknown), 'civil' An-12BP 9U-BHO (ex-Renan ER-ACK, c/n 8345503) and 9U-NHN – have been sighted to date. Unfortunately the operators are unknown in all cases, as the aircraft were devoid of titles.

Cambodia (Kampuchea)

- **Cambodia Cargo** (later renamed **Kampuchean Airlines**) leased 'civil' An-12BP RA-11034 (c/n 7345010) from Aeroflot's Irkutsk division in 1993.

- **Imtrec Aviation Cambodia [–/IMT]** of Phnom Penh has a single An-12 registered XU-365. There are indications this may be ex-Uzbekistan Avialeasing An-12BK UK 11109 (c/n 02348005).

- **President Airlines [TO/PSD]**, a subsidiary of Holiday Group Cambodia, operates An-12BP XU-315 No. 2 (c/n unknown)[85] and XU-355, a converted An-12PP ECM aircraft bought in September 2000 (ex-Inter Trans Air LZ-ITD, c/n 00347107). Some sources claim the latter aircraft was later sold to Sri Lanka as 4R-AIA.

- **Yana Airlines** leased An-12s as required until it suspended operations in 2001. For example, the above-mentioned XU-315 was reportedly operated in January 1999; another aircraft registered XU-345 (c/n unknown) was sighted in April 2000.

- An all-white and unmarked An-12 registered XU-395 was reported in September 2002, but its exact version and c/n are unknown.

Canada

Toronto-based **Skylink Aviation, Inc.** operated 'civil' An-12BP RA-11114 (c/n 01347909) leased from Komiinteravia in December 1994.

Central African Republic

'Military' An-12As TL-ACJ (ex-Air Pass 3D-AKV, ex-Air Cess TL-ACV, ex-RA-48971; c/n 1340107) and TL-ACR (c/n and ex-identity unknown) were registered in 1998. The former aircraft had basic Air Pass colours without titles, while the other was white overall. The chances are that they belonged to **Centrafricain Airlines [GC/CET]** founded in 1998 which bought almost the entire fleet of the defunct Air Pass (see Swaziland section). Interestingly, besides Bangui (the capital of the Central African Republic), the airline was also based at Sharjah, UAE – as was Air Cess, a sister company of Air Pass (see Liberian section). It makes you wonder if all three airlines had a common owner and Centrafricain Airlines is simply the successor of Air Cess/Air Pass incorporated under a new name.

China (People's Republic of China)

- Chinese developments paralleled those in the former Soviet Union in that originally the huge country had just one huge airline, **CAAC (Civil Aviation Administration of China)** – the 'Chinese Aeroflot' (even the livery was extremely similar to Aeroflot's 1973-standard colour scheme). In 1984, when deregulation set in, numerous new airlines (often based on CAAC's regional divisions – the equivalent of Civil Aviation Directorates in the USSR) started appearing; a few of these took over the former CAAC *Cubs*, some of which are listed below.

Registration	Version	C/n	Notes
B-201	An-12BP (+)	6344402	To Air China as B-3151
B-203	An-12BP (+)	8345303	To Air China as B-3152
B-1056	An-12BP (+)	7345107	Ex-PLAAF 51056 Red?
B-1059	An-12BP (+)	7345207	Ex-PLAAF 1059 Red, transferred after 1988. Preserved PLAAF Museum, Datangshan AB, Changping
B-3101	Y8F-100	1001	Registered 1985. To China Postal Airlines
B-3102	Y8F-100	1002	Registered 1985. To China Postal Airlines
B-3103	Y8F-100	1005	Registered 1985. To China Postal Airlines
B-3104	Y8B	?	
B-3105	Y8B	070802?	To ACA Air Changan Airlines, see below

All-white An-12 TL-ACR (c/n unknown) seen here at Ras al Khaimah, UAE, in March 2002 probably belonged to Centrafricain Airlines. (Nikolay Ionkin)

An-12BP B-3151 (c/n 6344402), seen here after retirement, illustrates the blue/white livery worn by the type with the Civil Aviation Administration of China (CAAC). (*China Aircraft*)

B-3196	Y8	?	Ground instructional airframe at Xian Aeronautical Institute
B-3198	Y8	?	Ground instructional airframe at Xian Aeronautical Institute
B-3199	Y8	?	Ground instructional airframe at Xian Aeronautical Institute
B-4101	Y8	?	Preserved PLAAF Museum

• **ACA Air Changan Airlines [2Z/CGN]** based in Xian operated a single Y8B registered B-3105. The aircraft was leased to the Sri Lankan Air Force as CR873 pending the return to service of a damaged sister aircraft (CR871), but eventually was never returned to the lessor.

• **Air China International [CA/CCA]** (formerly CAAC Beijing) operated two Soviet-built 'military' An-12BPs registered B-3151 (ex-B-201, c/n 6344402) and B-3152 (ex-B-203, c/n 8345303). Both were retired by 2000.

• **China Postal Airlines [–/CYZ]**, the flying division of the Ministry of Posts & Telecommunications based in Tianjin, operates five Y8F-100s registered B-3101, B-3102, B-3103, B-3109 and B-3110 (c/ns 1001, 1002, 1005 and 1303 respectively; the c/n of the last aircraft is unknown). The airline has also ordered a single Y8F-400 due for delivery in 2002.

• **China Southern Airlines [CZ/CSN]** based at Huanzhou-Baiyun leased 'civil' An-12BP RA-11116 (c/n 01348006) from Baikal Airlines at an unknown date.

- **China Xinjiang Airlines [XO/CXJ]** (formerly CAAC Xinjiang Regional Administration) based at Urumqi-Diwobao has a single Shaanxi Y8B, B-3105 (c/n unknown).

- The **People's Liberation Army Air Force** (PLAAF, or *Chungkuo Shen Min Taie-Fang-Tsun Pu-tai*) was the largest An-12/Y8 operator in China. Known aircraft are listed below. (**Note:** In the five-digit PLAAF serials currently in use the first two digits may be a code denoting one of the 11 defence districts, the fourth digit a unit code, while the third and fifth digits make up the individual number of the aircraft in the unit.)

Serial	Version	C/n	Notes
181 Red	Y8	?	
182 Red	An-12BP (+)	?	
182 Black	Y8C	001802	Prototype
980 Red	Y8	?	
982 Red	Y8	?	
983 Red	Y8	?	
987 Red	Y8	?	
989 Red	Y8	?	
4139 Red	Y8E	?	Prototype. Ground instructional airframe at Xian Aeronautical Institute
8711 Red?	Y8X (Y8MPA)	?	Serial not 100% sure!
9271 Red	Y8	?	Ground instructional airframe at Beijing Aeronautical Institute
9281 Red	Y8	?	Ground instructional airframe at Beijing Aeronautical Institute
31045 Red	Y8	?	Preserved PLAAF Museum
31046 Red	Y8	?	Ground instructional airframe at Xian Aeronautical Institute
31048 Red	Y8	?	
31141 Red	Y8	?	Ground instructional airframe at Beijing Aeronautical Institute
31146 Red	Y8	?	
31147 Red	Y8	?	Ground instructional airframe at Xian Aeronautical Institute
32042 Red	An-12BP (+)	?	Preserved PLAAF Museum
32045 Red	An-12BP (+)	?	
51056 Red	An-12BP (+)?	7345107?	To CAAC as B-1056?
94001 Red	Y8	?	Also marked 'LH' on fin

Colombia

The cargo airline **SADELCA (Sociedad Aérea del Caqueta, Ltda)** [–/SDK] based in Villavicencio and Neiva leased An-12BP RA-12980 (c/n 00347103) from Tyumen' Airlines at an unspecified date.

Congo-Brazzaville

- **Trans Air Congo [Q8/TSG]** operates an An-12B registered in Equatorial Guinea as 3C-QQL (previous identity unknown, c/n 3341803). The aircraft was leased from the Russian company Troika Leasing in 2001.

- **Air Atlantis** operated 'military' An-12BP TN-AGC (ex-TN-AFW, c/n 4342305) in 1999.

- The above-mentioned An-12BP TN-AFW (ex-Soviet Air Force '14 Red') has been reported as operated by **Aviaputsk**.

The second prototype Y8C wears the AVIC (Aviation Industry Corporation) logo but is believed to be operated by the PLAAF. (*China Aircraft*)

- **Hellier International** operated An-12BK TN-AGE (ex-Polyot Russian Airlines RA-11320, c/n 4342409) in 1999.

- The operators of An-12 TN-ACM, 'military' An-12B TN-AFJ (ex-Von Haaf Air D2-FVG No. 2, c/n 401908), 'civil' An-12 TN-AFR (ex-RA-12951, c/n 8345502), 'civil' An-12BP TN-AGK No. 1 (ex-Mikma ER-ACG, c/n 9346504; sold to Forner Airlines as ST-AQQ) and demilitarised An-12B TN-AGK No. 2 (ex-Aviostart LZ-ASY, c/n 402006) are unknown.

Cuba

- The fleet of **Empresa Consolidada Cubana de Aviación** [CU/CUB], the Cuban flag carrier (often called Cubana for short), included a single demilitarised An-12B registered CU-T827 (c/n 401504). The aircraft was built to the same specification as the Indian Air Force An-12Bs but featured additional underfloor fuel cells, and so was like an An-12BP with a narrow cargo door. Unfortunately, CU-T827 was lost in a fatal crash near Mexico City on 9 February 1967.

- It has also been reported that the **Cuban Air Force** (FAR – *Fuerza Aérea Revolucionaria*) took delivery of several An-12s, but none have been identified so far.

Czechoslovakia, Czech/Slovak Federal Republic, Czechia

Two Tashkent-built 'military' An-12s (c/ns 4342105 and 4342209) were delivered to the **Czech Air Force** (CzAF, or ČVL – *Československé Vojenské Letectvo*) in 1964. In keeping with the then-current (and still current) Czech practice they received serials matching the last four digits of the c/n – 2105 Black and 2209 Black respectively. The transports were based at Prague-Kbely AB.

In 1989 Václav Havel's 'gentle revolution' put an end to socialism in the country and the Czechoslovak Socialist Republic became the Federal Republic of Czechoslovakia. On 1 January 1993, however, the 'gentle revolution' was followed by an equally gentle divorce, and the once-united CzAF (including the tiny An-12 fleet) was divided between the Czech Republic and Slovakia; the 'new' **Czech Air Force** (*České Vojenské Letectvo*) retained the example serialled 2105 Black. The aircraft belonged to the 1.SDLP (*šmíšený dopravní letecký pulk* – composite transport air regiment).

However, operating just a single aircraft of a given type didn't make much sense. After making its final flight in CzAF service on 26 May 1996 the An-12 was placed into storage at Prague-Ruzyne International airport. The following year it was sold to the Bulgarian carrier Air Sofia (which took delivery of the aircraft on 8 October 1997) and registered LZ-SFJ.

Djibouti

Daallo Airlines [D3/DAO] operated 'military' An-12BP UN-11001 (c/n 5343408) in January–February 2000.

Egypt

- The **Egyptian Air Force** (EAF, or *al Quwwat al-Jawwiya il-Misriya*) had 25 *Cubs*, including 15 Voronezh-built An-12Bs delivered in 1964–7 and ten Tashkent-built An-12BPs purchased in 1966–72. The aircraft were operated by a single squadron (No. 16?) based at Cairo-West. At first they wore a restrained civil-style colour scheme with EAF serials and large Egyptian flag fin flashes but no roundels. Civil registrations were added soon afterwards, and these were apparently changed from time to time on some aircraft for security reasons.

Serial	Registration	Version	C/n	Notes
1216	a) SU-AOJ	An-12B (+)	402302	Registration confirmed worn in 1968
	b) SU-AOS?			Registration reported in 1969 but unconfirmed!
1217	none	An-12B (+)	402303?	Destroyed Cairo-West by Israeli air strikes 6-6-67?
1218	none	An-12B (+)	402304?	Destroyed Cairo-West by Israeli air strikes 6-6-67?
1219	SU-AOI	An-12B (+)	402305	
1220	SU-AOR	An-12B (+)	402306	
1221	SU-AOZ	An-12B (+)	402307?	
1222	SU-APB	An-12B (+)	402308	
1223	SU-AOS	An-12B (+)	402309	Was a testbed for the Brandner E-1 engine in 1962
1224?	SU-AOP	An-12B (+)	402906	
1225?	SU-AOJ	An-12B (+)	402907	
1226	a) SU-AOI?	An-12B (+)	402908	Registration reported in 1966 but unconfirmed!
	b) SU-AOT			Registration confirmed
	c) SU-BAW			Registration confirmed
1227	SU-APA	An-12B (+)	402909	
1228	a) SU-AOI	An-12B (+)	402910	
	b) SU-APZ			
1229	a) SU-AOK	An-12B (+)	402911?	
	b) SU-APC			
1231?	a) SU-AOZ	An-12B (+)	402912	Not confirmed if carried EAF serial!
	b) SU-ARB			
1233	SU-ARC	An-12BP (+)	6344107	
1234	a) SU-AOR	An-12BP (+)	6344108	
	b) SU-APX			
1240	SU-APY	An-12BP (+)	9346706	
1241	SU-ARA	An-12BP (+)	9346707	
1242	SU-ARE	An-12BP (+)	9346709	
1243	SU-ARD	An-12BP (+)	9346710	
1251	SU-ARY	An-12BP (+)	02348209	
1252	SU-AVA	An-12BP (+)	02348210	
1253	SU-ARZ	An-12BP (+)	02348302	
1254	SU-AVB	An-12BP (+)	02348305	

...AND ABROAD (NON-CIS OPERATORS)

The Egyptian Air Force was the second-largest military *Cub* operator outside the USSR; the 25-strong fleet included An-12B 1220/SU-AOR (c/n 402306). (RART)

An interesting view of two EAF An-12BPs – 1241/SU-ARA (c/n 9346707) and 1254/SU-AVB (c/n 02348205, the last aircraft delivered), probably at Cairo-West; note the difference in window placement. Neither aircraft has the cannon installed. (RART)

Starting in 1976, the *Cubs* were supplemented and gradually replaced by 23 Lockheed C-130Hs, the last of which arrived in 1982 (later augmented by three 'stretched' C-130H-30s). This was in line with Egypt's new allegiance to the West. The last of the An-12s reportedly remained in service until the early 1990s; eventually, however, all the *Cubs* were retired and progressively scrapped.

• According to *Aircraft Illustrated*, in June 1970 **United Arab Airlines [MS/MSR]** (the precursor of present-day Egyptair) ordered two An-12s. However, the order never materialised.

Equatorial Guinea

• **Atlas Air** operated 'civil' An-12BP 3C-ZZD bought from Santa Cruz Imperial (ex-EL-ALA, c/n 00347305) in 1999; however, the aircraft was sold to Lotus Airways in September of that year.

• **KNG Transavia Cargo [–/VCG]**, a Sharjah-based subsidiary of CNG Transavia, operates 'military' An-12BPs 3C-AAG (ex-RA-98119, c/n 7344801) and 3C-AAL (ex-RA-98103, c/n 00347003).

- **Space Cargo, Inc. [–/SGO]** based at Sharjah, UAE, acquired two *Cubs* in 2001; these are demilitarised An-12BK 3C-QRD re-equipped with an ROZ-1 radar (ex-Hellier International D2-FBZ, c/n 8346010) and 'civil' An-12BP 3C-QRI (ex-Tiramavia ER-ACJ).

- **Lotus Airways** (also based at Sharjah) purchased 'civil' An-12BP 3C-ZZD from Atlas Air.

- Additionally, 'military' An-12BP 3C-AAQ (c/n unknown), 'civil' An-12BP 3C-OOZ (ex-RA-12975, c/n 9346509) and demilitarised An-12BK 3C-QRN spotted in 2000 belong to as-yet unidentified operators. (3C-OOZ was reported for Air Cess long after the airline had ceased to exist!)

Ethiopia

The **Ethiopian Air Force** (*ye Etiopia Ayer Hail*) operated 16 ex-Soviet Air Force An-12BPs delivered in 1977 when Mengistu Haile Mariam seized power. Originally they wore ex-Soviet Air Force grey colours, but with the exception of three aircraft lost to enemy action or in accidents, the surviving *Cubs* were repainted in three-tone green/brown camouflage by 2000.

Serial	Version	C/n	Notes
1501	An-12B (+)?	?	
1502	An-12B (+)	401802	
1503	An-12BP (+)	4342009?	Also reported as An-12B c/n 402009!
1504	An-12B (+)?	?	
1505	An-12BP (+)	5342907	
1506	An-12B (+)	402002	Destroyed by enemy action Tesenni 15-1-84
1507	An-12B (+)?	?	
1508	An-12B (+)?	?	
1509	An-12B (+)?	?	Damaged beyond repair at Addis Ababa-Haile Selassie Int'l before 5-84, derelict
1510	An-12B (+)?	?	
1511	An-12B (+)?	?	
1512	An-12BP (+)	5343206	
1513	An-12B (+)?	?	
1514	An-12B (+)?	?	
1515	An-12B (+)?	?	
1516	An-12B (+)?	?	

Fiji

Hellier International operated 'civil' An-12BP D2-FBY bought from Sakha Avia (ex-RA-12959, c/n 8345510) in 1999. Another Fijian-registered *Cub*, 'military' An-12B DQ-FBS (ex-Ukraine Air Alliance UR-UAF, c/n 3341108) probably also belonged to this airline; it was sold to Moldova in 2001 as ER-ACP.

France

- In May 1999 'military' An-12BP EX-11001 (c/n 6344104?) was seen at Sharjah operated by the French petroleum company **Motul**, with appropriate titles.

- The airline **Heli-Union [–/HLU]** based in Paris, Grenoble, Tarbes and Île d'Yeu wet-leased An-12BP UR-11819 (c/n 6344009) from Vitair in 1995.

'Civil' An-12BP 3C-ZZD (c/n 00347305) served with Lotus Airways since September 1999. The previous registration (EL-ALA) can still be seen under the paint.
(Sergey and Dmitriy Komissarov archive)

The Ethiopian Air Force operated 16 second-hand An-12s, including this early An-12BP '1505' (c/n 5342907). Note the overpainted Soviet flag and registration. (RART)

Ghana

- On 4 October 1961 **Ghana Airways [GH/GHA]** took delivery of an Irkutsk-built 'military' An-12A registered 9G-AAZ (c/n 024009). Among other things, the freighter was used for flights to the UK to pick up spares for Ghana Airways' fleet of Bristol Britannia 309s, Vickers Viscount 838s and Vickers VC.10 Srs 1102s.

The *Cub*'s career in Ghana proved to be brief. In 1962 the aircraft was withdrawn from use at Accra – to quote the *Royal Air Force Flying Review* magazine (Vol. XVIII, No. 4, December 1962), 'owing to its inadequate operating economy. Sources in Ghana state that the An-12's payload is only 14,000 lb. The Ivchenko AI-20 turboprops have been removed and will be used by Ghana Airways' Il-18s, and it has been suggested that the An-12 airframe be placed in a public park as a playground for children!'

About the same time, on 2 November 1962, *Flight International* reflected on 'Ghana's lunatic obsession with air transport as an instrument of prestige' and wrote: 'In fairness, the An-12 was not as priceless a collector's piece [of air transport lunacy] as it might have been, as there appeared to be no guns installed. Perhaps the empty turret will be used, for a surcharge of course, as an observation lounge. No doubt if guns are installed on regular services, this will be in furtherance of a policy of "if you can't beat 'em, shoot 'em".'

Articles in the same vein appeared in *The Aeroplane and Commercial Aviation News* and in *Newsweek* the same year, the authors describing Ghana Airways' Soviet airliners as 'an economical nightmare' and claiming they were driving the country into bankruptcy. The Soviet press answered in kind: in April 1962 the **Novoye vremya** (*New Time*) magazine let loose with a venomous editorial entitled 'They're jealous'. The main thrust of this article was that the assertions of the Western press were 'malicious lies from beginning to end' and that 'the Western aircraft industry monopolies, which are losing lucrative contracts, are starting to use the dirtiest tricks against their competitors and trying to undermine the reputation of Soviet civil aircraft'. Of course, one has to remember that this was the height of the Cold War and that the media on both sides of the Iron Curtain were past masters at stirring up anti-Soviet (or anti-Western) sentiment. The truth probably lies somewhere in between.

Anyway, in 1963 An-12A 9G-AAZ was restored to airworthy condition and returned to the Soviet Union; its subsequent fate is unknown.

- According to *Royal Air Force Flying Review*, in 1961 the **Ghanaian Air Force** received three more An-12s donated by the Soviet government. No serials are known.

Guinea

- Conakry-based **Aero Trans Guinée** leased 'civil' An-12BP RA-12986 (c/n 00347201) from Samara Airlines in June 1993.

- Four 'military' An-12BPs registered 3X-GBA to 3X-GBD (c/ns 02348008, 02348009, 7345001 and 02348301 (?)) were delivered to Guinea; 3X-GBC could be ex-CCCP-11030. Though nominally owned by flag carrier **Air Guinée [GI/GIB]**, they were in fact operated by the **Guinea Air Force** (*Force Aérienne de Guinée*).

- An obscure company named **Minenta Labell Guinée** leased demilitarised An-12TB RA-11049 (c/n 9346109) from Yermolino Airlines in early 2002.

India

The **Indian Air Force** (IAF, or *Bharatiya Vayu Sena*) was the first export customer, ordering an initial eight An-12s in 1961; No. 44 Sqn 'Mountain Geese' at Agra, Uttar-Pradesh, took delivery of the first *Cub* on 1 March. A second batch of eight was ordered in 1962 for delivery to No. 25 Sqn 'Himalayan Eagles' at Chandigarh, Uttar-Pradesh. The IAF was also the largest foreign customer; according to available sources, 46 aircraft built by all three factories producing the type were delivered to the two squadrons, but more than 50 serials have been reported. Of course, it is possible that some of the *Cubs* were reserialled.

Serial	Version	C/n	Notes
BL532	An-12A (+)	024001	Grey c/s
BL533	An-12A (+)	1901601	Damaged 15-8-61 but repaired
BL534	An-12A (+)		
BL535	An-12A (+)		
BL536	An-12A (+)	1901603	No. 25 Sqn. Crashed Chandigarh AB 5-8-61
BL539	An-12A (+)	024008	
BL711		?	Coded 'C', grey/white c/s
L727		?	Later reserialled BL727. Coded 'G', grey/white c/s, later 'I', grey c/s; preserved IAF Museum, Palam AB
BL730		?	Coded 'P', grey c/s
BL731	An-12B (+)	2401303	Coded 'U', later 'Z', still later 'Q', grey/white c/s
BL732	An-12B (+)	2401304?	Grey/white c/s
BL733	An-12B (+)	2401305?	
BL734	An-12B (+)	2401306?	Crashed Palam AB 16-7-63
BL735	An-12B (+)	2401401	
BL736	An-12B (+)	2401402	Coded 'N', later 'U'
BL737	An-12B (+)	2401403	Coded 'B'
BL738	An-12B (+)	2401404	Coded 'C', grey/white c/s
BL739	An-12B (+)	2401405	Coded 'D', callsign VU-FPG
BL740	An-12B (+)	2401406?	Coded 'L'
BL741	An-12B (+)	2401501	Coded 'Q', later 'F', still later 'G'
L742	An-12B (+)	2401502?	Later reserialled BL742. Coded 'E', later 'T', grey/white c/s
BL743	An-12B (+)	2401503	Coded 'D'
BL748		?	
BL913		?	Reported as c/n 401504/sold to Cubana as CU-T827 but this is doubtful!
BL914	An-12B (+)	2401505	Coded 'M', later 'Z', callsign VU-PGH
BL915	An-12B (+)	2401506	Coded 'R', grey/white c/s
BL916	An-12B (+)	401507?	
BL917	An-12B (+)	401508?	
BL918	An-12B (+)	401509?	
BL919	An-12B (+)	401510?	
BL920	An-12B (+)	401511?	
L450		?	
L451		?	
L452		?	
L645	An-12BP (+)	6344205	Coded 'H', later 'S', callsign VU-PPA, grey c/s
L646	An-12BP (+)	6344206	Coded 'J', later 'W', still later 'G', callsign VU-PPB, grey c/s
L647	An-12BP (+)	6344207	Coded 'K', later 'Q', still later 'X', grey c/s
L648	An-12BP (+)	6344208	Coded 'B'
L649	An-12BP (+)	6344209	Coded 'X', later 'J', still later 'Q', grey c/s
L650*	An-12BP (+)	6344210	Coded 'M', grey c/s
L651	An-12BP (+)	6344301?	Coded 'T'
L652	An-12BP (+)	6344302?	Coded 'M'
L653	An-12BP (+)	6344303?	Coded 'Y'
L1471		?	
L1472		?	
L2170		?	Coded 'J', grey c/s
L2171		?	Coded 'K'???
L2172	An-12BP (+)	5343401	Coded 'L', grey c/s; No. 25 Sqn
L2173		?	
L2174		?	

* Some sources claim L650 was sold to the Iraqi Air Force as I.A.F.685, but this is wrong (see Iraqi section).

Ghana Airways An-12A 9G-AAZ (c/n 024009) was one of only 12 *Cub*s having c/ns in the so-called Aviaexport system not revealing the factory of origin (actually Irkutsk), batch number and number of the aircraft in the batch. Its African career proved to be brief.

...AND ABROAD (NON-CIS OPERATORS)

Indian Air Force An-12BP L647/K (c/n 6344207) visiting the UK, most probably to pick up spares for British-supplied combat aircraft; note Avro Vulcan B.2 XM647 in the background. (RART)

This IAF An-12BP, L649/Q (c/n 6344209), wears appropriate 'Indian Air Force' titles. The white top of the forward fuselage was meant to stop the flight deck from getting excessively hot. (RART)

Some of the *Cub*s wore overall medium-grey camouflage with a white top to the flight deck to prevent it from turning into a steam bath for the crew, while others sported a more high-visibility colour scheme, with a white upper fuselage/vertical tail, a grey belly and a thin black cheatline. Individual tail codes within each unit were introduced soon after service entry; these were very conspicuous and so were changed from time to time for security reasons.

In 1984 the IAF decided to replace the An-12, which had done sterling service but was getting long in the tooth, in order to meet the HETAC (**HE**avy **T**ransport **A**ir**C**raft) requirement. The decision was speeded by the discovery of fatigue cracks in the wing spars of some *Cub*s. The choice fell on the Ilyushin Il-76MD *Candid-B* four-jet transport; deliveries began in February 1985 and the two squadrons gradually phased out the An-12 as deliveries progressed.

Indonesia

• When President Soekarno was in office, Indonesia was on fairly good terms with the Soviet Union and enjoyed Soviet military aid. In 1964 the **Indonesian Air Force** (AURI – *Angkatan Udara Republik Indonesia*) bought nine An-12s serialled T-1201 to T-1209; no c/ns are known. T-1205 was named 'Ardjuna' after a famous warrior in the Hindu religion. The first six aircraft became quasi-civil at some stage, receiving the registrations PK-PUA to PK-PUF.

In 1966, however, Dr Soekarno was overthrown by the staunchly anti-Communist Gen. Soeharto. A wave of repressions against Communists swept through Indonesia, and Soviet support was promptly withdrawn. Predictably, all Soviet-built aircraft were soon grounded by lack of spares. An-12s PK-PUA, -PUB, -PUD and -PUF had crashed by then; the five surviving aircraft were returned to the USSR and their fate is unknown.

• **Mandala Airlines [RI/MDL]** based in Jakarta wet-leased two Cubs – 'civil' An-12BP LZ-SFA (c/n 02348007) and 'military' An-12BP LZ-SFL (c/n 4342101) – from Air Sofia in October–December 1997 and March–May 1998 respectively.

• An-12B CCCP-11236 (c/n 402111) and 'civil' An-12BP CCCP-11130 (c/n 02348205) were leased by a Jakarta-based airline with the almost unprintable name of **Penas Air Cargo [–/PNS]** in May 1992.

Iran

Bon Air (Bonyad Airlines) **[–/IRJ]** operated two Y8F-100s registered EP-BOA and EP-BON No. 2[86] (c/ns unknown) in 1998. There have been reports of a Y8 registered EP-ART and purportedly previously operated by Bon Air.

Iraq

In 1961, 1965, 1966 and 1968 the **Iraqi Air Force** (IrAF, or *al Quwwat al-Jawwiya al-Iraqiya*) took delivery of 11 An-12s equipping a single squadron. In the early 1970s five of the *Cubs* received a civil-style colour scheme with a green cheatline and the titles and logo of **Iraqi Airways [IA/IAW]** to facilitate flights abroad (e.g. in order to pick up spares for IrAF combat aircraft).

Serial	Version	C/n	Notes
505	An-12A (+)	024010	Grey c/s
506	An-12A (+)	024011	Grey c/s
507	An-12A (+)	024012	Grey c/s
I.A.F.636?	An-12B (+)	402709	Reported as 636 (exact serial presentation and c/s not known)
I.A.F.637	An-12B (+)	402710	Grey/white c/s
I.A.F.638	An-12B (+)	402711	Grey/white c/s
I.A.F.685	An-12BP (+)	6344305	Grey/white c/s. To YI-AES. Returned to the USSR by 2-81 as CCCP-11650 No. 2
I.A.F.686	An-12BP (+)	6344306	Grey/white c/s. To YI-AGD
I.A.F.805	An-12BP (+)	8345909	Grey/white c/s. To YI-AEP; sold to the Sudan Air Force 1992 as ST-ALV No. 1
I.A.F.806?	An-12BP (+)	8345910	Reported as 806 (exact serial presentation and c/s not known). To YI-AFJ
I.A.F.807	An-12BP (+)	8345908	Grey/white c/s. To YI-AER

As already mentioned, one of the *Cubs* was converted locally into a flight refuelling tanker, but it is not known which one.

Though wearing a civil registration and 'Ministry of Air Communication' titles, An-12 PK-PUB Ardjuna *is an Indonesian Air Force aircraft (ex AURI serial T-1205). It was lost in a crash in the mid-1960s.* (RART)

An-12BP 'I.A.F.807' (c/n 8345908), the last example delivered to the Iraqi Air Force, illustrates the grey/white colour scheme and serial presentation worn by the greater part of Iraq's *Cub* fleet. The first three aircraft were grey overall and had purely numeric serials. (RART)

Ivory Coast

Air Afrique [RK/RKA] wet-leased five An-12s from Air Sofia at different times. These were An-12B LZ-SFC (leased in February 1992 and returned before1997), An-12P LZ-SFG (September–October 1994), An-12B LZ-SFK (January–September 1994), An-12BP LZ-SFL (November 1992–October 1993) and An-12B LZ-SFN (March 1996–September 1999).

(**Important note:** Air Afrique is the multinational state carrier of Benin (TY-), Burkina Faso (XT-), Chad (TT-), Congo-Brazzaville (TN-), Ivory Coast (TU-), Mali (TZ-), Mauritania (5T-), Niger (5U-), Senegal (6V-) and Togo (5V-); however, since Air Afrique's own fleet is entirely registered in the Republic of the Ivory Coast, the airline is listed here under this country.)

Jordan

The **Royal Jordanian Air Force** (RJAF, or *al Quwwat al-Jawwiya al-Urduniya*) operated two An-12BPs serialled 351 and 352 in the early 1980s. The aircraft were operated by No. 3 Sqn in Amman, serving alongside three C-130Bs and four C-130Hs.

Lesotho

Anton Air International [–/ANP], a sister company of Aviakompaniya Pilot (see the previous chapter), leased all three of its An-12s in 1997. A fourth aircraft was sourced elsewhere.

Registration	Version	C/n	Notes
7P-ANA	An-12B (+)	2340709	Demilitarised. Ex-RA-11038, leased from Aviakompaniya Pilot ?-97
7P-ANB	An-12BP	4342404	Ex-RA-11760, leased from Aviakompaniya Pilot ?-97
7P-ANC	An-12BP	9346608	Ex-RA-11658, leased from Aviakompaniya Pilot ?-97
TN-AGF	?	?	Operated in 1998

Liberia

- **Air Cess [–/ACS]** based at Sharjah operated four An-12s.

Registration	Version	C/n	Notes
EL-AKN	An-12A (+)	1901706	Ex-von Haaf Air D2-FVD, bought ?-95, named 'Flying Cat'; transferred to Air Pass 1998 as 3D-SKN
EL-AKR	An-12BP (+)	9346801?	Ex-Special Cargo Airlines RA-11321?, bought ?-96; sold to Pamir Air same year as YA-PAA
EL-AKV	An-12A (+)	1340107	Ex-Aviastar RA-48971, named 'Voyager'; transferred to Air Pass 9-98 as 3D-AKV
EL-RDL	An-12B (+)	2340809	Ex-RA-11734, named 'Lastochka' (Swallow); transferred to Air Pass 11-98 as 3D-RDL

- **Flying Dolphin**, another Sharjah-based cargo airline, later rebranded **Santa Cruz Imperial [–/SCI]**, operated nine An-12s.

Registration	Version	C/n	Notes
EL-ALA	An-12BP (–)	00347405	Ex-RA-12991, bought ?-96; sold to Atlas Air ?-99 as 3C-ZZD
EL-ALB	An-12B (+)	402108	Ex-Special Cargo Airlines RA-12116, bought ?-96
EL-ALD		?	
EL-ALF	An-12BP (+)	9346801?	Ex-Pamir Air YA-PAA, bought ?-96
EL-ALJ	An-12BK	8346202	Ex-Pamir Air YA-PAB, re-equipped with ROZ-1 radar; bought ?-97
EL-ANB		?	
EL-ASA	An-12A (+)	3340909	Ex-Special Cargo Airlines RA-11890, bought 8-10-97. Leased to Savanair; crashed Luanda 2-2-99
EL-ASC	An-12B (+)	3341206	Ex-Southern Cross 3D-ASC, ex-Amuraviatrans RA-11831, bought ?-97
EL-ASS	An-12B (+)	?	Reported as ex-RA-11890 in error; reregistered EY-ASS (!) 27-7-98

- **ACS Air Charter Service [–/ACH]** leased 'civil' An-12BP UR-LTG (c/n 00347201) from Volare Aviation Enterprise in April 2000. The aircraft wore full Volare colours – except for the tail logo, which was that of ACS!

Macedonia

Avioimpex [M4/AXX] leased a demilitarised An-12B, LZ-SFL (c/n 4342101), from Air Sofia in June 1995; the aircraft was reregistered Z3-AFA. In mid-1996, however, it was returned to the lessor, regaining its former identity.

Maldives

Air Cargo Maldives leased 'military' An-12BP LZ-SFE (c/n 5342708) from Air Sofia in 1992.

Mali

Transair Mali leased 'civil' An-12BP CCCP-12981 (c/n 00347104) from Aeroflot's Norilsk UFD in 1992.

Malta

Air Malta [KM/AMC] operated 'civil' An-12BP CCCP-12965 (c/n 9346409) wet-leased from Aeroflot (Rostov-on-Don UFD) between 19 May and 19 July 1992.

Mozambique

The **Mozambique People's Air Force** (FPA – *Força Popular Aérea de Moçambique*) had at least two An-12s serialled 011 and 012 (c/ns unknown). Both were apparently on lease from the Soviet Air Force (or masqueraded in FPA markings for appearance's sake) and were eventually returned to the USSR.

Myanmar

The **Myanmar Air Force** has four Shaanxi Y8Ds on strength delivered between September 1992 and November 1994. These wear a civil-style colour scheme and are serialled 5815–5818 (c/ns 080803, 080804 (?), 090801 and 090802).

New Zealand

Air New Zealand [NZ/ANZ] wet-leased 'military' An-12BP LZ-SFL (c/n 4342101) from Air Sofia between August and 5 December 1997.

Nigeria

- **Fresh Air Cargo [–/FRR]** based at Sharjah, UAE, operates a single 'civil' An-12BP, 5N-BCN (ex-RA-12965, c/n 9346409), leased from Aeroflot-Don in May 2001.

- **Harco Air Services [–/HCO]** based in Kaduna leased 'civil' An-12BP RA-11114 (c/n 01347909) from Komiavia in August 1992. The aircraft was also operated for **Nigeria Mail** at the same time.

Peru

In 1991 **Compania de Aviación Peruana** operated two *Cubs* leased from the Soviet Ministry of Aircraft Industry's Moscow UFD/201st Flight – An-12BK OB-1448 (ex-CCCP-11868, c/n 9346310) and 'civil' An-12BP OB-1449 (ex-CCCP-12990, c/n 00347304). Both aircraft were returned in 1992, regaining their original identities.

Poland

For several years the Polish Armed Forces had to rely on Big Brother to provide aircraft for landing major airborne assaults. For instance, in May 1963 the troopers of the 6th Airborne Division (6. PDPD) made use of Soviet Air Force An-8s and An-12s to carry out their training. On 26 October 1965 a group of 6. PDPD paratroopers was air-dropped over the Erfurt training ground in East Germany during the Warsaw Pact exercise *Oktyabr'skaya grozah* (*October Storm*).

In 1966, however, the **Polish Air Force** (PWL – *Polskie Wojsko Lotnicze*) got its own strategic airlift capability, taking delivery of two An-12BPs, which were serialled 50 Red (c/n 6344307) and 51 Red (c/n 6344308). The *Cubs* equipped a squadron of the 13th Transport Regiment (13. PLT – *Pulk Lotnictwa Transportowego*) which was based at Kraków-Balice.

The PWL put the type to good use, participating in various WarPac exercises. Real-life airlift missions were also performed;

Polish servicemen in BMP-1 infantry fighting vehicles cross in front of a Polish Air Force An-12BP at Kraków-Balice. (*Wojskowa Agencja Fotograficzna*)

for example, in November–December 1973, as related in Chapter 7, the *Cubs* airlifted the Polish contingent of the United Nations Peace Forces to the Middle East to help maintain peace in the days after the Yom Kippur War. The contingent largely consisted of 6. PDPD personnel.

The first such mission was flown on 13 November when a PWL An-12 delivered ten officers, three GAZ-69 jeeps with drivers and various equipment to Cairo-West. Starting on 16 November, a steady stream of Polish servicemen doing the first tour of UBPF duty poured into Egypt, accompanied by all the necessary materiel and supplies – right down to firewood for the stoves! The non-stop flights took them from Kraków through Budapest, Skopje and Crete; the flights lasted an average of 5 hours 20 minutes. The last sortie was flown on 12 December.

The PWL's transport element was regularly used in the interests of civilian organisations, and the An-12s were leased to **LOT Polish Airlines [LO/LOT]** several times, receiving civil registrations and an appropriate colour scheme. The aircraft flew cargo charters to Astrakhan (USSR), Hanoi, Cairo, London, Benghazi, Rome, Tokyo, etc. Thus, 50 Red was registered SP-LZA from 8 June to 17 July 1967 and on 27 September 1972; unfortunately on 13 May 1977 it crashed on approach to Beirut. 51 Red was registered SP-LZB from 8 June to 17 July 1967, from 29 May 1968 to 24 July 1972 and on 9 October 1972; on 2 July 1993 it made its final flight in Polish service and was withdrawn from use at Kraków-Balice. Fortunately this was not the end of the road: on 10 February 1995 the aircraft was sold to Air Sofia as LZ-SFS.[87]

Portugal

Air Luxor [–/LXR] leased An-12B LZ-SFG (c/n 3341605) from Air Sofia in late 1997 or January 1998. Unfortunately, on 4 February 1998 the aircraft was lost in a crash at Santa Maria, Lajes, the Azores.

São Tomé & Principe

- **British Gulf International Airlines [–/BGI]** have two An-12BPs – civil-configured S9-BOS (ex-RA-11102, c/n 01347704, named 'Julia') bought in December 2000 and 'military' An-12BP S9-BOT (ex-D2-FDT, c/n 5343305) bought in 2001. Both aircraft are leased to Sarit Airlines of Sudan. Additionally, in September 2002 British Gulf International Airlines operated a 'civil' An-12BP with the non-standard Kyrghyz registration EX-160 (c/n unknown).

- **Natalco Airlines** purchased a 'military' An-12 (RA-11236, c/n 402111) from Sakha Avia in 1999; the aircraft was reregistered S9-BAN.

- **Zanex Airlines** operated an An-12 registered S9-SAT (c/n unknown). The aircraft was lost in a crash landing at Saurimo, Angola, on 17 December 1998.

- Additionally, four An-12s registered in São Tomé & Principe – demilitarised An-12BP S9-CAN (ex-RA-11013, c/n 6344002), An-12B S9-CAQ (ex-D2-FRT, c/n 3341408, named 'Akula'),[88] An-12B S9-CDB (ex-D2-FCV, c/n 401901, named

A Polish Army GAZ-69 jeep rigged for paradropping on a PGS-500 pallet is about to be loaded aboard An-12BP '50 Red' (c/n 6344307) during a military exercise. (*Wojskowa Agencja Fotograficzna*)

'Emmanuel') and An-12 S9-GRC (c/n unknown) – belonged to unidentified operators. The first aircraft was written off in a crash-landing at Lukapa, Angola, on 20 January 1999.

Sierra Leone

A 'military' An-12B registered 9L-LCR (possibly ex-RA-12166, c/n 4341801) was operated by an unknown airline in February 2002.

Singapore

Air Mark Aviation based at Singapore-Seletar operated 'military' An-12P LZ-SFG and An-12Bs LZ-SFK wet-leased from Air Sofia in 1997. In May 2002 the airline leased An-12BP LZ-SFT from the same carrier.

Slovakia

The **Slovak Air Force** (*Slovenské Vojenské Létectvo*) received one of the two CzAF An-12s, 2209 Black, after the breakup of

Czechoslovakia. However, with just one *Cub* on strength, the same problems were encountered as in neighbouring Czechia. Eventually the Slovaks sold the aircraft to Moldovan carrier Tiramavia in 1998 as ER-ACH.

South Yemen (People's Democratic Republic of Yemen)

The **South Yemen Air Force** (PDRYAF) operated at least four 'military' An-12s registered 7O-ABH, 7O-ABM, 7O-ACI and 7O-ACJ. The last two aircraft also wore PDRYAF serials 625 and 626. No c/ns are known.

Sri Lanka

• No. 2 Transport Wing of the **Sri Lankan Air Force** (SLAF) based at Ratmalana AB operated three Shaanxi Y8s.

Serial	Version	C/n	Notes
CP701	Y8D	060802	C/n often reported as 060801 but photoproof exists! Probably directly reserialled to
CR871			Shot down near Palaly AB 18-11-95
CP702	Y8D	060804	Probably directly reserialled to
CR872			Blue/white PLAAF-style c/s. Crashed 5-7-92
CR873	Y8B	070802	Ex-ACA Air Changan Airlines B-3105, leased as a replacement for temporarily unserviceable CR871; was to have been returned 4-95 but retained after loss of CR871. Basic ACA c/s.

By July 1996 CR873 had been transferred to the civil register as 4R-HVC in order to facilitate flights abroad.

• **Expo Aviation (Pvt) Ltd. [8D/EXV]** has a 'civil' An-12BP, 4R-EXC (ex-RA-12956, c/n 8345507) purchased from Samara Airlines in early 1999.

• **Skycabs Ltd** operated four 'military' *Cubs*.

Registration	Version	C/n	Notes
4R-SKL	An-12B (+)	3341505	Ex-U-UAPO RA-12174, bought ?-98; sold to Inter Trans Air ?-00 as LZ-ITS
RA-11408	An-12B (+)	3341209	Leased from Aviaobschchemash in 1995
RA-12116	An-12B (+)	402108	Leased from Special Cargo Airlines
RA-13357	An-12BK	8345604	Leased from Impulse-Aero ?-95

• **Srilankan Airlines [UL/ALK]** wet-leased An-12B LZ-SFK (c/n 4341901) from Air Sofia in the autumn of 2001.

• An unidentified Sri Lankan airline acquired demilitarised An-12PP 4R-AIA (ex-XU-355, c/n 01347107) from Air Sofia in March 2002. On 16 August the same year the aircraft suffered a landing accident in Karachi.

Sudan

• **Air West Co. Ltd [–/AWZ]** has operated several *Cubs* registered both in and outside Sudan.

Registration	Version	C/n	Notes
ST-AWM	An-12BP (+)	5343704	Demilitarised. Ex-FLight Air Company RA-11003, bought by 12-98, basic SPAir c/s
ST-AWU	An-12BK	8345804	Ex-Russian Air Force, bought ?-99, previous identity unknown
ER-ACW	An-12BP (–)	8345510	Ex-Savanair D2-FBY, bought ?-00; basic Savanair c/s, no titles. Sold to Bright Aviation Services ?-00 as LZ-BRC
RA-11734	An-12B (+)	2340809	Demilitarised; leased 12-94, ex-UNPF white colours
S9-BOT	An-12BP (+)	5343305	Reported for Air West 3-02; also reported as An-12B c/n 402102 (ex-Sarit Airlines ST-SAR)!

• **AZZA Transport Co. Ltd [–/AZZ]** operates Y8F-100 ST-ALV (the second *Cub* to wear this registration, c/n unknown) and a genuine An-12 registered ST-AQG (version and c/n unknown).

• **Coptrade Air Transport** operated 'civil' An-12BP ST-AQF (ex-Sakha Avia RA-12953, c/n 8345504) in October 1999. The aircraft was sold to Trans ATTICO (see below) in the same year.

• **Data International Aviation Ltd [–/DTN]** had three An-12s – ST-APG (c/n unknown), An-12A ST-APJ (previous identity unknown, c/n 2400701) and An-12 ST-APU (c/n unknown).

• **El Magal Aviation [–/MGL]** leased 'civil' An-12BP RA-12988 (c/n 00347206) in late 1998.

• **Forner Airlines** operated 'civil' An-12BP ST-AQF (ex-Mikma ER-ACG, c/n 9346504) in March 2002.

• **Sarit Airlines [–/SRW]** operate demilitarised An-12B ST-SAR leased from Lasare Air in October 2000 (ex-4L-CAA, c/n 402102) and 'military' An-12BP S9-BOT leased from British Gulf International Airlines.

• The **Sudan Air Force** (*al Quwwat al-Jawwiya as-Sudaniya*) operated eight *Cubs*.

Serial/ registration	Version	C/n	Notes
700	An-12B (+)?	?	C/n reported as 402602 but this is RA-11652, see previous chapter/Russian AF!

Data Airlines An-12A ST-APJ (c/n 2400701) unbuttoned for maintenance at Sharjah in March 2002. The No. 1 engine is apparently due for a change. (Nikolay Ionkin)

711	An-12B (+)?	?	C/n reported as 402603 but unconfirmed
722	An-12B (+)?	?	C/n reported as 402802 but unconfirmed
733	An-12B (+)?	?	C/n reported as 402803 but unconfirmed
744	An-12B (+)?	?	C/n reported as 402809 but this is also stated for Algerian Air Force 7T-WAH/516!
755	An-12B (+)?	?	C/n reported as 402902 but this is RA-13387!
ST-ALU No. 1	Y8D	070804	Registration passed to An-26 c/n 11805 in 1999!
ST-ALV No. 1	An-12BP (+)	8345909	Ex-Iraqi Air Force I.A.F.805. Registration later to Y8F-100 (see AZZA Transport)

• In 2001 an airline called **Sudanese States Aviation Co. Ltd** [–/SNV] bought an An-12 registered ST-AQQ (version and c/n unknown).

• **Trans Arabian Air Transport** [–/TRT] operates demilitarised An-12AP ST-AQE (ex-RA-12188, c/n 1400106) on lease from United Arabian. The aircraft retains the faded colour scheme of previous owner Mostransgaz.

• **Trans ATTICO** (African Transport, Trading & Investment Co.) [–/ETC] based in Khartoum and Sharjah operates the above-mentioned An-12BP ST-AQF and demilitarised An-12BP ST-AQP (ex-TN-AGC, c/n 4342305).

• The above-mentioned An-12AP ST-AQE belongs to **United Arabian Co.** [–/UAB].

Swaziland

• **Air Pass**, a sister company of Air Cess (Liberia),[89] operated most of the latter carrier's fleet which was transferred to the Swazi register in 1998. 'Pass' is an acronym for Pietersburg Aviation Services & Systems; this was because, though nominally a Swazi company, the airline was based at Pietersburg-Gateway International airport, South Africa. In 1998 Air Pass suspended operations, selling almost its entire fleet to Centrafricain Airlines.

Registration	Version	C/n	Notes
3D-SKN	An-12A (+)	1901706	Ex-EL-AKN, named 'Flying Cat'
3D-AKV	An-12A (+)	1340107	Ex-EL-AKV, named 'Voyager';
3D-RDL	An-12B (+)	2340809	Ex-EL-RDL, named 'Lastochka'

• An airline called **Southern Cross** bought 'military' An-12B RA-11831 (c/n 3341206) from Amuraviatrans in 1997. The registration 3D-ASC was allocated but possibly not taken up, and the aircraft may have been directly resold to Santa Cruz Imperial as EL-ASC.

Turkey

• **THY Turkish Airlines** (Türk Hava Yollari) [TK/THY] briefly operated 'military' An-12B LZ-SFK (c/n 2341901) wet-leased from Air Sofia in 1993.

• On 3 August 1994 **CAT Cargo** leased demilitarised An-12B RA-11366 (c/n 402808) from Magadanaerogrooz; the aircraft was reregistered TC-KET. By 1997 the aircraft had been withdrawn from use at Istanbul-Atatürk International (Yesilköy) airport and was still stored there in 2000.

United Arab Emirates

• **Aerocomplex**, a Soviet/UAE (later Russian/UAE) joint venture, leased An-12s and Il-76s from Aeroflot as required. These included red/white 'civil' An-12BPs CCCP-11108 No. 2 (c/n 01347810) and CCCP-11118 (c/n 01348002) leased from the Leningrad UFD in the summer of 1990.

• Sharjah-based **Phoenix Aviation [–/PHG]**, a division of the Phoenix Free Zone Enterprise, operated An-12BK EK-46741 (c/n 8345408) leased from Armenian Airlines (?) in August 2001. The aircraft was named 'White Bird'.

UK

• **HeavyLift Cargo Airlines [NP/HLA]** operated 'civil' An-12BP LZ-BAE (c/n 402001) leased from Balkan Bulgarian Airlines between late 1995 and mid-1996 in full HeavyLift colours. Later in 1996 it was supplanted by a sister aircraft, RA-12995 (c/n 00347402) leased from Pulkovo Avia.

• Veteran Airlines 'military' An-12AP UR-PAS *Andrey* (c/n 2401105) was based at Manston-Kent International at one time, flying cargo charters for **Skyline Aviation**. Its customers included DHL, Rolls-Royce and the Ford Motor Company.

Yugoslavia

The **Yugoslav Air Force** (JRV – *Jugoslovensko Ratno Vazduhoplovstvo*) took delivery of two An-12BPs in November–December 1971. The aircraft wore dual markings, carrying the civil registrations YU-AIC (c/n 01348007) and YU-AID (c/n 01348010), as well as the JRV serials 73311 and 73312 respectively. Curiously, the aircraft were built in unarmed commercial configuration; another unusual feature was that a Collins DME set had been integrated at the customer's request.

Little is known about the actual operational use of the Yugoslav *Cubs*. On 12 December 1988 YU-AID crashed on approach to Yerevan while making an earthquake relief flight. The surviving example had a chance to participate in the civil war in Yugoslavia before it was sold to SiGi Air Cargo as LZ-SGA in 1991.

Zaïre (now Democratic Republic of Congo)

ATO – Air Transport Office briefly leased 'civil' An-12BP RA-11101 (c/n 01347703) from GosNII GA in December 1993.

Operators from unknown nations

• An-12A EK-11304 (c/n 0901304) was leased by **Africa West Cargo** from Dvin Avia in June 1999.

• **Camp Aviation Services** leased 'military' An-12BP CCCP-11343 (c/n 00347503) from the Soviet Air Force in 1992.

• 'Civil' An-12BP RA-11526 (c/n 02348206) of Komiavia was leased by **GAZ Airways** in June–August 1991.

• An airline called **Miras Air** leased 'military' An-12BP RA-93913 (c/n 4342609) and 'military' An-12B RA-93915 (c/n 4342103) from Atran – Aviatrans Cargo Airlines in 2002. Both aircraft wore full Atran livery with 'Operated for Miras Air' stickers on the forward fuselage.

• **Southern Air Group** leased An-12BP RA-11339 (c/n 6344310) from the Penza Air Enterprise in 1995.

• An airline called **TASCO** leased demilitarised An-12PP RA-11301 (c/n 00347107) from Antey in 1998–9. The aircraft was in basic Antey colours without titles.

• 'Civil' An-12BP RA-12984 (c/n 00347109) was operated by a carrier called **The Atlantic Airlines** (!) in 1995.

• The above-mentioned An-12BP RA-11526 was also operated by **Victory Airlines** in May 1996.

• **Westrac Air Cargo** leased demilitarised An-12TB RA-11025 (c/n 6344103) from NPO Energiya in 1995.

APPENDIX I

Accident Attrition

The following is a brief rundown of known An-12 accidents as of 1 January 2002. Only fatal and non-fatal accidents of varying seriousness are listed here; flight incidents and cases of ground damage to parked aircraft are not dealt with because with most aircraft types the number of such incidents per year runs into the hundreds![90] Some accidents dealt with in previous chapters are not mentioned here.

(A list of accidents in chronological order admittedly makes pretty depressing reading. However, lest the reader should get the wrong idea that the aircraft in question is 'accident prone' or even 'inherently unsafe', please remember that all these unfortunate events occurred over a 42-year period. Besides, as we've already pointed out, many crashes were caused by the tell-tale human factor – pilot or ATC error, bad judgement or even negligence.)

• On 5 August 1961 a brand-new Indian Air Force/No. 25 Sqn 'Himalayan Eagles' An-12A serialled **BL536** (c/n 1901603) suffered a nose-gear collapse as it touched down at its home base in Chandigarh, Uttar-Pradesh. A fire erupted in the nose section, caused by the friction against the runway, and the *Cub* burned out completely.

• Ten days later another IAF An-12A (**BL533**, c/n 1901601) suffered an accident during its 101st landing. The nose gear failed, digging into the soft ground, but this time the aircraft could be stopped without sustaining further damage. It turned out that the ground personnel had neglected to change the nosewheels after each 85 landings as prescribed by the manual.

• On 23 December 1962 a Soviet Air Force An-12 (tactical code unknown, **c/n 0901406**) collided with a mountain near Norilsk, Russia. Only the tail gunner survived.

• On 6 March 1963 An-12 **CCCP-11007** (version and c/n unknown) suffered an accident in Samarkand, Uzbekistan, but was repaired to fly another four years.

• On 2 April 1963 An-12 **CCCP-11338 No. 1** (version and c/n unknown) of the North Caucasian CAD/Rostov UFD was damaged beyond repair when it ran off the side of a snow-covered runway at Magadan's Sokol airport because the captain had failed to correctly align the aircraft for take-off. The registration was reused the same year for a Tashkent-built An-12B (c/n 3341506).

• On 16 July 1963 Indian Air Force An-12A **BL734** (c/n 2401306?) crashed on landing at Palam AB.

• On 7 December 1963 An-12 **CCCP-11347** (version and c/n unknown)[91] of the East Siberian CAD crashed in Kirensk, Russia, when both engines on the port wing flamed out immediately after take-off because of a vapour lock in a fuel line. The propellers did not feather automatically, causing tremendous drag; with the two live engines running at full power, the result was inevitably an irrecoverable departure. Yawing and rolling to port, the aircraft plunged into the ground; all six crew were killed.

• There were four accidents with civil *Cubs* in 1964; no details are known, except that none of the aircraft was written off.

• On 11 September 1965 An-12 **CCCP-11337 No. 1** (version and c/n unknown) of Aeroflot's Polar Aviation Directorate descended prematurely and collided with the ground on approach to Ulan-Ude's Mookhino airport, killing the six crew and two passengers. It turned out that the pilots had incorrectly set the atmospheric pressure (QNH) on the altimeters, causing them to give false readings. The registration was later reused for another An-12 – which, oddly enough, also crashed (see below). Five other fatal crashes involving Air Force aircraft reportedly occurred in 1965, plus two minor accidents.

• Two minor accidents with civil An-12s occurred in 1966.

• On 14 January 1967 another Polar Aviation An-12B with the non-standard registration **CCCP-04343** (c/n unknown) crashed at Novosibirsk-Tolmachovo airport. A fire had broken out in the freight hold soon after take-off and the pilots attempted an emergency landing, but the aircraft exploded on touchdown, the five crew members and sole passenger losing their lives.

• On 6 March 1967, exactly four years after the previous accident, An-12 **CCCP-11007** (by then operated by the Polar Aviation Directorate) stalled and crashed at Salekhard, Russia, when the crew forgot to set the flaps for take-off. All five crew members were killed.

• On 4 June 1967 the An-12TP-2 survey aircraft of Antarctic expedition fame (**CCCP 04366**, c/n unknown) had its port main-gear collapse and slewed off the runway when landing at Blagoveschchensk, Russia. No one was hurt but the aircraft was declared a write-off. There were also five minor accidents that year.

• On 29 January 1968 An-12B **CCCP-11015 No. 1** of the Yakutian CAD (c/n unknown) was damaged beyond repair in a hard landing at Magan, Yakutian ASSR, Russia. The registration later passed to a demilitarised An-12BP (c/n 6344006?).

• On 2 November 1968 An-12 **CCCP-11349 No. 1** (c/n unknown) belonging to the East Siberian CAD (probably the Irkutsk UFD/134th Flight) hit high ground 15.6 km (9.69 miles) from Lensk

The charred remains of TsUMVS/64th Flight An-12BP CCCP-11107 (c/n 01347809) which burned out after aborting a take-off at Novyy Urengoy on 24 April 1982. The taxiway where the aircraft collapsed its landing gear can be seen in the background. (Courtesy CIS Interstate Aviation Committee)

airport during a late-night approach in bad weather, killing the six crew members.[92] There were also three minor accidents that year.

• On 25 June 1969 East Siberian CAD An-12 **CCCP-11380** (c/n unknown) was written off in a landing accident at Mirnyy airport, Russia, when the starboard main gear ripped away.

• On 12 August 1969 demilitarised An-12BP **CCCP-11018** (c/n unknown) operated by the Polar directorate fell into a forest 13 km short of Novosibirsk-Tolmachovo when the No. 2 engine failed with another engine already shut down. Four of the occupants died in the crash.

• On 13 November 1969 demilitarised An-12B **CCCP-11376** (c/n 402406), another Polar Aviation aircraft, crashed on approach 15 km (9.3 miles) from Amderma, Russia, because of heavy icing.

There were no survivors among the nine crew and three passengers.

• A very similar accident occurred on 6 December 1969 when An-12PL (An-12B) **CCCP-11381** (c/n 402807) operated by the Polar division crashed 13 km (8 miles) short of Khatanga, Russia, owing to heavy icing. Again all six crew and both passengers were killed.

• On 26 February 1970 civil-configured An-12BP **CCCP-12966** (c/n unknown)[93] of the North Caucasian CAD/Rostov UFD was damaged beyond repair in a heavy landing at Beryozovo, Tyumen Region, when the pilots flared out too early, misjudging the altitude during a landing on a misty day.

• On 1 October 1970 An-12BP **CCCP-11031** (c/n 7345003) of the Tyumen CAD/2nd Tyumen UFD/435th Flight crashed on take-off from Mys Kamennyy

('Stone Cape'), Russia, when two engines failed completely and a third lost power because of malfunctions in the fuel system. An attempt to make a forced landing failed, and the aircraft was totally destroyed, all seven crew and the sole passenger losing their lives. There were also five minor accidents with civil Cubs that year.

• On 22 January 1971 An-12BP **CCCP-11000** (c/n unknown) of the Komi CAD/Syktyvkar UFD 318th Flight crashed 15 km (9.3 miles) from the runway at Surgut, Tyumen Region, after completing the downwind leg of the landing pattern. The cause was loss of control through heavy icing; it is not known how many of the 13 occupants were killed.

• Nine days later the scenario was repeated with uncanny accuracy when a brand-new 'civil' An-12BP, **CCCP-12996** (c/n 00347403?) of the Tyumen CAD/2nd Tyumen UFD/435th Flight, crashed just 1 km (0.62 miles) from the same spot for the same reason. Again the death toll is unknown (there were seven crew members aboard).

• On 16 February 1971 An-12B **CCCP-11374** (c/n 402404?) of the Komi CAD/Syktyvkar UFD 318th Flight was damaged beyond repair at Vorkuta, Russia, when it veered off the runway after touching down with left bank and collided with a snow berm.

• On 25 May 1971 Yakutian CAD An-12 **CCCP-11024** (c/n unknown) was written off after a crash landing at Batagai, Russia, in which the starboard main gear collapsed.

• On 29 July 1971 the crew of 'civil' An-12BP **CCCP-12993** (c/n unknown) belonging to the Central Directorate of International Services (TsUMVS)/64th Flight chose not to make a go-around when landing at Calcutta in torrential rain with reduced visibility. As a result, the aircraft undershot by 198 m (650 ft) and was declared a write-off. Five minor accidents with Aeroflot An-12s also occurred that year.

• On 21 November 1972 An-12B **CCCP-11360** (c/n unknown) of the Moscow Territorial CAD (MTU GA) landed 140 m (460 ft) short of the runway at Vorkuta on its second approach, running into a ravine and breaking up. No one was hurt but the aircraft was a total loss. There were also seven minor accidents that year.

• On 17 February 1973 another MTU GA *Cub*, An-12B **CCCP-11341 No. 1** (c/n 401702), flared out too late landing at Amderma, touching down hard and sustaining irreparable damage. The registration was later reused for an ex-Soviet Air Force An-12BP (c/n 00347606).

• On 2 October 1973 'civil' An-12BP **CCCP-12967** (c/n unknown)[94] of the Yakutian CAD strayed off the intended course while making a go-around at Magadan-Sokol and hit a mountain side 13.7 km (8.5 miles) from the runway threshold and 5.6 km (3.47 miles) to the right of the extended runway centreline. All eight crew and both passengers perished. There were also two minor accidents that year.

• The 1974 May Day celebrations were marred by a fatal accident in the Arctic Ocean. On 1 May 'civil' An-12BP **CCCP-12950** (c/n unknown)[95] of the Krasnoyarsk CAD flew a support mission to the drifting research station SP-22. As the aircraft was being unloaded the icefield started shifting and the station's ice floe cracked, forcing an urgent evacuation before the runway became completely unusable. As it became airborne the *Cub* clipped an ice pinnacle with one wing, groundlooping and bursting into flames. The nine passengers escaped from the wreckage but one of the seven crew members perished.

• On 18 October 1974 'civil' An-12BP **CCCP-11030** (c/n 7345002) of the Krasnoyarsk CAD/Krasnoyarsk UFD/214th Flight crashed on final approach to Yeniseysk, Russia, inbound from Kamensk-Uralskiy. The crew had become disoriented in poor weather, and the aircraft sank below the glide path, cutting a 612 m (2,007 ft) swath through the forest; the main wreckage came to rest 1,321 m (4,334 ft) short of the runway. The navigator lost his life, but the other four crew members and six passengers survived. Interestingly, the aircraft used the ATC callsign CCCP-12423 at the time of the crash.

• On 4 December 1974 ATC incompetence led to disaster. That fateful day **CCCP-12985**, a civil-configured An-12BP operated by the East Siberian CAD/Irkutsk UFD/134th Flight (c/n 00347110), was making training flights at Irkutsk-1 airport, the crew practising ILS approaches. At 04.58 Moscow time, coming in to land after the fifth approach, the freighter collided with An-2 CCCP-49342 (c/n 1G1226) of the East Siberian CAD/Irkutsk UFD/190th Flight which had taken off eight minutes earlier, outbound for Kachug. The biplane crashed out of control, killing all 17 on board. The *Cub*, which was of sturdier construction, managed an emergency landing in the valley of the Ushakovka River within the city limits, but was a write-off; there were no fatalities among the crew of five. The crash was caused by an error of the feeder traffic ATC officer who had cleared the An-2 to take off into the An-12's flight path without informing the approach controller.

• Sometime in 1975 Balkan Bulgarian Airlines 'civil' An-12BP **LZ-BAA** (c/n 8346001) was damaged beyond repair in a landing accident in Egypt (date and location unknown).

• There were three minor accidents in 1975. One of them, which occurred in Fergana, Uzbekistan, on 15 December, involved **CCCP-11005**, a demilitarised An-12BP of the Yakutian CAD/Yakutsk UFD/139th Flight/2nd Squadron (c/n 6343907). The crew accidentally retracted the undercarriage before the aircraft had become airborne, taking off on a post-modification check flight. Slithering along on its belly in a shower of sparks and shedding the No. 1 propeller, which had struck the tarmac, the aircraft came to rest on the runway shoulder with both outer engines on fire; luckily the fire was quickly extinguished. Despite the heavy damage to the fuselage, the aircraft was soon rebuilt and flying again.

• There was one minor accident in 1976 and one more in 1978; no details are known.

• On 13 May 1977 LOT Polish Airlines 'military' An-12BP **SP-LZA** (c/n 6344307) crashed on approach to Beirut International airport.

• In November 1977 (the exact date is unknown) Soviet Air Force An-12BP **CCCP-11815** (c/n 7345101) was damaged beyond repair in a crash landing at Masawa,[96] Eritrea, during the massive Soviet airlift to Ethiopia.

• On 23 August 1979 another *Cub* was written off near Yeniseysk. 'Civil' An-12BP **CCCP-12963** (c/n 9346407), belonging to the Krasnoyarsk CAD/Norilsk UFD/434th Flight, took off from Norilsk-Alykel at 19.22 Moscow time, winging its way to Krasnoyarsk on flight 22200. At 21.40, as the aircraft was cruising at 7,800 m (25,590 ft), the starboard engines flamed out because of fuel contamination, followed three minutes later by the port engines. The crew requested an emergency landing in Yeniseysk but the freighter crashed and burned in a forest 18 km (11 miles) short of the airport. All six crew and five out of ten passengers died.

• Two minor accidents involving Tyumen CAD/2nd Tyumen UFD/435th Flight 'civil' An-12BP **CCCP-11128 No. 2** (c/n 02348003)[97] and Yakutian CAD 'military' An-12B **CCCP-11403** (c/n 401906) occurred in 1979; no details are known.

• On 1 March 1980 'civil' An-12BP **CCCP-11111**, a Magadan CAD/1st Magadan UFD/181st Flight aircraft (c/n 01347906), was on short finals to Novyy Urengoy's Yaghelnoye airport when the crew discovered that the No. 1 engine would not throttle back to ground idle because of a jammed control cable. Then the pilots made the mistake of setting the propellers of the outer engines to fine pitch. With No. 1 engine still running at flight idle, the aircraft veered off the runway into soft snow and swung to starboard, slithering sideways until the port main gear collapsed and the port wingtip dug in. Nobody was hurt; the *Cub* suffered damage to the fuselage, port wing and No. 1 engine but was repaired to fly another 12 years.

• On 26 August 1980 'civil' An-12BP **CCCP-11110 No. 2** (c/n 01347906)[98] of the Tyumen CAD/2nd Tyumen UFD/435th Flight/4th Sqn suffered a mishap at Kuibyshev-Kurumoch airport. The aircraft was inbound from Tyumen on flight 33053 PF with an ultimate destination of Kiev. After touching down on runway 05 the *Cub* ran onto the right runway shoulder, collapsing the starboard main gear and suffering damage to the wing and No. 4 engine. The aircraft was repaired and subsequently transferred to the flying division of the Kuibyshev Aircraft Factory No. 18.

• On 28 October 1980 **CCCP-11104**, a TsUMVS/64th Flight 'civil' An-12BP (c/n 01347710), was making flight SU1531 from Sofia-Vrazhdebna to Kabul via Mineralnyye Vody and Tashkent. On the last leg of the journey the crew encountered bad weather with low cloud and rain; yet the pilots persisted with the approach, descending below the minimum safe altitude. As a result, at 10.32 local time the aircraft smacked into Mt Vaïsi-Karnibaba 25 km (15.5 miles) from Kabul airport, disintegrating utterly; all six crew were killed, of course.

• A Soviet Air Force (7th VTAD/16th VTAP) An-12BK (**c/n 9346702**; identity unknown but possibly CCCP-12162 No. 1) was damaged in unknown circumstances. The aircraft took a year and a quarter to repair; it was finally returned to service on 18 April 1982 and transferred to MAP on 12 January 1983 (see below).

• On 23 April 1981 'military' An-12A **CCCP-48975** (c/n 1400101) operated by MAP's Moscow UFD/201st Flight suffered a port main-gear collapse after touching down at Tyumen-Roshchino, but was repaired.

• On 12 May 1981 'civil' An-12BP **CCCP-12957** (c/n 8345508) of the Krasnoyarsk CAD/Norilsk UFD/329th Flight had its starboard main gear collapse as it taxied in at Anadyr after making a supply flight to an *ad hoc* ice airfield in the Franz Joseph Land archipelago (known as Ledovaya Baza – 'Ice Base'), serving a Soviet polar expedition. The cause was fatigue failure of a drag strut owing to the augmented loads on the uneven ice strip; the damage was relatively minor and the aircraft was soon back in service.

• On 26 September 1981 'civil' An-12BP **CCCP-11106**, a Magadan CAD/1st Magadan UFD/181st Flight/1st Sqn aircraft (c/n 01347808), 'bit the dust' at Pevek. Coming in on flight 26052 from Magadan, the aircraft landed hard, bounced, and the nose gear gave way after the second touchdown. Yet again the aircraft was repaired and is still in service.

• On 13 February 1982 'civil' An-12BP **CCCP-11113 No. 2** belonging to the same unit (c/n 01347908)[99] got broken up very badly after skidding off an icy runway at Pevek. The aircraft, which was departing for Magadan at 03.55 local time on flight 26096, initially ran onto the right runway shoulder. Instead of aborting the take-off as he should have done, the captain applied left rudder, hoping to straighten out the course: as a result the aircraft swerved across the runway onto the *left* shoulder, wiping out four runway lights. Even this did not discourage the captain, who now gave a bootful of right rudder. Crossing the runway again, the An-12 careered over rough ground, spun 180° to the right and came to rest on the bank of Chaunskaya Bight 2,320 m (7,610 ft) from the runway. Despite serious damage to the starboard main gear, starboard wing and fuselage, the aircraft was repaired and is still in service; the crew of five were unhurt.

• On 24 April 1982 TsUMVS/64th Flight lost yet another *Cub*. 'Civil' An-12BP **CCCP-11107** (c/n 01347809) was departing from Novyy Urengoy, bound for Moscow-Sheremetyevo via Syktyvkar. As the aircraft lined up the captain neglected to set the nosewheels neutral, leaving them turned about 3° to the right. Seconds after commencing its take-off run CCCP-11107 ran off the side of the runway, yet for some reason the captain was late in aborting the take-off. When he did resort to emergency braking it was too late: the freighter careered over an elevated taxiway, shearing off the landing gear, slid into a drain culvert and burst into flames as the forward underfloor fuel cells ruptured. The crew escaped unhurt but the entire forward fuselage up to the wing centre section was consumed by fire before the firefighters managed to put out the blaze.

• On 24 August 1984 Balkan Bulgarian Airlines An-12BP **LZ-BAD** (c/n 6344001) crashed in Addis Ababa.

• On 19 September 1984 an Angolan Government (i.e. obviously an Angolan Air Force) An-12 registered **D2-EAD** (c/n unknown) crashed somewhere in Angola. (Incidentally, if you delete the digit from the registration you get the word 'dead'. Talk about bad omens!)

• On the night of 6 December 1984 'civil' An-12BP **CCCP-12986** (c/n 00347201) of the Volga CAD/Kuibyshev UFD/368th Flight had a tailstrike while landing at Kharkov-Osnova airport in bad weather. The aircraft was staging through Kharkov on flight 29001 from Kuibyshev with an ultimate destination of Dnepropetrovsk. The result: a nasty gash in the lower fuselage skin just ahead of the cargo door lip and some structural deformation in the aft fuselage.

• On 25 September 1985 a fire broke out in the No. 1 engine of 'military' An-12A **CCCP-69321 No. 1** (c/n 1901708)[100] belonging to the Komsomolsk-on-Amur aircraft factory (KnAAPO) as it cruised along at 7,500 m (24,600 ft), en route from Dnepropetrovsk to Moscow-Domodedovo. The crew sent out a distress call at 20.51, requesting an emergency landing at Kharkov-Osnova. Seven minutes later the crew radioed they had lost control. Eyewitnesses saw the aircraft diving almost vertically before it plunged into a forest 31 km (19.25 miles) from the airport, exploding in a fireball; of course, all five crew and four passengers died on the spot.

Investigation of the wreckage revealed that the port outer wing and the affected engine had broken away in mid-air, the fire being fierce enough to affect the aircraft's structural integrity. The fire had been caused by a severe fuel leak but it was impossible to establish where and why the leak had occurred.

- On 25 March 1986 demilitarised An-12AP **CCCP-11795 No. 1** (c/n 1400103)[101] belonging to the Polyot (Flight) Production Association (an MOM enterprise) crashed on approach to its home base of Omsk-Severnyy, inbound from Tbilisi. The aircraft came in too low in below-minima weather conditions; undershooting, the Cub hit three visual approach slope indicators (VASIs), cartwheeled and exploded. There were no survivors among the six crew and three passengers. In this instance both the pilots and the ATC officers were at fault.

- On 2 April 1987 'military' An-12BP CCCP-06105 (c/n 5343606) belonging to the Kamensk-Uralskiy Radiotechnical Plant (a division of NPO Vzlyot) was making a series of training flights at Tashkent-Vostochnyy. After landing, the trainee pilot attempted a U-turn on the runway with a view to taking off in the opposite direction, but the aircraft went wide, running onto the runway shoulder. As it did so, the starboard main-gear bogie ran into a drainage ditch; the aircraft banked sharply and was wrecked when No. 4 propeller struck the ground.

- 'Civil' An-12BP **CCCP-12962** of the Krasnoyarsk CAD/Norilsk UFD/434th Flight (c/n 9346406) may well qualify for the title of 'the Unluckiest Cub Ever'! On 3 May 1986 this aircraft undershot while landing at the aforementioned Ledovaya Baza airfield 53 km (33 miles) north of Graham Bell Island in the Franz Joseph Land archipelago; the pilots had misjudged the altitude because the white surface of the icefield offered little or no reference. Since the aircraft was damaged and unflyable and there were no repair facilities on site, there was no choice but to dismantle it and tow it to terra firma where repairs could be made. After the engines, outer wings, tail surfaces and as much of the equiipment as possible had been removed to lighten the airframe, the recovery job began. However, icefields are treacherous things; on 12 May the ice started shifting and cracking, and at 23.00 Moscow time (equals 03.00 local time on 13 May) a crack opened up and swallowed the aircraft! Hard luck indeed.

- On 19 October 1987 another Cub belonging to KnAAPO – An-12BK **CCCP-12162 No. 1** (c/n 9346702) – crashed at its home base, Dzemgi, while taking off on a flight to Kirov via Irkutsk and Moscow-Domodedovo with 2,399 kg (5,288 lb) of cargo. Commencing the take-off in a 6 m/sec (12 kt) tailwind at night from a snow-covered runway, the freighter failed to lift off in time, and seconds after becoming airborne it ploughed through the airfield vehicle garage and exploded. All seven crew and both passengers died in the blaze.

- On 16 May 1988 'military' An-12A **CCCP-11886** (c/n 2340302) of the Krasnoyarsk CAD/Norilsk UFD descended prematurely and undershot into piled snow at Chelyuskin when arriving on flight 22225 from Norilsk, suffering minor damage to the fuselage underside.

- On the night of 4 October 1988 demilitarised An-12B **CCCP-11418 No. 1** (c/n 401712) of the Yakutian CAD/Yakutsk UFD/139th Flight was approaching Batagai, inbound from Tiksi on flight 40066 with 15.5 tons (34,170 lb) of apples. For some reason the crew intentionally departed from the prescribed approach pattern. The result was predictable: in the darkness the aircraft hit a mountainside 25 km (15.5 miles) from the airport and exploded, all six crew members losing their lives. The registration was later reused for a demilitarised An-12BK (c/n 7344705).

- When a disastrous earthquake hit Armenia on 7 December 1988, killing 25,000 people and flattening the cities of Kirovaliasn and Spitak, rescue teams and humanitarian aid came to the stricken region from all over the world. Unfortunately some of the relief flights ended in new tragedy. On 12 December a Yugoslav Air Force 'civil' An-12BP appropriately registered **YU-AID** and serialled **73312** (c/n 01348010) was approaching Yerevan-Zvartnots on Flight YAF312 from Skopje, bringing 10,736 kg (23,668 lb) of humanitarian cargo. Landing at an unfamiliar airport, the crew became disoriented, causing the aircraft to stray from the designated course. At 02.18 local time the An-12 crashed into a road bridge and exploded, killing all seven occupants. Part of the blame lay with the approach controller at Zvartnots, who had not informed the crew of the deviation.

- On 13 January 1989 'civil' An-12BP **CCCP-12997** (c/n 00347404) of the Urals CAD/Sverdlovsk UFD departed from Sverdlovsk-Koltsovo airport on flight 37051, heading for Kharkov via Kuibyshev with 14,844 kg (32,725 lb) of cargo. Soon after take-off the crew found that Nos 3 and 4 engines would not throttle back to flight idle (the control cables had snapped owing to faulty repairs). The crew elected to return and make an emergency landing. Unfortunately the captain retarded all four throttles without thinking at the moment of flareout, forgetting that the starboard engines were not responding. Losing control, the aircraft bounced: 4.7 seconds later the starboard wing struck the ground, the An-12 groundlooped and caught fire. The crew escaped with injuries but the aircraft was totally wrecked.

- On 11 March 1989 'military' An-12B **CCCP-11996** (c/n 402504) of the East Siberian CAD/Irkutsk UFD/134th Flight was approaching Mirnyy, inbound from Irkutsk on flight 15007, carrying 12.8 tons (28.220 lb) of cargo. For training purposes the pilot in command made the approach with the blind-flying curtains drawn. When the curtains were opened it was apparent that the aircraft had strayed from the glide path. Instead of initiating a go-around the pilots took vigorous corrective action; as a result the Cub landed hard with 3.0 G, bouncing and collapsing the nose gear. The aircraft was soon repaired and returned to service.

- In November 1989 Soviet Air Force An-12BP **CCCP-11875** (c/n unknown) crashed and burned on landing at the Soviet naval airbase in Cam Ranh, Thânh Hoa province, southern Vietnam. Most of the occupants died in the blaze.

- A minor accident involving Magadan CAD/1st Magadan UFD/181st Flight 'military' An-12B **CCCP-11983** (c/n 401806) occurred in 1989; no details are known.

• On 21 June 1990 demilitarised An-12P **CCCP-11765** (c/n 401705) owned by the Antonov OKB and using the callsign CCCP-10622 was making flight 91792 from Kiev-Gostomel to Kishinyov (where cargo was uplifted) and thence via Pechora and Batagai to Tiksi. However, things started to go wrong when the airport authorities in Batagai refused to refuel the aircraft because there was no fuel on site. As a result the aircraft had to take off with insufficient fuel to make Tiksi. En route the crew consecutively shut down three engines in an effort to conserve fuel. Eventually, however, the last engine also died during the landing approach, and the crew made a wheels-up landing on a dirt strip adjacent to the main runway, the aircraft suffering substantial damage. Fortunately, CCCP-11765 was deemed repairable.

• Eight days later 'civil' An-12BP **CCCP-11130** (c/n 02348205) of the Yakutian CAD/Yakutsk UFD/139th Flight suffered a mishap at Rostov-on-Don. As it was taxiing out to depart for Chelyabinsk on flight 40036 the starboard wingtip struck the tail-gunner's station of An-12A **CCCP-11976** owned by the Rostov helicopter factory which was parked incorrectly. Both aircraft were soon repaired.

• Probably the best-known accident with an An-12 occurred on 12 December 1990 – and, ironically, again one of the OKB's own aircraft was involved. A 'military' An-12B wearing the non-standard registration **CCCP-29110** (c/n 402502) and an equally strange colour scheme – medium-grey overall with a dark blue cheatline – was making a 'tangerine flight' from Batumi, Georgia, to Kiev-Gostomel, carrying 12 tons (26,455 lb) of the juicy fruit. As it descended towards Kiev, the aircraft dived into clouds at 4,150 m (13,615 ft) – and the first officer mistakenly shut down all four engines instead of activating the de-icers. The error was because the fuel shut-off cocks were located right next to the de-icing system switches.

Four attempts to restart the engines failed. The crew then attempted a dead-stick landing in an open field 12 km (7.45 miles) north-west of Borispol airport, but as it touched down the *Cub* hit the embankment of the Brovary–Borispol highway and came apart, scattering tangerines all over the field as the fuselage broke in two and the port wing ripped away completely. All 17 occupants received injuries but survived – thanks to the skill of the captain, Anatoliy V. Slobodyaniuk, though luck was undoubtedly on their side.

• On 23 September 1991 the demilitarised An-12BP **CCCP-13320** (c/n 8345407), owned by Special Cargo Airlines, a division of NPO Vzlyot, ran out of fuel on final approach to Khatanga where it was to make a refuelling stop en route from Petropavlovsk-Kamchatskiy to Yermolino. The engines quit 5–6 km (3.1–3.7 miles) from the airport. The pilots managed a smooth touchdown 1,450 m (4,760 ft) from the runway threshold, but 640 m (2,100 ft) further on the aircraft rammed the brick building of the inner marker beacon and broke up. The crew of seven survived but one of the nine passengers was killed. It turned out that not enough fuel had been filled at Petropavlovsk-Kamchatskiy and the aircraft was overloaded as well.

• On 8 November 1991 'civil' An-12BP **CCCP-11129** (c/n 02348204) operated by SiGi Air Cargo overran the runway at Yanina, Bulgaria, suffering extensive (possibly irreparable) damage.

• Two Yakutian CAD 'civil' An-12BPs, **CCCP-11120 No. 2** (c/n 02348102)[102] and **CCCP-11129** (c/n 02348204), suffered minor accidents in 1991 (in Angola and Sudan respectively). No details are known.

• On 9 June 1992 'civil' An-12BP **CCCP-11105 No. 2** (c/n 01347801)[103] of the Leningrad CAD/Leningrad UFD landed at Khmelnitskiy, inbound on flight 24013 from St Petersburg with an ultimate destination of Samara. After touchdown the captain neglected to set the throttles to ground idle and activated the wheel brakes without resorting to reverse thrust. Emergency braking was to no avail: the tyres burst, and as the aircraft overran into the mud beyond the runway the nose gear buckled. Despite substantial damage to the forward fuselage, the freighter was repaired and returned to service.

• On 22 June 1992 'military' An-12B **CCCP-11896** (c/n 3340906) of the Krasnoyarsk CAD/Norilsk UFD/434th Flight crashed at its home base. The aircraft was inbound from Andizhan, Uzbekistan, via Omsk, on flight 22238, carrying 12 tons (26,455 lb) of fruit and vegetables. Because of bad weather the crew messed up the approach to Alykel airport, straying to the left of Runway 14. However, the pilots were reluctant to make a go-around, knowing that the weather might not permit another try and they might have to go to Igarka, the alternate airport – which they'd rather not. (For one thing, they wanted to complete the flight quickly and save fuel; for another, the cargo was perishable and if it went bad the Norilsk air enterprise would face heavy fines.)

Hence the pilots made an S-turn to try and get the aircraft onto the runway centreline. Next, realising they would not succeed, they hauled back on the control columns to initiate a go-around. Losing speed, the An-12 stalled and 'fell through', striking the runway with the port main gear and wingtip before becoming airborne again. Then it turned to the right and crashed with a 45° right bank just outside the perimeter fence, 605 metres (1,985 ft) from the runway. There was no fire, but six of the seven crew and four of the five passengers were killed.

• On 14 July 1992 'civil' An-12BP **CCCP-11111** (c/n 01347906) belonging to the recently established Magadanaerogrooz (Magadan Cargo Airlines)[104] was due to be employed on flight 26163 from Magadan-Sokol to Moscow-Domodedovo, with refuelling stops at Lensk, Novosibirsk and Yekaterinburg, carrying 11,060 kg (24,382 lb) of cargo. En route, however, the captain suddenly changed his mind, deciding to fly via Irkutsk. The available fuel was not enough for a non-stop flight to Irkutsk and the captain soon had misgivings about that; yet, inexplicably, he stubbornly pressed on towards Irkutsk, wasting several chances to land at alternate airports.

The result was as predictable as it was deplorable: 120 km (74.5 miles) from Irkutsk the outer engines quit, followed one minute later by the inboard ones when the aircraft was at 1,600 m (5,250 ft). The pilots had to make a wheels-up, flaps-up landing in a ploughed field 100 km (62 miles) from the airport. In so doing the An-12 bounced four times and the fuselage snapped in two at the production break; the forward fuselage and wings came to rest 690 m (2,260 ft) from the impact point, turning right through 153°. The crew walked away but the aircraft was totalled, of course.

- On the night of 18 December 1992 the aforementioned An-12BP **CCCP-12957** was damaged again when leaving Norilsk on flight 22233 to Sochi via Volgograd with 1.5 tons (3,300 lb) of cargo. Drifting to the left as it accelerated, the aircraft ran off the side of the runway. The take-off was aborted but the An-12 ended up in deep snow, collapsing the port and nose gear units and suffering damage to No. 4 propeller. Yet again the freighter was repaired and is still in service at the time of writing.

- According to press reports, a *Cub* (apparently a VTA aircraft) crashed fatally in Nakhichevan, Nakhichevan ASSR, in 1992 and another was damaged beyond repair in Aden, Yemen, that year.

- On 27 February 1993 'military' An-12BP **CCCP-11399** (c/n 4342501) belonging to MOM/the Omsk 'Polyot' Production Association was being used for flight 93232 from Omsk to Gyumri, Armenia, via Volgograd with six crew members, four passengers and 13,235 kg (29,177 lb) of cargo instead of the authorised 10,000 kg (22,045 lb). The weather in Gyumri was poor, with fog and driving snow; to make matters worse the localiser and glideslope beacon had failed, forcing the crew to make a visual approach. Horizontal visibility was 2,100 m (6,900 ft), but the approach controller mistakenly informed the crew it was 3,100 m (10,170 ft). One and a half minutes before touchdown the runway lighting also partially failed, which is why the pilots did not discover that the aircraft was off the runway centreline. When the landing lights were switched on six seconds before touchdown they created a so-called reflection screen, causing the crew to become disoriented. An involuntary jerk of the control wheel was enough to cause the *Cub* to touch down with right bank and run onto the right runway shoulder, where the starboard main gear collapsed in the deep snow. Turning 60° to the right, the aircraft slithered across the runway, tail first, and came to rest on the other side. No one was hurt and the An-12 was deemed repairable.

- A month later, on 26 April, 'civil' An-12BP **CCCP-11121** (c/n 02348103) was hit by a Stinger missile fired by UNITA rebels while it was on a mission somewhere in Angola; mercifully the aircraft remained in one piece, but it was damaged beyond repair in the ensuing crash-landing.

- On 23 July 1993 An-12BK **CCCP-11342** (c/n 00347607) of Volga Dnepr Airlines was making charter flight VDA 003 from its home base, Ulyanovsk-Vostochnyy, to Skopje via Simferopol; the aircraft was empty and was to collect a cargo in Skopje for the return trip. The Macedonian capital's airport lies in mountainous terrain and is quite difficult to fly into, especially in bad weather. This was exactly the case on 23 July when a thunderstorm raged over Skopje – of which the Macedonian approach controller had not informed the crew. To make matters worse the airport's DME system was out of order. As the pilots turned the aircraft on a heading of 163° for the downwind leg of the landing pattern, a piloting error caused CCCP-11342 to deviate 2.8 km (1.74 miles) to the right of the intended flight path. Then, seeing storm activity ahead, the pilots started circumnavigating it without knowing their true position or altitude above the ground (the An-12 had no ground-proximity warning system). As a result, CCCP-11342 crashed into the wooded slope of Mt Lisec at 1,524 m (5,000 ft) above sea level 24 km (14.9 miles) south of the airport and exploded, killing all six crew and both passengers.

- On 21 (some sources say 23) August 1993 yet another Russian Air Force An-12 crashed fatally near Volgograd when three engines quit, followed shortly thereafter by the remaining engine.

- On 7 August 1993 An-12BP **RA-11110**, by then operated by Aviacor (some sources say Aviaobschchemash), was damaged beyond repair at El Fasmer, Sudan, when it landed on rough ground, missing the runway after all the airport's navigation systems failed. Such cases when airports are disabled by power failures are not uncommon in many parts of Africa.

- On 20 August 1993 demilitarised An-12TB **RA-11375** (c/n 402405) of Komiavia (Syktyvkar UFD/318th Flight) took off from Slavgorod, Altai Region, bound for Syktyvkar via Samara on Flight OG9117. There were seven crew members aboard and the aircraft was carrying 10.8 tons (23,810 lb) of cargo comprising forty 55-gallon drums of liquid detergent. Immediately after becoming airborne RA-11375 collided with a large flock of birds, several of which were ingested by Nos 2 and 4 engines, knocking them out. The pilots initiated a U-turn, hoping to make an emergency landing at the airport of origin, but the power of the two remaining engines was not enough to keep the heavily loaded aircraft aloft. Crash-landing on rough ground 8.6 km (5.3 miles) from the runway, the *Cub* was completely destroyed by the resulting fire, and four of the occupants were injured.

- On 25 September 1993 an An-12B with the non-standard registration **RA-13387** (c/n 402902) belonging to the Rostov helicopter factory (RVPP Rostvertol) was heading from Khabarovsk to Tyumen on Flight FD9112 with 10,172 kg (22,425 lb) of cargo. The take-off weight was estimated at 67,079–67,347 kg (147,880–148,472 lb); therefore the aircraft was 6,079–6,347 kg (13,400–13,992 lb) overweight. This, together with strong headwinds, increased fuel consumption, and the crew soon realised they were not going to make it; yet they pressed on towards Tyumen instead of heading to the alternate airport of Tobolsk. As the aircraft approached Tyumen-Roschchino, descending through 3,500 m (11,480 ft), the engines cut one by one owing to fuel starvation, and there was no choice but to make an emergency landing in marshland a few kilometres from the airport. Mercifully there were no fatalities and the aircraft was repairable.

- On 19 December 1993 'military' An-12A **RA-12187** (c/n 1340201) belonging to the Petrolada company made a flight from St Petersburg to Lensk via Novyy Urengoy, carrying 9.1 tons (20,060 lb) of cargo. The crew were tired because of working overtime (which, as the investigation showed, was common practice at Petrolada), and crew fatigue is always dangerous.

On final approach to Lensk the crew discovered that half the runway lights (along one side of the runway) were out of action because of a broken power cable. The best solution would be to head for an alternate

ACCIDENT ATTRITION

airport and come back in daylight conditions. However, the alternate (Ust-Kut) was 700 km (435 miles) away, which meant a large expenditure of fuel; besides, the cargo would be damaged by the extreme cold at Ust-Kut. That said, the crew's decision to land at Lensk was justified.

However, crew fatigue led to two errors which caused the accident. First, the QNH had been set incorrectly (without making corrections for the low air temperature), causing the altimeter to give false readings; hence the aircraft came in too low. Then, the captain began retarding the throttles too early as the aircraft passed the inner marker beacon. The No. 4 engine was throttled back more vigorously than the rest, causing a braking effect; as a result the starboard wing stalled and 'fell through', the aircraft rolling 5–7° to the right and losing altitude fast. RA-12187 touched down 50 m (164 ft) short of the runway with 3.7–3.8 G; collapsing the starboard main gear and wrecking the No. 4 engine, the aircraft turned 80° to the right and came to a standstill on the runway shoulder. None of the eight crew and two passengers suffered any injuries and the aircraft was repairable.

• On 8 February 1994 'military' An-12BP **RA-11340** (c/n 6344502) was damaged in a landing accident when it missed the runway at Anadyr in bad weather.

• On 4 (some sources say 5) August 1994 a Russian Air Force An-12 (identity unknown) crashed on final approach to Bada AB 225 km (139.75 miles) south-west of Chita, Transbaikalian Defence District. Landing at night, the aircraft dropped below the glide path and hit a hill 4.5 km (2.79 miles) from the runway. There were no survivors among the six crew and 41 passengers.

• On the night of 24 October 1994 'military' An-12A **RA-11790** (c/n 1400302) departed from Yuzhno-Sakhalinsk (Khomootovo airport) on flight 9223, bound for Yermolino via Ust-Ilimsk and Omsk. The aircraft, which belonged to the Yermolino Flight Test & Research Enterprise (YeLIIP) but was leased by an airline called Aero-Nika, was carrying 12.1 tons (26,675 lb) of cargo – four (!) used Japanese cars plus 7.5 tons (16,535 lb) of seafood, part of the cargo being destined for Ust-Ilimsk. Besides, jet fuel was always abundant in Ust-Ilimsk (unlike the alternate airports of Ust-Kut and Bratsk), and the airport handling fares were lower; this prompted the crew to carry on with the landing approach, even though the weather conditions were below minima.

At 13.21 UTC, 15 minutes before the crash, the ATC shift supervisor instructed the approach controller to send the aircraft off to an alternate and went to inspect the runway in a service van. The van was not equipped with an air-to-ground waveband radio, which meant the supervisor could not monitor the exchange between RA-11790 and the approach controller, but believed the latter had complied with his orders. Instead, the controller asked the pilots about their decision; the aircraft was then 85 km (52.75 miles) away. Requesting weather information and learning that the weather at Ust-Ilimsk had briefly improved above minima, the crew confirmed their decision to land.

Shortly afterwards, however, the weather deteriorated again. Trying to establish visual contact with the ground on short finals, the captain caused the aircraft to descend below the glide path. Sensing that the approach was unsafe, the navigator called out, 'Too low. We're too low.' Ten seconds before the crash the flight engineer urged the pilots to go around but the captain did not react – apparently owing to psychological stress.

At the same time the ATC shift supervisor returned to the control tower, and seeing that the An-12 was on final approach, he told the controller to order an immediate go-around. However, the crew never received these instructions. At 13.36 UTC the aircraft hit a 30 m (98 ft) hill 2.1 km (1.3 miles) from the runway threshold and exploded, only the tail unit remaining intact. All nine crew and 14 passengers, including five children, were killed.

• On 24 December 1994 'civil' An-12BP **RA-11118** (c/n 01348002) of Pulkovo Avia, North-Western Regional Air Transport Directorate (ATD),[105] plunged into the ground on final approach to Nalchik, the capital of North Osetia, with a cargo of coins; all six crew and the seven guards accompanying the valuables were killed. The cause was traced to the problem which afflicted the type decades ago – a sudden pitch-down caused by heavy icing. The crew had forgotten that it would have been enough to set the flaps 5° (take-off position) to prevent loss of control.

• On 14 March 1995 Penza Air Enterprise 'military' An-12B **RA-11337** (c/n 3341204) was winging its way from Yerevan to Turkmenbashi, Turkmenia, when the crew realised they did not have enough fuel. Requesting an emergency landing at Baku-Bina, the pilots began a visual approach to Runway 35L; however, at the last moment the approach controller discovered the aircraft was heading for Runway 35R, on which some construction work was under way, and ordered a go-around. On the second try the engines quit, one after another, and the pilots had to make a belly landing in a field 6 km (3.75 miles) from the airport. All nine crew and six passengers escaped with minor injuries but the aircraft was declared a write-off.

• On 25 March 1995 An-12BK **RA-13340** (c/n 00347504) of the Far Eastern Regional ATD suffered an engine fire after landing at Bunia, Zaïre. Jumping clear of the aircraft, the crew attacked the flames with portable fire extinguishers; yet these efforts were fruitless and within minutes the fire completely gutted the aircraft.

• On 9 May 1995 'civil' An-12BP **LZ-PVL** of Global Air (c/n 02348202) overran at Lukapa, Angola, collapsing the nose gear, but was repaired and returned to the lessor (Pulkovo Avia) as RA-11127. Pilot error was the cause of the accident.

• On 17 June 1995 an unidentified An-12 suffered an engine fire 80 km (49.6 miles) from Kishinyov when cruising at 8,100 m (26,570 ft), en route from Larnaca to Moscow-Sheremetyevo. All attempts to tackle the blaze with the on-board fire-fighting system failed; luckily the crew, captained by GosNII GA Flight Centre Vice-Director Ruben Yesaian, managed a safe landing at Kishinyov, where the fire was finally extinguished. For this performance Yesaian was awarded the Personal Bravery Order.

• On 22 November 1995 'military' An-12B **RA-11008** (c/n 402612) was written off when it overran at Huambo, Angola, because of pilot error, and hit an obstacle, shearing off the landing gear and suffering heavy damage to the fuselage.

- On 24 February 1996 'military' An-12B **RA-11403** of Sakha-Avia (c/n 401906) was damaged beyond repair in an off-field landing near Lyudino, Russia, after running out of fuel.

- Three days later the civil war in Angola claimed its next victim. 'Military' An-12B **ER-ACE** (c/n 402812) belonging to the Moldavian carrier Mikma but operating for the local airline Aerotropical, Lda, was shot down by a shoulder-launched surface-to-air missile on short finals to Lukapa airport. The crew of five, all Russian nationals, and the three Angolan passengers perished. As usual, UNITA rebels were blamed for the shootdown and a formal protest was filed with the United Nations.

- On 14 September 1996 'military' An-12A **RA-11916** (c/n 2400901) owned by YeLIIP made a hard landing with left bank at Bryansk airport, pulling 3.9 G and suffering structural damage to the centre fuselage. Nevertheless, the aircraft was repaired and was still operational in 1998.

- Quite apart from the civil war, Angola is generally known as an 'accident black spot' owing to appalling flight safety standards. On 6 October 1996 'civil' An-12BP **RA-11101** of GosNII GA (c/n 01347703) was making a night approach to Lukapa when all the runway lights suddenly went out. Losing sight of the runway limits, the pilots could not stop the aircraft in time and the An-12 overran, crashing through a residential building 65 m (213 ft) beyond the runway and turning through 180°. In so doing part of the cargo became dislodged, crushing five passengers and one of the crew members to death; the other eight passengers and five crew escaped with minor injuries. One person on the ground was fatally injured as well; infuriated by this, local residents torched the aircraft the same night.

- On 2 November 1996 'military' An-12TB **RA-11851** (c/n 402003) of Aviaobschchemash was extensively damaged in a crash-landing in Nizhnevartovsk, Tyumen' Region.

- On 17 December 1996 a Russian Air Force *Cub* (identity unknown) crashed at Andreapol AB, Pskov Region, while taking off on a flight to Krasnodar in foul weather. The crash claimed the lives of 18 persons, including Leningrad Defence District Commander Col. Gen. S.P. Seleznyov.

- On 12 March 1997 another Russian-crewed 'military' An-12BP, **D2-FVG No. 1** of Air Nacoia (c/n 6344506), landed on rough ground beside the runway at Lukapa and broke up, killing 15 people.

- On 13 April 1997 'civil' An-12BP **RA-11112** (c/n 01347907) reportedly suffered serious damage in a hard landing at Verkhnevilyuisk but was repaired and back in service by the end of 1998. Strangely, the aircraft was reported for Baikalavia at the time of the accident.

- On 8 November 1997 'military' An-12A **RA-11327** (c/n 1400103) of Aviaobschchemash was damaged in a hard landing in Bryansk but subsequently repaired.

- 11 December 1997 saw another disaster caused by ATC error. 'Military' An-12BP **RA-12105** (c/n 5343404), seconded to NPO Vega-M by the Russian Air Force, was making a late-night approach to Naryan-Mar in heavy snow. Unbeknown to the crew, a Mil Mi-8T *Hip-A* transport helicopter (**RA-24247**, c/n 98730918) of the Naryan-Mar UFD/73rd Flight came in at the same time on an ambulance flight, bringing a pregnant woman who was due to give birth shortly. Touching down at 16.57 Moscow time, the *Cub* rammed the helicopter which had just landed on the runway immediately ahead and was taxiing in. The Mi-8 burst into flames, eight of the 18 occupants losing their lives; the An-12 suffered irreparable damage as well. The responsibility for this tragedy lay with the air traffic controller who had authorised the chopper to land squarely in the path of the incoming transport.

- On the night of 13 January 1998 an An-12 operated by the Taliban militia (identity unknown) crashed in western Pakistan. The aircraft had departed Kandahar (where Taliban had their south-western HQ), bound for Herat; however, both Herat and the alternate airfield of Shindand had closed because of foul weather. After circling in the vain hope of a change in the weather the crew requested an emergency landing in Quetta, Baluchistan Province. However, the *Cub* collided with a mountain slope near the Khojak Pass 44 km (27 miles) north of Quetta, possibly after running out of fuel. All 45 passengers and six crew perished.

- On 4 February 1998 demilitarised An-12B **LZ-SFG** (c/n 3341605), wet-leased by the Portuguese carrier Air Luxor from Air Sofia, stalled and crashed seconds after taking off from Santa Maria (Lajes, the Azores) on a flight to Lisbon. All seven occupants were killed.

- 'Civil' An-12BP **RA-12973** (c/n 9346505) of Tyumen Airlines reportedly crashed on 11 May 1998. No details are known.

- On 23 July 1998 An-12 **RA-***** crashed and burned after taking off from Pushkin, near St Petersburg. Pushkin is a test airfield used by the avionics manufacturer Leninets Holding Company; however, **RA-***** was not a testbed but an ordinary transport *Cub*. The aircraft took off at 03.42 local time, outbound for Norilsk with 13 tons (28,660 lb) of foodstuffs; seconds later it banked sharply to starboard, lost altitude, crashed 200 m (660 ft) beyond the runway threshold and burst into flames. The seven crew and two expeditors escaped from the wreckage, one of the pilots suffering severe burns; the aircraft was completely destroyed by the fire. The cause of the crash was traced to birdstrike in No. 4 engine; the propeller could not be feathered, the resulting drag causing the heavy aircraft to lose control.

- On 11 August 1998 An-12 **D2-FAZ** of ALADA (version and c/n unknown) was damaged beyond repair in Saurimo (Lunda Sul province, Angola).

- Fifteen days later 'military' An-12BP **EW-11368** (c/n 4342010) owned by the Belorussian airline Techaviaservice crashed near Kalomboloka 80 km (49.5 miles) south of Luanda, its point of origin, after suffering problems with two engines. All five crew and eight Angolans accompanying the cargo were killed.

- On 11 November 1998 'civil' An-12BP **RA-12955** (c/n 8345506) operated by the Viliuy Air Company crashed five minutes after take-off from Krasnoyarsk-Yemelyanovo, outbound for Mirnyy with 13 tons (28,660 lb) of cargo. The aircraft came down in a thick forest 25 km (15.5 miles) from the airport; there were no survivors among the six crew and four passengers.

• On 25 October 1998 An-12BK **RA-83962** (c/n 402210) owned by the Flight Research Institute went missing in a region of Angola controlled by the UNITA guerrillas. According to press reports the aircraft was operated by a local airline called Maveua (or some such) at the time.

• On 17 December 1998 Zanex Airlines An-12 **S9-SAT** (c/n unknown) was about to touch down at Saurimo, Angola, when the pilots saw a vehicle on the runway and initiated a go-around. However, the heavy aircraft was slow in reacting and came down hard, tail first; losing control, it careered across the field, suffering irreparable damage in the process.

• On 20 January 1999 demilitarised An-12BP **S9-CAN** (c/n 6344002, operator unknown) was damaged beyond repair after veering off the runway on landing at Lukapa, Angola.

• On 2 February 1999 'military' An-12B **EL-ASA** (c/n 3340909) of Santa Cruz Imperial took off from Luanda about 4 o'clock in the morning, outbound for Lukapa on flight SVN131 for Savanair. Immediately afterwards the crew reported an engine failure, requesting an emergency landing. However, the loss of power was so grave that the freighter ploughed through Cazenga township (a slum city on the outskirts of Luanda) and exploded, killing all four crew and 13 (according to some sources, more than 30) people on the ground.

• On 1 July 1999 'civil' An-12BP **TN-AFR** (c/n 8345502) of Savanair was hit by a Stinger missile near Luzamba (Lunda Norte Province, Angola) while en route from Luanda to Saurimo with a cargo of live chickens. The pilots managed a perfect emergency landing; the Russian crew of five and the two Angolans accompanying the cargo were captured and held hostage by UNITA.

• On 14 December 1999 Khors Air Company 'military' An-12BP **UR-11319** (c/n 4342510) with five crew members aboard went missing near Cuito-Cuanavale, Angola. It was later established that the aircraft was shot down by UNITA guerrillas.

• Sometime before August 2001 Russian Air Force An-12BK **'18 Red'** (c/n 00347007) was damaged in a ground accident at Chkalovskaya AB near Moscow when a taxiing aircraft struck the port side of the *Cub*'s nose with the starboard wingtip.

• On 31 January 2000 'military' An-12BP **LZ-ITB** of Inter Trans Air (c/n 8346006) was reportedly damaged in a minor accident at Hahn AFB, Germany.

• On 24 March 2000 demilitarised An-12BP **RA-11302** (c/n 8346004) of Antey crashed on landing at Colombo-Bandaranaike International airport.

• At 17.16 Moscow time on 22 May 2001 a Russian Air Force An-12BP (**RA-12135**, c/n 00347002) crashed about six minutes after take-off from Rzhev, Tver Region. The aircraft, which belonged to the 226th OSAP at Kubinka AB, was carrying an aircraft engine and other spares. Apparently the No. 2 engine failed as the aircraft climbed through 2,000 m (6,560 ft). According to preliminary reports, the propeller autofeathering system also failed, the dead engine causing tremendous drag and loss of control; the aircraft rolled and dived into marshland near the village of Myakotino, crashing in an 80° nose-down attitude and exploding. All seven crew – pilot Maj. Sergey Grischchenko, co-pilot Lt. (sg) Igor Yeremeyev, flight engineer Lt. (sg) Aleksandr Novikov, navigator Capt. Dmitriy Bashkov, the regiment's chief navigator Maj. Sergey Svischchev, radio operator Ens. Roman Popov and loadmaster Capt. Mikhail Aksyuchitz – were killed.

Initial attempts to recover the bodies and the 'black boxes' were foiled by the impassable terrain. A 3 km (1.8 mile) road had to be constructed in order to get to the crash site. The wreckage was completely submerged and the 'tin kickers' had to drain the area in order to recover it. The airmen were buried in their home town of Kubinka on 30 May. All Russian Air Force An-12s were grounded pending investigation.

• On 10 July 2001 'military' An-12B **LZ-SFK** of Air Sofia (c/n 4341901) was damaged in a landing accident at Exeter airport. The freighter, inbound from Casablanca on a charter flight, ran off the side of the runway in a strong crosswind, collapsing the starboard main gear and bending No. 4 propeller blades, blocking the runway for several hours. The damage was not so bad and the aircraft was returned to service on 30 July after spares and a repair crew had been brought in by Air Sofia's An-26 LZ-SFH.

Flight hours of An-12s written off in accidents (where known)

Aircraft (c/n)	Manufacture date	Total time since new	Total cycles since new	Overhauls
An-12A/military **CCCP-69321 No. 1** (1901708)	31-8-1961	14,251 hrs	5,707	4
An-12AP/military **CCCP-11795 No. 1** (1400103)	18-7-1961	11,980 hrs	6,026	4
An-12A/military **RA-11790** (1400302)	28-12-1961	7,748 hrs	3,966	4
An-12B/military **CCCP-11418 No. 1** (401712)	30-6-1963	16,419 hrs 41 min	9,041	5
An-12TB/military **CCCP-11375** (402405)	31-12-1964	30,840 hrs	13,112	8
An-12B/military **CCCP-29110** (402502)	28-12-1964	4,461 hrs 34 min	2,703	3
An-12B/military **CCCP-11896** (3340906)	11-1-1963	15,654 hrs 11 min	6,487	4
An-12BP/civil **CCCP-11030** (7345002)	29-7-1967	11,123 hrs 32 min	4,629	2
An-12BP/military **CCCP-13320** (8345407)	30-4-1968	3,872 hrs 45 min	2,150	2
An-12BP/civil **CCCP-12962** (9346406)	23-5-1969	26,140 hrs 09 min	9,696	7
An-12BP/civil **CCCP-12963** (9346407)	23-5-1969	18,235 hrs	7,006	2
An-12BK **CCCP-12162 No. 1** (9346702)	13-8-1969	7,411 hrs 16 min	3,162	3
An-12BP/civil **CCCP-12985** (00347110)	27-5-1970	5,811 hrs 43 min	2,617	1
An-12BP/civil **CCCP-12997** (00347404)	31-8-1970	24,967 hrs 36 min	10,249	6
An-12BK **CCCP-11342** (00347607)	26-12-1970	4,537 hrs 51 min	4,868	2
An-12BP/civil **CCCP-11104** (01347710)	24-3-1971	19,130 hrs	6,217	3
An-12BP/civil **CCCP-11107** (01347809)	25-5-1971	20,359 hrs	6,710	4
An-12BP/civil **CCCP-11111** (01347906)	12-8-1971*	32,700 hrs	12,972	7
An-12BP/civil **YU-AID/73312** (01348010)	19-12-1971	8,388 hrs	4,727	3

* Also stated as 1 September 1971 in some documents.

- Two weeks after this accident, on 24 July, two Cubs – 'military' An-12BP **LZ-SFS** of Air Sofia (c/n 6344308) and 'civil' An-12BP **4R-EXC** of Expo Aviation (c/n 8345507) – were caught in a crossfire in Colombo. At about 04.40 local time LTTE rebels attacked Bandaranaike International airport, blowing up four SLAF aircraft (two Israel Aircraft Industries Kfir C2 fighters, a MiG-27 *Flogger-F* attack aircraft and an An-32B) and two Sri Lankan Airlines Airbus Industrie A330s. In the ensuing shoot-out between the Tigers and the government forces both An-12s were riddled with bullet holes; several slugs hit the engines, rendering the aircraft unflyable. Eventually, however, both Cubs were repaired.

- On 16 October 2001 'military' An-12A **ER-ADT** of Aerocom (c/n 2340605) was damaged beyond repair in a landing accident at Henderson Airport, Honiara, Solomon Islands.

- On 27 January 2002 Angolan Air Force An-12 **T-304** (c/n unknown) crashed on landing at Kanyengue.

- On 7 February 2002 Volare Airlines An-12BK UR-LIP *The Spirit of Cornwall 2* (c/n 9346405) flew into the Atlas mountains 80 km (49.5 miles) from Agadir, Morocco, and exploded, killing all on board. This is all the more deplorable because UR-LIP was one of the best-equipped Cubs.

- On 15 February 2002 'military' An-12BP **ER-ADL** of Tiramavia (c/n 4342610) crashed at Monrovia's James Spriggs Payne International airport during an attempted emergency landing.

- Finally, on 16 August 2002 demilitarised An-12PP **4R-AIA** (c/n 00347107) suffered an accident at Karachi when the nose gear failed to extend before landing.

APPENDIX II

An-12 Drawings

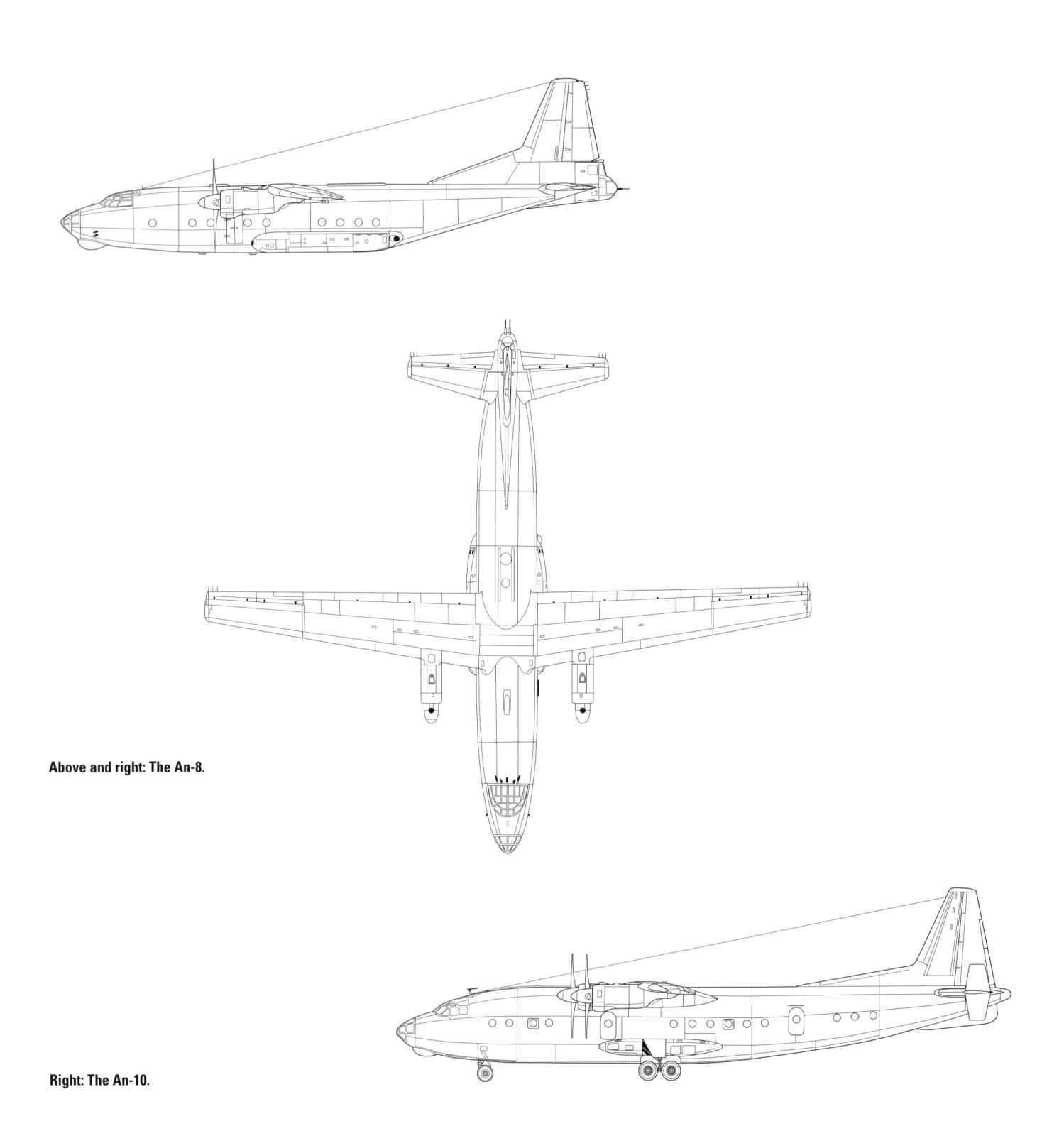

Above and right: The An-8.

Right: The An-10.

180

AN-12 DRAWINGS

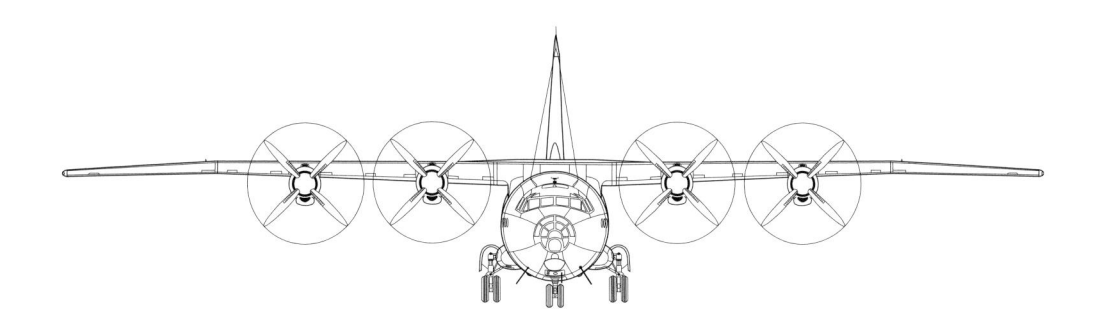

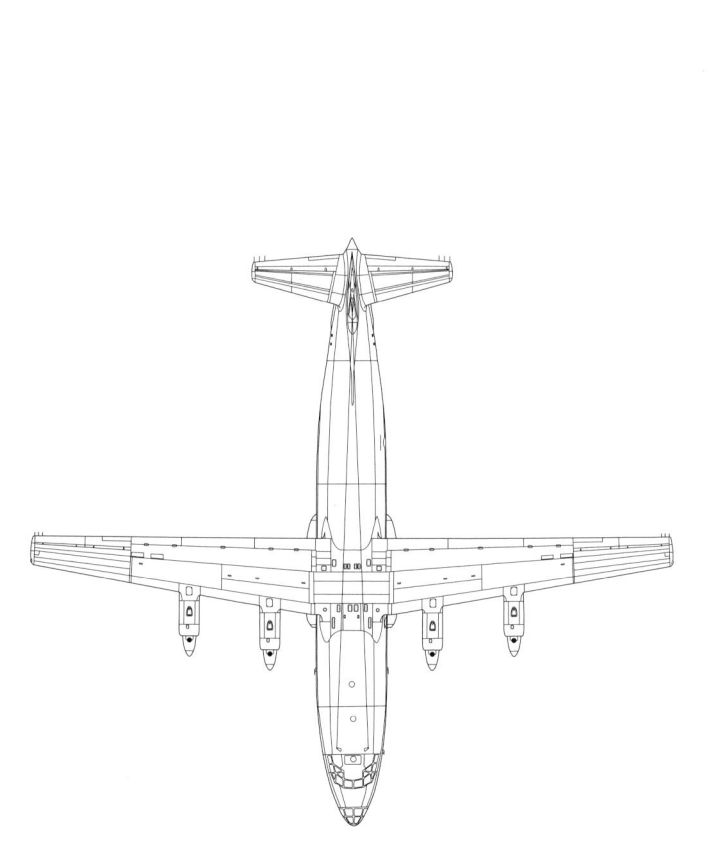

Above, top and left: The An-10.

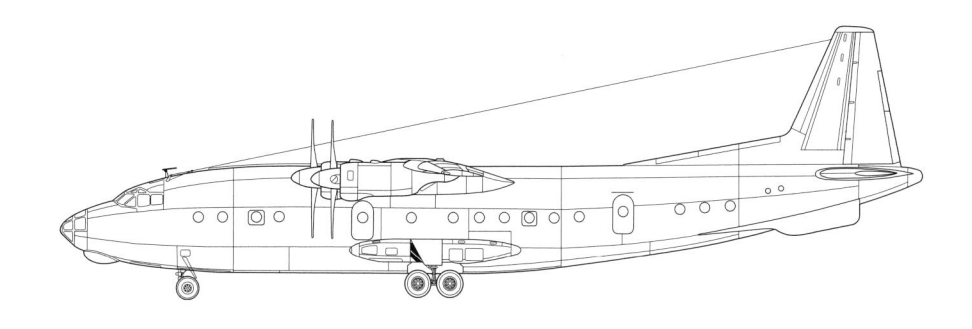

Right: The An-10A.

AN-12 DRAWINGS

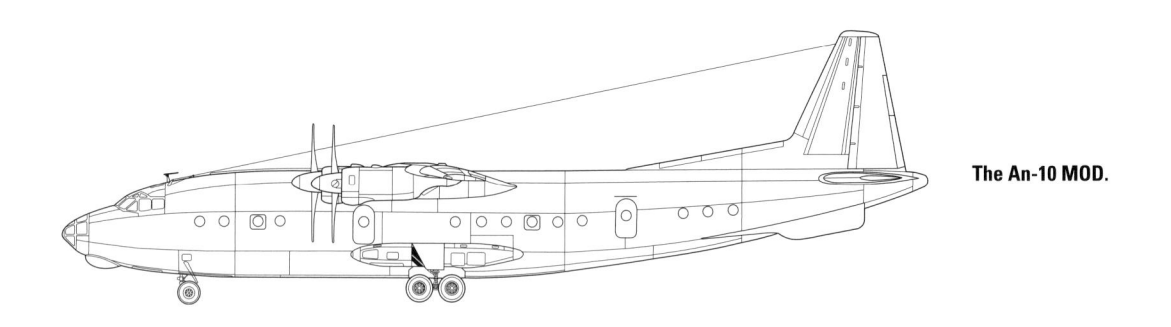

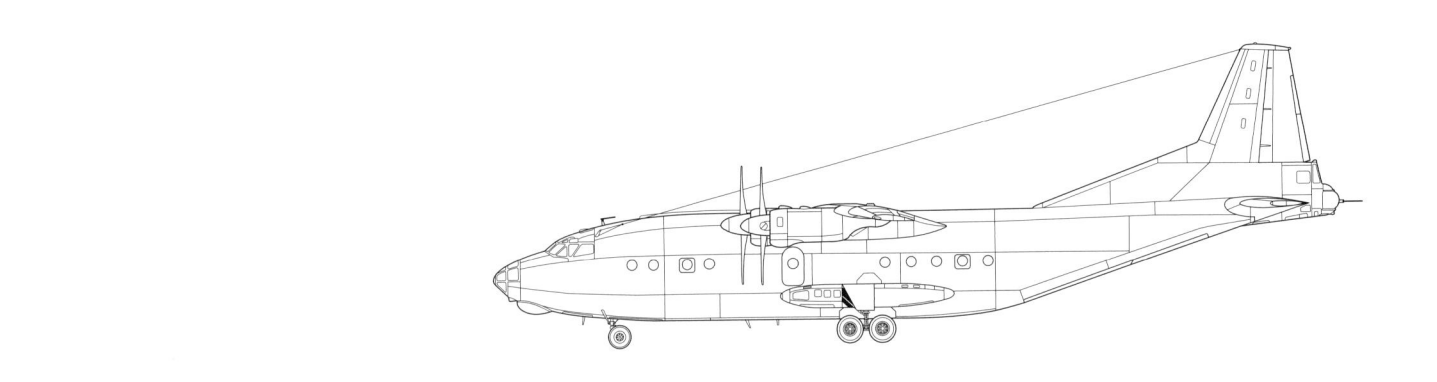

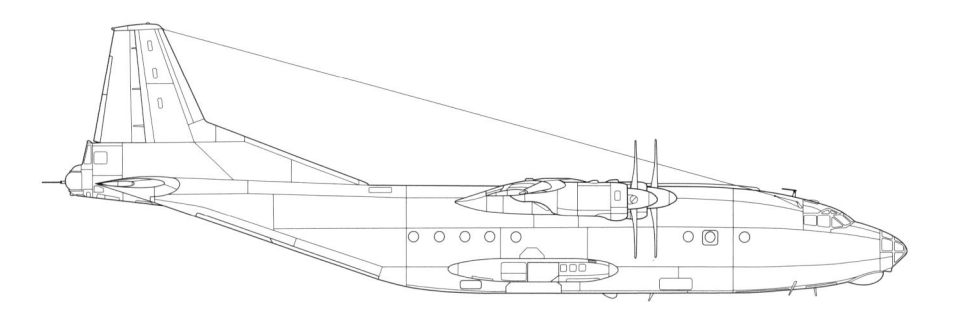

The An-10 MOD.

Above and left: The An-12A.

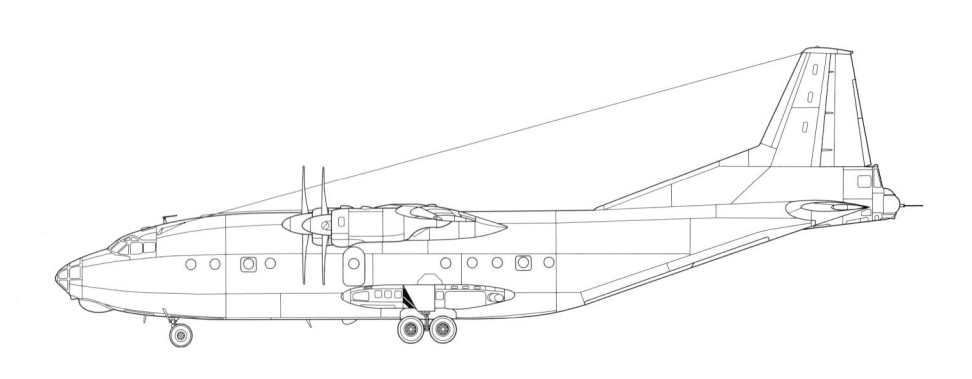

The An-12B-1.

Left, below left and below right: The An-12B-1.

The An-12B-2.

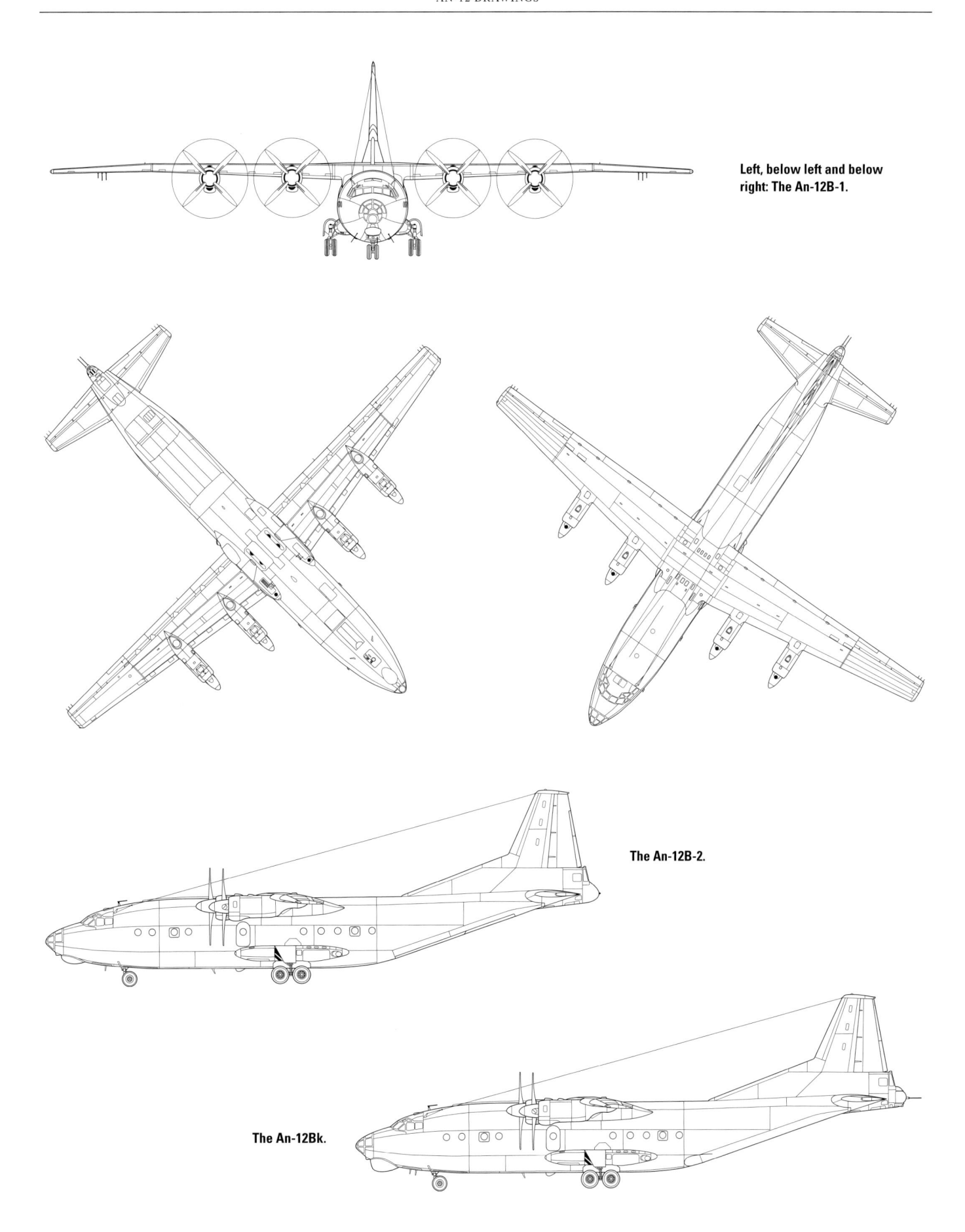

The An-12Bk.

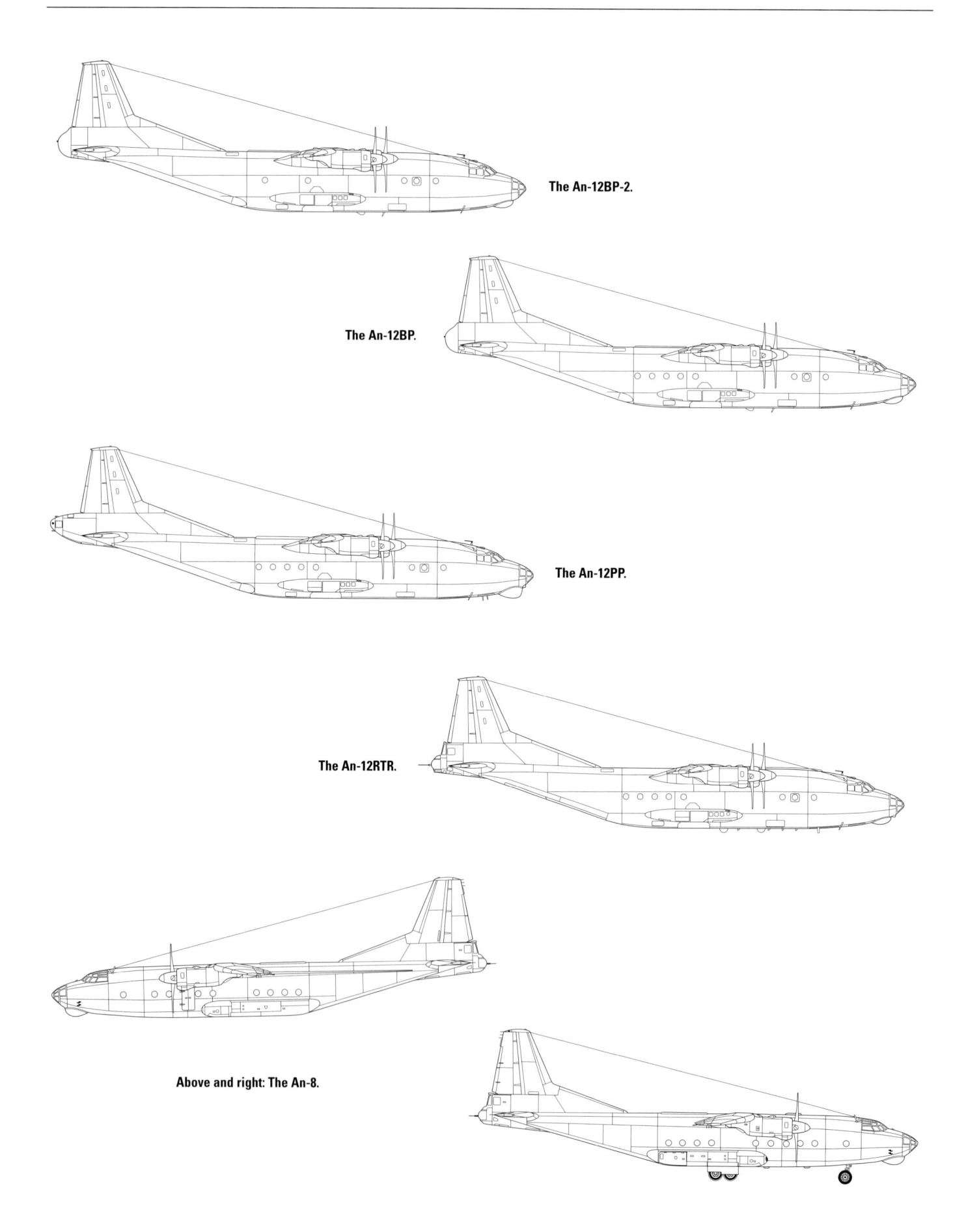

AN-12 DRAWINGS

The An-12BP-2.

The An-12BP.

The An-12PP.

The An-12RTR.

Above and right: The An-8.

AN-12 DRAWINGS

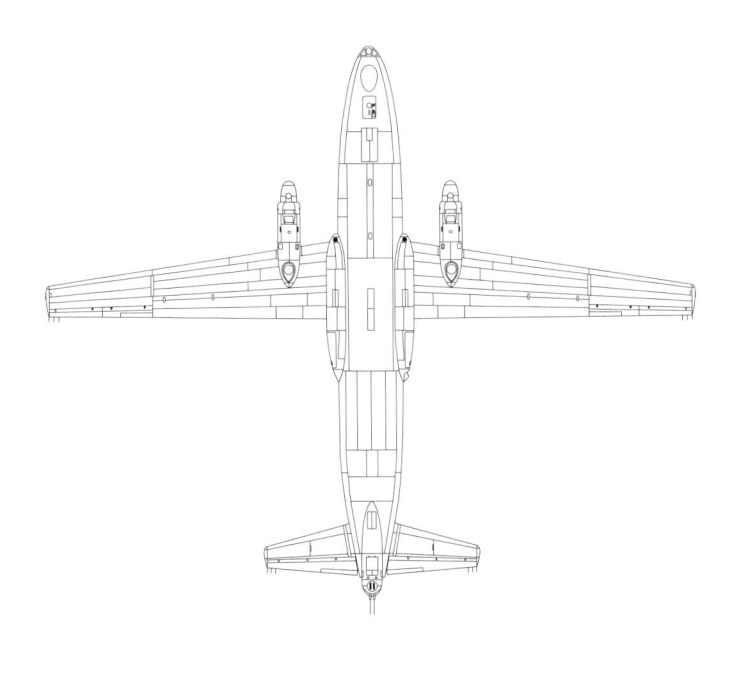

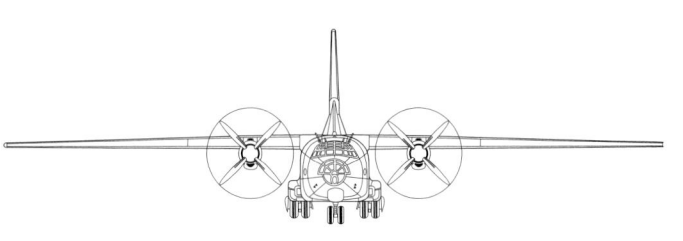

Above and left: The An-8.

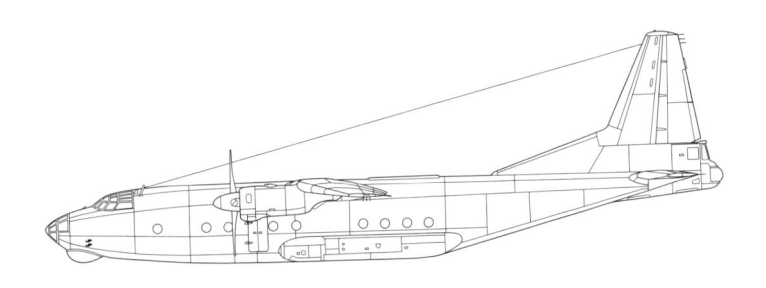

The An-8PRD.

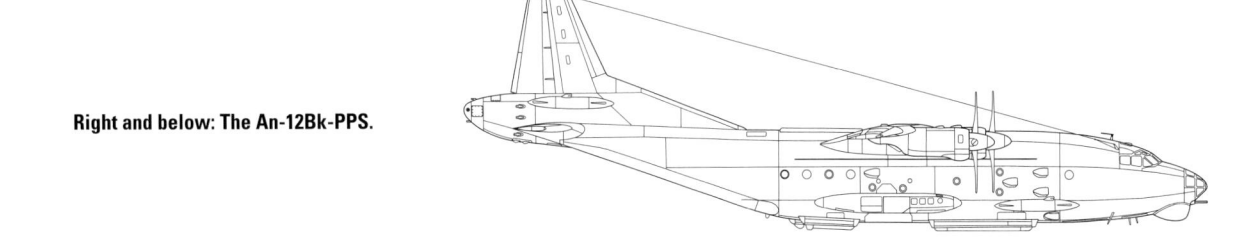

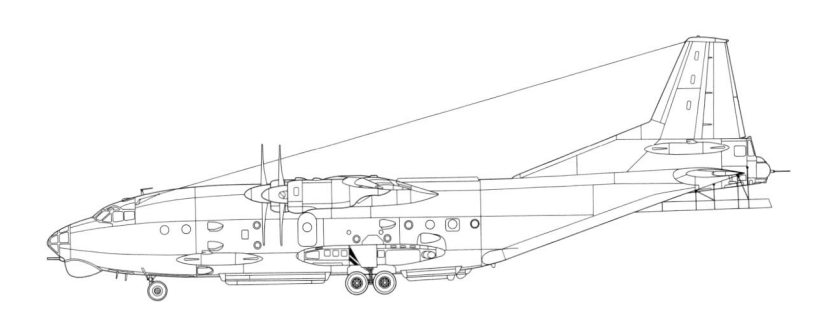

Right and below: The An-12Bk-PPS.

Notes

1. OKB – *opytno-konstrooktorskoye byuro* – experimental design bureau; the number is a code allocated for security reasons.
2. He later went on to become Minister of Defence, a post which he held until his death in office.
3. TV = *toorbovintovoy* [*dvigatel'*] – turboprop engine.
4. KMZ = *Kiyevskiy mashinostroitel'nyy zavod* – Kiev Machinery Plant No. such-and-such. GSOKB = *Gosoodarstvennoye soyooznoye opytno-konstrooktorskoye byuro* – State All-Union Design Bureau, meaning that the OKB had national importance.
5. *Izdeliye* (product) such-and-such was/is a commonly used code for Soviet/Russian military hardware items.
6. MMZ = *Moskovskiy mashinostroitel'nyy zavod* – Moscow Machinery Plant No. such-and-such.
7. It was, in fact, a demotion from ministry status. Later, when Nikita S. Khrushchev had been ousted and Leonid I. Brezhnev became head of state, the Ministry of Aircraft Industry was reinstated.
8. Originally Plant No. 84 was located in Khimki, a northern suburb of Moscow, producing PS-84 (Li-2) airliners. In late 1941 the German offensive against Moscow forced an evacuation to Tashkent, where the plant was established at the site of the unfinished Aircraft Factory No. 34 (which, as such, never built a single aircraft). Yet the c/ns of Li-2s built in Tashkent initially still featured the true factory number as 84; it was not until 1952 that someone got the idea of using the number of the (for all practical purposes) non-existent Plant No. 34 as a code for the Tashkent factory, obviously in order to confuse would-be spies.
9. Some sources claim the change in the c/n system was because the plant was preparing to build the An-12, which was to have all-digit c/ns. However, this won't hold water – for two reasons. Firstly, knowing that different types of aircraft are involved eliminates any possible confusion; in any document the aircraft type comes first. Any fool can see that An-8 c/n 0503 is not the same as An-12 c/n 0503. Secondly, the c/n system was changed in early 1960, whereas An-12 production in Tashkent did not begin until mid-1961. That said, it is clear that the reason for the change must have been different!
10. On military *transport* aircraft, however, three-digit tactical codes do not relate to the c/n or f/n; they are the last three of the former civil registration (many Soviet/Russian Air Force transports were, and still are, quasi-civilian).
11. RBP = *rahdiolokatsionnyy bombardirovochnyy pritsel* – radar bombsight; ARK = *avtomaticheskiy rahdiokompas* – ADF; MRP = *markernyy rahdiopreeyomnik*; SP = [*sistema*] *slepoy posahdki* – blind landing system; SPI = *samolyotnyy preeyomoindikahtor*; SRO = *samolyotnyy rahdiolokatseeonnyy otvetchik* – aircraft-mounted radar [IFF] responder; RV = *rahdiovysotomer* – radio altimeter; NKPB = *nochnoy kollimahtornyy pritsel bombardirovochnyy* – night-capable collimator bombsight; AIP = *aviatsionnyy infrakrahsnyy pritsel* – aircraft-mounted infra-red sight (the AIP-32 was a standard OPB-1R optical bombsight with an IR imaging adapter); VB = *vychislitel' ballisticheskiy*.
12. DYa-SS = *derzhahtel' yashchichnyy sredstv signalizahtsii* – 'box-type rack for signal means'; KD = *kassetnyy derzhahtel'* – cassette-type rack; FotAB = *fotograficheskaya aviabomba* – flare bomb; TsOSAB = *tsvetnaya oriyenteerno-signahl'naya aviabomba* – coloured marker/signal flare bomb.
13. TG = *toorbogenerahtor* – lit. 'turbo generator'. This specific reference to the generator is because the TG-16 had no provisions for using bleed air for engine starting, since the engines were started electrically.
14. An honorary appellation given for the unit's part in liberating the town of Mga during the Great Patriotic War (the 12th was then a bomber division).
15. Nowadays renamed Velikiy Novgorod (Great Novgorod) in order to distinguish it from Nizhniy Novgorod ('Lower Novgorod', i.e. the one down south; formerly Gorkiy).
16. Now renamed back to Samara.
17. Now an aviation industry enterprise.
18. Now SNTK *imeni Kuznetsova* (the Samara Scientific and Technical Complex named after N.D. Kuznetsov).
19. Now ZMKB 'Progress' (the 'Progress' Zaporozhye Engine Design Bureau).
20. Up to 1959 the CCCP- registration prefix of Soviet civil aircraft was followed by a code letter designating the operator plus up to four digits. E.g. the code letter Л (L in the Cyrillic alphabet) stood for *leeneynyy samolyot* (aircraft in airline service) and denoted passenger and cargo aircraft operated by the Main Directorate of the Civil Air Fleet. Н (the Cyrillic N) stood for the Main Directorate of the Northern Sea Route, i.e. Polar Aviation; A was allocated to agricultural aircraft, K (for *Krahsnyy Krest* – Red Cross) to ambulance aircraft, С (the Cyrillic S) to aircraft operated by the OSOAVIAKHIM organisation managing the air clubs, etc. However, U was definitely **not** among the official codes; it stood for 'Ukraine'!
21. An-10 c/ns are deciphered as follows. The first digit denotes the year of manufacture; the next digit (4) refers to Plant No. 64, the first digit being omitted for security reasons to confuse would-be spies, which is why the Voronezh aircraft factory was for many years mistakenly believed in the West to be No. 40. The next three digits are the batch number followed by the number of the aircraft in the batch (six per batch).

Initially the c/n was stencilled on both sides of the ventral fin; later, when most aircraft were updated to feature twin ventral fins instead of the original single ventral fin and endplate fins, the c/n was stencilled either on the outer faces of the ventral fins or on both sides of the vertical tail. Additionally, Soviet Air Force

An-10s had the c/n stencilled on the starboard side of the forward fuselage, just aft of the flight deck.

22 These words are quoted in V. Moiseyev's book *A Winged Name*, published by the Soviet 'Dnepr' publishing house in 1974.

23 This airfield is the seat of the Lookhovitsy Machinery Plant (LMZ – *Lookhovitskiy mashinostroitel'nyy zavod*), now part of the Moscow Aircraft Production Association (MAPO – *Moskovskoye aviatsionnoye proizvodstvennoye obyedineniye*). During the years of its existence the plant manufactured Mikoyan/Gurevich MiG-23 *Flogger* and MiG-29 *Fulcrum-A/C* fighters, Interavia I-1 and Ilyushin Il-103 light aircraft and the RosAeroprogress T-101 *Grach* utility aircraft.

24 The official title of Soviet OKB heads.

25 FAB = *foogahsnaya aviabomba* – high-explosive bomb.

26 AFA = *aerofotoapparaht* – aerial camera; NAFA = *nochnoy aerofotoapparaht* – aerial camera for night operations; FotAB = *fotograficheskaya aviabomba* – 'photo bomb' (i.e. flare bomb for aerial photography).

27 Some sources say An-12A production in Voronezh continued up to and including c/n 401604. Indeed, CCCP-11916 (c/n 2400901) and UR-PAS (c/n 2401105) have been reported as An-12APs. Strangely enough, so has Tashkent-built CCCP-11906 (c/n 2340802)!

28 Second use of registration. The original CCCP-11145 was an An-10 which crashed in Voroshilovgrad on 31 March 1971.

29 Second use of registration. The original CCCP-83962 was a Lisunov Li-2 Meteo (*Cab*) weather research aircraft.

30 ASO = *avtomaht sbrosa otrazhahteley* – automatic chaff/flare dispenser; PPI = *peeropatron infrakrahsnyy* – infra-red [countermeasures] cartridge. It should be noted that some An-12s had these chaff/flare dispensers removed in the post-war years to save weight.

31 The tactical code of the VVS example has been retouched away by military censors on the only available photo. A photo exists of a ski-equipped An-12 in basically natural metal finish with Aeroflot titles and a 'lightning bolt' cheatline but apparently no registration, but this could be a fake.

32 Normally the re-entry modules of Soviet/Russian manned spacecraft touch down in the plains of Kazakhstan; thus a splashdown in the world ocean is only possible if an emergency forces a premature return from the orbit.

33 ROZ = *rahdiolokahtor obzora zemlee* – ground-mapping radar. The radar had been borrowed from the An-12 *Cub-A* transport, hence the primary mission and the designation.

34 Ex CCCP-12108 No. 2; the original CCCP-12108 was a Voronezh-built An-12A (c/n 401908) which became Soviet Air Force '16 Red' and then RA-11318.

35 LNPO = *Leningrahdskoye naoochno-proizvodstvennoye obyedineniye* – Leningrad Scientific & Production Association. LNPO Leninets is now known as the Leninets Holding Company.

36 Pronounced *izdeliye* – 'product', a term often used for coding Soviet military hardware items.

37 ASLK = *avtomatizeerovannaya sistema lyotnovo kontrolya* – automated flight checking system; KPA = *kontrol'no-poverochnaya apparatoora* – calibration equipment.

38 RPSN = *rahdiolokatsionnyy pribor slepoy navigahtsii* – blind navigation radar device. This radar is fitted to the An-24 (Groza-24), An-26 *Curl* and An-32 *Cline* transports (Groza-26), An-30A/B/D *Clank* photogrammetry/photo recce aircraft (Groza-30), some versions of the Ilyushin Il-14 *Crate* airliner (Groza-40), export versions of the Tupolev Tu-134A/Tu-134AK airliner and the Tu-134B *Crusty-A* (Groza-M134), Tu-154 *Careless* airliner (the Groza-154) and Yakovlev Yak-40 *Codling* feederliner (the Groza-40).

39 The registration was later reused for a Yakovlev Yak-42 (c/n 4520424711399, fuselage number 1308).

40 The registration was later reused for an An-12A (ex RA-11318, c/n 401908).

41 This Russian term is used indiscriminately and can denote any kind of testbed (avionics, engine, equipment, weapons, etc.), an aerodynamics research aircraft or control configured vehicle (CCV), a weather research aircraft, a geophysical survey aircraft, etc.

42 The word *konversiya* (conversion) means the adaptation of military technologies and defence industry enterprises to civilian needs.

43 The registration had been previously worn by a Li-2.

44 The registration CCCP-48974 was used for the third time in late 1987 for a brand-new An-32A (c/n 1407).

45 UPAZ = *oonifitseerovannyy podvesnoy agregaht zaprahvki* – 'standardized suspended (i.e. external) refuelling unit', or HDU. The 'standardised' part of the name means it can also be used as a 'buddy' refuelling pack by tactical aircraft – e.g. the Su-24M, Su-30 and Su-33 (Su-27K).

46 Now the Samara State Aviation University (SGAU).

47 Y8 construction numbers are deciphered as follows: the first two digits are the batch number, followed by 08 to denote the type (Y8) and then the number of the aircraft in the batch (probably five to a batch). The c/n is normally stencilled on the fin and sometimes under the wing leading edge at the roots. On some aircraft the type designator has been omitted; e.g. Y8F-100 B-3101 has the c/n painted on as 1001, though logically it should be 100801.

48 Now called the South Motive Power & Machinery Co. (SMPMC).

49 In Y8C c/ns the version designator is changed to 18 to stress the scope of the changes.

50 Different sources quote different figures.

51 Now renamed back to Tver.

52 Penkovskiy was a colonel in the Soviet Army's Main Intelligence Department (GRU – *Glahvnoye razvedyvatel'noye oopravleniye*) who worked in a government agency called the State Committee for Science and Technology (GKNT – *Gosoodarstvennyy komitet po naooke i tekhnike*). In the line of duty he had dealings with British citizens and was soon recruited by the British MI5 Intelligence service, divulging a lot of highly classified information to the West before he was exposed, arrested and sentenced to death.

53 PGS = *parashootnaya groozovaya sistema* – parachute cargo system.

54 Soviet Air Force An-22s also took part in the airlift. Tragically, one of them (An-22 *sans suffixe* CCCP-09305 No. 1, c/n 9340205) was lost with all hands in the notorious Bermuda Triangle on 18 July 1970; the registration was later reused for another *Cock* (An-22A c/n 043481240).

55 Called GSVG (*Grooppa sovetskikh voysk v Ghermahnii* – Group of Soviet Forces in Germany) until 1989.

56 Also spelled Massauua.

57 Unless there were two different *Cubs* registered CCCP-11408, this was a Tashkent-built An-12B (c/n 3341209) which was repaired and later transferred to the Ministry of General Machinery (Minobshchemash), ultimately becoming

RA-11408 with the Aviaobschchemash airline and then with the Russian cargo carrier Aerofreight Airlines.
58 Later renamed Sheikh Mansour International airport by the Chechens.
59 Some sources quote a different figure – 25,793 km (16,020 miles).
60 Other sources say 48 hours 27 minutes or 44 hours 34 minutes.
61 Other sources say 580 km/h (360 mph).
62 The Tu-134AK is a VIP version of the Tu-134A identifiable by the extra entry door in front of the port engine which is missing on regular 'As (including those converted to VIP configuration). The Tu-134 *Balkany* (Balkans) is an airborne command post derivative of the Tu-134AK often erroneously referred to as 'Tu-135' (which was really a bomber project of 1963) and identifiable by the HF aerial 'sting' under the APU exhaust and four small additional blade aerials.
63 The registrations were later reused for An-12BK c/n 00347409 and An-12BP c/n 5343203 respectively.
64 The registration was reused for a Tashkent-built An-12B (c/n 3341910).
65 The 46xxx block is allocated to the An-24 airliner, and the registration **CCCP-46741** belonged to a Kiev-built An-24 *sans suffixe* (c/n 47300803). It is not known if the An-12 in question ever had the CCCP- prefix.
66 CCCP-11418 No. 1 was An-12B c/n 401712 which crashed on 4 October 1988.
67 The original **CCCP**-11006 had been a different aircraft.
68 Thus there were **three different An-12BPs** with this registration: **CCCP**-11001 (c/n 5343702), **EX**-11001 (c/n 6344104) and **UN** 11001 (c/n 5343408)!
69 CCCP-11650 No. 1 was An-12A c/n 9901006; CCCP-98102 No. 1 was a Yakovlev Yak-40 *Codling* feederliner which crashed on 14 August 1982.
70 The registration CCCP-11110 was originally worn by a grey-painted Soviet Air Force An-12B.
71 The name has nothing to do with the French oil company Elf-Aquitaine. The E6 flight code was used only briefly; in 2000 it was passed to a Russian charter carrier, Aviaexpresscruise [E6/BKS].
72 Not to be confused with Volare Aviation Enterprise [F7/VRE] (see Ukrainian section) and the Italian airline Volare Airlines SpA [8D/VLE, later VA/VLE].
73 The flight code OP was reallocated to Chalk's International Airlines (Miami, FLA.).

74 CCCP-12162 No. 1 was an An-12BK owned by the Komsomolsk-on-Amur aircraft factory (c/n 9346702) which crashed on 19 October 1987 (see Appendix 1).
75 The crash of An-32B RA-26222 at Kinshasa-N'dolo on 8 January 1996 when the aircraft ploughed through the adjacent Simba Zikita market, killing some 260 people, was the last straw. Some sources, however, claim that Moscow Airways' licence had already been suspended at the time of the crash and the aircraft had no business being there in the first place!
76 CCCP-11325 No. 1 was a Mi-6 (c/n 3681406V).
77 Now coded [–/REV].
78 The name has also been rendered as SP Air and Spaero (not to be confused with Spaero JSP, see Ukrainian section).
79 The new flight code is also assigned to Omni Air International [X9/OAE] of Tulsa, OK.
80 UR-UAF has been reported as ex Soviet Air Force '13 Blue' but this is extremely doubtful because the tactical code 13 was never used for superstitious reasons!
81 This was the **third** An-12 to be registered 11109.
82 The PQ flight code was reassigned to Tropical International Airways (Basseterre, St Kitts & Nevis). However, the new flight code is also used by AIRES Colombia [4C/ARE].
83 The name has also been spelled 'Bourfarik'.
84 Some sources claim that the three An-12s were traded in for used but quite fresh Il-76TDs, while others indicate they were sold to Angolan carrier ALADA (Empresa de Transportes Aéreos, Lda).
85 The registration was previously worn by an Ilyushin Il-14.
86 The original EP-BON was a Tu-154M (ex RA-85746 leased from the Russian airline KMV, c/n 92A929).
87 Some sources claim there was a third An-12, 53 Red (c/n 6344309) which became SP-LZC; however, no confirmation has been found for this.
88 'Akula' means 'shark' in Russian; possibly the name was a play on the last two letters of the registration and the grey colour scheme.
89 Air Pass was just a trading name; the official name was Air Cess (Swaziland) Ltd.
90 Russian terminology is used here. Thus, the word 'accident' refers to fatal and non-fatal accidents when the aircraft suffers more or less serious damage to the airframe and/or engines, applying to both total hull losses and cases where the aircraft is eventually repaired. 'Incident' means situations not serious enough to be rated as a non-fatal accident, such as avionics or systems malfunctions not causing major damage, in-flight engine shutdowns, tyre explosions, birdstrikes (unless they result in a crash), lightning strikes, near-misses, departures from pre-designated air routes, landings in below-minima conditions, go-arounds because of obstacles on the runway, etc.
91 Much later there was an An-12BP or BK registered UR-11347 (c/n 8346105), but this probably never had the CCCP-prefix!
92 The registration was subsequently reused for another An-12 (c/n 401807?) first noted in 1971 and for An-12BK UR-11349 (c/n 9346302) which never had the CCCP- prefix.
93 Could be c/n 9346501.
94 Could be c/n 9346502.
95 Could be c/n 8345501.
96 Also spelled Massauua.
97 CCCP-11128 No. 1 was a grey-painted 'military' An-12BP (c/n unknown).
98 CCCP-11110 No. 1 was a grey-painted 'military' An-12BP (c/n unknown).
99 CCCP-11113 No. 1 was a grey-painted 'military' An-12BP (c/n unknown).
100 The registration was subsequently reused for an An-32 *Curl* transport operated by MAP/the Gorkiy Aircraft Factory No. 21 (c/n unknown). The c/n 1901708 has been reported in error for a Soviet Air Force An-12A coded 84 Red which served as a ground instructional airframe in a technical school at Chortkov AB in the Ukraine and was scrapped in the late 1990s; the aircraft in question was probably c/n 1901709.
101 The c/n is sometimes reported in error as 6343805. The registration was later reused for another *Cub*, an Irkutsk-built An-12A (c/n 8900704) which stayed around long enough to become RA-11795 after the demise of the Soviet Union.
102 CCCP-11120 No. 1 was an An-10A (c/n 0402001).
103 The registration originally belonged to a grey-painted 'military' An-12BP.
104 The aircraft was still in full Aeroflot colours at the time.
105 Former Leningrad CAD.

Index

Page numbers in **_bold italic_** refer to illustrations. Airlines and other operators are listed here only if mentioned **outside the operators section**; otherwise refer to Chapters 8 and 9.

Aero L-29 Delfin 117
Aeroflot 27
Aeroflot colour schemes 17, 22, 25, 123
Aeroflot units operating the An-12 123
Afghan War 118–120
Afghan civil war 120–121
AI-20 *see* Ivchenko
Airborne troops *see* VDV
Airbus Industrie:
   A320-200 179
   A330-200 179
   A340-300 179
Aircraft factories:
   Kumertau helicopter plant 125
   No. 18, Kuibyshev 15, 125
   No. 22, Kazan' 7, 22, 125
   No. 23, Moscow-Fili 11
   MMZ No. 30, Moscow 7, 22
   No. 39, Irkutsk 15, 44–45, 125
   No. 64, Voronezh 26, 33, 44–45, 125
   No. 84, Tashkent 11, 44–45, 125
   No. 99, Ulan-Ude 15, 125
   No. 116, Arsen'yev 14, 15, 125
   No. 126, Komsomol'sk-on-Amur 15, 125
   No. 153, Novosibirsk 15
   No. 166, Omsk 15, 125
   No. 168, Rostov-on-Don 15
   No. 473, Kiev 7, 9
   Ul'yanovsk Aircraft Production Complex 125
Aircraft overhaul plants 125
Airshows:
   Airshow China 94, 95
   Kubinka AB open doors days 115
   MAKS-97 80
   MosAeroShow-92 80
   1967 Moscow-Domodedovo show 115
   Royal International Air Tattoo 115
   Tushino flypast 9
All-Union Electronics Research Institute *see* LNPO Leninets
Angolan civil war 122
Antonov, Oleg K. 4, 6, 8, 9, 22–24, 29, 47, 113
Antonov:
   'aircraft P' 6, **_6_**, **_7_**
   An-8 4, 6–18, **_9–17_**, 124

An-8 airliner version project 17
An-8 radiation reconnaissance version 16
An-8M project 18
An-8PS project 18
An-8RU 17
An-8Sh project 18
An-8T 17
An-10 19–40, **_19–25_**, 41, 123
An-10A **_25–27_**, 30, **_32_**, **_34–36_**, 124
An-10AS **_28_**, 30
An-10B (project) 30
An-10B (real) **_29_**, 30
An-10D project 33
An-10KP 35
An-10TS 33–34, **_33–34_**
An-10V (An-16) project 30–32
An-112 90
An-12 'Tanker' de-icing systems testbed 81–82, **_86–87_**, 123, **_125_**
An-12 avionics testbeds 71–76, **_72–75_**
An-12 ejection seat/APU/recovery systems testbed
An-12 ELINT version 64, **_65_**, 114
An-12 engine testbeds 70, **_71_**
An-12 instrument calibration laboratory 76
An-12 Iraqi refuelling tanker conversion 70, 122
An-12 *sans suffixe* 41–45, **_41–45_**, 48, **_48_**
An-12 trailing wire aerial testbed 79, **_80_**
An-124 Ruslan 115, 124
An-12A 49, **_50_**, 114, 115, 121, **_122_**, 124, 126, **_144_**, **_159_**
An-12A ballistic missile transporter version 59
An-12A/B/BP/BK demilitarised version 66, **_68–69_**
An-12AP 50, **_52_**
An-12AP geophysical survey version 82, **_85_**
An-12B (civil) 69, **_70_**, **_135_**
An-12B (LIAT) 76
An-12B (military) 49, **_51_**, **_110_**, **_112_**, 114, 115, **_116_**, 126, **_129_**, **_130_**, **_134_**, **_148_**, **_156_**, **_160_**, **_161_**

An-12B communications relay version 59, 60, **_138_**
An-12B-30 89
An-12B-I 62
An-12BK 54, **_54–55_**, 93, 96, **_116_**, 118, 119, **_119_**, **_120_**, 124
An-12BK (SAR version) 59
An-12BK-IS 62, **_63_**
An-12BKK *Kapsoola* 66
An-12BK-PPS 64, **_64–65_**
An-12BKSh 66
An-12BKT 59
An-12BKV 66, 94, 122
An-12BL 65
An-12BM 59
An-12BP (civil) 69, **_123_**, 124, **_124_**, **_130_**, **_149_**, **_151_**, **_157_**
An-12BP (military) 50, **_53_**, 93, **_117_**, 118, **_122_**, 124, **_131_**, **_142_**, **_153_**, **_156_**, **_158_**, **_162_**, **_164_**, **_165_**, **_167_**
An-12BP (polar) 55, **_56_**
An-12BPTs 'Tsiklon' 76–79, **_76–78_**, 114
An-12BSh 66
An-12BSM 70
An-12BZ-1 90
An-12BZ-2 90
An-12D 89
An-12DK 89
An-12M 66
(An-12M LL) 79, **_81–83_**
An-12P 49, **_52_**, 115
An-12PL 55, **_56–58_**, 81
An-12PP (An-12B-PP, An-12BP-PP) 62, **_62–63_**, 114
An-12PS 59, **_61_**
An-12R 89
An-12RR 66, **_67_**, 114
An-12RU 89
An-12SN 89
An-12T 59
An-12TB/An-12TBK 69
An-12TP-2 81, **_84–85_**, 123, **_125_**
An-12U 86
An-12UD/An-12UD-3 55
'An-12V' ('An-12MGA') 69
An-12VKP (An-12B-VKP) *Zebra* 66, **_68_**
An-16 project 33

An-22 76, 115, 118, 124
An-24 70
An-24B 117, 124
An-24RR 16
An-24RV 124
An-26 78, 90, 118, 124
An-26 'Tsiklon' 79
An-2F 8
An-32 90, 179
An-38 90
An-3T 124
An-40 91
An-40PLO 91
An-42 91
An-72 82, 86, 89
An-72S 124
An-74 89
DT-5/8 6
Antonov OKB Tashkent branch 17
An-8 service 14–16
An-10 service 35–39
An-10 accidents and incidents 26, 35, 39
An-10 to An-12 conversion 22, 30, 41, 47
An-12 accidents and incidents (*see also* Appendix 1) 43, 44, 109, 113
Armament:
    Afanas'yev/Makarov AM-23 cannon 13, 41, 93
    DB-65U turret 41, 71, 93
    DB-75 turret 90
    DK-7 turret 93
    Gryazev/Shipoonov GSh-23 (AO-9) cannon 90
    Kh-28 anti-radiation missile 66
    PV-23U turret 13
ASU-57 self-propelled gun 111, **112**
ATC callsigns (phoney registrations) 71, 114
AV-68 propeller 92
Aviation Industry Corporation (AVIC) 94
Aviation Industry Corporation II (AVIC II) 95

Balandin, V. (GKAT) 110
Ballistic missiles 59
Bartini, Robert L. 4, 7
Bartini:
    T-108 4, 7
    T-117 4, 7
    T-200 4, 7
Beijing University of Aeronautics and Astronautics (BUAA) 94
Belolipetskiy, A. Ya. 6, 9, 47
Beriyev Be-12 15
Brandner, Ferdinand, Dr. 71
Brandner E-300 70
Bristol Britannia 8
Britten-Norman:
    BN-2 Defender 96
    Searchmaster 96
Brovtsev, S. G. 14

Chang Hong-1 target drone 94, **95**
China Aircraft Technology & Industry Corporation (CATIC) 95
Chinese People's Liberation Army Air Force (PLAAF) 92–95
Chinese People's Liberation Army Naval Air Force (PLANAF) 95–96
Chou En-Lai 92
Civil Air Fleet Research Institute *see* NII GVF
Civil Aviation Administration of China (CAAC) 93
Civil registration blocks (Soviet/CIS aircraft) 114
Collins avionics 94
Containerised cargo transportation 70, 124
Czechoslovak uprising of 1968 117

Dassault Aviation:
    Mirage III 122
    Mirage F1EQ-200 122
Davydov, I. Ye. 12, 24, 26, 44
Davydov, V. N. 14
Dement'yev, Pyotr V. (GKAT/MAP) 110
Demilitarised An-8s/An-12s *12*, *14*, 61–62, 66, **68–69**
Douglas DC-3 Dakota 4, 117

Eisenhower, Dwight D. 27
Eskin, A. P. 7
ESM upgrades (An-12BK) 55
Ethiopian airlift operation 118
Ethiopian/Eritrean war 121
Ethiopian/Somalian war 121

Fairchild:
    C-119G Flying Boxcar 4, 121
    C-123 Provider 4
Filippov, V. F. 113
First Chechen War 120
Flight Refuelling Ltd. 96
Flight Research Institute *see* LII

Gamaris, M. M. 110, 111
GEC-Marconi 95
General Electric CT7 turboprop 94
Georgian civil war (Georgian-Abkhazi conflict) 120
Ghel'prin, V. N. 7, 23, 47
GK NII VVS 9, 26, 30, 44, 54, 59, 71
GosNII GA 37, 38, 79
Ground instructional airframes 126

Helwan HA-300 71
Holy Day War (Yom Kippur War) 117, 121
Humanitarian airlift missions 113, 124

ICAO Annex 16 Chapter 3 noise regulations 125
Il'yushin, Sergey V. 7, 22, 26, 29

Il'yushin:
    Il-12B 4
    Il-12D 4
    Il-14 11
    Il-14G 123
    Il-14T 9
    Il-18 (Moskva) 22, 30, 126
    Il-18D 'Tsiklon' 79
    Il-18V 123
    Il-28 7, 22, 117
    Il-76 90, 115
    Il-76 *sans suffixe* (military) *Candid-B* 114, 118
    Il-76M 115, 118
    Il-76M Iraqi refuelling tanker conversion 70
    Il-76MD 118, 120, 126, 160
    Il-76T 124
    Il-76TD 124, 125
    Il-78 115
    Il-114 81
Il'yushin/Beriyev A-50I 96
Indo-Chinese conflict 121
Indo-Pakistani conflict 121
In-flight entertainment systems 29
Infra-red countermeasures 119
Iraq wars:
    Gulf War (Operation *Desert Storm*) 122
    invasion of Kuwait 122
Irons, Gen. 117
Israel Aircraft Industries Kfir C2 179
Ivchenko, Aleksandr G. 6, 11, 22
Ivchenko:
    AI-20 (TV-20) 11, 24, 26, 43
    AI-20A 27, 30
    AI-20D 11, 13
    AI-20DK 89
    AI-20K 30, 92
    AI-24 70
    AI-24VT 70
    AI-30 89, 90

Kabanov, A. N. 4
Kalinin, V. A. 24, 26
Kamov Ka-25Ts 74
Khrunichev, Mikhail V. 4, 6
Khrushchov, Nikita S. 18, 22, 27
Kolesov RD36-35 90
Koorlin, Yuriy V. 44
Korol', R. S. 9
Kuznetsov, Nikolay D. 6, 22
Kuznetsov:
    TV-2 6
    TV-2T 6, 8, 11
    2TV-2F 6
    NK-4 24, 26, 27, 41, 43

Lebedev, V. I. (Maj. Gen.) 8
Liberation Tigers of Tamil Eelam (LTTE, Tamil Tigers) 94, 122, 179

INDEX

LII (Mikhail M. Gromov Flight Research Institute) 9, 38, 79
Lisunov Li-2 4
Litton avionics 94, 96
LNPO Leninets 71, 74, 125
Lockheed Company 94
Lockheed:
  C-130 Hercules 4, **5**, 41, 93, 94
  C-130E 89
  C-130H 147, 156
  C-130H-30 147, 156
  C-130K Hercules C.1K 82, 90
  C-130K Hercules C.1P 89, 90
  C-130K Hercules W.2 77
  DC-130E 94
  F-104 Starfighter 74
  GTD-21 79
  HC-130H 79
  JC-130 79
  LC-130 89
Lotarev D-36 89
Lysenko, G. I. 42, 44
Lyul'ka AL-7 8

Malenkov, Gheorgiy M. 8
Malinovskiy, Rodion Ya. (Marshal of the Soviet Union) 111
Man-portable air defence systems *see* Surface-to-air missiles
Marghelov, A. V. 111
Marghelov, V. F. (Army General, VVS C-in-C) 111
McDonnell Douglas F-4E Phantom II 117
McMurdo polar research station 123
Mikoyan/Gurevich:
  UTI-MiG-15 117
  MiG-17F 115, 117
  MiG-19 89
  MiG-21F-13 115
  MiG-21PFM 118
  MiG-23BN 122
  MiG-25RBS 71
  MiG-27 179
Mikulin RD-9 89
Mil', Mikhail L. 6
Mil':
  Mi-4P 32M
  Mi-8MT 118
  Mi-24 118, 119
Military exercises:
  Dvina 55, 111, 116
  Oktyabr'skaya Groza 163
  Stal'noy Shchit 15
Ministry of Aircraft Industry (MAP) 15, 125
Ministry of Electronic Industry (MRP) 15, 71, 125
Ministry of General Machinery (MOM) 15, 125
Ministry of Shipbuilding (MSP) 15, 125
Mirnyy polar research station 123

Museum exhibits and preserved aircraft **11**, 15–16, 39, **48**, 126
Myasishchev 3M 55
Myasishchev, Vladimir M. 4

Nanchang Q-5 (A-5) 96
Nigerian civil war 117
NII GVF (*see also* GosNII GA) 26, 30
Northrop F-5E Tiger 16
NPO Vega-M 125
NPO Vzlyot 74, 125

Ojukwu, Col. 117
Operation *Enduring Freedom* 146, 147
Osipov, Boris S. 123
Overseas deployment (Soviet/Russian Air Force units):
  Czechoslovakia 114
  (East) Germany 35, 114–115
  Poland 114

Pen'kovskiy, Oleg 110
PGS-500 parachute cargo delivery system 111, **112, 113**
Polar research missions 123

Racal avionics 96
Republic of Korea Air Force 16
Royal Norwegian Air Force 73–74
Ryan AQM-34N Firebee 94

Saunders-Roe Princess 24
Scale models 126
Sever air cushion vehicle 91, **91**
Shaanxi Transport Aircraft Factory 92
Shaanxi:
  Y8 92–96, **92, 93**
  Y8A 93
  Y8B 93, 122, 166
  Y8C 94, **94, 154**
  Y8D 94, 122, 163, 166, 167
  Y8E 94, **95**
  Y8F 95
  Y8F-100 95, **96**, 166
  Y8F-201 95
  Y8F-300 95
  Y8F-400 95
  Y8F-600 95
  Y8G 95
  Y8MPA (Y8X) 96
  Y8 AEW version 96
Shakhatooni, Ye. A. 7, 47
Shevelyov, Mikhail I. 123
Shvetsov ASh-73TK engine 94
Sikorsky:
  MH-60G Black Hawk 93
  S-70C 93
  UH-60L Black Hawk 93
Six-Day War 115, 121
Skydiving records 115

Soviet Air Defence Force (PVO) 15
Soviet Air Force evaluation 109
Soviet Air Force Research Institute *see* GK NII VVS
Soviet Air Force units operating the An-12 109
Soviet Air Force units operating the An-8 14
Soviet Naval Air Arm 15
SP-9 polar research station 123
Spacecraft re-entry capsule tests 86, **88**
Speed record attempt 39
Sri Lankan civil war 122
State Committee for Hydrometeorology and Environmental Control 76
State Research Institute of Civil Aviation *see* GosNII GA
Stepankov, V. A. 9
Sudanese civil war 122
Sukhoi Su-7BMK 115
Surface-to-air missiles:
  9K32 Strela-2 (SA-7 *Grail*) 118
  9M319 Igla-1E (SA-18 *Grouse*) 122
  General Dynamics FIM-43A Redeye 118
  General Dynamics FIM-92A Stinger 118
  Raytheon HAWK 117
  Shorts Blowpipe 118
Syrian deployment 117

T-54 main battle tank 89, 117
Technical schools 126
TG-16 APU 14, 49, 51, 93
Troonchenkov, N. S. 23
TsAGI (Central Aero- & Hydrodynamics Institute) 4, 8, 26
Tsybin Ts-25 4
Tupolev, Andrey N. 4, 7, 9
Tupolev:
  Tu-4 4, 94
  Tu-4D 4, 9
  Tu-4LL engine testbed 8
  Tu-16 7, 22, 23, 93
  Tu-16K-26 79
  Tu-16R 16
  Tu-75 4
  Tu-95 6
  Tu-95KM 16
  Tu-95K-22 16
  Tu-104 9
  Tu-104A 29
  Tu-104A 'Tsiklon' 79
  Tu-104B 29
  Tu-114 Rossiya 24
  Tu-124 79
  Tu-134A (Tu-134A-3) 120
  Tu-134AK 124
  Tu-134B 124
  Tu-134 *Balkany* 124
  Tu-142MR 79
  Tu-154B 120
  Tu-154B-2 124

191

UNITA 122, 175, 177, 178
United Nations World Food Programme (WFP) 124

VDV (Soviet Airborne Troops) 111
Vernikov, Yakov I. 9, 24, 42
Vershinin, Konstantin K. (Air Marshal, VVS C-in-C) 110
Vickers:
  Viscount 8
  VC.10 C.1K 96
VNIIRA see LNPO Leninets

WJ-6 engine 92, 94
World Exhibition in Bruxelles (Brussels) 30

Xian Aircraft Factory 92
Xian H-6 93

Y8 et seq see Shaanxi
Yakovlev:
  Yak-14 4
  Yak-25RRV 16
  Yak-28RR 16

Yak-42 124
Yemen airlift 115
Yemeni civil war 121
Yermolino flight test centre 74
Yugoslav civil war 122

Zaïtsev, N. F. (Maj.-Gen.) 113–114
Zhigarev, P. F. (Air Marshal, VVS C-in-C) 8
Zhuzhou engine facory 92
Zvezda K-36 ejection seat 79